# FOCUSED
# READING INSTRUCTION

# FOCUSED
# READING INSTRUCTION

**WAYNE OTTO**

The University of Wisconsin—Madison

**ROBERT CHESTER**

The University of Wisconsin—Madison

**JOHN McNEIL**

The University of California—Los Angeles

**SHIRLEY MYERS**

The University of Georgia

▲
▼▼

ADDISON-WESLEY PUBLISHING COMPANY, INC.

Reading, Massachusetts · Menlo Park, California · London · Don Mills, Ontario

This book is in the
*Addison-Wesley Series in Education*

ISBN 0-201-05511-2
ABCDEFGHIJ-MA-787654

To kids—

who need all the help
we can give
as they slide down
the razor blade of life.

# Preface

We are convinced that in order to get down to the business of *individualization* and *accountability*—two of the main challenges that face us in reading education—we must be able to *focus* our teaching. *Focused Reading Instruction* presents a rationale for, and an approach to, focusing instruction through the use of objectives and objective-based teaching. The first five chapters deal with the nature of the reading process, the facilitation of children's learning, and the essential prerequisites to reading instruction. Chapters 6 through 10 present first an introduction to focusing instruction through the use of objectives, and then specific objectives and ways to assess and pursue them. The final four chapters get down to the nitty gritty of how-to-do-it.

*Focused Reading Instruction* is not a conventional reading methods text. There is no attempt at omnibus coverage of reading methods and materials. To the contrary, our purpose is to present a point of view and an approach that is workable. The objective-based approach to focusing reading instruction is presented in sufficient detail to permit prospective teachers to get started and to enable experienced teachers to get on with it.

*Focused Reading Instruction,* then, is for both teachers in training and teachers in the field. It is perhaps best viewed as a how-to-do-it manual to assist with the difficult tasks of individualizing reading instruction and accounting for instructional efforts through demonstrated results. As such, it could serve as the text for undergraduate courses in elementary reading, as the text or a text supplement for graduate courses designed to improve reading instruction, and as a text/reference for in-service courses designed to improve reading instruction.

*Madison, Wisconsin*                                                            W. O.
*March 1974*

# Contents

# 1 / **Introduction**

Our intent in *Focused Reading Instruction* is to present a point of view: Efficient reading instruction, instruction that is responsive to the needs of individuals, is objective-centered. In other words, we feel that if teachers are to succeed in their attempts to focus reading instruction in light of the needs and attributes of individual readers, they must start with clearly stated objectives. This book, then, is an introduction to objective-based reading instruction.

## Overview of the Book

Before we tell you more about what this book is, let us tell you what it is not. This book is not another omnibus *elementary reading methods* text. There is no attempt to survey in any general way the methods and materials that are available for teaching reading. Nor is there any attempt to cover the more or less standard topics that are usually included in such texts. Both of those kinds of things have been done, and the books are readily available. You ought to consult one or more of them to get a breadth of coverage.

 The focus of this book is on the elementary school. We present specific objectives that are clustered to cover kindergarten through grade six. But it will become clear that we are talking as much about an *approach*—an *objective-centered* approach— to the teaching of reading as about the content of an elementary school reading program. In fact, we are less interested in covering all possible behavioral objectives related to reading than in providing prospective teachers and in-service teachers with: (a) a rationale for using objectives to focus reading instruction, (b) a set of guidelines for implementing an objective-centered approach, (c) a coherent set of objectives that covers the skills that appear to be essential for success in elementary school reading, and (d) procedures for making use of objectives to assess performance and to focus instruction. At the same time, we recognize the need to humanize an objective-centered approach in order to keep it from becoming too mechanistic or too lock-step.

We are not so hung up on objectives as to suggest that teaching can be reduced to a set of behavioral objectives. Yet based on our collective experience, we have become convinced that when it comes to teaching skills, instruction can be focused most efficiently through the use of objectives. And we are convinced that in elementary reading, *teaching skills* is the name of the game. In the chapters that follow we have tried to develop a framework that both provides structure and permits flexibility.

To sum up, this book is for in-training and in-service teachers. Our main purpose is to acquaint you with a specific approach to reading instruction *that works*. But before you go on to Chapter 2, study the section that follows. There, we give you a brief look at each chapter and tell you how the chapters are related. You will be able to proceed more smoothly if you have some notion of what to expect.

## Overview of the Chapters

This book has four authors, which means that four different people with four different writing styles have written chapters. We have not attempted to "edit out" the differences in style, because we feel that each author has something to say and that he says it best in his own way. We got together in the first place because we share an orientation toward reading instruction. We feel that to teach reading effectively and efficiently, there is a need for *focus*. And we have learned that instruction can best be focused when attention is paid to the essential skills and to the objectives that are associated with them. We decided to write a book together when we realized that each of us had accumulated certain experiences that are relevant to the successful implementation of an objective-centered approach to reading instruction. What we have done, then, is to pool our experiences in order to deal with a topic that we feel is worthwhile: focused reading instruction. Each of us wrote the chapters for which we felt best qualified in terms of our personal experience. Thus, we have a single purpose and a single plan, but we have a variety of styles.

The purpose of Chapter 2, "The Reading Process," is to help you take a look at the reading process from several angles in order to gain perspective. "Reading" is an active experience, and the process includes psychological, sensory, perceptual, biological, and pedagogical aspects. Each aspect is examined.

In Chapter 3, "The Reader," the aim is to consider the human being who is engaged in the process of reading, to examine some ways in which learning to read can be facilitated, and to get down to some specific suggestions as to how teachers can become facilitators of learning. In practice, *to facilitate* means *to individualize*. Much of the discussion has to do with ways in which a teacher can facilitate children's learning by individualizing instruction.

Chapters 4 and 5 deal with prerequisites to reading, early language development, and critical skills that serve as a basis for success in reading. The aim in Chapter 4 is to establish a language base for reading instruction. Our experience has been that in many cases the diagnosis of severe reading problems does not go back far enough in the developmental sequence. As a result, remedial efforts fail simply because the instruction begins at a point that is beyond the child's language development. In Chapter 4 we seek to acquaint you with certain linguistic facts that will enable you to sequence early instruction and to use whatever strength a child may have in language development. Chapter 5 is in line with the relatively new notion that almost *anyone* can learn almost *anything* regardless of ability so long as the instruction is properly sequenced and paced. The focus of the chapter, then, is on the identification of the specific skills that must be mastered in order to reasonably assure success in beginning reading.

In Chapter 6 we talk about the nature and function of objectives. The trend toward accountability in education is noted, and the role of objectives in responding to the challenge is considered. Then, we examine the limitations as well as the benefits of *behavioral* objectives and present you with some instruction on how to write functional behavioral objectives. Finally, we consider the need for "open," or "expressive," objectives as well as behavioral objectives in a well-rounded, objective-based system; and we describe an approach to implementing an objective-based approach to reading instruction.

Specific objectives for reading instruction are presented in Chapters 7 through 10. Behavioral objectives are given for word attack, study skills, and comprehension; expressive objectives are given for self-directed, interpretive, and creative reading. Criterion-referenced guides to assessment are given for all the behavioral objectives, which are clustered to correspond roughly to traditional grade levels. The objectives given are stated at a level of specificity that has been found to be appropriate for use by teachers as they plan instruction.

The remaining chapters have to do with "what to do in the classroom." We have attempted to provide guidelines and examples that will be useful as you attempt to implement an objective-centered approach—as you begin to be a *facilitator of learning*.

Chapter 11, "Organizing Learning Situations for Individual Differences," includes the following: a review of individual differences; approaches to diagnosis, particularly through the use of criterion-referenced tests; classroom management, ranging from effective seating arrangements through the use of centers and stations for *focused* teaching; grouping techniques; and the management of materials so that they can be most useful in *individualizing* instruction. In Chapter 12 we deal specifically with the individualization of instruction through the use of objectives. We consider ways in which different approaches and materials can be focused to meet individual needs, and we present examples of how specific objectives can be taught.

Reading problems and problem readers will always be with us, so Chapter 13 deals with the matter of meeting *special* needs for instruction in reading. An essential point is that *most* deviant learners can (and should) be taught effectively in the regular classroom *if instruction is adequately focused*. Problems encountered by children with specific language disabilities, disadvantaged children, and slow learners are dealt with. In each case the problem is defined, special needs are identified, and required "instructional adjustments" are examined. Special methods for teaching disabled learners are also presented.

The aim in Chapter 14 is to show how improvement of reading instruction can be built into an ongoing situation through in-service education. Techniques for evaluating teachers and, more specifically, teaching procedures are presented; and models for helping teachers improve are given in sufficient detail to permit school people to use them with little adaptation.

# 2 / The reading process

We often use the term "reading process" in our attempts to describe what happens when an individual "reads." In one sense, the term is a misnomer because, in fact, reading is not a single process. Instead, it is the synthesizing of several processes culminating in a single act. This suggests that we view reading as an active rather than as a passive experience— something that the child does, rather than as something that he experiences. This is not to say that the experience of the child does not contribute to the reading act; for indeed, this is not true. Rather, it means that the final manifestation, the bringing together of the various processes, is expressed by an act— the reading act.

The purpose, then, of this chapter is to point out a number of important processes that comprise the reading process. Beginning with the psychological process, we will briefly examine some of those factors that influence reading growth. We will then examine the sensory and perceptual processes as they relate to reading. In the last two sections, the developmental and skill-development processes, we discuss the variety of tasks and abilities associated with the unfolding nature of the reading process.

## Reading as a Psychological Process

The reading process must, by its very nature, involve the total child. Contrary to the opinions of those critics who accuse the educational system of being impersonal and uninvolved, the fact remains that today, more than ever before, we are looking at the child as an individual with individual strengths and needs. In no area is this more true than in reading. Evidence of this is seen in the abundance of reading-research literature, which is accumulating at a present rate of about 300—500 publications annually. The child and the various aspects of reading are being examined and reexamined in order to capitalize on the strengths and deficits unique to each learning situation.

Our main purpose here is to point out some of the more important and relevant findings and to relate them to the total reading process. Among the more frequently encountered correlates of reading ability are the following:

| | | |
|---|---|---|
| 1. intelligence | 5. language | 9. physical growth |
| 2. mental age | 6. race | 10. perceptual skill |
| 3. sex | 7. personality | 11. rate of reading |
| 4. socioeconomic level | 8. attitude | |

This list represents only a few of the reading correlates. In view of their number and nature, it is impractical to examine them all at this time. However, it does appear necessary to look more closely at a few of the more important ones.

### Intelligence quotient and mental age

The terms Intelligence Quotient (IQ) and Mental Age (MA) are usually used to express the results of tests of general intelligence. The IQ of a six-year-old child represents the ratio between his particular score on a given intelligence test and the score which an average individual of his exact chronological age would attain on that same test. In differentiating between MA and IQ, one might define IQ as a measure of mental growth, whereas MA might more appropriately be described as a level of mental maturity. Although there are exceptions, IQ is generally thought to remain relatively stable as the individual grows olders. MA, on the other hand, tends to increase at a rather constant pace until sometime in midadolescence. Consequently, MA seems to be a better, short-range predictor of performance, whereas IQ is more appropriate for accurate, long-range predictions.

The following formulas are helpful in further explaining the relationships between Chronological Age (CA), Mental Age (MA), and Intelligence Quotient (IQ):

$$MA = IQ \times CA$$

and

$$IQ = \frac{MA}{CA} \times 100.$$

We might derive the MA for a child whose IQ is 110 and whose CA is 6.0 in the following way.

$$MA = IQ \times CA$$
$$MA = 110 \times 6.0 \text{ (yrs.)} = 110 \times 72 \text{ (mos.)} = 79.2$$
$$MA = \frac{79.2}{12} = 6.6$$

Similarly, given his MA (6.6) and his CA (6.0), we might derive his IQ:

$$IQ = \frac{MA}{CA} \times 100$$

$$IQ = \frac{6.6}{6.0} \times 100 = 1.1 \times 100 = 110.$$

Of all the many factors correlated with reading readiness and achievement, none has been more consistently or frequently studied than intelligence. Although there is general agreement that intelligence is an important factor, educators are divided about the extent of that importance. The fact that there is so much conflicting information about the importance of intelligence has tended to compound rather than clarify the issue.

For example, according to Harris (1970), "The most important single factor in reading readiness is general intelligence, which, being an average of many phases of mental growth, is significantly related to most of the other factors" (p. 23). Similarly, Witty and Kopel (1949) concluded that an individual with a Binet IQ score below 25 ordinarily will never reach a level of mental development sufficient to learn to read; those with an IQ score below 50 will experience difficulty in reading both abstract and other types of difficult material; and those with an IQ score between 50 and 70 may ultimately become able to learn to read, but probably never above a fourth-grade level.

While reading achievement tends to be related to intelligence at all academic levels, the exact nature of this relationship seems to vary. In a study with elementary children, Strang (1943), for example, found correlations of .80 to .84 between the language score on the *California Tests of Mental Maturity* and scores on the *Gates Basic Reading Tests*. On the other hand, the correlations were only .36 to .56 for the nonlanguage intelligence score and the reading tests. These findings were very similar to those of Traxler (1939) based on high school pupils. He found a correlation of .69 between the language score of the *California Tests of Mental Maturity* and the score of the *Iowa Silent Reading Test*. For the nonlanguage score and reading, the correlation was only .36. This seems to suggest that verbal group intelligence tests generally correlate more highly with reading comprehension than do nonlanguage group intelligence tests.

Just as the relationship between intelligence and reading may vary between verbal and nonverbal types of measures, it may also vary from academic level to academic level. Bond and Wagner (1966) report:

The correlation between mental age, as measured by individual Stanford-Binet tests, and reading comprehension at the end of the first grade is approximately .35; at the end of the fifth grade, it is approximately .60; during the high school years it approaches .80.

Cohen and Glass (1968) found no significant relationship between IQ scores and reading ability in the first grade, but they found a significant relationship in the fourth grade.

Possibly the best-known study of intelligence and reading readiness was published by Morphett and Washburne (1931). They found that the subjects in their study whose mental ages were below six when they entered school usually failed the first grade. They also reported that the proportion of failures dropped as mental age increased, up to about six and one-half years. Many educators, in reading their report, have ignored the fact that the reading materials used in the study would be considered difficult by today's standards and that the standard set in the study would be considered high in many schools in our present-day educational system.

For many years the Morphett and Washburne findings dominated the field. However, we have since come to recognize that other factors may be as, if not more, important than mental age. One of the studies that helped to bring about this change in attitude was carried out by Gates (1937). His classroom studies indicated that the necessary mental age for successful reading is relative. He pointed out that differences in class size, procedures, and teaching methods may allow some children to read as early as at the age of four and one-half, whereas other may begin to read as late as at age seven.

Gray (1956) advocated the mental age of six for beginning reading, but readily admitted that materials, teaching procedures, and a variety of other factors may be more important than mental age. He called attention to the fact that Scotland and several other European countries have developed successful readers at the mental age of five.

Smith and Dechant (1961) reported that mental-age scores are closely related to both reading readiness and reading achievement. They further stated that the correlations between mental age and reading-readiness test scores range from about .35 to .80. They concluded that, to a large extent, tests of reading achievement, reading readiness, and intelligence measure the same factors.

Although there is conflict of opinion about the exact nature of the relationship of IQ and MA to reading, several points of agreement can be found.

1. IQ and MA are relatively good predictors of a child's minimal performance level. Barring other serious handicaps, most children with mental ages of six can be taught to read in the first grade.

2. Most children who fail to succeed in reading in the first grade have mental ages below six years.

3. Although IQ and MA are important, other factors such as class size, procedures, motivation, and teaching procedures may be just as important to successful reading performance.

4. Even though IQ and MA are relatively sound predictors in most cases, they should never be used in isolation to determine expectations. The fact that a first grader has an IQ of 130 is no more of a guarantee that he will learn to read than is the fact that a child with an IQ of 80 will not.

5. Correlations between IQ and reading scores tend to increase with grade level. This is due largely to similarities in test factors, measuring instruments, and skill performance. A high IQ score at the sixth-grade level is a much better predictor of reading performance than is the same score at the first-grade level.

## Socioeconomic factors

One of the factors most often correlated with reading achievement during the last decade has been socioeconomic status. Riessman (1962) quoted the rather conservative estimate that, in general, 15 to 20 percent of American school children have some degree of reading disability. However, he estimated that among the lower socioeconomic classes, and particularly among the disadvantaged, the disability estimate may rise as high as 50 percent. Benson (1969) in a less conservative estimate claims that "in middle class communities, the number of children retarded in reading averages between ten and twenty percent while in low socioeconomic areas it may range as high as eighty percent" (p. 266).

Although these findings are disturbing, they should come as no surprise. As far back as 1940, Coleman found a high relationship between socioeconomic status and reading ability. Studying a national sample of school children grouped into three socioeconomic levels, he found socioeconomic level related to a variety of subjects, including reading. Similarly, when Gough (1946) compared sixth-grade students in schools ranked as high, medium, and low according to socioeconomic levels, he found significant differences favoring the high-status schools.

There appear to be a number of reasons for these findings. Among the more obvious are malnutrition, poor health, crowded living conditions, unstable home environment, and economic pressures. However, these are the extremes and are conditions over which the teacher generally has little control. There are, on the other hand, a number of other reasons for poor achievement which may be associated with socioeconomic status. Most of these may be summed up under three headings: (1) background experience, (2) level of motivation, and (3) language.

### Background experience

The statement is too often made that children from low socioeconomic levels lack background experience. This simply isn't true. *All* children have background experience. The fact that their experiences are not the same as those of middle-class children or those represented in traditional teaching materials should not be interpreted as meaning that these children have none. Rather, it must be understood that their experiences are different. Unfortunately, many teachers overlook this or assume that it doesn't exist and fail to capitalize on the experiences that the child brings to the learning situation.

On the other hand, it is unrealistic to suggest that certain children are not handicapped by their background experience. Since the educational system is geared toward middle-class standards with middle-class subject matter and vocabulary, the child who has never experienced these is at a disadvantage. Again, the child in the lower socioeconomic class has less opportunity to travel, handle books and magazines in his home, or meet people outside his immediate environment. Because of restricted social environment and economic limitations, many avenues of enrichment are closed to him. Frequently, both parents work, and there is no opportunity for them to contribute to widening the child's experiences. In other cases, because of social and economic pressures, parents simply neglect to do so. Consequently, the child may be attitudinally unprepared to accept the changes that accompany school.

### Level of motivation

To assume that all children want to learn to read is both naive and unrealistic. Because many children come from homes in which the parents do not or cannot read, the motivation for learning to read may be lacking. This is especially true of children from low socioeconomic environments. They are less likely to see their parents or other members of their families and peer groups placing importance on reading. Also, they are less likely to have opportunities to examine books, magazines, newspapers, etc., in their homes. They have neither the encouragement nor any reason to learn to read.

Another reason that some children may be poorly motivated is that they rarely find reading to be a rewarding experience. Because of a number of factors associated with their backgrounds and preparation, they come to school without the proper level of readiness. Because they are ill-prepared, they fail, and reading too often becomes equated with failure. Nobody enjoys failing, so it is not surprising that negative associations are built up. Rather than motivating them to read, constant failure motivates them to leave school.

### Language

A third area in which the student from a low socioeconomic environment is handicapped is language. The fact that the student may have a language quite adequate for communication with his family and peers is not sufficient. The language of the home and community may not necessarily be the language of the school. As Patin (1964) points out, the student often has an adequate "public" language, but little or no "formal" language. His public language is adequate for conveying simple items of information, making requests, or indicating agreement or disagreement. It is characterized by simple, declaratory sentences and imperatives. Structural complexities, dependent clauses, and more elaborate speech patterns found in formal language are not in his public language. Since the language of the school is formal, the student from a low socioeconomic level is at a disadvantage from the beginning.

These findings are in agreement with those of Thomas (1962), who found language deficiencies in white and Negro children in low socioeconomic areas. He indicated that children living in areas covered by his study use only about 50 percent of the words in school readers and that they fail to use about 20 to 50 percent of the words on the Dolch, Gates, International Kindergarten Union, Rinsland, and Thorndike lists recommended for primary grades.

## Reading as a Sensory Process

Whatever else we may say about reading, we must acknowledge that it begins as a sensory process. The cues and stimuli for reading come in through the ears, eyes, and in the case of braille, through the fingers. No matter how intelligent, well adjusted, and psychologically ready the child is, he cannot learn to read unless he has some way of experiencing the stimulus material. And if he is handicapped here, it may well be reflected in his reading progress. This is not to say that if handicapped, he will not learn to read; we know this isn't true. Children have the remarkable ability to compensate. Also, this should not be interpreted as meaning that an impairment in vision or hearing will alone impede progress. Stating that reading is a sensory process does not mean that it is only a sensory process. There are many factors involved, and reading disability is usually the result of a number of factors working singly or in combination. Whereas a hearing or visual weakness alone may not cause severe problems, you rarely find either alone. To the contrary, they quite often combine with, or cause, other problems such as fatigue, restlessness, discomfort, poor self-image, etc.

### Reading and vision

Reading begins with seeing, i.e., the stimulus enters through the eye. At an early age children begin to perform in a way that might loosely be called reading. That is, they begin to recognize that certain signs or symbols represent names of things. Later, they learn that when certain signs and signals are put together, they represent talk. They begin to recognize and interpret bill-boards, road signs, labels, and the like. But when are they ready to read books? Or, to state the question more specifically, when is their vision ready?

Research tells us that the child is usually visually ready for reading books when he reaches the age of five or six. By this time he has reached some competency in binocular coordination, depth perception, focus and refocus, and changing fixations at will. On the other hand, at this age he's generally farsighted. But, since children are individuals with individual patterns of growth and development, there are likely to be considerable differences among pupils in any first-grade class. Therefore, you should have some knowledge of what to look for.

The most common type of visual disability is *refractive error*, which simply means that the eyes are out of focus. As already mentioned, many first graders suffer from various degrees of one type of refractive error, *hypermetropia* (farsightedness). Unfortunately, many schools still use only the Snellen-type wall charts for testing vision. This type of test does not check for close vision, and many cases of hypermetropia go undetected. Although quite able to focus on distant objects such as wall charts, blackboards, etc., the child may experience various degrees of discomfort when required to read from a book. The alert teacher, aware of this condition, can aid the child by not giving as much close work and by not requiring him to read for long periods at one time. Even though there is little research directly relating hypermetropia with reading disability, we can be relatively sure that the discomfort caused by extended periods of eyestrain can result in restlessness, tension, and a dislike for reading.

A second type of refractive error is *myopia* (nearsightedness). This is less common in beginning readers and except in extreme cases, appears to have little detrimental effect on reading. In fact, many teachers feel that moderate myopia favors, rather than hinders, reading. Considering the fact that most reading first graders read at a distance of about 14 inches, this may well be true. In either case, myopia is unlikely to be a problem with beginning readers.

A third, infrequently encountered type of refractive error is *astigmatism*, a condition of uneven focus of the eyes. This may involve hypermetropic, myopic, or mixed conditions. Although generally not attributed as a cause of reading disability, it can be a contributing factor. As with other types of refractive error, it tends to create discomfort, tension, and disinterest in reading.

There are, of course, other types of visual problems involving such things as inadequate conversion and fusion deficiencies, but these are less frequent, and unless you know exactly what to look for, you are unlikely to spot them. Nevertheless, there are a number of more general symptoms of which you should be aware and should be able to recognize as indications of visual difficulty. In a study of third graders, Know (1953) found the following 11 symptoms to be most reliable for picking out visual defects: (1) facial contortions, (2) book held close to face, (3) tension during visual work, (4) tilting head, (5) head thrust forward, (6) body tense while looking at distant objects, (7) assuming poor sitting position, (8) moving head excessively while reading, (9) rubbing eyes frequently, (10) avoiding close visual work, (11) losing place in reading. These overt symptoms, combined with results from a screening test, appear to be relatively good indicators of visual difficulty.

Results of research dealing with the relationship between vision and reading are inconclusive. For instance, in investigating the relationship between various eye conditions and reading, Park and Burri (1943) found that good readers had fewer than average visual deficiencies for their chronological and mental age groups. Conversely, poor readers had more than average visual deficiences for their chronological and mental age groups. Also, both Betts (1934) and Spache and Tillman (1962) determined that fusion is directly related to reading difficulty. Other studies relating reading disability and visual deficiencies are those by Harris (1970), Kephart (1953), Eames (1964), and Dearborn and Anderson (1938). However, there are a large number of studies reporting evidence to the contrary. Among the numerous studies suggesting no relationship between visual defects and reading abilities are those by Witty and Kopel (1936), Betts and Austin (1941), Ball (1961), and Shearer (1964).

Spache (1963) attributes most of the conflict of research findings to the fact that: (1) a variety of tests have been used in investigations, (2) visual tests are generally low in reliability, (3) many researchers do not consider the age of their sample or the developmental nature of vision, (4) many researchers measure each visual function separately and ignore the interrelationships between various functions, and (5) many tests have absolute and arbitrarily set standards which do not allow for human variance.

Our own position is that visual defects may be the cause, a contributing factor, or unrelated to reading performance, depending on the individual. Since most of the evidence is inconclusive, it seems premature at this time to make generalities, especially since in the final analysis we are dealing with individuals whose strengths, weaknesses, and abilities to compensate are largely unknown.

## Reading and hearing

Just as reading may be said to begin with seeing, reading readiness, to a large extent, may be said to begin with hearing. A child's auditory preparation begins at home in the form of vocabulary development, effective listening, and discrimination skills. If, either because of physical defects or environmental and social conditions, his experiences are limited, effects of this limitation may show up in his early reading development. If within his own family and among his own peers he has trouble distinguishing differences between similar-sounding words or is unable to detect certain sounds within words, there is reason to believe that he will have the same difficulty in school. Until he can detect and identify these discriminations, he is unlikely to recognize that they exist and even less likely to learn them. This is especially true when reading instruction relies heavily on some sort of phonics or oral system of sounding out words. Whether the disability is physical, as in certain types of hearing loss, or learned, as in the case of dialectical differences, it is nevertheless real and may influence the child's language and reading.

The beginning reader should be able to hear likenesses among letter sounds as they occur in words, detect words that begin and end with the same sound, detect rhyme, determine that words contain a given sound, and recognize that words are composed of a sequence of sounds in a given order. In most cases, children who cannot do this can be trained to do so. Where training is unsuccessful, a program with heavy emphasis on phonics should not be implemented.

Although most attention is generally given to *auditory discrimination* (ability to hear likenesses and differences in letter sounds as they occur), *auditory acuity* (ability to hear sounds of varying pitch and loudness) is equally important. At its extreme, disability in auditory acuity describes the condition often referred to as hard of hearing, but this is relatively uncommon among first graders and requires the help of a specialist to detect. Much more often, poor auditory acuity is exhibited as an inability to detect high-pitched letters and combinations of letters such as b, p, s, t, k. c. v. fl, th, ch. Because vowels are pitched lower than consonants, they are more easily heard.

Although the research dealing with hearing and reading achievement is sketchy and inconclusive, there is ample evidence suggesting a relationship between hearing disability and beginning reading problems. Certainly, every child who is experiencing serious reading problems should have a hearing test. You might also suspect hearing problems if a child exhibits such symptoms as requesting numerous repetitions of statements, manifesting facial expressions indicating intense effort in listening, confusing words which are similar in sound, turning his head or cupping his ear to hear better, or using slurred or indistinct speech.

As mentioned above, research results in auditory discrimination and acuity are both limited and indecisive. Although neither space nor purpose dictates that a review of the literature be done here, it does appear worthwhile to mention a few representative studies. Bond (1935) and Goetzinger, Dirks, and Baer (1960) conducted studies involving the matched-pairs technique in efforts to determine differences in the performances of "good" and "poor" readers on selected auditory skills. In both studies, significant differences were found between the two groups of readers in auditory discrimination. Harrington and Durrell (1955) found similar results in a modified matched-pairs study of 500 parochial school second graders. In another study of second graders, Thompson (1963) found that of the 24 best readers, 16 had possessed adequate auditory discrimination upon entering the first grade. Of the 24 poorest readers, only one had exhibited adequate discrimination skills at the beginning of grade one.

Contrary findings were reported by Gates and Bond (1936). Working with four first-grade classes, they found only low correlations between reading-readiness skills and selected auditory skills. They also noted that tests of blending and rhyming ability failed to discriminate between those pupils who were failing and those who were passing reading. Similarly, studies of fourth graders carried out by Reynolds (1953) and Templin (1954) resulted in only low to moderate correlations between auditory discrimination and reading achievement. Results of these, as well as a number of other similar studies, remain inconclusive.

Our own position is that, as in the case of vision, hearing disability, unless severe, may or may not affect the child's reading achievement, depending on the individual child and the particular mode of instruction. If a child with an acute hearing loss has proper motivation, ability to compensate, and an adjusted mode of instruction, he may experience little or no reading difficulty. On the other hand, the child with only a mild hearing disability may have great difficulty because his problem is compounded by such things as poor motivation, poor self-image, and improper instruction. We cannot emphasize too strongly that reading is an individual process for each child; whether he succeeds or fails to succeed depends on a number of factors and how they relate uniquely to him.

## Reading as a Perceptual Process

Related to, but not to be confused with, the sensory process is the perceptual process. As in the sensory process, perception in its larger meaning refers to stimulus input from seeing, hearing, smelling, tasting, and touching; however, in reading we generally think in terms of only the first two. In relation to these, many people incorrectly confuse the reception of sound waves, or in the case of vision, light waves, with the total process of perception, when in fact, this is only one part of the process.

Vernon (1962) describes the perceptual process in reading as consisting of four parts: (1) awareness of the visual stimulus standing out from its background, (2) awareness of essential similarities for general classification of the word, (3) classification of visual symbols of the word within the general class, and (4) identification of the word, usually by naming it. Although Vernon intended these descriptive steps for visual perception only, they are equally applicable for auditory perception. Indeed, although there is some disagreement among educators as to what takes place within the different steps, there is substantial agreement as to what those steps are. Most agree that perception involves a stimulus, the association of meaning and interpretation from experience with that stimulus, and a response relating the meaning to the stimulus or symbol.

As mentioned previously, the first step, i.e., the stimulus, is often mistaken as the whole of perception. The error of this can be readily recognized by noting that the stimulus in itself has no meaning. We do not get meaning from a symbol or sound; rather, we bring meaning to it. For example, a black dot on a page has no meaning in itself. However, if the dot appears at the end of a sentence, we may interpret it as a period; if it appears on a map, we may interpret it as representing a city. In other contexts we may recognize it as an *e* in Morse code, or as a Hebrew vowel marker. Of course, if we've never associated a black dot with any meaning, it may appear as a meaningless black dot.

The major function of the stimulus is, as its name implies, to stimulate, to invoke. Obviously, an important part of this stimulation is the ability to isolate and discriminate between the various stimuli. Before a child is going to be able to respond to differences between *b* and *d*, he is going to have to be able to identify differences between them. On the other hand, noticing that *b* doesn't look like *d* or that the sound of *b* is different from the sound of *d* is of little use if they are both meaningless symbols. The same might be said in regard to figure-ground, position in space, and special relationships. Although this is perception in that the child perceives selected dimensions of the stimuli, it is only the initial input facilitating the recognition and identification process.

Visual perception tests such as Frostig's *Developmental Test of Visual Perception* and the *Monroe Reading Aptitude Test* have shown limited value as predictors of reading success. Furthermore, their scores have not been shown to be a successful basis for prescribing remedial treatment. Similar results have been found with auditory tests such as the *Wepman Auditory Discrimination Test* and the perceptual tests of the *Gates-McKillop Reading Diagnostic Tests*.

The second step in perception, the association of meaning with the stimulus, is obviously closely associated with the first step of isolating the stimulus. In fact, the two steps are complementary in that the more clearly we can isolate and identify the stimulus, the easier it is to associate meaning with it; the more meaning we can bring to a stimulus, the easier it is to isolate and identify it. An important part of the discrimination of stimuli involves having a reason for discrimination. Although the *T* and *H* are different because of differences in horizontal and vertical lines, the difference may not become significant until the child recognizes that the letters have different sounds which, in combination with letters, make up words. Similarly, unless the child has experienced a difference (through teaching or otherwise) between such words as *bear* and *bare*, his awareness of the difference will remain at the stimulus level (spelling) and will not modify his perception of meaning.

Thus far, we have talked about perception of stimuli in terms of letters and words. However, essentially the same points can be made about sentences, paragraphs, or even stories. Perceptual meaning is influenced by a number of factors, among which are past experiences, cultural background, and emotional and physical associations. For instance, children come from a wide variety of backgrounds. The child who has been read to by his parents, who had been surrounded by an abundance of reading materials, and who has been exposed to parents and peers who set a premium on reading will perceive reading differently from one who has had a different set of experiences. Also, the child who attends kindergarten, frequents the public library, travels frequently, and who is encouraged to think and talk with his parents and peers has an entirely different set of perceptions from the child who has experienced none of these.

Of course, the socioeconomic differences are the most obvious and the most dramatic, but real differences do exist elsewhere. For instance, a wide variety of differences may occur within a single socioeconomic level. The experiences of the children of a rural farmer, a migrant worker, and an innercity laborer will vary strikingly, even though they may all be from the low socioeconomic level. The perceptions of a middle-class suburban child will certainly be different from those of a middle-class rural child. The perceptual differences will exist not only because of differences in experiences and socioeconomic circumstances, but also because of cultures. This becomes a significant factor since to a large extent, the child's self-concept and attitudes are influenced by the culture in which he is raised. If his cultural environment happens to be one in which reading is esteemed and encouraged, he may be reinforced by that attitude. However, if his particular culture puts no value in reading or minimizes its importance, he will probably develop a similar attitude.

Not to be overlooked in the perceptual process is the influence of emotional and physical factors. Both may have a great impact on a child's perception of a word or event. The child who is uncomfortable because of either physical or emotional reasons cannot function at his level of potential. The experiences that he brings to a perceptual experience may be restricted, or distorted, or both. Experience has shown that although a visual or auditory handicap alone may not cause failure, it may combine with other factors to distort perceptual performance. Furthermore, the child who finds reading an uncomfortable experience or a threat will in all likelihood become a reluctant reader. This goes for emotional as well as physical factors.

In addition, the nature and intensity of the emotional experiences that the child brings to a word or event may color or distort meaning. The child who owns a pet mouse is certain to have a different perception of a story about mice from that of a child raised in a ghetto situation. Whereas the word *snow* may mean sledding and fun for one child, another might associate it with cold and deprivation. In fact, sometimes the emotional overtones associated with words and events are so strong as to completely distort and break down meaning entirely.

Up to this point, we have talked about the child's perceptual development as a growth process from sensation (experential background, culture, etc.) to identification and recognition. However, we cannot stop here. The child must not only be able to focus on the stimulus and identify and recognize it in terms of his experience, he must also be able to modify and relate his experience to the stimulus in its present context or environment. In other words, some sort of mediation must take place. Perception ranges over a wide area, from concrete and specific to abstract and generic, and it is at this latter extreme that conceptualization is most pronounced. Here, the child must learn to deal with such factors as categorization, generalization, analysis, synthesis, etc.

As numerous and as widely varied as the experiences of the young reader may be, there are many concepts which he will not have encountered and many others which, though encountered, will not have been assimilated to the point of conceptualization. His limitations will involve not only his experience, but also his maturity and mental ability. For example, he will generally learn concrete and specific concepts first. A *dog* is the brown collie that he sees at home, and a *flower* is the geranium that grows in the windowbox outside his window. Later, he will learn that dogs come in all sizes, shapes, and colors and that poodles, Chihuahuas, and schnauzers are all dogs. He will learn that flower can mean daisy, rose, tulip, etc., and that flowers are found in many places. Although at his early stages he will probably limit the meaning of objects to their functions, i.e., a cup is something from which you drink milk, he will move beyond this as he matures. As his experiences enlarge, he will learn not only that you drink other things from a cup and that cups come in many sizes and shapes, but also, hopefully concept of "cupness."

You see, then, how important it is to provide the beginning reader with as wide a variety of experiences as is possible. The greater his variety of experiences, the greater his opportunities to develop concepts and improve perception will be. Through field trips, games, and classroom activities, you will be able to provide him with some of the experiences he may lack. In other instances, you may have to rely on audio-visual presentations, stories, and pictures to develop vicarious experiences. In either case, time spent in this type of activity is not only important, it is essential.

Even from this brief glimpse of reading as a perceptual process, we readily see that it is extremely complex. Perception affects, and is affected by, many other factors in reading. We see that it is affected by not only the senses, but also such things as culture, experience, emotion, maturity, and even personality. Even though a breakdown of perception may occur at any one of a number of points for a variety of reasons, you can do much to lessen its impact or even head it off. By providing a wide variety of experiences, by attending to verbal and nonverbal symptoms of difficulty, and by being willing to adapt and modify in accordance to individual needs, you can facilitate perception in the classroom.

## Reading as a Developmental Process

Reading, by its very nature, is a developmental process spanning the life of an individual. We don't know when it begins or when it ends. We do know, however, that the mother's poor health during pregnancy or the occurrence of complications during childbirth may have detrimental effects later on the child's reading performance. We know that certain children develop reading readiness before others and that some children learn to read quite early, perhaps as early as at the age of three or four, whereas others do not learn until much later. We also recognize that individuals continue to develop additional reading skills at differing rates throughout their school careers and afterwards. In short, reading is an ongoing, ever-changing process. Just as we are unsure as to its beginning, we are equally unsure of its ending. No matter how well an individual reads, he will always be able to make improvement. Even after he leaves school, he will need to improve the proficiency of some old skills and to develop new ones. As he chooses a career, he will have to develop special skills associated with his work. The telephone operator must be proficient in the rapid reading of telephone numbers, digits, etc.; the architect must learn to read blueprints accurately; the truck driver must be able to read road maps and order sheets, and so it goes. New careers, new personal and social responsibilities, new life situations—all demand the continuous development of reading.

Although reading is a developmental process, it does not proceed at a fixed rate. Although most children go through the same developmental sequences, they do so according to their own individual schedules. Because one child stands only at seven months, walks at eight, and runs at nine, we cannot expect it of all children. In the same sense, we should not expect all children to proceed in reading at the same pace. Although progress in reading development is usually orderly and systematic, exceptions are to be expected. Sometimes, we can help facilitate a reader's progress by recognizing a problem and solving it; at other times, however, we may allow him to slip behind by our failure to diagnose a problem. Sometimes, the problem is merely one of maturation, and we simply have to wait until the child is ready. Even though we generally think of reading readiness as a prereading level, we should all be aware that readiness must be developed for each new level of learning. In this sense the developmental process is sequential in nature. What happens at one level of development influences subsequent levels. Each new level is in reality an outgrowth of earlier levels rather than an addition to them. The best way to ensure the child's readiness for the next level is to thoroughly prepare him at his present level.

One of the harsh realities of reading development is that the good readers get better and the poor readers fall farther behind. It is enough to say that there are many factors contributing to this dilemma. However, because this is true, expectations should be modified to meet the child's potential. Quite often we frustrate a slower child by expecting too rapid progress while we neglect another by underestimating his potential. To this end, we would caution the use of normed tests to decide where a child should or should not be. A norm-referenced test merely indicates where the student is in relation to group norms, not where he is in relation to his own potential.

Just as reading has been described as a developmental process, it might also be called an unfolding process; as each successive level of accomplishment unfolds, it reveals insight into successively higher levels of achievement. In addition, the unfolding process opens up an ever-increasing variety of opportunities for practice and application. Skills are mutually reinforcing, moving the student toward greater and greater independence in relation to both instruction and content. This is what the reading process is all about: a movement from dependence to independence, a movement from developing reading as a task to using it as a tool.

In looking at reading as a developmental task, two things immediately stand out. First, we must realize that reading is taught; it isn't something that occurs incidentally. No child learns to read by watching someone else read. Most of what occurs in reading is unobservable. Unlike in the teaching of swimming, we cannot throw the child into the pool and depend on his instinct for survival to save him. Reading isn't an instinct; it's a learned process dependent on the acquisition of certain skills and procedures. A child may understand that reading is a type of communication and even that certain symbols represent words. However, until he has been taught to decode those symbols and identify them with particular concepts and experiences in such a way as to get meaning from them, he isn't reading.

Second, without belaboring the point, it does seem important to emphasize that reading is a process, not a subject. Too often, a teacher allows reading instruction to deteriorate to the level of teaching a basal reader, a program, or a workbook, in much the same manner that he teaches social studies, health, or geography. The children wind up knowing more about Billy's father or Sally's pony than about the skills and abilities generalizable to other situations and materials. The point is, of course, that content should not be considered an end; rather, it is a means to an end. Agreed, content should and must be interesting and appropriate; however, its major reason for existence in the initial stages of learning is to provide a vehicle for the process. The process will be generalizable to other grades and subjects; the content will not.

One way of describing the relationship between reading as a task and reading as a tool is shown in Fig. 2.1. This diagram shows that emphasis on reading instruction decreases as emphasis on content development increases. Although this is essentially true, the major change is one of emphasis rather than of dimension—the change being a move from reading instruction to reading usage. In the primary

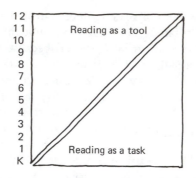

*Fig. 2.1    Reading is both a task and a tool.*

grades the reading process is given major focus, and content receives less emphasis. During these years the child learns nearly all of his decoding skills, as well as many of the basic comprehension and study skills. Because he has only limited reading ability, reading is still a relatively ineffective tool. Fortunately, most primary school programs demand relatively little use of reading other than in formal reading instruction. To repeat, the primary emphasis at this stage is, and must be, on learning to read. If the child fails to master basic skills, he is certain to have difficulty when confronted with a content load which demands their use.

As Fig. 2.1 further illustrates, during the elementary grades there is still an important emphasis on learning to read. Although further help must be given to those children who have failed to master decoding, the emphasis at this level shifts to comprehension and study skills. From this point on, the use of reading as a tool becomes increasingly important. The student must have the skills to handle many kinds of reading tasks and be able to derive meaning from a wide variety of reading materials. Instruction in reading comprehension must not be limited to performance in a basal reader or workbook; it must be applicable to such areas as history, geography, and science. Instruction in reading for the main idea, for facts, for inference, etc., usually takes place in a reading program, but most of the application of these skills will take place in the content areas. Although taught in the reading program, study skills such as map reading, graph interpretation, dictionary skills, and following directions will be used in geography, math, history, science, etc. Furthermore, there will be an increased need at this level for self-directed, interpretive, and creative reading skills. The student who does not have these skills is not only disadvantaged at his present level, he will also be severely handicapped at all subsequent levels. The emphasis must be on both teaching the basic skills and integrating them into the total program. Content becomes less important as a vehicle for the process and more important as an academic area.

The role of reading as a task tapers off sharply during junior high and high school. Many schools cease formal reading programs altogether after elementary school. However, in most cases instruction continues under the guise of English or language arts. Under such labels as reading for meaning, vocabulary development, and reference skills, comprehension and study skills still receive some instruction. In addition, some schools add developmental and/or special reading classes to their programs, but these are usually formed for the underachiever. Reading problems still materialize, but are labeled science problems, history problems, or social studies problems. Little, if any, help is available for the student who still hasn't gained independence in reading. At this point, reading should have reached a stage at which it can be considered a tool. If it is an inadequate one, the student has little hope of achieving success. If, on the other hand, the student has mastered the various levels in the reading process, he will find reading the single most important source of help in dealing with his daily work load.

In summing up the developmental process, we stress again that it is highly idiosyncratic. No matter how much we as teachers and educators talk about the average child, there's no such being. Each student in the classroom is an individual with highly personal abilities, needs, motives, and interests. And it is his ability, motivation, and interest that will largely determine his rate and route of reading development. As we have mentioned, if he has average intelligence, a relatively comprehensive background of experience, and no serious physical or emotional problems, he should progress normally. However, the fact that he is inadequate in one of these areas or that he does have some sort of handicap does not necessarily mean that he will fail to achieve satisfactorily. One cannot overestimate the ability of the properly motivated individual to compensate. With the right kind of motivation, the most unlikely candidates for reading have been known to succeed. On the other hand, the most able students often fail for lack of it.

## Reading as a Skill-Development Process

As has been amply illustrated, reading is a complex exercise dependent on a great variety of factors. We have thus far alluded to but not discussed reading as a skill-development process. Although this topic will be examined in considerable detail in later chapters, it seems relevant to introduce it here in a brief overview.

### The nature of the skill-development process

*Skills are objective*

One of the first things of which we become aware when examining the process of reading-skill development is that it is somewhat objective. It is objective in the sense that its development is dependent on neither one set of materials and methods nor academic grade levels. This is not to deny that there are reading skills within the process which are so related, but these are no more than specialized outgrowths of the basic skills.

One very important part of the development process is the identification of the skills to be taught. Once a specific skill has been identified, any one of a number of methods and materials can be used to instruct the child. A case in point might be the teaching of initial consonants. One child may learn best through a visual program, another through a program utilizing heavy auditory emphasis, and another may require some type of tracing or kinesthetic training. Three different children may be working on initial consonants, each utilizing the methods and materials most appropriate to him. Another example might be based on the skill of using an index. Although a basal reader or elementary storybook might provide appropriate material for teaching this skill to a primary school student, you would probably want to use materials such as newspapers, magazines, catalogues, etc., in teaching it to an adult. In both cases the skill is the same—only the materials and/or the methods in teaching will vary.

Just as skill development is not tied to specific materials and methods, neither is it dependent on grade level. In its truest sense, a skill is a skill—not a first-grade skill or a fourth-grade skill or a sixth-grade skill. Because of this, you as a teacher should be aware of the entire spectrum of skills. In order to meet the specific needs of the student at his individual level, you must know which skills precede his present skills and which follow. It is not enough to know that a particular student is a second grader who came from the first grade and who will go to the third. This gives you only minimal information about his skills.

### Skills are sequential

Even though skills are not sequentially tied to grade level, they are somewhat related sequentially. This does not mean that you must teach initial consonants before final consonants, the period before the question mark, or reading for facts before reading for the main idea. In fact, many teachers prefer to teach particular clusters of skills together. On the other hand, there are some skills that are prerequisites for other skills. For example, knowledge of vowel and consonant sounds should be introduced before work with diagraphs and dithphongs, and work in indexing depends on skill in alphabetizing. In such cases, nonmastery at one level will be reflected at subsequent levels. Skills build upon one another, and what often appears as a new skill is in reality an extension of an old one. Location of specific information for classroom research is an example of this. Although this is sometimes thought of as a single skill, it is in reality the extension and combination of a number of skills such as alphabetizing, using a card catalogue, decoding catalogue card data, locating sources by shelf numbers, using the index, and locating the information within the particular source of material. Until the student has some mastery of these prerequisite skills, he will not be independent in searching for resource material.

### Skills are generalizable

In addition to being objective and sequential, skills are generalizable in nature. Just as they span method, material, and grade level, they also span content. Except for those unique skills peculiar to the language and taxonomy of specialized subject matter, the same reading skills can be used in all content areas. When a student learns to attack words independently, it will be of no consequence to him whether they are located in a math text, a geography workbook, or a novel. Inferring the main idea of a paragraph from a history text involves the same skills as inferring the main idea of a paragraph from a science text. Using the context of a sentence to determine the meaning of an unknown word is the same skill, no matter in what subject matter. The basic reading skills are generalizable and the student who has mastered them should be able to apply them whenever and wherever the situation demands.

## Stages of skill development

The word *stages* used in the description of the skill-development process is not to be confused with or interpreted as meaning discrete levels. To be sure, one can speak of levels in the sense of levels of achievement within certain skill sequences; however, within the process itself, stages are more fluid. At times, different skills flow into one another, become immersed in one another, or parallel one another in development. The child does not cease to develop at one stage because he has begun to develop at another. On the other hand, some stages, particularly those involving interpretation and application, are dependent on some mastery of previous levels.

*The foundation of the skill-development process is concept development.* This begins with the child's earliest experiences and continues to grow throughout his life. Concept development is a prerequisite to reading in much the same way that it is to listening and speaking. It serves as a knowledge bank into and from which he will continually be putting and taking information. Just as the child grows and changes with growth, so will his concept load grow and change.

There is apparently no one right set of concepts that will guarantee reading success. However, several factors appear to contribute to adequate concept development. Possibly most important among these is the provision for a wide and varied background of experience. The child who is limited to one type of environment, one level of communication, or one set of experiences is very likely to be handicapped. Another factor of particular importance to concept development is language development. Parents who listen to their children and encourage them to express themselves verbally are providing valuable opportunities for language and vocabulary growth. Children learn the meaning of words from hearing them used and by using them.

*A second stage of skill development deals with recognition and identification.* Even as the child is building his basic concept base, he is also beginning to relate some of his concepts to particular stimuli. The most obvious example of this in reading is his recognition and identification of letters and words. He learns to relate certain letters and words or combinations of letters and words with concepts that have meaning for him. When he can successfully combine the two—the stimulus and the concept—he gets meaning from the experience.

*A third stage of development deals with interpretation of information.* Obviously, the child has been dealing with some type of interpretation of information from the beginning of the process. This is apparent in both the concept development and the recognition and identification stages. Those who argue that interpretation is a kind of reasoning and not limited to reading are correct; however, we cannot deny its importance to reading also. In the sense that reading deals with a particular set of stimuli and skills peculiar to its own process, it is somewhat unique, i.e., something more than general reasoning.

In dealing with interpretation of information, we must deal with two types—literal and inferential. Since interpretation is generally conceived to be a type of comprehension skill, it seems best to illustrate it in that context. Literal interpretation of information refers to the interpretation of facts as they are presented. As an example of literal interpretation as a comprehension skill, let us look at the following sentence and questions.

Columbus discovered America on October 12, 1492.

1. Who discovered America?
2. When did Columbus discover America?
3. What country did Columbus discover?

Although this example may be oversimplified, it is not unlike the procedures usually applied in testing for literal interpretation. As you can see, this task requires no more than a matching of fact with question. If the student is not allowed to look back at the stimulus sentence, we add the dimension of memory; however, it is still a relatively straightforward task. The student merely interprets the information in the sentence and translates it into what he understands to be an acceptable answer to satisfy the dimensions of the question. The question determines the expectation of the student, and it is this expectation that determines the nature of the interpretation. For instance, the same stimulus statement might be used as a basis for one type of inference question: *How do you think Columbus felt when he saw America for the first time?* This question changes the expectation and thus changes the nature of the task.

The major difference between literal and inferential interpretation, then, lies in the expectation of the student. Whether it be extrinsic, as in the case of a test question, or intrinsic, as in person knowledge-seeking, it is of primary importance. To further illustrate the difference between literal and inferential interpretation, let us examine the following paragraph and questions as an example of inferential comprehension.

Joey stopped his new bike on the sidewalk in front of Bill's house. Bill came out to look at it. He was wishing that he had a new bike. His squeaked and rattled and had lost most of its paint. But then, new bicycles cost money, and Bill was very poor.

*Questions*

1. What suggests to you that Bill didn't have a new bicycle?

2. Where did the story take place?

   a) in town
   b) in the country
   c) on a ranch

3. Why do you think Joe wanted Bill to see his new bike?

In looking at the questions, we immediately recognize that the task involved in answering them is more than straight matching. We also recognize that answering the three questions requires using three different types of information. For example, we have three pieces of information from which to infer an answer to the first question: (a) Bill's bike *squeaked*, *rattled*, and had *lost most of its paint*. This is the description of an old bicycle, not a new one; (b) Bill wished he had a new bike. This suggests that he didn't have one. This is a type of analogy; (c) New bicycles cost money, and Bill was poor. This analogy suggests that Bill didn't have a new bike because he could not afford one.

To answer the second question, we have only one piece of information from which to infer an answer. That there was a sidewalk in front of Bill's house suggests that the story takes place in town. By adding the additional constraint of multiple-choice format, we allow the question to be answered by use of the processes of analogy and elimination.

There is no correct answer for the third question. We have no facts on which to base an answer. In this case, any logical answer must be considered correct. Our answer will probably reflect our experiences dealing with reasons for showing someone a new possession which we have acquired.

Inference, then, as illustrated here, involves the interpretation and combination of whatever facts and experiences we have in such a way as to satisfy our expectations. At times it may involve analogy, the convergence of a number of facts and experiences, or the recognition, interpretation, and translation of a single fact. At other times it may require the scanning of our personal experiences in an effort to identify some particular piece of information relevant to the expectation.

*A fourth stage in the skill-development process is application and generalization.* Even though a child has achieved a relatively adequate concept base and has mastered the skills involved in recognition, identification, and interpretation of information, the process may not be complete. He may still lack the ability to apply and generalize the skills and information he has acquired. Until he has gained this ability, he will not achieve independence in reading.

As with interpretation, we see examples of generalization and application at all stages in the development process. These range from recognizing that roses, daisies, and tulips are all flowers and that *c* in lower case, *C* in upper case, and *c* in script all have the same sound, to certain analogies necessary for interpretation of inferential information. A student, for example, must not only recognize that the vowel combination *ea* is generally pronounced $\bar{e}$ and that alphabetizing by three or four letters involves the same process as alphabetizing by two letters, he must also be able to apply this knowledge to the words he encounters in reading. Only when the student can apply and generalize a skill can he be said to have mastered it.

## Conclusion

In this chapter we have tried to briefly describe the reading process. We have done so by examining it as a psychological process, a sensory process, a perceptual process, a development process, and a skill-development process. We have attempted to emphasize above everything else that it is an individual-oriented process. Each child is a unique and complex being with a unique and complex relation to reading. Only by recognizing this in our classrooms and emphasizing it in our daily teaching can we help each child reach his reading potential.

This chapter is not intended in any sense to be a definitive description of the reading process. Rather, it is intended to provide you with a cursory look at what goes into it. By looking at the process from a number of different angles, we have attempted to give you a better understanding of reading. We believe that by having a better understanding, you will be able to provide a more meaningful experience for each individual in your classroom.

## References

Ball, E. A. "Visual functioning in reading disability," *Education* **82** (1961): 175–178.

Benson, J. "Teaching reading to the culturally different child," in *Readings on Reading*, ed. Alfred R. Binter, John Diabal, and Leonard Kise, Scranton, Pa.: International Textbook Company, 1969, p. 259.

Betts, E. A. "A physiological approach to the analysis of reading disability," *Educational Research Bulletin* **13** (1934): 135–140, 163–173.

Betts, E. A. and A. S. Austin. *Visual Problems in School Children*, Chicago: The Professional Press, 1941.

Bond, G. L. "Auditory and speech characteristics of good and poor readers," *Teachers College Contributions to Education*, 1935, No. 567.

Bond, G. L. and E. B. Wagner. *Teaching the Child to Read*, 4th ed. New York: Macmillan, 1966.

Cohen, A. and G. G. Glass. "Lateral dominance and reading ability," *The Reading Teacher* **21** (1968): 343–348.

Coleman, H. A. "The relationship of socio-economic status to the performance of junior high school students," *The Journal of Experimental Education* **9** (1940): 1962.

Dearborn, W. F. and I. W. Anderson. "Aniseikonia as related to disability in reading," *Journal of Experimental Psychology* **23** (1938): 559–577.

Eames, T. H. "The effect of anisometropia on reading achievement," *American Journal of Optometry and Archives of American Academy of Optometry* **41**, 12 (1964): 700–702.

Gates, A. I. "The necessary mental age for beginning reading," *Elementary School Journal* **37** (1937): 497–508.

Gates, A. I. and G. L. Bond. "Reading readiness: a study of factors determining success and failure in beginning reading," *Teachers College Record* **37** (1936): 679–685.

Goetzinger, C. P., D. D. Dirks, and C. J. Baer. "Auditory discrimination and visual perception in good and poor readers," *Annals of Otology, Rhinology, and Laryngology* **69** (1960): 121–136.

Gough, H. G. "The relationship of socio-economic status to personality inventory and achievement test scores," *Journal of Educational Psychology* **37** (1946): 535–536.

Gray, W. S. *The Teaching of Reading and Writing*, Chicago: UNESCO, Scott, Foresman, 1956.

Harrington, S. M. J. and D. Durrell. "Mental maturity versus perception abilities in primary reading," *Journal of Educational Psychology* **46** (1954): 375–380.

Harris, A. J. *How to Increase Reading Ability*, 5th ed. New York: David McKay, 1970.

Kephart, N. C. "Visual skills and their relation to school achievement," *American Journal of Ophthalmology* **36**, Part I (1953): 794–799.

Knox, G. E. "Classroom symptoms of visual difficulty," *Clinical Studies in Reading: II*, Suppl. Educational Monograph No. 77, Chicago: University of Chicago Press, 1953, pp. 97–101.

Morphett, M. V. and C. Washburne. "When should children begin to read?" *Elementary School Journal* **29** (1931): 496–503.

Park, G. E. and C. Burri. "The relation of various eye conditions and reading achievement," *Journal of Educational Psychology* **34** (1943): 290–299.

Patin, H. "Class and caste in urban education," *Chicago School Journal*, **45** (1964): 305–310.

Reynolds, M. C. "A study of relationships between auditory characteristics and specific silent reading abilities," *Journal of Educational Research* **46** (1953): 439–449.

Riessman, F. *The Culturally Deprived Child*, New York: Harper & Row, 1962.

Shearer, R. V. "Eye findings in children with reading difficulties," *Journal of Pediatric Ophthalmology* **3**, 4 (1966): 47–52.

Smith, H. P. and E. V. Dechant. *Psychology in Teaching Reading*, Englewood, N. J.: Prentice-Hall, 1961.

Spache, G. D. *Toward Better Reading*, Champaign, Ill.: Garrard, 1963.

Spache, G. D. and C. E. Tillman. "A comparison of visual profiles of retarded and non-retarded readers," *Journal of Developmental Reading* **5**, 2 (1962): 101–109.

Strang, R. "Relationships between certain aspects of intelligence and certain aspects of reading," *Educational and Psychological Measurements* **3** (1943): 355–359.

Templin, M. C. "Phonic knowledge and its relation to spelling and reading achievement of fourth grade pupils," *Journal of Educational Research* **47** (1954): 441–454.

Thomas, D. R. *Oral Language Sentence Structure and Vocabulary of Kindergarten Children Living in Low Socio-economic Urban Areas*, Ann Arbor: University Microfilms, 1962.

Thompson, B. B. A. "Longitudinal study of auditory discrimination," *Journal of Educational Research* **56** (1963): 376–378.

Traxler, A. E. "A study of the *California Test of Mental Maturity: Advanced Battery*," *Journal of Educational Research* **32** (1939): 329–335.

Vernon, M. D. *The Psychology of Perception*, Baltimore: Penguin Books, 1962.

Witty, P. A. and D. Kopel. "Heterophoria and reading disability," *Journal of Educational Psychology* **27** (1936): 222–230.

——— *Reading and the Educative Process*, Boston: Ginn, 1949.

# 3 / The reader

If you read between the lines in Chapter 2, the main point is unmistakable: *Reading is a complex process*. This point has been made by many other writers and inferred by many other readers, but it remains basic to any consideration of the *whys* and *hows* of reading instruction. To ignore the complexity or to attempt to oversimplify the process would be naive. Naiveté in reading instruction gives rise to sure-fire methodology and one-shot cures. The purpose for pointing out the complexity, then, is not to titillate the ego and boggle the mind, but to help stamp out oversimplified solutions for complex problems.

Up to this point, the focus has been on the *process* of reading. In Chapter 3 the focus is on the *reader*. This amounts to a shifting of focus, not an attempt to divorce the reader from reading process. The latter would be like trying to interview Ted Kennedy without mentioning the Democratic Party. But the fact remains that each reader is a unique individual. We feel that this uniqueness bears special consideration.

## The Individual

The complex process of reading is translated to real-world behaviors only when human beings tackle the tasks of mastering the composite skills and of making sense out of printed symbols. The process is abstract and lifeless until a reader is involved. Yet each reader is an individual with unique characteristics. Thus, while the reader makes the process come alive, he also adds to the complexity of the process, for he brings to it the full range of his own idiosyncrasies. Focused reading instruction is possible only when both the process and the individual are given due consideration.

**Individual differences**

Leona Tyler (1969) wrote an article on individual differences for the fourth edition of the *Encyclopedia of Educational Research*. The article is extremely readable, and it would be worthwhile for you to study the whole thing. But in a very real sense, she summed it all up in a single sentence. "The uniqueness of the individual," she wrote, "is a fundamental principle of human life" (p. 639).

Tyler's statement was preceded by the point that even a teacher who deals with 300 pupils a year for 40 years will never encounter two who are precisely alike. They will differ in both physiological and psychological ways. In fact, they will differ so widely and in such a multitude of ways that if a number of characteristics are to be considered at once, there is no "normal" person who can serve as a standard to which the others can be compared.

But forget about Tyler and the *Encyclopedia* for a moment. Think about yourself and all the people you have ever known. If you are a teacher, think about the children in your classes. If you are still in training to become a teacher, think about your classmates, friends, and acquaintances. Can you think of any two—including the twins—who are exactly alike? The point, of course, is that there is no need to cite authorities or research studies to demonstrate individual differences. We are surrounded by individual differences! We are ourselves collections of individual differences that are unmatched in the whole of creation.

Perhaps we are belaboring an obvious point. Individual differences clearly exist, and virtually everyone admits that they do. But consider one more quotation from Tyler's article:

> It is psychological individuality which is of the greatest importance to education. Each student in a classroom, no matter how carefully selected as a member of a "homogeneous" group, will of necessity react in his own unique way to the situation ... when a teacher makes an assignment to a class of 30, it is actually 30 different assignments that are carried out.*

Are those of us who are prepared to accept the concept of individual differences prepared to accept the consequences of individual differences as well?

The concept is easier to accept than the consequences. Many teachers who fully accept, say, the normal, or bell-shaped, distribution of intelligence do little or nothing in their classrooms to adapt the instruction accordingly. But to single out just one dimension of individual differences, e.g., intelligence, is to greatly oversimplify the problem. Perhaps this tendency to oversimplify by fixating on but one dimension at a time is at least partly responsible for our typically poor attempts to cope with individual differences. If we would take a look at the larger, more complex picture, there would be no way to avoid the conclusion that instruction must indeed

---

\*    Robert L. Ebel and Victor H. Noll, eds., *Encyclopedia of Educational Research*, 4th ed., New York: Macmillan, 1969, p. 639. Reprinted by permission.

be individualized. Then, we could get on with the task of figuring out how to get the job done.

## Some points from individual psychology

A number of points are well supported by the existing work in individual psychology. Taken together, they demonstrate the wide range of concerns we must have in order to work effectively with each individual.

1. *Children achieve at different rates.* This point is obvious to anyone who has ever worked with children. Some of them learn almost spontaneously, whereas others learn only after much repetition and belabored effort. The tendency, though, may be to oversimplify the reason for these differences by explaining them solely in terms of intellectual ability, or worse, IQ scores. The fact is that achievement rates are also influenced heavily by such factors as previous experience, sex, physical ability, and a multitude of personality variables. All of the latter are as potent in their own way as is "intelligence." One result is that attempts to identify *homogeneous* groups on the basis of IQ scores never turn out to be very satisfactory.

The only effective way to deal with different achievement rates is to pace the rate of instruction so it is suitable to each individual's pace of learning. This is, of course, much more easily said than done, but it gets right to the heart of the matter of efficient teaching and learning. Efficient, or focused, reading instruction is properly paced. Proper pacing is based on: (1) a thorough knowledge of individual's achievement rates, and (2) an explicit knowledge of exactly what it is that we want them to learn. A major purpose in the remaining chapters of this book is to establish the knowledge base required to deal effectively with individual's learning rates.

2. *Differences in achievement increase as children advance through school.* Two additional facts seem relevant here. First, the *better* the teaching, the *greater* the differences. Certain critics of education seem to be suggesting that the goal ought to be a pre-established level of performance for all. What a waste of human potential that would be! Well-focused, effective teaching will maximize the realization of each child's full potential and ensure a range in achievement that is as great as the range in individual differences. Second, given *equal* amounts of practice, the differences in good and poor achievers' performance will, all other things remaining equal, *increase.* In a sense, this goes like the old song that says ". . . the rich get richer and the poor get poorer." (To add a bit of parenthetical nostalgia, the song goes on with ". . . In the meantime, in between time, ain't we got fun." The analogy, it appears, is strictly a one-liner.) Again, the outcome is an increase in the range of differences in achievement.

The more general issue of *teaching for mastery* is also relevant here. Reduced to essentials, mastery teaching amounts to setting specific objectives and then seeing to it that every child masters the objectives. Handled in a mechanistic, heavy-handed manner, mastery teaching *could* put a lid on achievement, thereby decreasing the range in differences. This would, of course, amount to a dreadful misuse of a sound idea. We feel that mastery teaching of the basic reading skills is essential. But we also know that the *pace* of such teaching must vary greatly from individual to individual and that there is more to *mature* reading than essential skills. In other words, *how fast* and *how far* will remain highly individual matters.

3. *Achievement is often marked by spurts and plateaus.* Achievement rate in any given area is a highly personal matter, but whether it is fast or slow it is likely to be marked by periods of relatively little progress and periods of rapid growth. This phenomenon is particularly apparent in remedial teaching situations, where the periods of no measurable progress may tend to be prolonged. Apparently, children have a need from time to time for an opportunity to assimilate new information, to fit it into existing cognitive frameworks, and to organize it all into a manageable whole.

The spurt-plateau phenomenon has rather obvious implications for pacing the instruction of individuals, but there are also implications for interpersonal relations. When both a teacher and a pupil know that a plateau period may be followed by rapid growth, they may find the teaching/learning situation a bit more palatable. The important point here is that learning is not a simple matter of continuous input-output. Also involved are such things as assimilation, adaptation, reality checking, idiosyncratic learning styles, and widely varied experiential and social backgrounds.

4. *Native endowment (biological factors) plays a large role in a child's development.* Up to this point we have been focusing mainly on psychological and experiential factors, both of which are powerful forces in shaping human differences. The fact remains, however, that each human being is bounded by his biological attributes. Consider a simple analogy: The *size* of a box establishes limits to what can go into it. The size does not dictate *what* can go in, nor does it determine whether it will be partially or completely filled. Similarly, biological attributes establish limits on potential without dictating whether that potential will be realized.

Suffice it to say here that human beings differ immensely in their biological attributes. The differences are real, and they ought to be considered when we look at individuals.

5. *Environmental factors play a large role in a child's development.* The old notion that intelligence is fixed by hereditary, unchangeable factors has now been quite thoroughly discredited. Certainly, as suggested in the preceding point, hereditary biological endowment establishes a base, but there is considerable evidence that such things as nutrition, experiences, and training can and do have a profound influence on human intelligence *as it is currently measured.* In his well-received book, *The Biological Time Bomb*, Taylor (1968) made a careful but optimistic statement: "There is a guarded belief that one may be able to effect considerable improvements in the level of intelligence of future generations, even if the idea of an 'intelligence pill' which turns us all into geniuses in a week or two remains chimerical" (p. 125). That belief is gaining support.

The essential point here is that environmental factors *could* serve as equalizers by offsetting many kinds of individual differences. Poor teaching could be a great equalizer by encouraging mediocrity. Poor nutrition could prevent the realization of potential, as could an impoverished experiential background. Conversely, enriched environments *could* make for even greater individual differences. And there is an optimistic footnote to the latter. Note that with enrichment and the full realization of potential, *everybody* does *better*!

6. *Membership in a group may lead to wrong attribution of a certain characteristic to an individual.* This point has strong social psychological overtones, but it focuses clearly on the individual. And it gets at an important matter, namely, if dealing with real individual differences is difficult, then dealing with false differences is just plain mind-boggling.

We could look to race, religion, or ethnic background for some rather obvious examples, but we have resisted that temptation. We're tired of Polish jokes! Consider, instead, the following: "Your brothers and sisters were all good students, so you must be . . ." "So you're in remedial reading. You must be . . ." "Are you saying, Johnny, that you'd really rather take home ec than go out for baseball? You must be . . ." "This medical report says that you were a premature baby. That means that you must . . ." The message, we think, is clear.

7. *Intra-individual differences may be as great or greater than inter-individual differences.* All the things we have said about individual differences have to do with the differences *among* individuals. The fact is that there are also differences *within* individuals that must not be overlooked. Each individual is a collection of both strengths and weaknesses. To cite an obvious example, good readers are not necessarily good spellers. Individual uniqueness is indeed an individual matter.

## The Person

The matter of individual uniqueness is, as Tyler put it, "a fundamental principal of human life" (1969, p. 639). First recognizing and then coming to cope with this uniqueness in some sensible way is, we are convinced, what efficient, focused teaching is all about. We feel that in order to cope with individual uniqueness in the teaching of reading, we must first decide *what* it is we want children to learn. Then, we must be able to determine which children already know it, how we can teach it to the rest, and how we will know when each of them has learned it. What this calls for is the focusing of instruction through the use of behavioral objectives and criterion-referenced assessment. In other words, we are convinced that sensible reading instruction must be based on two kinds of information: (1) a reasonably explicit knowledge of what reading skills we want to teach, and (2) a reasonably thorough understanding of the unique strengths and weaknesses of each individual learner.

So far, so good! Who could quarrel with such a goal? Yet we see a need for a few words of caution. Concern for individual differences and for carefully focused instruction can cause problems as well as help to solve them. These problems are implicit in two paradoxes that confront us. We shall call them the "individual-person paradox" and the "teaching-learning paradox."

## The individual-person paradox

One of the present authors wrote about the individual-person paradox in another context (Otto and Smith, 1970). Some of the relevant points are:

> In our zealous attempts to understand and to provide for the individual we tend often to forget about the person.

> Macdonald (1965) had discussed the individual-person paradox: "The *person*... in contrast with the individual, is not prized for his uniqueness .... The person is valued because of what he shares in common with all other persons: the human condition .... To treat persons as individuals (in the psychological sense) is in essence to treat them as objects for our study and control."

> Individuals are indeed unique, and they do indeed seem to respond to instruction that is sensitive to their idiosyncratic strengths and weaknesses. Ultimately, though, the acceptance of these factors can—and often does—cause students to be treated as if they were little more than "objects for our study and control," as Macdonald put it. In this case what began as a sound and desirable attempt to personalize instruction becomes an extremely impersonal complex of procedures and categories.*

Each child presents us with a paradox. He is, on the one hand, an individual unique in the world. Because there is no else like him, he must be treated like no other. We must cater to his strengths and minister to his weaknesses. Yet he is, on the other hand, a person who has a common human status with all other beings. He is valued not for his idiosyncrasies, but for his common human status.

But if the paradox is complex, its resolution is straightforward. We must not lose sight of the person as we focus on the individual. The individual can be assessed in terms of his unique strengths and weaknesses and taught accordingly; but the person must remain unclassified, free to strive and free to learn. But as teachers, we are confronted by still another paradox when we attempt to strike a balance in dealing with the individual-person.

## The teaching-learning paradox

Educators have traditionally addressed themselves to the methodology—the how-to-do-it—of teaching. That is, or so it would appear, as it ought to be, for if we

---

\*    Wayne Otto and Richard J. Smith, *Administering the School Reading Program*, Boston: Houghton Mifflin, 1970, pp. 5–6. Reprinted by permission.

are to focus instruction, we must first have a clear notion of what the task is and how to tackle it. Unfortunately, such an emphasis usually tends to stress the *manipulation* of pupils rather than the *participation* of each pupil in the learning process. Thus, if we truly believe that active participation is an important aspect of efficient learning, we can see a teaching-learning paradox. On the one hand, once we decide what we want children to know, we want to get on with *teaching* them. On the other hand, we want to ensure that they take major initiative for their own learning. In effect, we want to be free to *manipulate*, yet be assured that everyone will *participate*.

This paradox, too, can be resolved if we will make the main function of teaching the *facilitation of learning*. Here again, concurrent concern for the individual and the person is critical. We can facilitate learning by helping learners to focus on what they need to know. This must involve not only a thorough understanding of the idiosyncrasies of each individual, but also an abiding conern for the integrity of each person.

In the balance of this chapter, guidelines are given for the facilitation and organization of instruction. Application of the guidelines will help to resolve the paradoxes just discussed.

## The Facilitation of Learning

For many years now, Carl Rogers has been writing and talking about things like client-centered therapy and student-centered teaching. He is making a point that is both simple and profound: The most important consideration in a relationship—whether it be counseling or teaching or both—is the *person* involved. Not the techniques or methodology, not the jargon, not the external trappings, but the *person*.

In one of his recent books, *Freedom to Learn*, Rogers (1969, Chapter 7) listed what he calls "principles or hypotheses" about learning. Taken together they bespeak the great value he places on each person who becomes involved in the process of learning. Taken as a set of assumptions about human beings as learners, they amount to a basis for beginning to work with individuals in a way that will ensure the facilitation of learning. Rogers' points, with our comments, follow.

1. *"Human beings have a natural potentiality for learning."* This basic point springs from a belief that human beings are naturally curious and eager to learn. This enthusiasm can, of course, be blunted by unsatisfactory or inappropriate learning experiences encountered in school. Witness the fact that with so many pupils, teachers must resort to jelly beans and other gimmicks to "motivate" them "to learn." But the fact is that all children are constantly learning. The only real question is whether—or how—we can get them to learn what we want them to know.

Consider the child who fails in reading. Whatever the true cause for the failure may be, the fact is that not only will his enthusiasm for school-oriented learning almost certainly be blunted, but his belief in his "natural potentiality for learning" will be shaken as well. Failure in reading can very quickly become chronic and spread to all areas of the curriculum. A teacher's main task, then, is to ensure that each pupil has the success experiences that give him reason to believe in himself as a learner.

2. "*Significant learning takes place when the subject matter is perceived by the student as having relevance for his own purposes.*" Teachers who act as facilitators of learning will make it a point, *first*, to discover what subject matter is most relevant for an individual at a given point in time, and *second*, to demonstrate the relevance of subject matter as it is presented. This is not to suggest that teachers ought to turn the responsibility for determining the curriculum over to their pupils. But they ought to know all they can about each pupil's background, interests, attitudes, and instructional needs. If they do, the matter of relevance is something that can be worked out between teacher and pupil.

3. "*Learning which involves a change in self-organization—in the perception of oneself—is threatening and tends to be resisted.*" A child may, for reasons unrelated to school, build an elaborate set of ego defenses on his completely self-inflicted inability to read. Thus, he becomes a kind of voluntary invalid who cannot be expected to respond to certain demands and who can expect certain concessions because of his problem. He builds up a strong negative incentive *not* to learn to read, because to learn to read would be to change drastically his self-perception as a nonreader and nonparticipant in a variety of related activities.

Although this example may be extreme, it is not nearly so uncommon as we might hope. The fact is that "perception of oneself" is a powerful determiner of success in learning—and of response to instruction.

The next two points are closely related:

4. "*Those learnings that are threatening to the self are more easily perceived and assimilated when external threats are at a minimum.*"

5. "*When threat to the self is low, experience can be perceived in different fashion, and learning can proceed.*"

Taken together, points four and five underscore the need to remove external pressures and all potential sources of ridicule or scorn from the learning situation. The sources of external threats are virtually limitless. For example, the child who speaks a neighborhood dialect may be threatened by the standard English he encounters in his teachers and in the books he reads. The youngest of several siblings may be threatened by the prospect of learning to read if she thinks that doing so will eliminate her dependence, which she sees as her last remaining claim to parental attention. "Big girls" can read, but they cannot expect much attention from busy parents. And, of course, children who are already experiencing reading problems have good reason to feel threatened and inadequate. They do not need to be told that they are lazy, or that all they need to do is try harder, or that they are going to be given a failing grade.

6. *"Much significant learning is acquired through doing."* A case in point is the way children acquire oral language. As Carroll (1971) puts it "Language is *learned* whereas reading is *taught*. That is, there is normally no formal system for teaching children to speak, whereas there are a multitude of formal systems for teaching children to read" (p. 35). Adults may provide language models for children, but the children learn to speak by speaking.

The irony is that although hardly anyone fails to learn to speak, failure in reading is all too common despite—or perhaps because of—the more formalized teaching. But the contrasts are significant. Speech is acquired gradually, but strong, immediate, and highly individual reinforcers are usually available. Reading, on the other hand, is usually presented in group situations, and reinforcement is likely to be neither immediate nor personal. If we could make learning to read more like learning to speak, perhaps we could cut down substantially on the reading failures.

7. *"Learning is facilitated when the student participates responsibly in the learning process."* Earlier, we mentioned the desirability of deciding first *what* we want children to learn and then determining who already knows it, how to teach it to the rest, and how to decide when they have learned it. These are precisely the things that we, as teachers, must determine before we can seriously solicit students' participation in their own learning. We have to decide on the rules of the game before we can invite anyone else to play.

And three closely related, final points:

8 *"Self-initiated learning which involves the whole person of the learner—feelings as well as intellect—is the most lasting and pervasive."*

9. *"Independence, creativity, and self-reliance are all facilitated when self-criticism and self-evaluation are basic and evaluation by others is of secondary importance."*

10. *"The most socially useful learning in the modern world is the learning of the process of learning, a continuing openness to experience and incorporation into oneself of the process of change."**

All three final points call for the active involvement of the learner in his own learning. They underscore the need for each teacher to have a positive perception of each pupil's potential for learning. They bring us full circle, back to the key point that human beings will learn, that they have "a natural potentiality for learning."

## Role of the teacher

We have already suggested that the teaching-learning paradox can be resolved if we will make the facilitation of learning the main function of teaching. The role of the teacher, then, is to act as a facilitator of learning. We feel that this is com-

---

* Carl Rogers, *Freedom to Learn*, Columbus, Ohio: Charles E. Merrill, 1969. Principles reprinted by permission.

pletely consistent with our position that the way to deal with individual uniqueness is to first decide what it is that we want children to learn. Active teaching will not amount to coercion if the teacher proceeds as a true facilitator of learning.

The facilitation of learning proceeds from a belief in the value of each person and in each person's natural potentiality to learn. It is shaped by an understanding of and a respect for each person's uniqueness as an individual learner. But the learning can be focused only after some basic decisions have been made about what it is that we want children to learn. In reading instruction, what we *want* children to know is what they *need* to know in order to read successfully.

Perhaps we can put it another way. When you look at potential readers, you see unique individuals with common human attributes who are about to tackle an immensely complex task. As a reading teacher, what you see is what you get. To facilitate their learning, you must deal concurrently with human needs, individual differences, and a complex process. What you need is an organized approach, a way to get on with the individualization of instruction.

## The Individualization of Instruction

If your goal is to facilitate the learning of individuals, you need to consider some approaches to the individualization of instruction. Exactly how to get on with the individualization of instruction is, of course, a topic that has received a great deal of attention from a great many people. Some claim to have discovered the only way to do it, others suggest that there may be a number of workable approaches and that individual teachers need to pick the one that is best for them, and still others seem to have given up in despair. We certainly do not want to suggest that we have discovered the only way, but we do want to suggest one way to at least approach the problems involved. But first, let us decide exactly what we are talking about.

### What it is

Stahl and Anzalone (1970) have written a book entitled *Individualizing Teaching in Elementary Schools*. The book is excellent. The authors deal with the individualization of instruction in sensible, practical terms, and they present the goal as one that can realistically be attained by any dedicated teacher. This we find refreshing, because too much of what has been written presents individualized instruction as a kind of will-o'-the-wisp that could be handled only by "super teachers." Their comments on differentiated instruction are particularly relevant here.

> If your concept of individualized instruction is a continual series of paired situations, teacher and student, reason and experience will tell you that this kind of individualization is impossible. A strictly tutorial relationship is not only impossible but also not truly desirable if we value the social learnings and skills which are acquired only by working within groups. Occasionally it will

be necessary to work with one child, but you can use many other strategies to differentiate instruction. (p. 25)*

In practical terms, then, the suggestion is that individualizing instruction amounts to *differentiating instruction*. We agree, and we are convinced that this is the conception that can make the individualization of instruction workable. Stahl and Anzalone put it this way:

> To truly individualize instruction we would probably have to provide every child with a unique set of learning experiences. We might also find it necessary to provide each student with a unique set of teachers—teachers who are expert in recognizing and developing the many facets of that learner's potential. Differentiating instruction is a realistic step toward the ideal of individualized instruction. You differentiate when you recognize and accept the different learning needs within the class and modify your methods to meet some of those needs. (p. 26)†

In teaching reading, individualization through the differentiation of instruction can proceed most efficiently when we have a way to assess the individual's strengths and weaknesses and to adapt our teaching in view of what we know about each individual. This amounts to helping learners focus on what they need to know.

## How to do it

To do an effective job of focusing reading instruction, we must have a way to organize instruction. We are suggesting one way to proceed. The points that follow can provide a framework for organizing instruction (see Fig. 3.1).

1. *Identify essential skills.* We have already stated our belief that we must decide *what* we want children to learn if we hope to deal effectively with their individual differences as we teach them to read. This means that the first step toward organizing instruction in reading must be to identify the skills that are essential to success in reading. Until this is done, there is no basis for *focusing* instruction.

Unfortunately, at the present time there is no empirically derived list of essential skills in reading. That is, the massive task analysis and research job that will be required to determine precisely which skills must be mastered, and in what order, has not been done. One of the problems is that people in reading education and research are still having trouble in reaching agreement on how to define reading. In any event, an empirically derived and validated list of skills is not likely to be available in the near future.

---

* From the book, *Individualized Teaching in Elementary Schools*, by D. K. Stahl and P. M. Anzalone. © 1970 by Parker Publishing Co., Inc., West Nyack, N.Y.
† *Ibid.*

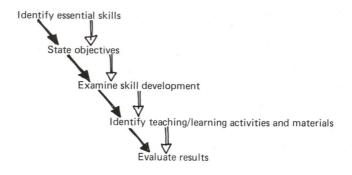

*Fig. 3.1    Flow chart for organizing instruction.*

This does not mean that nothing can be done now. The fact is that reading is being taught successfully, and there is reasonable agreement among teachers as to what the essential skills are. What we can do, then, is to make use of lists of skills that have the consensual support of successful teachers. One such list of essential skills is suggested in Chapters 7–10.

As a reading teacher, then, once you have decided which skills you consider essential to success in reading, you have a basis for proceeding with the differentiation of instruction. Your main task is to help each child to master the skills as rapidly and efficiently as possible. Continual progress—that is, moving each child along at a rate that is right for him, not at a rate that is tied to a curriculum guide or a basal reader—is possible because you know what you want each child to learn.

2. *State objectives in behavioral terms.* Having identified the essential skills, it is useful to pin down each one with a description of the behaviors that are expected from a child who has mastered it. Such a description is a *behavioral objective,* and it serves two purposes. First, since it makes explicit the behaviors considered relevant to each skill, it gives you a basis for discussing the skill with other people, and it sets a goal for teaching the skill. Second, it establishes an observable criterion that permits you to decide when a child has mastered the skill. (Objectives are discussed in detail in Chapter 6, and a behavioral objective is stated for each skill identified in the lists that are given in Chapters 7–9.)

3. *Examine the individual's skill development.* If we can decide which skills we consider essential and if we can describe our expectations regarding mastery of those skills, we are in a position to examine the skill-development status of individuals. We can observe the behavior of individuals to determine their strengths and weaknesses. Such knowledge about each individual is the practical basis for differentiated instruction in reading. Specific suggestions about ways to proceed are given in Chapters 11 and 12.

4. *Identify appropriate teaching/learning activities and materials.* Appropriate instruction involves more than focusing on strengths and weaknesses in skill development. It also involves providing differentiated instruction for different types of students. That is, given a common objective, some pupils will respond well to one instructional approach, some others will respond best to an alternative approach, and still others will do best with yet other approaches.

What this means is that teachers must not be lulled into a false sense of well-being by an objective-centered approach to teaching reading. They must remain *eclectics* in their approach to teaching. An eclectic does not follow any one system or approach; he selects and uses the best from all approaches. And, most important, an eclectic is in a position to adapt his approach with a given individual because he is aware of and comfortable with a variety of approaches.

So by all means, be an eclectic. But in order to avoid being overwhelmed by the vast quantities of materials and the varied procedures that are available for teaching reading, remember that your goals are described by objectives and they are prescribed by your list of essential skills. In other words, once you decide what is important, you have an efficient way to bring instruction and approaches to instruction into focus. You can organize your instruction and your instructional materials around your objectives. With an individual pupil you may follow any one of several paths, but you always know exactly where you are going.

5. *Evaluate the results.* Two levels of evaluation are essential when specific skills are the focus of instruction. First, there must be assurance that the skill-related objectives are being reached. Second, there must be assurance that the attainment of specific objectives is accompanied by functional reading ability, an ability to cope with the reading tasks encountered both in and out of school. The payoff for focused reading instruction comes at this second level.

We focus on essential skills and specific objectives in order to systematize teaching and encourage efficient learning. But the mastery of specific objectives is meaningless unless it is accompanied by an ability to get them all together and to read connected text. Many opportunities to apply the skills must be provided, and assurance that functional reading ability is increasing must be sought. Any evidence of a breakdown at either level is a signal to go back and re-evaluate the entire process.

A breakdown in specific skill development may indicate too rapid pacing, inappropriate teaching, overwhelming personal difficulties, or other problems that can be identified through careful re-examination. A breakdown in functional reading ability may indicate inadequate skill mastery, inability to apply known skills, or inappropriate choice of reading materials at a given stage of skill development. Such problems, too, can be identified through re-examination. The main advantage of a skill-centered approach to reading instruction is that it establishes a basis for tracing back to see what went wrong if the desired end results are not forthcoming. We can do a better job of teaching if we first decide exactly what we want children to learn.

## The Application of Learning Principles

This discussion may appear to have strayed away from our main concern in this chapter, the reader. But in a book that deals with *reading instruction*, we feel that the facilitation of learning and the organization of instruction are relevant to any consideration of the reader. As teachers, we cannot simply acknowledge the fact that each reader is unique; we must devise ways to deal with this uniqueness that are realistic in terms of the available resources and our own capabilities. And at the same time, concern for individual uniqueness must not be permitted to block our acceptance and appreciation of each person we deal with.

For a reading teacher, then, the facilitation of learning must be implicit in any discussion of the reader. Up to this point we have considered, first, some positive assumptions to guide the facilitation of learning and, second, a way to organize instruction to deal realistically with individual differences. We can turn now to some guidelines for instructional procedures that are consistent with Rogers' assumptions and our framework for organizing instruction.

## Learning principles

We have identified ten learning principles that have a great deal of support from both teachers in the field and research studies. In other words, the principles are sound in both theory and practice. The principles, with the related discussion, can serve as guidelines for planning instruction that gives concurrent consideration to the individual and to the person.

The discussion here is adapted from another source (Otto, McMenemy, and Smith, 1973), which was directed to remedial teachers and the remedial teaching situation. However, good remedial teaching is nothing more or less than good teaching at its best. The principles have to do with the facilitation of learning. While they can serve as guidelines for efficient teaching, the focus is clearly on the reader.

1. *"Secure the learner's cooperation."* This principle is basic to all the others. Unless and until a child becomes an active participant in the learning process, there can be no efficient learning. All of the principles that follow are designed to secure and enhance the learner's involvement by focusing on his personal strengths and weaknesses.

2. *"Offer instruction at the learner's level."* To do this you must first look carefully at each pupil's current level of skill development, at his mastery and nonmastery of essential skills, and at his personal needs and abilities. The next step is to bring to bear the most appropriate instructional materials and procedures. The goal is to match pupils and instruction.

Implementation of the framework for organizing instruction that we discussed earlier will be helpful. If you know *what* you want to teach and *how* to identify the needs of individuals, you have a very credible basis for offering instruction at the right level. Of course, you must also be familiar with and have access to a wide variety of materials at all levels in order to offer instruction that will meet the needs. Eclecticism is the name of the game!

3. *"Take small steps."* Borrow a basic idea from programmed instruction: Make each step so small that a correct response is assured. This means, of course, that you must know exactly where the child is and exactly where you want him to go as each step is taken.

Consider some examples. Given the goal of improved comprehension, it is not realistic to expect a child to move directly from a general inability to extract the main idea from a written passage to success in dealing with questions that have to do with the main ideas of passages. Instead, it is desirable to start with the understanding of words, phrases, and sentences; then to move to the literal comprehension of stated facts; then to identify a stated topic sentence or main idea; and finally, to infer a main idea that is implicit but unstated. Or, given the goal of independence in attacking words not known at sight words, it is not realistic to expect a child to begin at once to "sound out" such words. Instead, it is desirable to start with the discrimination of sounds within words and then to move through a sequence of instruction that builds sound-symbol associations.

In any case, careful analysis of the task is required before a sensible sequence of small steps can be planned. The fact that the steps are small does not detract from their importance. The identification of essential skills and the statement of related objectives will help to ensure that small steps move in the right direction.

Careful consideration of each pupil's personal goals is also required. A child must perceive a small step as one that is significant for him, or he will not derive any satisfaction from taking it; the next principle is closely related to this point.

4. *"Reinforce success."* The first assumption in programmed learning is that small steps will ensure correct responses. The second assumption is that correct responses are inherently reinforcing to the learner; that is, the learner derives satisfaction directly from the success experience. The assumption is undoubtedly sound in most instances. Most of the things we do, we do not because they yield immediate, tangible rewards, but because they give us a feeling of satisfaction, possibly because they move us toward a long-range goal.

Of course, a learner who successfully completes a step must know at once whether or not his response was correct if the experience is to be self-rewarding. That is, he must have *immediate knowledge of results.* Programmed instruction provides this knowledge of results, which is an important key to its effectiveness. A one-to-one tutorial situation also offers at least the possibility of immediate knowledge of results. In group situations a good teacher must be constantly on the alert to provide pupils with immediate feedback about the results of their efforts.

Some teachers make extensive use of tangible reinforcers (gold stars, jelly beans, dimes), as contrasted with the intangible reinforcement provided by knowledge of success. Tangible reinforcers are, in our opinion, most appropriately used with so-called reluctant learners, pupils who are improperly motivated to participate in school-related activities. Such reinforcers can be used to get the action started and then be withdrawn the moment learning becomes reasonably self-sustaining. The effective teacher is one who knows *when* a student perceives success and *what* constitutes reinforcement for him at that particular moment in time.

5. *"Keep learning tasks and materials meaningful."* Tasks that are meaningful are mastered much more quickly than tasks that are unclear or irrelevant. Likewise, materials must be meaningful in terms of their relevance and difficulty level to be worthwhile for a given child. The problem that teachers need to be aware of is that materials and directions for tasks may have *inherent meaning* and yet be *meaningless* to the children to whom they are directed.

Consider, for example, the statement, "Intelligence quotient equals mental age divided by chronological age." It has inherent meaning, and it means something to most teachers because they have the conceptual background to understand it. Yet it is meaningless to most elementary school pupils because they do not have the conceptual background that is required to understand it. The moral of the story is very simple: Do not assume that any set of directions or any piece of material will be meaningful for a given child simply because it has inherent meaning. Do try to know as much as possible about each pupil's conceptual and experiential background. The more you know, the less often you will miss the target when you assign a task or suggested materials.

6. *"Facilitate remembering."* Actually, we know more about forgetting than we know about remembering, so the best way to facilitate remembering is to combat forgetting. Most psychologists agree that the primary cause for forgetting is interference. That is, previous learning tends to block new learning, and new learning tends to blur old learning because similarities in what is known and what is newly learned tend to merge, thus interfering with both efficient learning and remembering.

The best way to combat interference is to see that the unique features of each new learning are stressed and understood. The more clearly you can differentiate between the old and the new, the less likely that interference will cause forgetting. In letter perception, for example, the difference between similar letters like *d* and *b*, or *p* and *q* should be stressed; in sight word recognition, the significant difference between similar words like *then* and *than*, or *horse* and *house*; in sound perception, the difference between *close*—as in *"close* the door"—and *close*—as in "a close call."

Remember, though, that while merging together may cause interference and forgetting, a similar process enables us to grasp useful relationships and to generalize. Do not hesitate to point out similarities and relationships when appropriate.

With some tasks, the best way to facilitate remembering is to provide for *overlearning*. This amounts to providing for repetitive practice beyond the mastery level. ("Repetitive practice" seems to have a five-letter synonym: DRILL. For this we offer no apology. Sensibly used, in moderate doses, drill is, in our opinion, a perfectly legitimate activity for which there is no effective substitute.) Common service words that appear very frequently in written materials, e.g., *this, that, the, and, but, for,* should, for example, be overlearned to the point where they are recognized instantly at a fairly early stage in the learning-to-read process.

7. "*Encourage pupil discovery of relationships.*" A phonics principle that is presented by the teacher and memorized by the pupil is not as likely to be applied in independent reading as is a generalization that he discovers for himself. When pupils are able to discover relationships and generalizations for themselves, they are in a much better position to transfer their understanding to new tasks and situations.

We are not suggesting that pupils be abandoned to proceed without direction to discover relationships. To facilitate instruction is to structure a learning sequence so that the learner is led to the discovery of relationships and generalization. The teacher's role is not to impose relationships, but to provide the kind of learning situation that permits them to emerge.

8. "*Guard against motivation that is too intense.*" Too much motivation can be harmful in the same sense that too much caution, which usually has positive effects, can be harmful. We want children to be cautious enough not to dart into the street, but we do not want them to become so fearful that they will not cross at intersections under safe conditions. We want children to be sufficiently motivated to become active participants in their learning, but we do not want them to become so anxious and fearful that their learning efficiency deteriorates. Motivation that is too intense causes distracting emotional reactions and a tendency to fixate on limited, and perhaps unimportant, bits of a total learning situation.

Motivation appears to facilitate learning up to an intermediate level of intensity; after that it tends to produce anxiety, fear, and decreased learning efficiency. The problem is complicated by the fact that different children start at different points on the continuum that runs from no-motivation to adequate motivation to anxiety. As a result, one child may benefit from a pep talk or the promise of a reward (or punishment), whereas the same talk or promise might cause another child extreme anxiety. We must, therefore, be sensitive to signs of anxiety or fear and be prepared to adapt out motivational techniques as needed.

9. "*Provide spaced practice.*" Both common sense and research results suggest that learning is likely to be more efficient when the available time is broken down into relatively short sessions than when it is massed into long sessions. The research suggests that this is particularly so when the learning task is one that involves high *response similarity*, e.g., similar-appearing sight words like *horse* and *house* or similar-appearing letter forms like *d-b, p-q, m-n,* and there is evidence that long-term memory is best after spaced practice. The implication is that the kinds of performance that seem to call most clearly for overlearning or drill also call most clearly for spaced practice. So be sure to break drill-type activities into short sessions.

10. *"Build a backlog of success experiences."** Ernest Hilgard, one of our leading learning theorists, believes that tolerance for failure is based largely on a backlog of success experiences. A child with a history of success experiences has that to sustain him when he encounters difficulty. Contrast this with the child who has experienced continuous failure or limited success. He has little reason to try again when he fails at a given task, for he has no reason to expect success. Thus, a teacher's most important function may be to ensure that every child gets many opportunities to add to his store of success experiences.

This brings us back to Rogers' basic assumption: "Each human being has a natural potentiality for learning." If you can do even a mediocre job of helping your pupils to build a backlog of success experiences, you will have contributed significantly to ensuring that they will recognize that potentiality in themselves.

## A Final Word

In this chapter we have suggested that the complex process of reading is complicated even further by the uniqueness of each individual who reads. To be an effective reading teacher, one must have a reasonably clear understanding of the reading process; equally important, one must have a profound respect for the reader as a unique individual, as a human being, and as a learner. But most important, one must be able to cope simultaneously with the process and the person in order to facilitate learning, which is what teaching is all about. We have suggested some ways to begin to cope with the immense task that confronts the reading teacher who would be a true facilitator of learning. Our suggestions about the organization of instruction and the application of learning principles represent movement toward a technology of education that can, in our opinion, lead to more effective teaching and more efficient learning.

But how far we can, or should, go with the technology remains to be seen. Eric Hoffer (1955, p. 12) once observed that "where there is the necessary technical skill to move mountains, there is no need for the faith to move mountains." We believe that in teaching reading there will continue to be a great need for the faith. We can use the technology to analyze the reading process, to assess the skill development needs of individuals, and to guide instruction; but when it comes to facilitating the learning of each reader, we must have faith in the judgments of perceptive teachers.

---

* Wayne Otto, Richard A. McMenemy, and Richard J. Smith, *Corrective and Remedial Teaching*, 2nd ed., Boston: Houghton Mifflin, 1973. Principles reprinted by permission.

# References

Carroll, John B. "Learning to read and learning one's language: some relationships," *Teaching Reading—Not by Decoding Alone*, ed. Joseph P. Kender, Danville, Ill.: The Interstate Printers and Publishers, 1971, pp. 31–42.

Hoffer, Eric. *The Passionate State of Mind*, New York: Harper & Row, 1955.

Macdonald, James B. "The person in the curriculum." Speech delivered at the 1965 Teachers College Curriculum Conference, Columbia University, November 1965.

Otto, Wayne, Richard A. McMenemy, and Richard J. Smith. *Corrective and Remedial Teaching*, 2d ed., Boston: Houghton Mifflin, 1973.

Otto, Wayne and Richard J. Smith. *Administering the School Reading Program*, Boston: Houghton Mifflin, 1970.

Rogers, Carl R. *Freedom to Learn*, Columbus, Ohio: Charles E. Merrill, 1969.

Stahl, Done Kofod and Patricia Murphy Anzalone. *Individualized Teaching in Elementary Schools*, West Nyack, N.Y.: Parker, 1970.

Taylor, Gordon B. *The Biological Time Bomb*, New York: World, 1968.

Tyler, Leona E. "Individual differences," in *Encyclopedia of Educational Research*, 4th ed., ed. Robert L. Ebel and Victor H. Noll, New York: Macmillan, 1969.

# 4 / Language development in young children

There are many reasons for attending to the development of language in young children. The linguist seeks to observe in the child's language clues to how language is acquired, e.g., Is language acquisition chiefly a matter of learning through imitation and other instructional processes, or is it an innate ability that follows a universal structure of language itself and emerges in accordance with the biological growth of the child? Those interested in reading instruction look to the child's language in order to: (1) match reading materials to the child's competence in language, (2) determine what language the child must learn so that he can adjust to the reading material, and (3) explain why the child is having difficulty in reading aloud and comprehending particular printed materials.

## Linguistic Competence Demonstrated by Children at Various Age Levels

Descriptions of linguistic competence typically have been reported in terms of the following features: sounds or phonemes used, intonation patterns-pitch, number of words used, mean sentence length, number of different words used, variety of parts of speech, variety of sentences, complexity of sentences, coherence and completeness.

Most recently, investigators have attempted to report developmental changes in the use of certain syntactic structures of children at different age levels as revealed by both nonverbal responses to verbal stimuli and actual oral production. One way to examine syntactical structure has been to determine mass/count noun subclasses in order to determine childrens' ability to distinguish mass nouns like *bread*, *cheese*, *green,* and *pie* from count nouns like *eggs, cookies,* and *carrots.* The adult, for instance, would say, "I want two pieces of bacon." The four-year-old might say, "I want two bacons."

### Before four

Babies are able to learn any language when they are born, and children every-where learn to speak their native language in a similar way. Until about six months of age, the child is in what is called the cooing stage. Lenneberg (1970) indicates that unlike crying sounds, cooing sounds show resonance modulation in that organs such as the tongue move. By about six months, the baby's cooing sounds become dif-ferentiated into vowels and consonants and by the end of the first year, the baby is uttering sounds like the syllables and intonations of the language used by his parents. Before the child says his first words, he imposes intonation patterns on his babbling and seems to babble statements and questions. At about 18 months the child is using one-word utterances and may even put two words together into a minimal sentence. At first, the one-word utterance is overgeneralized—"hot," for example, may refer to either the sensation felt by touching ice or a hot plate.

> Brown and Bellugi (1964) analyzed the verbal behavior of three children into three stages from the eighteenth to the twenty-eighth months. At stage one, inflections, auxiliaries, articles, and most pronouns were absent. The children used intonation to make a question. They asked mostly *yes* or *no* questions and only a few beginning with *who* or *what* or *where.* Interrogatory structures appeared to be understood. At stage two, articles, pronouns, and some negative forms appeared; auxiliaries were still not present. Stage three marked the emergence of auxiliaries, auxiliary inversions ("I can go out; Can I go out?"), and transformations ("Did you break that boat?"; "Do you get two ice creams?"). Inversion and transformation were found in *yes* or *no* questions but were absent in *who, what, where* questions. Children responded to questions, but did not use tag questions, e.g., "—, can he?" "—, didn't she?"*

By the age of four, most children have learned many of the essentials of gram-mar and have a well-developed *phonological system*—speech sounds of one's language. Thus, by age four the normal English-speaking child has probably learned all the phonemic elements of English and can combine these sounds into meaningful units. As a result of work with a small group of children, Miller and Ervin (1964) concluded that variations from adult speech of even the two- or three-year-old child are few. Those that occur are omissions ("I'll turn water off."), overgeneral-izations or predispositions for consistence ("foots"), incorrect subclassification of lexical class ("a Billy"), and doubly marked forms ("mine's"). Further evidence

---

*    Roger Brown, and Ursula Bellugi, "Three processes in the child's acquisition of syntax," *Harvard Educational Review* **34**, 2 (1964). Reprinted by permission.

that most four-year-old children have mastered the basic structures of their language in that they use them rests on the work of Menyuk and of Slobin. Menyuk (1963) found that nearly all basic syntactic structures could be found in upper-middle-class children as early as two years and ten months. Slobin (1966) reviewed Russian data on language development in children and suggested that the order in which different structures appeared in children's use depends on relative semantic difficulty rather than grammatical complexity.

A cautionary note must be added. Although certain linguists claim that the major language acquisitions may take place by the age of four, children do not have the linguistic abilities of adults, nor do all children have the same competencies. Linguists have perhaps overgeneralized about language development from the small populations of children observed. Seldom has the linguist attended to sociological and motivational variables. Children brought up in a dialect different from standard English do not develop the same structures as appear in the standard form.

Similarly, oral competence may develop differently in different groups. Also, few descriptions of children's language take into account cognitive differences at various age levels and in social groups. Indeed, there is evidence that ethnic differences exist in the organization of spacial and verbal abilities. Jewish children, for example, were found to excel on verbal skills, whereas Chinese children ranked higher in space conceptualization (Lesser, Fifer, Clark, 1965). One must keep in mind the research of Piaget indicating the development of intelligence as well as information about the development of syntax and phonology. Piaget's observations remind us that until four, most children are in a preconceptual phase, where they have difficulty in classifying and are unable to verbalize how classes relate to one another.

## Language development after age six

By age six, the child probably possesses the basic elements and structures of adult speech; however, the intellectual content of what he is saying does not match the forms he produces. The six-year-old child can project thought and actions into the future and can also speak of ideas and events in the past. Nevertheless, significant development occurs in all children after the age of six. Chomsky (1972) found, for example, that although a child's grammar, as revealed in spontaneous speech, did not appreciably differ from adult grammar, children did differ in the way they integrated complex linguistic structures. She tested different age groups of children, requiring them to apply relatively uncommon specific principles of sentence analysis. Three examples follow:

1. Interpretation of the construction *easy to see* in the sentence "The doll is easy to see." The complexity derives from the fact that the word order is misleading—*doll* is the implicit object of the verb *see*. ("The doll is eager to see" versus "The doll is easy to see.")

2. Interpretation of the construction *promise,* as in "Bozo promises Donald to stand on the book" versus "Bozo told Donald to stand on the book." Here, the child must draw on his knowledge of the verbs *promise* and *tell* in order to determine who is to stand on the book in each instance.

3. Interpretation of the construction *ask,* as in "The girl asked the boy what to paint" versus "The girl told the boy what to paint." The child must tell who is to paint in the two sentences (the girl in one sentence and the boy in the other).

The results indicated that the selected tasks were acquired in a sequential order and that there was high variability in age of acquisition—sometimes the oldest children failed. After age seven, it seems as if age is less of a factor in learning than is the individual rate of development.

Certain kinds of sentences are especially difficult for seven- and perhaps eight- and nine-year-olds to comprehend. For example, Olds (1968) and Hatch (1969) found that children of these ages consistently interpreted *unless* as *if* rather than as *if not.* But it is the work of Strickland and of Loban that has had the most profound influence on what we believe about the language of school-age children. Strickland (1962) found the most commonly used sentence pattern in grades one through six was that consisting of subject, verb, and direct object. Ten sentence patterns used by older children did not appear at all in the speech of first graders. Also, the older children made more frequent use of adverbial expressions. The child of eight, for instance, used five times as many subordinate clauses as did children age three, but the differences varied according to the type of clause.

Loban (1970) made a 13-year longitudinal study of the language used by certain pupils over time—from kindergarten through twelfth grade. All of the children were found to say more words at each succeeding year, but perhaps his most striking finding dealt with the difference in ability and the persistency of ability among groups of pupils. At the first-grade level, for example, members of the high group were producing 7.91 words per communication unit, a level not reached by the low group until fifth grade. Further, all groups ended the twelfth grade with virtually the identical percentages with which they began the first grade, despite the fact that increasing chronological age produced an increasing complexity in language.

Loban studied "mazes" of language—hesitations, false starts, and meaningless repetitions which interrupt sentence patterns. During kindergarten and the first three grades, many children showed a steady decrease in the number of these tangles, or mazes. However, initially low performers increased both the number of mazes and the average number of words per maze during the same four-year period. The high group, also, was distinguished from the kindergarten group by their ability to express tentative thinking as revealed by such words as *perhaps, maybe,* and *I'm not exactly sure.*

By age six, most children have control of the phonemes associated with their dialect, although misarticulations may be present. Poole (1934), for instance, found that children correctly articulated consonant sounds, as follows:

| Age in years | Sounds associated with these letters |
|---|---|
| $3\frac{1}{2}$ | b, p, m, w, h |
| $4\frac{1}{2}$ | d, t, n, g, k, ng, y |
| $5\frac{1}{2}$ | f |
| $6\frac{1}{2}$ | v, th (as in *the*), zh, sh, l |
| $7\frac{1}{2}$ | z, s, r, th (as in *thin*), wh |

Templin (1957) analyzed the articulations of children aged three to eight and found that three-year-olds have about 50 percent of the accuracy of eight-year-olds and that eight-year-olds achieved about 95 percent accuracy. Later, Carroll (1960) showed that the only phonemes not correctly articulated by 90 percent of Templin's population by age six were the fricatives /s/ /š/ /z/ /ž/, the affricatives /č/, and the semivowel /hw/. Parenthetically, it should be mentioned that misarticulation is not a serious obstacle in learning to read, but inability to discriminate among speech sounds is.

Differences in children's use of morphology (forms of words) have been examined by Jean Berks Gleason (1969), who compared the responses of kindergarteners and first-grade children with responses of adults in applying morphological rules to new situations, e.g., "This is a wug", "There are two _____", and the subjects were expected to say *wugs*. She found that the children did not yet generalize the rule for adding /əz/ sounds to words ending in *s* and that children, unlike adults, did not add the /əd/ sound to new words ending in *t* or *d* in the past tense. They said, for instance, "Yesterday he *mot*" instead of "Yesterday he *motted*." Also, adults tended to use suffixes, whereas children used compound nouns, e.g., the adult would say, "A tiny wug was a 'wuglet,' 'a wugling,' or a 'wuggie'"; children would say, "It was a 'baby wug.'" We should remember, however, that just because a child does not use uncommon forms in his speech does not mean that he cannot comprehend these forms when others use them in speech and writing.

## Implications of language problems for instruction in reading

Certain language structures should be avoided in reading materials used with young children or, if these structures are used, children must be given systematic help in learning how to interpret them. Among those situations likely to present special difficulty are the following:

1. Sentences that use many "structures" or function words, e.g., *and, so, mine, after, some,* in relation to "content" words, e.g., nouns, adjectives, and verbs, e.g., *father, table, red, big, run.* Structure words relate words to each other; content words have independent meaning.

2. *Why* and *how* questions which require *because* and *so* clauses in response. Children seem to acquire *because* clauses first, followed by *if this* clauses, and finally *so* clauses.

3. Sentences using *unless/then* clauses.

4. *When* questions which require an exact time reference. These sentences are difficult for many first-grade children.

5. The prepositions *during, near, beside*. Children have difficulty in interpreting these prepositions.

6. Passive transformations of basic subject-verb-object sentences. Children use the *got* passive instead of the *be* passive and seldom include the agent in passive sentences, e.g., "It was thrown" versus "It got thrown."

7. Irregular participles with perfect tenses and with the passive. Children are likely to misread irregular participles inasmuch as they have a predisposition for consistency of form, e.g., "I digged a hole" versus "I dug a hole."

8. Reversed order in sentence. Children give fewer correct responses to questions and statements made in reversed order, e.g., "Neither did Bill" versus "Bill didn't either."

9. Time connective. Young children comprehend better when the order of mention is the same as temporal order, e.g., Do *A* then *B*, versus do *B* but first *A*. (Children will comprehend better if asked, "If Susan started out with three marbles and she found two marbles, how many did she end up with?" than if asked, "How many marbles did Susan end up with if she found two marbles and she started with three marbles?")

## Practices for the Advancement of Language Skills

Thus far, we have seen that young children possess an innate ability to learn any language. Upon entering school, the typical child has a fine control over his native language. He uses the same sounds as those the adults are using; he has an excellent, though not perfect, control over syntax; he has an active and passive vocabulary of somewhere between 2000 and 24,000 words; and he has the amazing capacity to produce and comprehend an infinite number of sentences that he has never heard before. How, then, can the school best maintain this ability to acquire language? If our "track record" in the schools is not too good in this respect, it might be because we are trying to teach language skills that differ from those already acquired, i.e., the skills of written English and a new dialect, standard English. The fact that language growth sought by the school may be perceived by the child as unnecessary to learn, as something different or in conflict with what he already possesses constitutes one kind of problem (attitudinal problem).

Another problem for teachers is how to provide opportunities for the child to immerse himself in "natural" learning situations such as using the new language with playmates (the learning environment problem) and how to artificially yet systematically order instances of the new patterns and concepts so that the child can abstract the common attributes in each instance and learn to apply the pattern in fresh instances (the instructional sequence problem).

### Practices to improve attitude toward a new language

The young child is likely to greet a new experience with eagerness if he does not perceive it as threatening. Perception of threat can be minimized by having those he knows and trusts—parents, brothers, friends—enter the learning situation with him. A mother's participation in the language lesson within the classroom and in follow-up activities at home often is enough for learning to continue. Other ways of strengthening attainment for the new is to link it to the familiar. Children who have acquired enjoyment of games and songs may find it easier to learn a new language as they sing new verses and play games demanding different language structures and skills.

Language growth is probably associated with the teacher's positive rather than punitive responses to the child's present language. To the kindergarten child who says, "Look what I brang you," the teacher might reply, "I'm glad you brought that. You are very thoughtful to bring things to help us. You brought something the other day, too." The most effective teacher probably is able to take into account the child's previous language experience and blocks to learning. In some instances, this means learning the linguistic variations of different social and ethnic groups so that a link with the child can be effected. It also means giving more attention to what the child understands and showing less concern about his pronunciation and articulation. The teacher who can establish a warm and approving relationship with the child can increase that child's language skills. However, it may be too much to expect a single teacher to relate to all pupils. Hence, the increasing use of older children and other adults as tutors and models seems desirable. Quintillian long ago caught an essential for learning from others: "Indeed the whole conduct of life is based on the desire of doing ourselves what we approve in others. It is a universal rule of life that we copy what we approve in others."

### Improving the learning environment

Children learn language through verbal interactions with more mature speakers— by using the language. Teachers should give each child frequent opportunities to talk in school. This includes providing the child with something to talk about. As one child said, "Boy, when I have something to tell, I can sure tell a good story."

Illustrations are readily available to show how learning experiences in content fields can advance language growth. Science materials have been used to assist children in sequencing, distinguishing similarities and differences, separating inferred causes from the evidence of the event, and abstracting common elements.

Mathematics, art, music, and the like have been used as sources for children's oral language experiences. Cooking, dramatic plays, playwriting, dialogues, and telephone conversations have been found to improve oral language at several age levels. Analysis of words used in advertisements and origins of place names are helpful language activities with older children. The dictating of compositions has contributed to communication skills. Reading aloud from good books, of course, is a must—stories with an adequate theme, a lively plot, memorable characters, and a distinctive style. This includes old literature—folk tales and fairy tales—poetry, and new literature—books that the teacher, too, enjoys, books that will make the children weep, laugh, give them "gooseflesh and glimpses of glory."

## Systematic focus

Improvement in specific language skills, e.g., use of negation, conjunctions, disjunctive statements, have occurred through programs that focused on specific objectives and provided for numerous opportunities to practice the skills in concentrated periods of time—programs that offer the maximum redundancy and deliberate variation. Three kinds of activities are associated with such targeted programs:

1.  Programmed materials such as the Bereiter and Englemann program that have contributed to specific, immediate changes in a particular verbal behavior.

2.  Oral drills, e.g., choral speaking techniques and pattern drill exercises that elicit from the child predetermined linguistic structures. These drills may be humorous and should proceed at a fast pace. A variant of such drills is systematic language modeling, as when the teacher models correct pronoun forms or expands on the child's responses to a combined situation, e.g., Mike: "I see hot"; José: "I see smoke"; Teacher: "That smoke that you think you see is called steam."

3.  Gamelike activities that result in the child's acquiring a new language skill or reinforcing a previously learned one. Nearly any word-form skill, e.g., comparative and superlative forms of adjectives, formulation of past tense in verbs, or syntactical skills (transforming an active sentence into a passive construction) can be taught through simple games in which children are given examples of the pattern and are then asked to "play the game" by contributing examples which match the pattern. For example: Teacher: "The car is big, but the truck is bigger" or "The dog is fast, but the bird is faster"; student: "The bread is hot, but the soup is hotter."

## Relating Oral Language to Reading

### Differences between oral language and reading

Writing is not just talk written down. Written materials rely on the formal meanings of words and may require more words than in oral speech to convey the same ideas.

Most writing lacks the musical intonational qualities of oral speech. In speech, one must listen at the same rate as the speaker; but in reading, the reader can set his own pace, can skip ahead and go back. A frequently overlooked advantage of print is that it allows one to see the close connection in meaning of words that do not sound alike, e.g., *nation, national*; *commit, committee*; *major, majority*; *critical, critique*. Spelling patterns and their lexical meanings are more universal than pronunciation patterns. Most children require little deliberative instruction in learning to talk, but they must be instructed in order to read. The benefits for learning to speak are immediate; those for learning to read are often deferred.

It is not a simple matter to relate print to speech. The learner must acquire the necessary visual discriminations, including giving at times different oral responses to the same visual stimulus, e.g., *house* in "my house" and in "Where did he house it?", and at other times giving the same oral response to different visual stimuli ("*c*, is it /k/ or /s/?"). In speech, the flow of language is continuous but patterned enough so that it can be broken down into phonemes. In reading, the learner must learn to blend discrete letters into the flow of continous patterns. Also, there are many symbols to learn in order to know what pitch (rise and fall of voice), stress (words or parts of words to emphasize), and juncture (pause) to place on the printed words and to determine which words are meant to be spoken by a particular character or speaker in the written discourse.

### Language-based programs in reading

Successful instruction in beginning reading is usually dependent on the child's oral language. The child's knowledge of the structural system of the sound and grammar he uses in speech influences his perception of written words and allows him to comprehend their meaning. Ruddell (1965) found that children comprehended passages better when the written language patterns were similar to the children's oral language patterns. This implies that the child who does not have a fluent grasp of the language he is to read might be taught the pattern found in the reading material or that the reading material can be changed to conform to the language he has.

Several approaches have been taken to bring the child and the reading material into closer agreement with respect to structural sequencing and vocabulary. One strategy is to use materials for reading instruction invented by the children themselves. If the children generate the material, it is assumed that the material is consistent with their own language competence. A more common strategy is to provide oral activities based on the language and concepts children will need in order to profit from the printed material they are about to read. (One teacher rewrites stories, inserting familiar words and sentence structure. After children read those stories, the teacher modifies the same stories by adding new vocabulary and sentence structure as a means to extend the children's comprehension.)

Most language-based programs in reading are characterized by their breadth. The objectives for such programs include far more than the child's recognition of certain sight words and the ability to "sound out" printed words. A language-based program includes the teaching of: (1) many ways to identify printed words, e.g., phonics (ascribing sound values to letters) and (2) ways to derive meaning from printed expressions, e.g., identifying humor as revealed by exaggeration and incongruity, interpreting figurative language, and attending to signal words—*if, when, that, then, so,* etc.—marking the fact that a clause is about to unfold.

One initial instructional task in a language-based program is to make the pupils conscious of the language patterns they have mastered on the preconscious operational level. To this end, it is customary for the teacher to arrange instances of oral patterns and to have pupils both label them or point out what they have in common and produce other instances consistent with the pattern. Recognition of oral patterns are then followed by teaching the pupils graphic counterparts of these patterns. Examples of oral patterns and graphic correspondences follow.

| *Oral patterns* | *Graphic correspondence* |
|---|---|
| 1. Phonemic patterns— identifying rhyming elements, initial sounds that are the same, open-closed syllables | Letters, phonograms, spelling patterns:<br>*an*    *sh*<br>can    she<br>Dan    shed<br>man    shirt<br>ran    show |
| 2. Intonation patterns— stressing certain words, recognizing sentences that rise and fall in pitch, identifying pauses between words and statements | Punctuation marks (question mark, comma, semicolon, italics, ellipses), bold face type |
| 3. Sentence patterns— identifying questions versus commands and statements | Word order (*Is he?* versus *He is.* )<br>Question markers (*why, when, who, what, which* and verb forms of *do, does, did*) |
| 4. Patterns for word-form changes—forming plurals, making adjectives from nouns | Spellings of inflectional endings (ly, ed); suffixes (ous, ful, less); changes in spelling of singular and plural (thief-thieves) |

A more encompassing aim of language-based programs is to make children more sensitive to their language. This includes (1) learning various meanings of particular words such as the origin, evolution, and very different usage of certain words in two given cultures, and (2) being able to identify indicators of irony and satire as conveyed through sentence structure, e.g., a formal, serious style for the presentation of a trivial idea. Another broad aim is the development of thinking itself, e.g., to help pupils tell facts from opinion, to judge relevant from irrelevant statements, and to evaluate cause-and-effect relationships. Language-based programs are sometimes criticized because of the magnitude of the tasks undertaken. Do language and thinking aims make the teaching of beginning reading too complicated? Although all agree that reading should ultimately contribute to the development of the reader's language and that thinking for reading is a key to the wisdom of the world, there are differences of opinion about whether the child should be helped (1) to relate the graphic system only to the language he already speaks and understands or (2) to develop his oral speaking and thinking skills in the process of acquiring a second symbol system, i.e., reading.

## Spelling Patterns and Sentence Patterns

Among the problems of relating speech to reading, two appear large. One is the problem of relating particular letters (graphemes) to corresponding spoken sounds (phonemes). This task is associated with decoding, the process of looking at a previously unencountered word and being able to pronounce it. A second problem is the matching of printed sentences with entire speech patterns, being able to orally read phrases with proper intonation.

### The problem of reconstructing speech from written symbols

The history of instruction in reading reveals different beliefs about sounds and letters. When reading instruction was first initiated in this country, each word was spelled and pronounced in turn. Many people had the mistaken idea that the names of the letters were their sounds and that when one could name the letters, he could read. Others thought that spelling was the key to reading. By the nineteenth century, however, two different methods were in use: (1) the analytic method, whereby one memorized whole words with little reference to individual letters and sounds, and (2) the synthetic method, by which one pronounced a sound when shown a given letter (even though the sound was often somewhat distorted because it was isolated from a vowel) and then tried to pronounce several sounds from a number of letters, putting them together (blending them) to form a word.

During the midtwentieth century, the following views of prominent linguists began to be considered by reading specialists:

1. Phonemes (a significant unit of speech sound—probably 45 of them in English) are represented by graphemes (the spelling of phonemes, e.g., /ch/ in *chief*). Letters do not have sounds, but stand for them.

2. Learning to read requires learning phoneme-grapheme relationships. It does not require learning to say sounds, for the child already knows the sounds of his language (dialect), i.e., give less attention to articulation.

3. The phoneme-grapheme relationship should not be taught as isolated letter-sound correspondence, e.g., h = "huh," but as parts of words, for that is how sounds and letters occur.

4. The first word that a child reads should be selected to show consistent relationships between sound and spelling. That is, don't confuse the child with examples of words that are not representative of a common pattern. Don't present *stop*, *go*, *come*, all of which have a different sound for the letter *o*. Instead, first present the child with words that have a single sound for the letter *o* so that the child can identify the sound-letter correspondence, e.g., *no*, *go*, *so*.

The writing system in English is technically called *aphabetic* because it is based on the principle that there should be one sound (phoneme) for each letter. In fact, this ideal is far from realized in English spelling. There are many different letters for a single phoneme, e.g., the letter *i* in *bride* and the letter *y* in *fry* have the same /i/ sound. Further, a single letter may represent a variety of different phonemes, e.g., *c* in *cent* has the sound of /s/, and *c* in *cat* has the sound of /k/. This is not to say that there are not regularities in the spelling of English. A study by Hanna and others (1966) showed that there are more consistent relationships between sounds and letter representations than had been thought. It was found, for instance, that (1) the great majority of consonants have single spellings which are used 80 percent of the time in more than 17,000 words, and (2) many phonemes, particularly vowels, have quite predictable spellings in certain positions, e.g., /ā/ is spelled *a* 81 percent of the time when it ends a syllable that does not end a word, e.g., *lady*. This finding is in agreement with the assumption that the correspondence between written and spoken English can be strengthened by attending to letter patterns, words, and word groups instead of trying to relate individual letters and sounds.

Two different kinds of responses have been made to the irregularities of our printed language and the problem of helping pupils relate to it. These responses can be termed the linguistic and phonics approaches and revised alphabet proposals.

## Linguistic and phonics approaches

A word pattern approach typically involves the learning of four different orderings of letters. Each ordering indicates an invariant pronunciation for the vowel.

1. Pattern cvc (consonant-vowel-consonant), e.g., *cat*, *let*. This is the most common spelling pattern in English. The child learns that the vowels in this pattern have particular sound values subsumed by an old term "short vowel."

2. Pattern cvc(e) (consonant-vowel-consonant with letter *e*), e.g., *cane*, *like*. The child learns that the vowels in this pattern probably are associated with a restricted number of sound values, or "long vowels."

3. Pattern cvvc (consonant-vowel-vowel-consonant), e.g., *pain*, *meat*. The child learns that the first vowel is probably "long."

4. Pattern cv or cvv (consonant-vowel or consonant-vowel-vowel), e.g., *go*, *so*, *see*. The child learns that words ending in this pattern have a "long" vowel.

Typically, these patterns are not taught as verbalizations, i.e., rules to be memorized. Neither must a child learn the terms *long* and *short*. Rather, examples within each pattern are presented in such number and order that the child formulates the generalization himself. Contrasts between patterns may aid in making the generalization, e.g., contrasting words like *so*, *go*, *no* with words like *hot*, *pot*, *lot*; *we*, *he*, *she* with *wet*, *net*, *get*; and *kit*, *tap*, with *kite*, *tape*.

Generalizations about the sound values of particular consonants in various positions occur after seeing a number of words in which these consonants employ a regularity in sound. For example, after studying initial *h* in *he*, *hen*, *hop*, *hot*, the child can generalize that *h* in *his* is likely to have the same sound. Or, after seeing and hearing the *t* in words such as *hit*, *hot*, and *hat*, he can predict that the *t* in *but* will have the same sound.

Parenthetically, if teachers expect children to be able to transfer the ability to associate a particular sound-letter correspondence when encountering a new word, the child must have many opportunities to practice applying the generalization to fresh instances. Also, the systematic isolation of words that follow particular patterns can be overdone. Levin and Watson (1963), for instance, found that although it is more difficult to teach conflicting associations in the first place, there is greater transfer to new tasks. Perhaps the child should be exposed early to a certain amount of irregularity in the correspondence between written and spoken forms of the language, though not to the total range of variations (*come* might be treated in sentences along with *go*, *no*, *so*). Indeed, today most reading materials that stress regularities in patterns also include unpatterned speech units, e.g., function words such as *the*, *were*, *are*, *have*. The inclusion of these irregular words is believed necessary because they are among the most frequent words in print; they permit the construction of meaningful sentence patterns and contribute to the transfer task of reading "lifelike" materials. (Can you think of reasons why it has been recommended that function words should not be taught in isolation?)

Although the question as to what element (letter, syllable, spelling, or word pattern) is most useful in learning how to decode new words is unresolved, Groff (1971) has marshalled strong evidence in favor of the *phonogram* as the natural unit for the beginner. Phonograms are frequently occurring vowel/consonant combinations, usually closed syllables (those that begin with a vowel and end with a consonant), e.g., *at*, *ed*, *ing*. The phonogram is a highly stable unit whether it occurs in initial, medial, or final position, e.g., *an* in *an*imal, adv*an*cing, r*an*.

The sounding of vowels is usually regulated by the letter pattern which follows the vowel, and the phonogram with vowel and letter pattern enables the reader to see the entire pattern as a unit not restricted to letter-by-letter perception. After mastering beginning consonants and 50 phonograms, the learner should be able to decode many hundreds of words.

**Revised alphabets**

In contrast to helping the child use the letter-to-sound correspondence rules already present in English, the revisionist would present the beginning reader with special materials that use a regularized spelling of English. Many such proposals are now available. The Initial Teaching Alphabet (i.t.a., formerly the Augmented Roman Alphabet) is one such system. This alphabet uses 43 characters, of which 24 are conventional. The 19 new characters somewhat similar to the conventional forms, aid the child in making the transition to orthodox spelling at a later time (Downing, 1964).

In addition to being an alphabet, i.t.a. is also a medium for the teaching of reading. Data in support of the procedure have been collected by Block (1973) and indicate that using the i.t.a. approach has positive effects on teaching reading. On the other hand, i.t.a materials have been criticized as a medium for making the fit between letter and sound because they do not reflect dialectical differences in pronunciation and in some ways are closer to British than to American speech. (In the United States, the materials have occasionally been modified to replicate the characteristic sounds of a given region in which the children live.) MacDonald (1970) has argued that conventional spelling is more effective because it corresponds to a common sound representation among many dialects. The point is that what is wanted in a letter-sound system is spelling that generates corresponding speech sounds in the reader's own dialect rather than phonetic distinctions he does not make.

Another revised alphabet is UNIFON, which makes use of corresponding sound and written symbols. Unlike i.t.a., which is "transitional," UNIFON is designed for spelling reform, not just for teaching reading. According to Malone (1962), the isomorphic spelling system, which uses a different letter for each phoneme, regularizes English spelling and is easy to master.

A third example is a scheme for beginning readers that makes use of diacritical markings to indicate how each of the letters in conventional orthography is pronounced. The markings provide for an almost perfect correspondence between letters and sounds. After the reader gains a certain proficiency, the marking appears on fewer and fewer words (Fry, 1964).

One final comment about the relating of the child's phonological system to the spelling system of English: Teachers should not try to change the child's sound system, i.e., modifying his patterns of articulation so that he speaks language more artificial than the actual sounds he hears around him. Wardhaugh (1970) has commented on the unproductive practice of trying to teach a child "his sounds" and his language.

> If he is really unlucky, he gets special attention in pronouncing final r's in *here* and *far*, even though he is from New England; or in differentiating *which* from *witch*, even though both words sound alike to him; or *pin* from *pen*, even though the teacher has her problem with these words herself, being careful

to specify whether she wants a *writin'* one or a *stickin'* one—except, of course, when she's also working on final *ng's* in which case she says *writing* and *sticking.**

## Relating sentence patterns of speech to graphic counterparts

An important skill in reading is getting meaning from a printed message. This is often interpreted as something more than being able to pronounce printed words. It requires comprehending the general grammatical patterning of the sentence. There are occasions, too, when recall of the pronunciation of a word is easier in the context of a sentence than when seen in isolation, such as on a flash card or word list. A child may find it easier to decode the new word *out*, as in the sentence "We go in and out," by using the contextual structure prompts of sequence and phrase familiarity rather than by trying to apply a phonic generalization. But this can be done *only if he can already read most of the other words in the sentence.*

It should be noted that it is the child's mastery of syntax and semantics that allows him to profit from context clues in reading. A child can learn to attend to:

1. known happy and sad words to guess the tone of the new word;
2. familiar synonyms in the same passage as a clue to the meaning of the new word;
3. metaphors and other expressions which compare and contrast the unfamiliar term;
4. reoccurring expressions and clichés as indicators of what an unfamiliar word might be, e.g., *beautiful* is likely to be followed by *woman* [However, this example illustrates a problem of minority group pupils who do not share stereotypes of expression. The Navajo child, for example, would seldom associate *woman* with *beautiful*. Pather, he would tend to say *beautiful horse.*]
5. the kind of word that probably follows a particular word. For example, given the familiar words *the kite* and an unfamiliar word, the child can be led to suspect that the unfamiliar word is more likely to be *spins* than *big, Tom* or *hardly* just on the basis of sentence sense or syntax.

We show understanding of sentence structure when we use one word in the same position more frequently than we do other words in that position. Four sentence patterns are established as especially important in our language:

1. Noun verb:

        *The boy runs.*

        *Jill plays well.* (nv + adverb)

        *The gate swung open.* (nv + adjective)

---

* Ronald Wardhaugh, "Linguistics and Phonics," in *Language, Reading, and the Communication Process*, ed. Carl Braun, Newark, Delaware: International Reading Association, 1971, p. 106. Reprinted with permission of R. Wardough and the International Reading Association.

2. Noun verb noun:                 *The cat likes milk.*

3. Noun verb noun noun:            *Bill gives his dog bones.*

                                   *Meg calls her cat Puff.*

4. Noun linking verb noun:         *The dress is pretty.*

                                   *The dog is in the house.*

These patterns can be varied. One way to vary a statement is to convert the basic active-voice pattern to the passive. For example, sentence pattern (2) can be changed to the passive by either changing the word order or using the word *is* plus *by*, e.g., *The milk is liked by the cat.* Similarly, by changing the word order and using the verb *be* plus *by*, sentence pattern (3) can express the passive, e.g., *The bones were given his dog by Bill.*

Changing the word order is, or course, the way in which a basic sentence can be "transformed" to a question. Sentence patterns with the verbs *be* and *have* commonly signal a question when the linking verb (lv) is placed before the noun, as in *They are* versus *Are they?* Also, the noun-verb pattern becomes a question by prefacing it with a form of *do*, e.g., *The boy runs* becomes *Does the boy run?*

The teacher of reading might use a knowledge of sentence patterns in order to:

1. Compose sentences most likely to prompt the children's correct response to an unfamiliar word;

2. Determine the reading difficulty of particular materials;

3. Determine what sentence pattern the child must acquire in order to profit from given reading material.

Hypotheses about what makes a sentence difficult are derived from findings, such as those by Loban (1966), indicating that certain sentences are seldom used by children, i.e., sentences with a complement, as in "Mary threw the dog some biscuits" and sentences with the passive pattern, as in "Strawberries were eaten by Mary." Contrary to what many persons believe, sentence length does not reliably determine the complexity of a sentence. Estimation of the difficulty of a passage is made by noting the presence or absence of certain relatively easy and difficult structures:

*1. Easy to read*

   a) The four basic sentence patterns, including the variation nv plus infinitive (*He wanted to eat*). The very easiest of sentences will have no more than three lexical items, e.g., noun-verb-object, although sentence patterns with four lexical items, e.g., noun-verb-object-complement (*We called him Spot*) are still relatively easy to read.

   b) Elliptical sentences (*Oh!*, *Yes*)

   c) Simple transformations for questions and exclamations (*What is it? What a car!*)

d) Coordinate clauses joined by "and" (*He saw and he cried*). Slightly more difficult are the coordinates *for, but, so, yet, or*. (*She will go or he will come.*)

e) Modifiers—adjectives (little, happy), possessives (boy's, Jim's), participles as adjectives (*The running dog*), gerunds as subjects (*Singing is fun*), prepositional phrases (*The girl on the bike*).

2. *Difficult to read*

a) Passive patterns (*He was seen by Bill*).

b) Appositives with commas (*Betty, my sister, came*).

c) Infinitives as subjects (*To work is good*).

d) Conjunctive adverbs (therefore, hence, so, nevertheless, thus, since, being, as).

e) Paired conjunction—neither-nor, either-or (*Either he goes or I do*).

3. *Very difficult*

a) Clauses as subjects (What you think is your business).

b) Absolute constructions (*This being so, let's go. The work done, he left*).

Children can be taught to read language structures which are not in their speaking repertoire. Much of what we read after the primary level does not parallel oral language in that there is less redundancy, more formal vocabulary, and greater variety in sentence patterns, e.g., more frequent use of passive sentences. Many persons believe, however, that in the beginning stages of reading, the learner should have much practice in reading familiar patterns. Among these reasons are:

1. To make clear that there is a relation between written language and spoken language;

2. To use spoken language as a "prompt" in recognizing printed words;

3. To prevent the habit of "word calling," that is, reading orally without proper intonation.

The question of how best to introduce familiar language patterns in reading is not settled. Some advocate a *language experience approach*. A characteristic of this approach is that children are stimulated to use their oral language in connection with the materials to be read. The source of the materials may differ. A teacher and group of pupils may generate their own reading material. Or, the teacher may use commercial textbooks in reading, being careful to provide children with the oral language experience that relate to the printed selection the children are about to read.

Teacher-generated reading material is usually provided after children have interacted with a mouse, dog, party, or the like—something that provides a need for expression. Under teacher leadership, a descriptive account, a narrative, or some other kind of purposive communication is created. Typically, a group of children create a "story." Each child offers an idea (oral expression); the teacher writes it down and reads it back to the group. The completed account can be read in many ways—choral, echoic, or individual responses to words, parts of words, phrases, or sentences. Proponents of this technique claim that the children learn to read "meaningful" material and, therefore, are likely to read with natural intonation and with interest. A disadvantage is that the words and sentences spontaneously generated are so diffuse in kind that the child has difficulty in abstracting common patterns, thereby failing to learn the generalizations by which he can greet fresh instances of useful patterns. Attempts to overcome this weakness include the use of "word banks," isolated words that can be taken from the original compositions and grouped together in order to illustrate a pattern.

Commercially prepared materials stressing the language experience base list specific suggestions for preparing pupils for each reading selection, e.g., oral language activities that relate to the new vocabulary, concepts, syntax, and intonation patterns of a given selection. Well-prepared materials provide for the systematic introduction of consistent patterns of orthography, phonology, and syntax, yet ensure the development of the oral language background necessary for recognizing and using these patterns in reading.

## Linguistically Different Readers

### Black dialects

Teachers of pupils with black dialects will find this experiment suggested by Hageman and Saario (1969) helpful.

1. Select one difference in the dialect between nonstandard Negro English and standard English, i.e., third singular inflection: *He has* versus *He have*; *He does* versus *He do*; *He runs* versus *He run*. Recall that the speaker of standard English must use a rule that requires inflection of the third singular very (*I do, You do, He does*); the speaker of black dialect must use a rule that requires all verbs except *be* to remain the same without inflection (*I do, You do, He do*). In accordance with the first rule, a speaker can say, "He has long legs, and he runs the mile in record time. He really does!" But the nonstandard, black speaker using the second rule must say, "He have long legs, and he runs the mile in record time. He really do!" Each speaker is correct in terms of his own dialect.

2. Prepare to use this rule: No verb inflection in the present tense except with *be*.

3. Construct a sentence using no inflection on the third singular.

4. Record yourself describing an activity, e.g., an activity of a child. This recording should be continuous speech of at least three minutes in length. Each time you use a verb other than *be*, do not inflect.

5. Listen to the tape, count hesitation, corrections, and verbs which are inflected according to the standard English rule, not the rule for black dialect.

6. Describe how you felt as you made the recording.

According to Hageman and Saario (1969), teachers of standard English who have tried this experiment report that they have no difficulty understanding what they are supposed to do; however, teachers find that when they try to apply this simple rule in connected speech, they must make a conscious effort to edit their native dialect before speaking. This editing appears on the tape as a hesitation. They also have to make much conscious effort to sustain speech which requires just one difference in dialect. The conflict between the two morphologies interferes with the ability to speak freely. Only a small number of standard English speakers can sustain connected speech using a nonstandard morphological difference.

There are even more complex dialect differences in the area of syntax. For instance, the subordination of some conditional clauses in nonstandard, black dialect requires a change in word order similar to the standard English question: "Billy doesn't know *if he can go* on the bus with me" versus "Billy don't know *can he go* on the bus with me."

Linguists (Labon 1968; Baratz, 1970) have reported many syntactic and other differences between black and standard English. For example:

Linking verb: He *is* going.      He———goin'.

Verb form: He *drank* the milk.      He *drunk* the milk.

Past marker: Yesterday he *walked* home.      Yesterday he *walk* home.

Plural marker: I have ten *cents*.      I got ten *cent*.

Preposition: He is over *at* his friend's house.      He over *to* his friend house.

Be: He *is* here all the time.      He *be* here.

The purpose of this exercise was to call attention to the phenomenon of contractive differences in black and standard English and to generate a predisposition to consider the hypothesis that black dialect might be an important factor to consider in teaching reading to those who speak this dialect.

Phonological differences include: (1) frequent omission of the last consonant sounds in words ending in consonant clusters, e.g., hold-hoe; past-pas; disk-dis; (2) dropping the final sound represented in writing by the letters *r* and *l*, e.g., door-dough; tool-too; and (3) substituting the terminal sounds represented in writing by the letter *f* for the sounds represented by *th*, e.g., mouth-mouf; with-wif.

The experiment prompts one to believe that a conflict between one's native dialect and the second dialect creates interference in using the second dialect. Hence, a speaker of black dialect might have difficulty in learning to read standard English. One conclusion that follows is that there should be reading materials in black dialect for the beginning reader who speaks this dialect. Such a conclusion is hasty, however. There is still argument as to whether there is a single, regularized black dialect that would be easier for black speakers in all parts of the country than standard English. Also, there are questions such as, "Will the black speaker be handicapped in making a transition from reading materials in black dialect to standard English?"

Speech samples from Negro children inWashington, D.C., New York, Detroit, Chicago, and San Bernardino have been found to be very similar in sound and structure. Indeed, the black speakers had more in common with one another than with middle-class white children from the same cities (Hageman and Saario, 1969). However, some experimenters have systematically varied standard English and black dialect in teaching those who spoke black dialect and in teaching those who spoke standard English. They found that Negro children achieved approximately the same or higher levels when instructed in standard English as when instructed in black dialect (Keislar and Stern, 1969). Perhaps there are wide regional variations in dialect so that no single dialect, however "typical," can communicate equally to all children as well as can standard English. Unlike the speaker of standard English who has much interference in trying to use black dialect, the speakers of black dialect can understand both nonstandard and standard forms, although they may produce only the nonstandard. Even black speakers who have had little personal contact with the white community are accustomed to hearing standard English on the television. Furthermore, the issue of adjusting materials to the child is more than matching written language to the child's oral patterns. There are content (culture) changes that might be important in building ego support and motivation in the black speaker.

There are those who respond to language differences by trying to train black pupils to approximate standard English. To date, however, the effect of such training on reading achievement has been insignificant (Rystrom, 1970). One explanation for the failure to find transfer effects is that the reading tests did not match the language skills taught in the training program. Moreover, there remains a question about the purpose of this kind of training endeavor. Is it to produce some linguistic pattern which will make it easier for the learner to "decode" a new word or to answer questions about passages written in conventional English? Or is it an attempt to get the learner to articulate a passage in standard English? The latter effort is less defensible.

Most readers read orally in their own dialects. The speaker of black dialect who reads standard English, changing the written vocabulary and syntax to his own patterns, is probably demonstrating a high proficiency in reading. It can be theorized that competent readers sample enough from the standard English print to anticipate what is coming and are, therefore, able to express themselves in their own dialect. In short, teachers must be able to differentiate between: (1) black dialect-speaking pupils who are not able to apprehend printed materials, and (2) black dialect-speaking children who apprehend very well what they are reading, but correct the standard English to the vocabulary, pronunciation, and syntax of their own speech. The teacher who knows the rules for black dialect should be able to recognize when a child is making a conversion to dialect as opposed to making a reading error.

### The Spanish-speaking child

Those who speak Spanish can learn to read English. They profit a great deal from the language experience approach, whereby the teacher prepared them orally for the selection they will read. Preparation includes placing much emphasis on both the vocabulary that will be found in the material to be read and the vocabulary to be used during instruction. Teaching the vocabulary of instruction allows the learner to comprehend what he is to do during the lesson and what he must know to respond to such directions as: "Read aloud," "Look at the first letter," and "Put a mark by the word that sounds the same." Successful teachers first try to find out whether or not a child can respond in either Spanish or English to the concepts in particular lessons. If not, it is better to first explain the concept in the native language and then to make sure that the learner has practice in using the corresponding English term.

The Spanish speaker will master English syntax if given frequent opportunity to talk in English with others in meaningful situations. A classroom with a group of children learning to speak a new language is not a quiet one, for children must try out the language they are learning. Repetition drills, including substitution drills, where one noun replaces another without changing the sentence pattern; conversations; short talks; role-playing, and dialogues are all activities in preparing the language base for reading.

During oral reading the teacher should expect Spanish-speaking children to pronounce English words differently from the English speaker. The following are English vowel sounds not common in the Spanish language: /i/ as in *it*; /ə/ as in *the*; /ä/ as in *got*; /u̇/ as in *full*; /ȯ/ as in *all*.

The Spanish speaker will experience difficulty in pronouncing these consonant sounds: /th/ as in *thank*; /š/ as in *show, vision*. The Spanish sound system does not contrast /š/ and /č/, and substitutions of these English phonemes are common. The Spanish-speaking child may say: /čuw/ for *shoe* or /šer/ for *chair*. His intonation patterns also differ. He uses less stress, probably pronounces every syllable for the same length of time, shortens syllables stressed in English, and puts stress on the wrong syllables.

However, as in the case with speakers of black dialect, the teacher must not confuse articulation with comprehension. Certain basic differences in the structure of Spanish and English may prevent the child from getting the cues he needs for both word recognition and comprehension. There are some differences in word order, e.g., *The hand right* versus *The right hand*; *To him he gives the hat* versus *He gives him the hat*. Also, some inflectional endings differ, e.g., Spanish does not use the possessive—*The head of the dog* versus *The dog's head*. Nor does it use irregular plurals, e.g., *men, mice, feet*.

Currently, there is some interest in the idea of teaching Spanish-speaking children to read in Spanish before teaching them to learn to read in English. This suggestion parallels another goal—the development of bilingual competencies in children—usually through programs where, for example, reading lessons can be taught in Spanish one day and in English the next.

To date, there are few schools in the United States where English- and Spanish-speaking children learn to read both English and Spanish. There are, however, many teachers who bring the beauties of the Spanish language to all their children while teaching them to read English. Koch (1971), for instance, has described his language experience lesson involving Spanish words. He has children do such things as invent a new holiday and use Spanish words (some of which he writes on the board) in describing its main features, with results like the following:

"The estrellas are many colors, and the grass is verde."

"On my planeta named Carambona La Paloma, we do a fiesta called Luna Estrella . . ."

"We do a baile named Man of Nieve."

## Conclusion

Linguistics can be used as a heuristic. Theories and studies of language promise to help teachers find better ways to teach reading. Both new instructional objectives and different options in teaching procedures have followed from the writings of language specialists. Cases in point are: (1) objectives calling for the teaching of punctuation marks as a means for interpreting pitch, stress, and juncture, and (2) arranging instructional sequences so that the learner can recognize regular language spelling patterns and interpret various sentence patterns. Most of all, linguists have created a climate favorable to inquiry in reading by challenging many of the assumptions which formerly guided instruction and by themselves engaging in arguments about priorities in language acquisition. Newer knowledge about the five-year-old's extensive facility in language has led to increasing the sophistication of the materials now used in reading (richer vocabulary, more varied sentence patterns). Also, those who have studied dialects other than standard English have influenced the teaching of reading by both enhancing appreciation of dialects and making teachers consider ways to link the dialects of their pupils to the reading of standard English.

Linguists have not resolved the problem of teaching reading. On the contrary, they have, if anything, intensified recognition of problems. For example, among the *problems of sequence in instruction* are: Should spelling come before reading (sound to letters versus letter to sound)? Should the recognition of patterns in words precede the reading of sentences with proper intonation (reading for meaning versus decoding of words)? In addition, there are *problems of purpose*: Should reading materials match the oral speaking repertoire of the child? Or, should he meet reading materials that extend his language beyond that found in his oral expression, even perhaps increasing his ability to think?

Language studies do not offer a prescription for effective teaching of reading. Linguistics is a resource field, like psychology or sociology, from which one can find ideas and information that might be useful in directing attention to important elements in teaching reading that would otherwise be overlooked. But the ideas have to be tested in the classroom and adapted in the light of other knowledge and practical circumstances.

Our hope is that the teacher who reflects on the content of this chapter will have acquired two outcomes: first, more defensible instructional objectives—those that are considered in the light of linguistic scholarship, are more comprehensive, and are more potentially useful to learner; and second, additional powerful factors or variables to take into account when engaging in instructional planning—selecting or designing methods and materials, and interacting with pupils and guiding and interpreting the responses of learners during the reading process.

## References

Baratz, Joan C. "Teaching reading in an urban Negro school system," Chapter in *Language and Poverty*, ed. Frederick Williams, Wisconsin: Markham, 1971.

Bereiter, C. and S. Engelman. *Teaching Disadvantaged Children in the Preschool*, Englewood Cliffs, N. J.: Prentice-Hall, 1966.

Brown, Roger and Ursula Bellugi. "Three processes in the child's acquisition of syntax," *Harvard Educational Review* **34**, 2 (1964): 133–151.

Carroll, John B. "Language development," *Encyclopedia of Educational Research*, ed. Charles Hain, New York: MacMillan, 1960, pp. 744–752.

Chomsky, Carol. "Stages in language development and reading exposure," *Harvard Educational Review* **42**, 1 (1972): 1–33.

Downing, J. A. *The ITA Reading Experiment*, London: Evan Brothers, 1964.

Fry, Edward. "A diacritical marking system for beginning reading instruction," *Elementary English* **41** (May 1964): 526–529.

Gleason, John Berko. "Language development in early childhood," *Oral Language and Reading*, ed. James Walden, Urbana, Illinois: National Council of Teachers of English, 1969, pp. 18–19.

Groff, Patrick. *The Syllable*, Portland, Oregon: Northwest Regional Educational Laboratory, 1971.

Hanna, P. R., et al. *Phoneme-Grapheme Correspondences as Cues to Spelling Improvement*, Washington, D.C.: U.S. Office of Education Project 1991, OE-32008, 1966.

Hageman, Barbara and Terry Saario. "Non-standard dialect interference in reading," in *Thirty-third Yearbook Claremont Reading Conference*, Claremont, California: Claremont Graduate School, 1969, pp. 158–167.

Hatch, E. *Four Experimental Studies in Syntax of Young Children*, TR No. 11. Inglewood, California: Southwest Regional Laboratory, 1969.

Keisler, Evan and C. Stern. "Research projects in early childhood," *Learning Newsletter*, Los Angeles: University of California, June 1969, 2,1.

Koch, Kenneth. *Wishes, Lies, and Dreams*, New York: Random House, 1971.

Lenneberg, Eric H. "On explaining language," in *Language and Reading—An Interdisciplinary Approach*, compiled by Doris V. Gunderson, Washington, D.C.: Center for Applied Linguistics, 1970.

Lesser, G. S., G. Fifer, and D. H. Clark. *Mental Abilities of Children in Different Social and Cultural Groups*. Monographs of the Society for Research in Child Development **30**, 4 (1965).

Levin, Harry and John Watson. "The learning of variable grapheme- to phoneme correspondence; and the learning of variable grapheme- to phoneme correspondence: variations in the initial consonant position," in *A Basic Research Program on Reading*. Ithaca, N.Y.: Cornell University and the U.S. Office of Education Cooperative Research Project No. 639, 1963.

Loban, Walter. *Language Ability—Grades Seven, Eight, and Nine*, Cooperative Research Monograph No. 18, OE-30018. Washington, DC: U.S. Government Printing Office, 1966.

——————. *Stages, Velocity, and Prediction of Language Development: Kindergarten through Grade Twelve*, Final Report, Berkeley: University of California, 1970.

——————. "Teaching children who speak social class dialects," *Elementary English* **45** (1968): 592–599, 618.

MacDonald, John W. "Book reviews—i.t.a.: *An Independent Evaluation*, by F. W. Warburton and Vera Southgate; *Alphabets and Reading*, by Sir. James Pitman and John St. John, *Harvard Educational Review* **40**, 2 (1970): 317–325.

Malone, John R. "The larger aspects of spelling reform," *Elementary English* **39** (1962): 435–445.

Menyuk, P. "Syntactic structures in the language of children," *Child Development* **34** (1963): 407–422.

Miller, W. and Susan Erwin. "The development of grammar in child language," *Acquisition of Language*, ed. U. Bellugi and R. Brown, Monographs of the Society for Research in Child Development **29**, 1 (1964).

Olds, H. F. *An Experimental Study of Syntactical Factors Influencing Children's Comprehension of Certain Complex Relationships*, Report No. 4, Cambridge, Mass.: Harvard Research and Development Department, 1968.

Poole, I. "Genetic development of articulation of consonant sounds in speech," *Elementary English Review* **11** (1934): 159–161.

Ruddell, R. B. "The effect of oral and written patterns of language structure on reading comprehension," *Reading Teacher* **18** (1965): 270–275.

Rystrom, R. "Dialect training and reading: a further look," *Reading Research Quarterly* **5** (1970): 581–599.

Slobin, D. I. "The acquisition of Russian as a native language," in *The Genesis of Language: A Psycholinguistic Approach*, ed. F. Smith and G. A. Miller, Cambridge: M.I.T. Press, 1966.

Strickland, R. G. "The language of elementary school children: its relationship to the language of reading textbooks and the quality of reading of selected children," *Bulletin of the School of Education*, Indiana University **38** (1962): 1–131.

Templin, Mildred C. *Certain Language Skills in Children, Their Development and Interrelationships*, Institute of Child Welfare Monograph No. 26. Minneapolis: The University of Minnesota Press, 1957.

Wardhaugh, Ronald. "Linguistics and Phonics," *Language, Reading, and the Communication Process*, Newark, Delaware: International Reading Association, 1971.

# 5 / Prerequisites to reading

## Introduction

Procedures for preparing children to read are changing rapidly. This can be seen by examining some of the newer diagnostic-prescriptive instructional materials: *Individually Prescribed Instruction in Reading* (University of Pittsburgh, 1970); *Program for Learning According to Needs* (Westinghouse, 1970); *READ System* (American Book Company, 1971); *Communication Skills Program* (Southwest Regional Laboratory, 1971); and *Wisconsin Design for Reading Skill Development* (Wisconsin, 1971). The thrust of the fundamental change can also be noted in policy statements such as those in the State of New York (New York, 1971) emphasizing precise descriptions of the specific skills each individual must acquire to become a proficient reader. Further, numerous school districts, e.g., Los Angeles, are implementing the change to diagnostic-prescriptive learning, whereby teachers identify appropriate objectives for each individual pupil and then use instructional materials from a variety of sources keyed to the specified objectives.

Most of these newer developments are based on the cumulative learning model, that is, learning to read is seen as the acquisition of skills and chains of skills which interact to produce complex reading competencies, including the capacity to generalize particular learnings and to apply concepts to fresh situations. One basic assumption of the newer approaches is that regardless of initial aptitude, most learners (one author suggests perhaps over 90 percent) can achieve what we have to teach them (Bloom, 1968). Aptitude itself is now thought by many to be largely a matter of prior learning, hence modifiable. A central key to ensuring that nearly all pupils gain mastery of reading is believed to be found in increasing their engagement in those learning tasks that are prerequisite elements to the desired competency.

*73*

A comparison of prereading programs based on older views of learning and those developed in accordance with the cumulative learning model usually reveal the following differences:

| *Conventional model* | *Cumulative learning model* |
|---|---|
| Teacher has a general idea of each learner's needs, e.g., vocabulary weakness as revealed by informal inventories and standardized tests. | Teacher has results of child's performance on a pretest that measures a specific skill, e.g., given three pictures, two of which are identical, the child can point to the pictures that "are the same." |
| Teacher has one or more readiness books available for use with groups of pupils. Classroom activities contribute to general learning rather than to specific objectives. | Teacher has a variety of resources, e.g., games, independent activities, programmed materials, and tapes, all of which are targeted to specific prereading tasks. |
| Pupils are placed in particular study groups, membership in which is relatively constant and based on an assessment of "ability to learn." | Study groups are reconstituted after short intervals so that instruction can be focused on specific needs. |
| Teacher has few materials that can be used in self-instruction or with paraprofessionals, tutors, parents, peers, aides, for helping a child overcome a specific deficiency. | Teacher has a number of teaching-learning activities that match the skill needed by the child. These activities are structured so that a teacher is not needed to prepare the instructional sequence. |
| It is difficult for the teacher to know which children have succeeded in learning a lesson or series of lessons. | Criterion-referenced tests are used to provide evidence that a given concept has been attained from instruction. Following a lesson and after a unit of instruction, short, easy-to-score tests are available for all children. |
| Classroom management tools are gross, i.e., achievement tests are available for use after child has been exposed to activities during a semester or year. | Check-up tests are used continually—daily, weekly, monthly—to certify pupil progress. |
| Teacher lacks a record of what skills child has mastered and what must yet be attained. | Simple record system indicates specific tasks mastered and allows planning for individual child and providing a means for reporting to parents on the specific accomplishments of pupil. |

Children have opportunities to read together and to discuss the stories they have read in common.

By participating in the reading of selected pieces, children gain integrative experiences. However, many of the prerequisites for participation in these activities have been identified and previously taught so that the learner has more success in the integrated task.

It is also true that participation in the integrative task is likely to reveal the child's need for learning additional prerequisites.

Component, or task, analysis is the fundamental operation for designing programs for reading programs that follow the concept of cumulative, or mastery, learning. Such an analysis begins with selecting a reading task or objective. It then asks, in effect, "To perform as called for on this objective, what prerequisites, or component, tasks must the child be able to do?" The technique can be applied to any objective at any level of the reading program. The importance of the backward (no pun) analytic procedure for a prereading program is that it offers a way to identify those learnings that are critical to the reading objectives to follow. Thus, the teacher is less likely to develop learnings that are "blind alleys," i.e., that do not contribute to the subsequent instruction in reading.

In this chapter we try to bring out issues that arise in connection with prereading programs in general and in programs based on cumulative learning theory in particular. In addition, we deal with problems and strategies for identifying skills that are necessary for success in beginning reading. We present a listing of the prereading skills that seem to be surviving empirical and logical screening, and we also designate tasks that are of lower priority but that are frequently taught to young learners. Finally, we show some practical ways to implement the mastery model in readiness programs—illustrating strategies for making a task analysis, diagnosing, and prescribing for individual learners.

## Issues in Prereading Programs

### Maturation and environment

Those who plan early learning programs (whether preschool, kindergarten, or first grade) that are targeted toward reading accept the importance of young children learning to read and tend to view reading ability as primarily the result of intervention by a teacher (an environmental influence) rather than as an ability that is inherited and fixed. They also place less importance on the evidence of maturation and natural development in the academic progress of the child. In contrast, those who had strong beliefs in the importance of maturation-growth-readiness dominated much of primary education until the last decade. According to the maturation view, associated with the ideas of such eminent psychologists as G. Stanley Hall and Arnold Gesell, certain organized patterns of growth of neural structure had to be present before environmental factors could be effective. Modern growth-readiness proponents are likely to be pessimistic about instruction aimed at speeding up the reading achievement of learners who are lacking in maturation. Their assumption is that the intellectual development for reading depends on the individual's internal biological mechanism and that growth proceeds in orderly states—spontaneously with time rather than as the result of inputs from the environment.

A middle position to the environment-maturation theories is that both should be considered in planning reading programs. Developmental factors associated with age may be relatively important in determining the probable success one would have in teaching children how to read complex language structures. Carol Chomsky, for instance, has postulated developmental skills in language and found empirical data indicating that certain language patterns are not present before a given age (Chomsky, 1972). Accordingly, a comprehension task such as the following would not be appropriate for a child under the age of seven:

> Given two sentences which differ only in the use of *and* and *although*, the child can say what is meant by "I would have done the same" in each sentence:
> 1. "Mike scolded Bill for eating it, *and* I would have done the same."
> 2. "Mike scolded Bill for eating it, *although* I would have done the same."
> (answer to first sentence: would have scolded Bill)
> (answer to second sentence: would have eaten it)

Environmental factors might be given more weight in deciding whether or not to teach associational learning tasks, e.g., letter-sound correspondence or conceptual learning tasks such as decoding previously unencountered words composed of familiar elements, e.g., initial consonant and spelling pattern.

Dolores Durkin has written an historical account indicating a relation between the maturational view and the issue of when to begin reading instruction (Durkin, 1970). She believes that because the 1920's were permeated by the ideas of Hall and Gesell, failure to read was attributed to a lack of readiness—children that had not yet reached the stage of development which would allow them to be successful. The proposed solution to reading failure was to postpone instruction until the children matured. Other factors that might have accounted for failure, e.g., teacher incompetency and inappropriate instructional materials were not considered. Singer (1970), too, has indicated how the bias in the 1930's toward maturational explanations was associated with postponement of instruction. He attributes delayed instruction in reading to the influence of the previously mentioned Morphett and Washburne recommendation (Chapter 2) that reading be postponed until the child had a mental age of six years and six months on the *Detroit First Grade Intelligence Test* or seven years and six months on the Stanford-Binet. This recommendation was based on the finding that 78 percent of the children in one school system with the given mental ages made satisfactory progress, i.e., progressed through 13 steps in a particular structured program and learned to recognize a minimum of 37 sight words by February. Possibly because of Washburne's prestige (he was both superintendent of schools in Winnetka, Illinois, and leader in the then popular Progressive education movement), his findings were generalized to all tests of intelligence, programs of instruction, and evaluation instruments.

The 1960's marked the rise of the interventionist (environmental) position, the belief that the teacher, not nature, must assume responsibility for equipping young children with the skills necessary for learning to read and that readiness was not something to wait for, but to produce. The interventionist approach to readiness in reading drew upon the cumulative learning model, i.e., (1) define what the beginning reader must do when confronted with print, (2) specify the constituent dependent parts (skills) that are subsumed in the more complex skills of beginning reading, and (3) deliberately elicit from the learner responses so that each component in the overall task is mastered.

Many forces contributed to the popularity of trying to teach reading skills at an early age. There were societal influences such as equalitarian interests demanding that poor children be given early compensatory training in reading and prereading so that they might achieve as well as their more affluent classmates. Such educators and psychologists as Benjamin Bloom and Jerome Bruner emphasized the importance of the environment to the very young child's intellectual development and hypothesized that whatever the ultimate objective, the child at any age can learn something from deliberate instruction that will move him toward that objective more rapidly than if he is left to unguided activity.

Just as the final verdict about the value of early intervention programs in general is not yet in, so too, there is no final answer about the value of preschool programs in which there is specific training in prereading and reading skills. Kohlberg, for example, finds some value in early teaching of reading, but not because it is likely to lead to greater cognitive development. Rather, he feels that the child might enjoy learning reading skills early, especially since those tasks that require much drill can be more interesting to younger children than to older ones. He also feels that the child who begins school with word-attack skills already acquired could be freed for more cognitively valuable activities (Kohlberg, 1968).

Although a few studies have indicated positive effects from early training (Brzeinski, 1967; Durkin, 1968; and Sutton, 1969), extensive longitudinal studies measuring durability of early educational effects are awaited. Recently there have been voices expressing concern that too great an enthusiasm for the early teaching of reading skills—other than those demanding simple associative learning—and too much faith in the power of component analyses may bring disillusionment. Jensen, for example, feels that results from efforts to enhance desired cognitive processes in disadvantaged children on the basis of cumulative learning experiences and specific training will not meet expectations; hence, he is fearful that there will be a swing of the educational pendulum to some other extreme. Therefore, he suggests that the cumulative learning model be supplemented and modified by taking into account biological developmental factors, i.e., differentiating the skills which are susceptible to training from those which are better explained by reference to developmental factors such as maturation of brain structure (Jensen, 1969).

Rohwer, too, has argued for restricting objectives in the early years to those which can be readily learned and deferring the teaching of many "thinking skills," i.e., those requiring formal operations, until adolescence. He claims that there is no compelling evidence to support the notion that delaying the onset of reading instruction by one or several years would retard the rate at which the component skills are acquired (Rohwer, 1971). All children are ready at every age to learn some skill of importance in reading. The challenge is to select skills that intervene between the child's present capabilities and a desired future competency in reading. Thus, the issue of when to teach reading skills is being reformulated into a problem of what skills to teach and to whom.

### Determining cruciality of a reading skill

The question of which reading skills to teach a particular learner requires that the teacher know the immediately foreseeable objectives of reading, i.e., the kinds of reading tasks the learner will be expected to perform, and the status of the learner with respect to these objectives and to their prerequisites. Further, without the teacher's knowledge of the particular materials that will be used during instruction, it is difficult to predict what success the child will have and what is prerequisite. Although conventional methods of teaching reading often require considerable cognitive and psychomotor maturity, the use of innovative materials can sometimes shortcut some of the requirements and promote early learning of decoding and other reading tasks, e.g., using the typewriter to bypass maturing motor skills of handwriting. Shortly, we will present detailed ways to select and formulate prereading instructional objectives. However, in this general treatment of issues in prereading, we would be remiss not to present a schema that encourages wider considerations to be undertaken in determining the cruciality of any instructional objective. Professor Robert Stake of the University of Illinois has suggested such a schema in the following formula:

$$\text{cruciality} = \frac{\text{relevance to learner's need} \times \text{probability that (school) teacher can do job}}{\text{probability that the objective can be acquired outside of school}}$$

*Learner need* can include both psychological needs such as that for acceptance and anticipated future societal, e.g., instructional, demands that may be placed on the learner. The *probability that the teacher can do the job* can be estimated after noting: (1) whether the task is one of associative rote learning or conceptual problem solving, and (2) maturational factors in the learner. The teacher's capability to teach a given skill within the constraints of time and the materials at hand can also figure in determining the likelihood of success. The *probability that the objective will be acquired in a nonschool setting* can be based on analysis of what is learned from TV, parents, and the daily life of the neighborhood community. It would, of course, be an error to exclude the teaching of a particular objective to a given child who does not have the environmental influences available to the majority.

One group of teachers gave the following objective a mean rating of 8 after assigning probability values of 1–5 to each of the factors in the formula: "Given any of the letters—initial consonants f, m, s, p, w, g—the child can orally supply words which begin with the sound associated with each letter." The teachers arrived at this rating by averaging their individual estimates of probabilities with respect to the objective. Need was estimated at 4, teachability at 4, and alternative instructional sources at 2. Hence,

$$\frac{4 \times 4}{2} = 8$$

## The research basis for determining prerequisite skills to reading

An observer of the reading scene might have reason to wonder why there are so many conflicting ideas about what are essential prerequisites for learning, say, the reading tasks commonly taught in the first grade. Is it really necessary that the child first be able to name the letters of the alphabet? That he be able to alphabetize the letters? Or that he be able to tell whether two orally pronounced words are "exactly the same"? Must the child be able to pronounce the final phoneme in words like *going* and copy goemetric forms? One explanation for the variety of opinion is that the value of certain skills has gone unchallenged. Many tasks such as those mentioned are prized, not appraised. Teachers teach them because of habit, tradition, or convenience. Another, related, reason is that there has been a dearth of facts to substantiate personal opinion; few efforts have been made to determine the consequences for learning or not learning the tasks.

Validation of the component skills for learning to read requires empirical and experimental research. To date, most research in reading readiness has been correlational—the associating of test scores purporting to measure prereading skills with test scores purporting to measure reading achievement. Few researchers have tried to demonstrate that when one experimentally succeeds in equipping a sample of pupils from a common population with an assumed prerequisite skill, this sample achieves at a higher level on subsequent reading tasks than do those who were not taught the "prerequisite." We should not infer that we know what is a causal factor in successful beginning reading solely from correlational data. It is an error, for example, to think that letter-naming ability (given a letter, the child can say its name) is a prerequisite skill for beginning reading just because findings from a nationwide study show that upon entrance to the first grade, those children who are able to name letters generally achieve more in reading during the first year. It could be that those children who enter school with some familiarity with letters come from homes where reading is more valued, where parents are more ambitious for their children, or that they differ from other children in more fundamental ways. No, the value of such task variables as naming letters is best shown by experimentation. For example, one might:

1. choose a test which best represents a valued reading skill and a skill to which one has reason to believe that better knowledge might contribute;

2. randomly assign children who cannot name letters to either a group that will receive instruction in the naming ability or to one that receives nearly equivalent instruction (e.g., attention, praise, opportunity to respond) in all but the naming of letters;

3. test the children to make sure that they had mastered the "prerequisite task" as a result of training;

4. give equivalent instruction to members from both groups in the beginning reading task and subsequently assess their relative performance on the test which measures the objective.

Incidentally, when studies using procedures similar to that outlined above have been conducted on the value of letter-name knowledge as opposed to letter-sound knowledge, it has been found that the latter and not letter-naming facilitated learning to read new words made up of the same letters (Samuels, 1971). This is not to say that investigators are wasting their time if they only associate factors that accompany reading achievement, or suggest factors that might be important because of a theory about the reading process, or carefully describe the reading behavior of children. The results of such studies should draw out attention to skills that should be checked out experimentally to see if they are necessary components to other reading tasks.

Several straightforward designs exist for confirming the value of the skill or task. Base-line designs, for example, allow the experimenter to show the effect of prerequisite training and to compare the effect of different prerequisites:

$A + B$ vs. $B$, where $B$ is the reading program and $A$ is the training program that develops the prerequisite skill;

$A + B$ vs. $C + B$, where $A$ and $C$ are both prerequisite skills.

A correlational design that offers much statistical control and allows several presumed conponents to be studied in a comprehensive rather than a piecemeal fashion has been suggested by Samuels (1971). The essence of his suggestion is that tentative skills or factors be derived from psychological conceptions about how attention, visual and auditory discrimination, and memory function in reading. Next, data about the selected factors are collected early in the school year from all first-grade pupils in the sample. Then, at the end of the year, pupils are given reading achievement tests (presumably, tests that measure the objectives sought through the instructional program), and the relative contribution of each of the preassessed factors to the performance on the achievement test are determined by analyses. A possible problem with this procedure is that the tests given to measure the presence of the "prerequisite skills" may not be of equal difficulty or sensitivity. Therefore, an easy test of visual discrimination vs. a difficult test of auditory discrimination may lead one to conclude that the latter is a more important prerequisite.

Criticisms of research in readiness to read have been made by MacGinitie (1969) and Calfee and Venezky (1968). Most of these criticisms center on the embarrassing fact that the "factors" being related to reading achievement are not clearly defined and that indeed, the measures of reading achievement used in different studies are not comparable. There is no consistent definition of the things counted under the rubrics of "comprehension" and "visual discrimination." By way of illustration, the following are but a few examples of different operational definitions for "auditory discrimination":

1. Given matched pairs of words such as *tub, tug, zest, zest,* and asked if two words are exactly the same, the child can identify those that are and are not the same.

2. Given sentences, each of which contains a number of words that begin with the sounds for *b, f, t, c* (Betty saw a baby bird that was not very big), the child can clap his hands each time he hears a word that begins with the same sound as the first word in the sentence.

3. Given a series of word pairs, the child can tell which one rhymes (cake, rake, cake, dog).

4. Given a number of environmental sounds played on a tape recorder (a bird whistling, a dog barking), the child can point to the picture among several that is associated with the sound.

5. Given an isolated speech sound /s/, the child can name a letter that is associated with that sound.

Examination of this list throws light on the reasons for the lack of agreement on the importance of auditory discrimination as a readiness skill for reading. One can see noncontrol of task variables, i.e., the tests make different demands on memory and/or the ability of the child to follow verbal instructions, and there is a confusion between visual and auditory skills. The resulting effect on reading of whatever is measured by such tests is not necessarily a test of a basic variable, but only an artifact of the particular test used. In interpreting readiness research, one must look at the actual tasks given children, regardless of the names that the investigator has given to these tasks.

The tests used for indicating reading achievement have also been found wanting, chiefly because they do not measure separable skills. In addition, they are too insensitive to measure the impact of a very specific segment of early reading.

A second kind of criticism of readiness studies is that they fail to specify instructional treatment. The effect of a prerequisite skill on achievement depends in part on what the teacher does during instruction. The teacher who teaches the skill of pronouncing phonograms by requiring the child to first identify rhyming elements may find that the concept *rhyme* is indeed a prerequisite, whereas a different instructional strategy could circumvent the need for rhyming.

The most persistent and damning criticism, however, is that too often in the field of reading, we have confused *correlates* to reading achievement with *causes* for reading achievement. Almost all attributes of a child's intellectual performance correlate to some extent with reading achievement. To reiterate, however, just because certain attributes are associated with higher scores on a beginning reading test, we cannot say that any or all of the attributes caused the higher score. Consider a negative example. For years it was observed that pupils who had difficulty on silent reading tests tended to vocalize while reading—they were "lip readers." Some teachers thought that the vocalization must contribute to poor performance. Hence, there were direct efforts to suppress vocalization rather than to teach the skills that might make vocalization unnecessary. Only recently has there been considerable evidence that vocalization indicates that a child is encountering difficulty, not that vocalization is the cause of the difficulty, indeed, it may even be an aid to the struggling child.

## Prereading Skills of High Promise

There are five high-priority prereading skills. These skills selected from many fulfill the requirements of cruciality. Also, they have a direct relationship to reading. They are not justified on the grounds that they may contribute to general learning and problem solving. More specifically, since a necessary aspect of beginning reading is the decoding of printed words, these prerequisite skills focus on this task rather than on all kinds of tasks subsumed under *"beginning reading."* There is evidence (empirical findings by partial correlations and logical relationships) to suggest that the acquisition of these skills is necessary if learners are to succeed in learning to decode printed words. Further, children are not likely to acquire these skills without deliberate instruction.

Three of the high-priority skills are visual—*letter orientation, letter order,* and *word detail*; two are sound skills—*sound matching* and *sound blending*.

Operational definitions (instructional objectives) and illustrative test items for each of the skills appear below:

1. *Letter orientation.* Given a sample letter(s) and two alternative sets of letters (one set identical to the sample and the other set having at least one letter different from the sample), the child can select the set that matches the sample.

    General instructions: "Show me one that looks just like this one." (Administrator points to the item in the first column.)

    | di | bi | di |
    |----|----|----|
    | qi | qi | pi |
    | d  | b  | d  |
    | op | op | og |
    | bi | bi | di |

2. *Letter order.* Given a sample of letters and two alternative sets of letters (one set identical to the sample and the other differing only in the ordering of the letters), the child can select the set that matches the sample.

General instructions: "Show me one that looks just like this one." (Administrator points to the item in the first column.)

| | | |
|---|---|---|
| gm | mg | gm |
| rf | fr | rf |
| nt | tn | nt |
| bc | cb | bc |
| kw | wk | kw |

3. *Word detail.* Given a sample set of three letters and two alternative sets of letters (one set identical to the sample and the other differing in a single, but similar, letter), the child can select the set that matches the sample.

General instructions: "Show me one that looks just like this one." (Administrator points to the item in the first column.)

| | | |
|---|---|---|
| oty | cfy | oty |
| uhg | ubg | uhg |
| ODA | QDA | ODA |
| hzp | hzp | bzp |
| uxs | uks | uxs |
| zua | zuq | zua |

4. *Sound matching.* Given a sound of spoken language (a phoneme) and three pictures, the name of one which contains the sound in initial, medial, or final position, the child can select the picture whose name contains the spoken word.

General instructions: "One of these has the sh-h sound. Point to the one that has the sh-h sound."

General instructions: "One of these has the *oh* sound. Point to the one that has the *oh* sound."

5. *Sound blending.* Given isolated sounds (a two-second pause between sounds), the child can put them together to pronounce (make) a word.

   General instructions: "Try to guess what word I'm making."

> "mou___se"
> "boa___t"
> "a___pe"
> "no___se"
> "lea___f"

The above prereading skills are drawn from the work of Richard L. Venezky and Associates at the University of Wisconsin.*

Calfee and Venezky have long been active in appraising component skills in beginning reading, giving special attention to uncovering visual and auditory-phonetic processes related to decoding (Calfee and Venezky, 1968, 1970). In addition, those with the Wisconsin prereading skills project have developed a program for teaching these skills. The program includes games, songs, and other activities, an assessment procedure, a teacher's handbook, and a resource file (*Wisconsin Prereading Skills Program*, 1971).

Often, a child doesn't learn because he doesn't know what the teacher is asking him to do. Therefore, a second category of important prereading skills includes those tasks dealing with the language of instruction—special terms and instructions that are used in beginning reading but are not common to out-of-school life:

---

*    *Wisconsin Prereading Skills Program*, Madison: The University of Wisconsin, Research and Development Center for Cognitive Learning, September 1971. Reprinted by permission.

1. *Matching to sample.* Given a sample (sound, letter, or picture), the child can select from among several alternatives the one that "is the same" (identical). Matching can be on the basis of such attributes as directionality, shape, size, function, and order.

2. *Position.* Given illustrations (e.g., pictures, letters, words) arranged in left-to-right order, the child can label the illustrations as *first, middle, last.*

   In addition, given the expression "beginning (or ending) with the same sound" and an example, the child can provide another example that begins (or ends) with the same sound. (The emphasis here is on the concept "beginning," "end," "speech sound." It is not to be regarded as a test of hearing.)

3. *Concept of "word."* Given the term "word" and name of object within a known category, the child can provide another "word" within the same category, e.g., "I'm thinking of a word; the word is red (color) or chair (furniture). You give me another "word.""

4. *Special vocabulary.* Given terms such as "top" or "bottom of page," "line," "row," "checkmark," the child can point to the referents of these terms.

Thus far we have stressed tasks associated with successful decoding in reading. Prerequisite skills for reading comprehension are likely to be similar to those necessary for comprehension in general. Before a child can infer how a character feels, for instance, he probably should be able to identify clues to emotions, e.g., stamping of foot, shaking of legs. It should be helpful if the learner can perform tasks demanding both literal and inferred comprehension. That is, for the former he can answer direct questions about what has been said, indicating his knowledge of the vocabulary used and his ability to comprehend grammatical relations. For the latter, he must have the experiential base for making the inferences required.

There is only modest hope that the young child can be taught to apply logical arguments in making inferences (e.g., "Mary's apple is either red or yellow. Here is a green, brown, and red apple. Which apple is Mary's?"). Most of the cognitive skills which would have long-run general beneficial effects may be influenced more by developmental and maturational factors than by training. Also, it would be nice if children could acquire this objective: Given word problems, the child can state whether the problem requires an inference ("educated" guess on his part) or whether he is being asked to directly ascertain the answer from what has been stated. By surveying the reading materials to be used during the first year, the teacher can identify the oral language skills most necessary as prerequisites, e.g., the particular vocabulary, sentence patterns, and syntactic structures, the child will encounter in printed form.

## Skills of Lower Priority

We have tried to narrow the number of prereading skills to be achieved. A manageable prereading program must be targeted on *crucial* skills, not those that are "nice to know" or ones that most children already have in their repertoire or will acquire concurrently with other tasks. It is known that when one teaches irrelevant skills, the child's progress toward priority skills is impaired. The discerning teacher will, of course, be prepared to augment prerequisite skills for particular learners.

There are several general categories of skills and activities which should not replace priority items. These skill categories are relegated to lower status for one or more of the following reasons: (1) they are not directly related to reading, (2) they can be acquired incidentally, (3) they are influenced more by maturation than by teaching, and (4) they can be taught more effectively in another branch of the academic program, e.g., aesthetics, special education. These categories of skills are:

1. *attending skills*    (persisting, cooperating, following directions)

2. *motor skills*    (balancing, left-to-right movements, path following, drawing)

3. *sensory skills*    (visual discrimination of color and geometric figures; auditory discrimination of pitch, sound intensity, sources and direction of sounds, rhythmic patterns; tactile discrimination of textures, shapes, and temperature)

4. *pattern recognition*    (counting, completing sequence, conserving number)

5. *problem solving*    (stating rules to self, searching systematically, reducing possibilities, using "hints," thinking of unusual uses, formulating questions, predicting outcomes, ranking alternative solutions)

6. *memory skills*    (recalling an array of objects, repeating a sequence of events, using mnemonic devices to recall a poem)

7. *geometric skills*    (identifying basic shapes, lines; determining congruence of forms).

## Making a Task Analysis

As indicated previously, task analysis consists of selecting one or more instructional objectives to be considered as "terminal" and then listing the component learnings that would seem to be necessary before the pupil could perform as demanded by the terminal objective. (An objective in reading is seldom truly terminal—an end in itself—but becomes a "stepping stone" to future objectives.) The product of a task analysis is a number of subtasks or objectives. Subsequently, these tasks may be arranged in a sequential order for teaching.

Johnson and Kress have provided an illustration to help clarify the process of tasks analysis (Johnson and Kress, 1971). This illustration, as paraphrased, follows.

*Terminal objective*: Given previously unknown words which follow the (consonant)-vowel-consonant(s) pattern, child can identify the vowel sound as "short."

*Subtask 1*:  Given patterns of words, child can identify those groups of words which fit the cvc pattern.

*Subtask 2*:  Given words, child can identify those which have the same final visual and rhyming elements, e.g., *Ed, Ted, red.*

*Subtask 3*:  Given words composed of different final consonants but same vowel, child can identify the vowel sound that is common to them, e.g., Given *Ed, pet, tell, bend,* child can select the word from several (*bat, bet, can*) that has the same vowel sounds as these words.

*Subtask 4*:  Given words with different vowels in the (c) vc (c) pattern, child can select another word from several that has the same vowel sound, (e.g., Child has generalized that *ed, end, ill, ock, ask,* all represent occurrences of a "short vowel sound).*

Any individual's analysis is likely to reflect his view of the teaching-reading process. The illustrative analysis just cited assumes that mastery of the terminal objective is best achieved when the learner makes a series of successively higher generalizations based on observations until he reaches a level for general application. Others making a task analysis of the same objective might arrive at different pre-requisites—perhaps omitting, for example, the need for teaching rhyming elements, and extending the subtasks farther down the hierarchy to skills of letter order and word orientation.

Skills that are prerequisite to the terminal objective need not always appear in the terminal performance. They might be considered prerequisite tasks because they facilitate learning of the higher-level skill. More precisely, if *A* (e.g., the ability to tell which spoken word begins like another spoken word) is prerequisite to *B* (e.g., the ability to say a word that begins with the sound that "goes with" a given letter), then learning *A* first should result in positive transfer when *B* is learned, and anyone able to perform *B* should be able to perform *A* as well. (If pupils can do *B* but not *A*, then *A* is not a prerequisite.) Prerequisites themselves are further analyzed to determine still simpler prerequisites. Analysis stops when a level of ability is reached which can be assumed in most pupils.

A psychological point of view regarding the making of a task analysis is found in the work of Gagné, who has classified eight types of learning which he thinks

---

*    Adapted from Marjorie Seddon Johnson and Roy A. Kress, "Task Analysis for Criterion-referenced Tests," *The Reading Teacher* **24**, 4, January 1971.

can be used to establish a hierarchy of capabilities in learning to read (Gagné, 1967). One of these types is *multiple discrimination*, whereby one learns to make different identifying responses to many different stimuli, e.g., to make the distinction between words having different vowel sounds when different combinations of letters are used, as in *rat* and *rate*. Another type is *concept learning*, the making of a common response to a class of stimuli that may differ widely from one another in appearance (e.g., "Which of these words does not belong? *later, yesterday, soon, here*", all but one being instances of the concept words of time.) Gagné contends that it is difficult for the child to acquire principles for use in reading until he has first attained capabilities in the use of concepts which require as a prerequisite multiple discrimination, which in turn requires other prerequisites such as verbal associations, e.g., associating a printed word with the saying of the word.

Although theorists from the disciplines—psychology, linguistics, sociology—are the sources for most of our heuristics in task analysis, common sense can be used to draw attention to possible prerequisites. Consider the prerequisites for a typical prereading task:

"Circle the word in each row that has two letters that are the same."

> pop    pan    mop
> men    mop    mom

Your answer might include (1) skills demanded in order to comprehend the language used in the directions—referents for the terms *two, circle, word, row, letter*, and (2) skills for discriminating letters visually—letter orientation.

## Diagnosing and Prescribing in Reading-Readiness Programs

Diagnosing reading difficulty is a controversial issue. There are arguments over the etiology of reading disability—the reasons children do not succeed in beginning reading; also, there are differences of opinion about how to respond to the different explanations and how to remedy the difficulties. The nature-nurture issue is ever present. Those with environmental-interventionist leanings are not interested in collecting information about a child's deficiencies and strengths solely to make predictions about the child's probable success; they want to use this information to upset "self-defeating" predictions. Currently, it is charged that too many teachers have been using "reasons" as "excuses" for not teaching effectively. Madeline Hunter, for instance, urges that diagnostic data be taken, "not as a cushion for failure but as a launching pad for successful learning."*

Consistent with the interventionist's position and the theory of "mastery learning," we hold that it is not enough to say that a child has a physical, emotional,

---

*    Remarks before the Claremont Reading Conference, Claremont California, February 7, 1969.

or cultural reason for not reading. We believe that the teacher has to do something about whatever difficulty is identified. As suggested by Wiener and Cromer, there are typically four courses of action available (Wiener and Cromer, 1970). Each course of action stems from a somewhat different assumption to account for unsuccessful reading.

1. *Circumvent the difficulty.* This practice rests on what Wiener and Cromer call an assumption of defect, i.e., something is not operating appropriately in the person, so he cannot benefit from his experiences. An example of circumvention is to teach a different way to read, as in the case of teaching a blind person to read by tactile means.

2. *Reverse the difficulty.* This is the practice most consistent with mastery learning—the cumulative-learning model which serves as the basis for so many of the newer reading programs. It rests on the assumption that a particular process or factor is absent in the learner and must be *added* before adequate reading can occur, e.g., teach a nonnative speaker of English the skill of recognizing questions on the basis of word order—*It is* versus *Is it.*

3. *Remove or lessen the problem.* The assumption is that something is interfering with reading, e.g., anxiety, anger at mother. Many clinical programs in reading for emotionally disturbed children are rooted in the belief that the interference must be removed (not necessarily the mother) before any missing components can be added.

4. *Making a better match between learner and instruction (method and materials).* The assumptions underlying this action are that there are not one or two best ways for all to learn and that there are background characteristics in the learner which should be respected in planning for instruction. Those who advocate that Chicanos and speakers of black dialect would learn to read more readily if given materials written in their own languages hold assumptions of difference. A further instance of matching learner characteristics and instructional procedure is found in classrooms where the teacher provides the highly active pupils, especially boys, with materials that allow for frequent overt responding, e.g., self-instructional programs.

## Purposes for diagnosing

A central purpose for diagnosis is to decide *what* to teach. Before attempting to teach a high-priority prereading skill like letter orientation, the teacher must find out which children "need" it. Need is defined as the gap between the desired behavior, i.e., performance that meets the objective, and what the learner can presently do with the task. Strange as it seems, many teachers fail to acquaint themselves with the patterns of skills pupils bring initially to their classrooms. Skager, for instance, found that the larger the proportion of pupils able to perform on a task at the beginning of a year, the more likely teachers were to rate that task as highly relevant to their own instruction (Skager, 1969).

A second purpose in diagnosing is to decide *how* to teach. This purpose is related to making the match between learner and means of instruction. Even when the selected objective is the same for several pupils, the route to the objective can be varied. The objective can be made more inviting by linking it with what the learner has previously found to be rewarding. Diagnosis in this case is finding out for what the child has previously been rewarded, e.g., his language, interests, activities, friendships.

A teacher may engage in diagnosis for other purposes too. General assessment of, say, the child's health (emotional and physical), intellect, and social adjustment can be very useful in identifying special children who may warrant clinical examination by qualified persons—physicians, psychologists, and the like. We believe, however, that as a teacher of reading, the classroom teacher must diagnose for the purpose of collecting information to be used in deciding (1) what reading and prereading skills to teach, and (2) the most promising instructional strategies to use.

## Tools for diagnosing

### *Measures for deciding what to teach*

Instruments must be related to purpose. Those measures most useful in deciding what prereading skills to teach given learners are criterion referenced tests—measures that reveal whether or not a pupil has already achieved some specific objective. A kindergarten or first-grade teacher might want to know whether or not pupils had mastered those skills presented on pages 20–22. The teacher might use the criterion-referenced tests that are available for measuring attainment of these practical skills (Wisconsin Prereading Program, 1972) or might prepare such a test. To develop a criterion-reference test, the teacher writes at least five problems equivalent to the kind of problem called for in the objective. The child who can respond correctly to each problem or test item is said to have mastered that particular task. The teacher must then find a subsequent task that the child cannot do.

We recommend pretesting all children who are about to begin formal instruction in reading on each of the five priority skills. The recommendation rests partly on the *principle of proximity*, i.e., in diagnosing a learner's competency in a task, it is better to first test his ability on the task itself rather than its prerequisite. If children do not perform well on the criterion-referenced test, the teacher can either make assumptions about what must be taught so that the child can achieve, or administer other criterion-referenced tests that measure particular skills believed to be prerequisite to the terminal task. The point to be made is that it is more efficient to first test the learner on the cumulative task, because if he does well on it, there is no need to test his competency on the component parts.

Some teachers may want to administer standardized tests for reading readiness as a basis for diagnosing needed skills. Tests such as the *Illinois Test of Psycholinguistic*

*Abilities—Revised* (ITPA, Kirk, *et al.,* 1972), *Metropolitan Readiness Test* (Harcourt Brace, 1965, *Lee Clark Reading Readiness Test* (McGraw Hill, 1962) are sometimes used. Information from these kinds of tests has been useful in the past in identifying those children most likely to succeed in reading. Now, however, that there is more interest in deciding what to teach so that all succeed, these tests are of lesser value. Standardized tests are criticized because the subtests often lack validity as "true prerequisites to reading," i.e., the variables measured may correlate with reading achievement, but they are not necessarily causal factors in learning to read. In other words, even if the teacher taught children to perform well on tasks comparable to those demanded by the standardized readiness test, it is not certain that the child will be any better able to profit from instruction in reading—to learn to decode. Most standardized tests are not useful as diagnostic tools, because if a child does poorly on the test, the teacher is still left with the problem of deciding what particular skill(s) to teach and what remedy to prescribe. This is because the subtests frequently measure more than a single skill. A test of "word meaning," for instance, is likely to measure visual discrimination and logical inference as much as vocabulary, requiring the teacher to find or develop further tests in order to know what particular skills to teach.

Results from a single criterion-referenced test may also require further testing. A child may not perform well because he cannot follow the instructions, cannot attend to visual detail, or has a memory defect. Descriptions of specific tests for assessing the child on these and other factors can be found in such sources as Buros' *Reading Tests and Reviews* (Gryphon, 1968), *Early Childhood Education,* a collection of sample instruments for measuring pupil attainment of more than 300 objectives common to early childhood education (Instructional Objectives Exchange, 1971), and *CSE Test Evaluations,* descriptions and ratings of kindergarten and elementary school tests as related to specific objectives (1971 and 1970).

We would be remiss in not mentioning the value of informal inventories in the readiness program to determine (1) how well the individual can perform on selected tasks, and (2) the point where the learner has need for instructional help and at which he can profit from it. The informal inventory can be used with both groups and individuals and usually consists of the teacher's selecting previously unintroduced instructional materials (exercises, games, programmed materials, instruction via casettes) similar or identical to that which the teacher is considering to use with the pupil(s). Subsequently, the teacher observes either the child's performance or the product of his performance. A check sheet for recording the kinds of errors made when working with the material is valuable. Analyses of the number and kind of errors made indicates what should be taught.

If one is using programmed materials in the classroom, it is relatively easy to determine the appropriateness of the material by asking the child to respond to the last part of the program. If he can do so, the material is probably inappropriate. Some early learning materials such as ABC's *Learning Activity Booklets* (American Book Company, 1969), have separate programmed sequences—each sequence is aimed at developing a separate skill, e.g., negation, prepositions, rhyming. By asking pupils to respond only to the last page on each booklet where there are "criterion frames" (unprompted problems), the teacher can quickly discover which of the booklets warrants the pupil's use.

### Using diagnostic tools to determine what to teach

It seems logical to first measure the child's ability to perform on the priority pre-reading items. Then, and only if there is good cause to do so, assess performance on those motor and intellectual skills associated with the general ability to learn. The teacher can usually effect desired progress with respect to the priority items, but will be unsuccessful in trying to improve the child's general psychometric intelligence. As indicated in Balow's penetrating analysis of nearly 50 investigations treating motor and perceptual efforts for the development of reading skills, there is little evidence to suggest that visual perceptual and cognitive motor activities can replace the careful diagnosis and direct teaching of reading skills (Balow, 1971).

### Responding to diagnostic findings

Thus far we have indicated that the best response to diagnostic findings is to select instructional objectives that are appropriate for a particular learner. A second kind of response follows from a different diagnosis—diagnosis of the learner's interests, attitudes, preferences, and other background information that might be useful in planning the activities for "bridging the gap" between where the learner is with respect to skills and where the teacher wants him to be. Self-reports of what the learner likes to do, observation schedules, and parent input can be used in collecting information for this kind of diagnosis. Typical of sources for such information-gathering devices are *Attitude Toward School* and *Self-Concept Measures*, collections of sample instruments for indicating pupil preferences (Instructional Objectives Exchange, 1973), and *The Handbook on Formative and Summative Evaluation of Student Learning*, especially the chapter entitled "Evaluation of Learning in Pre-school Education" (McGraw-Hill, 1971).

### Relating learner characteristics to instructional means

Diagnosis of interest and background provides clues about how to teach—the selection of learning activities. We want the learner to find the activities satisfying and to look forward to participating in them. The more we know about what the learner has been rewarded for in the past—what he has been taught to enjoy and value—the easier it is to select instructional activities that will be viewed favorably by him. Notice, however, that the challenge is not merely to select activities that accord with the child's predispositions, but also to select learning activities that will give the pupil opportunity to practice the competency called for in the objective.

The following is an illustration of matching objectives, characteristics, and activities:

| Objective | Background information | Choices in activities |
|---|---|---|
| When asked to point to letters on left or right of a reference, the child can do so. | Children from some cultures like to engage in cooperative group activity rather than to work alone or to engage in individual competition. Others prefer to work solo. | Offer (1) letter games group participation, e.g., those adapted from "Looby Loo" and "Simon Says," (2) structured, self-instructional activity teaching left-right orientation with letters. |
| Given words ending in "er" or "est," the child can select the alternative that best corresponds to the word, e.g., "smaller," "biggest," "loudest." | Some children have keen interest in things musical; others, in natural phenomena. | Draw alternatives which pupils select (1) from musical and instrumental sounds, and (2) natural objects and sounds. |
| Given incomplete oral sentences, the child can supply the missing word. | Children reveal differences in vocabulary and dialects. | Sentence patterns and kinds of words omitted are the same; however, sentences are drawn from both standard and dialectal speech |

## Conclusion

Newer programs in reading draw heavily from the theory that nearly all children can achieve in reading and that one way to facilitate this is to teach for mastery those component parts that constitute complex reading skills. The problem of identifying such parts and validating their contributions to particular reading tasks requires both analysis and experimentation.

Application of the newer theories at the prereading level is both upsetting traditional notions of readiness and greatly changing practice. Testing for purposes of determining readiness to read and of predicting success in learning to read is giving way to testing to determine what and how to teach. Instead of engaging in the teaching of general perceptual and motor skills and hoping that these efforts will transfer to reading, there is more careful specification of the beginning tasks in reading, e.g., decoding, and a narrower list of directly related prerequisites involving letter-sound correspondence.

Teachers now have a manageable number of objectives on which to focus, and the early learning activities they provide are not regarded as ends in themselves, but rather as means to these objectives. The ferment from newer thrusts of intervention and component analysis is rejuvenating older issues: the value of preschool reading on long-run reading achievement and the possibility of accelerating academic progress independent of genetic and maturational factors.

## References

*The ABC Learning Activities.* New York: American Book Company, 1969.

Balow, Bruce. "Perceptual-motor activities in the treatment of severe reading disability," *The Reading Teacher* **24**, 6 (March 1971): 513–525.

Bloom, Benjamin S. "Learning for mastery," *Evaluation Comment* **1**, 2 (1968): 1–12.

Brzeinski, Joseph. *Summary Report of the Effectiveness of Teaching Reading in Kindergarten in the Denver Public Schools*, Denver, Colorado: Cooperative Research Project No. 5-0371, 1967.

Buros, O. K. *Reading Tests and Reviews*, Highland Park, N. J.: Gryphon Press, 1968.

Calfee, Robert C. and Richard L. Venezky, *Component Skills in Beginning Reading*, Madison: Wisconsin Research and Development Center for Cognitive Learning, University of Wisconsin, July 1968.

————. *How a Child Needs to Think to Learn to Read*, Madison: Wisconsin Research and Development Center for Cognitive Learning, University of Wisconsin, July 1970.

Chomsky, Carol. "Stages in language development and reading exposure," *Harvard Educational Review* **42**, 1 (February 1972): 1–33.

Cohen, S. Alan. *Teach Them All to Read: Theory, Methods, and Materials for Teaching the Disadvantaged*, New York: Random House, 1969.

*Communication Skills Program.* Inglewood, California: Southwest Regional Laboratory, 1971.

Durkin, Dolores. "What does research say about the time to begin reading instruction?" *Journal of Educational Research* **64**, 2 (October 1970): 52–56.

————. "When should children begin to read?" *67th Yearbook of the National Society for the Study of Education*, Part II, Chicago: University of Chicago Press, 1968.

Gagné, Robert M. *The Conditions of Learning*, New York: Holt, Rinehart and Winston, 1967.

*The Handbook on Formative and Summative Evaluation of Student Learning.* New York: McGraw-Hill, 1971.

Hoepfner, R., G. Strickland, G. Stangel, P. Jensen, and M. Patalino. "CSE elementary school test evaluations," Los Angeles: Center for the Study of Evaluation, UCLA Graduate School of Education, 1970.

Hoepfner, R., C. Stern, and S. Nummedal. "CSE-ECRC preschool kindergarten test evaluations," Los Angeles: Center for the Study of Evaluation, UCLA Graduate School of Education, 1971.

*Individually Prescribed Instruction in Reading*, University of Pittsburgh, 1970.

Instructional Objectives Exchange. *Attitude Toward School* (1973), *Early Childhood Education* (1971), *Self-Concept Measures* (1973). Los Angeles, California, 90025.

Jensen, A. R. "How much can we boost IQ and scholastic achievement?" *Harvard Educational Review* **39**, 3 (Winter 1969): 1–123.

Johnson, Marjorie Seddon and Roy A. Kress. "Task analysis for criterion-referenced tests," *The Reading Teacher* **24**, 4 (January 1971): 355–359.

Kirk, Samuel A., James J. McCarthy, and Winifred D. Kirk. *Illinois Test of Psycholinguistic Abilities*, rev., Urbana: University of Illinois Press, 1971.

Kohlberg, Lawrence. "Early education: a cognitive-development view," *Child Development* **39**, 4 (December 1968): 1013–1062.

*Lee-Clark Reading Readiness Test.* Monterey: California Test Bureau, 1962.

MacGinitie, Walter H. "Evaluating readiness for developmental language learning: critical review and evaluation of research," in *Reading and Realism*, ed. J. Allen Figurel, *Proceedings from the Thirteenth Annual Convention* **13**, 1 (1969): 508–515. International Reading Association.

*Metropolitan Readiness Tests.* New York: Harcourt Brace Jovanovich, 1964.

Morphett, Mabel and Carlton, Washburne. "When should children begin to read?" *Elementary School Journal* **31** (1931): 496–503.

*Program for Learning According to Needs.* Westinghouse, 1970.

*READ System.* New York: American Book Company, 1971.

Regents of the University of the State of New York. *Reading*, Position paper No. 12 of a series, Albany: The State Education Department, July 1971.

Rohwer, William, D., Jr. "Prime time for education: early childhood or adolescence?" *Harvard Educational Review* **41** 3 (1971): 316–341.

Samuels, S. Jay. "The effect of letter-name knowledge on learning to read," *American Educational Research Journal* **1** (Winter 1972): 65–74.

————. "Letter-name versus letter-sound knowledge in learning to read," *The Reading Teacher* **24**, 7 (April 1971): 604–608.

————. *Success and Failure in Learning to Read: A Critique of the Research*, Occasional Paper #9, HEW Grant OE-09-332189-4533 (032), November 1971.

Singer, Harry. "Research that should have made a difference," *Elementary English* **47** (1970): 27–34.

Skager, Rodney W. *Student Entry Skills and the Evaluation of Instructional Programs: A Case Study.* Los Angeles: Center for the Study of Evaluation, June 1969.

Sutton, Marjorie H. "Children who learned to read in kindergarten: a longitudinal study," *Reading Teacher* **22** (April 1969): 595–602.

Venezky, Richard L., Robert C. Calfee, and Robin S. Chapman. "Skills required for learning to read," *Language and Reading—an Interdisciplinary Approach*, comp. Doris V. Gunderson, Washington, D. C.: Center for Applied Linguistics, 1970, pp. 37–54.

Wiener, Morton and Ward Cromer. "Reading and reading difficulty: a conceptual analysis," in *Language and Reading—an Interdisciplinary Approach, op. cit.*, 136–162.

*Wisconsin Design for Reading Skill Development.* Madison: The University of Wisconsin, Research and Development Center for Cognitive Learning, 1971.

*Wisconsin Prereading Skills Program.* Madison: The University of Wisconsin, Research and Development Center for Cognitive Learning, September 1971.

# 6 / Objectives: their nature and function

## Introduction

If you were to examine all of the textbooks on the teaching of reading that are presently available, you would find that few, if any, have a chapter or even a substantial part of a chapter devoted to the function of objectives in the teaching of reading. Yet it has been our observation that as objective-based materials have become available, they have had an enthusiastic reception from teachers. And, perhaps more important, they have been used with success to improve children's reading achievement. We have noted, too, that teachers in many schools—as they serve on various types of curriculum improvement committees or independently—have been working toward the identification of essential skills and the statement of objectives as a means for improving the teaching of reading. We see this as a positive trend for two main reasons.

First, the identification of objectives in reading reinforces the teacher's role as a *facilitator of instruction*. Remember the discussion in Chapter 3? We said that the facilitation of learning proceeds from a belief in the value of each person's natural potentiality to learn, but that learning can be focused only after some basic decisions have been made about what it is that we want children to learn. To state objectives for reading instruction is to pin down in behavioral terms what we want children to learn. The objectives permit us to come to grips with the task of facilitating children's learning.

Second, teachers' acceptance of objective-based approaches to reading instruction is in step with the trend toward greater accountability in education. The matter of accountability is given further attention in this chapter, but the point here is that teachers are not necessarily opposed, as certain critics suggest, to the notion of accountability. To the contrary, many of them have long been seeking ways to focus their efforts, to measure their success, and to work toward the self-correction of problems. This, we feel, is accountability at its best, for it comes from the professionals who are in the best position to see it through to its ultimate goal of improving learning.

The use of objectives in the teaching of reading, then, is both reasonably well accepted and, at least in our opinion, desirable despite the neglect of objectives in the traditional texts. In fact, as we have said repeatedly in the preceding pages, focused reading instruction is of necessity objective-based. Our general purpose in this chapter is to present a rationale for taking an objective-based approach to reading instruction. Specifically, we look first at the matter of accountability in education. Second, we consider behavioral objectives—what they are and what they amount to in terms of benefits and limitations. Then, we deal in turn with the general matter of objective-based instruction and with the specific matter of focusing instruction in reading through the use of objectives. Finally, we present an overview of the specific objectives that are offered in the four chapters that follow.

## Accountability in Education

*Accountable* is broadly defined in the dictionary. For example, the *Random House Dictionary* defines it as "subject to having to report, explain, or justify; responsible; answerable." Yet the word has taken on a narrower, more restrictive meaning for many teachers and other school people. More often than not, *accountability in education* amounts, operationally, to holding each teacher responsible for improving the reading and arithmetic scores of the pupils in his class. Certainly this is not an unseemly expectation, given the fact that much of what goes on in school and in the world revolves around the ability to deal with words and numbers. But whether reading and arithmetic scores constitute the only, or even the major, concern of teachers and of the schools is a question that has not been resolved. We shall not attempt to resolve it here, but we do want to consider the issue of accountability because it will help to put objective-based reading instruction into perspective. The discussion is developed in the responses to a series of questions.

1. *What does "accountability" in education really mean?* The answer to this question continues to emerge as new programs are implemented, as new techniques for assessment become available, as community pressures mount, and as professional perceptions mature. We have already pointed out what the operational answer has been: Accountability means that we hold each teacher responsible for improving the reading and arithmetic scores of his pupils. But the general answer is reasonably straightforward: Accountability means that the schools, the professional educators, should be held responsible for what children learn. The assumption behind the answer is that such accountability will result in improved professional performance, which will lead in turn to improved academic achievement and better attitudes on the part of pupils.

2. *Whose idea is it?* If the assumption that accountability will lead to improved educational outcomes is sound, then the notion ought to have the unequivocal support of professionals in education. But the fact is that the push for accountability has come, for the most part, from other sources or, at least, from sources that are outside the traditional mainstream of professional education. The notion has received much impetus from each of the following: (1) the demand for evaluation of school programs and entire school systems brought about as part of federal funding programs; (2) the budget crunch that has caused a re-examination of educational endeavors in view of cost effectiveness; (3) a focusing on the special needs of the disadvantaged as a high-priority responsibility of the schools; and (4) the trend to make the schools more responsive to their clientele and communities. These major thrusts turn out to be mutually reinforcing, and together they exert a powerful pressure for educational change—for accountability on the part of the educational establishment.

The idea spreads because it has all the seductive appeal of a siren song, e.g.:

> People in business have always been
> accountable for their products.
> Now is the time to make people in
> public education accountable for
> their product.
> Accountability in education will lead to
> improved educational outcomes.
> Accountability in education is a
> GOOD thing.

But like many other siren songs, it may be more seductive than fulfilling. There are many problems involved in making the idea operational. Two of the greatest problems are that there has been a tendency to oversimplify the whole process and to rush in with half-baked programs, and more often than not the teachers who will carry the main burden of accountability have had little or no voice in shaping approaches to accountability.

3. *Accountability for what?* The ultimate question about accountability is a very specific one: *For what?* There appears to be an idealistic answer and a realistic answer. Ideally, school people ought to be responsible for (1) selecting "proper," or "correct," objectives and assigning them appropriate priorities, (2) achieving the objectives, and (3) avoiding any adverse effects on pupils. One problem is that the selection of objectives can turn out to be a highly subjective matter that is influenced by both philosophical and political forces. And, even after objectives are stated, there are still problems of how to assess all of them and how to anticipate and avoid adverse effects. Compromises must, therefore, be worked out between what is desirable and what can be done.

Realistically, it is most feasible for school people to be responsible for educational outcomes for which objectives are well defined and output can be measured. Two kinds of performance meet these qualifications: first, *cognitive* performance in skill areas like reading and mathematics, where essential skills can be identified and described in behavioral terms; second, and perhaps a poor second, certain *affective* performance, for which there are indicators like drop-out rates, absenteeism, vandalism, and delinquency. Pragmatically, the basic skill areas at the elementary school level are most open to accountability because there is reasonable agreement as to what the skills are and how performance can be measured. There is no such agreement for the subject areas taught in the secondary schools.

A *simple* answer to our question, then, is that accountability will, or should for the forseeable future, continue to focus on the basic skill areas at the elementary school level. But even with such a simple answer, the implications turn out to be complex, because eventually we must devise ways to decide how much each member of the school establishment contributes to the measured results. The related problems are complex, even when we consider only the classroom teacher.

That the educational results obtained in a given classroom or school building are dependent on many things besides the skill of the teacher or teachers involved is well known and accepted. Pupils' experiential backgrounds, socioeconomic status, language development, peer-group relations, and many other factors all exert a powerful out-of-school effect that is reflected in school achievement. The problem is to separate out the teacher effect from all the others, and it must at least be considered before we can hope to hold individual teachers accountable for *any* educational outcomes. This means that accountability measures will need to be adapted in terms of pupil characteristics and in terms of comparisons with the performance of teachers in similar circumstances.

4. *Accountability to whom?* Underlying the notion of accountability is the assumption that each member of the school establishment is, or ought to be, expected to answer to someone for doing specific things according to established plans and guidelines in order to meet performance expectations. Each person who becomes involved presumably does so to contribute to the process of meeting the established expectations. Thus, the intent of accountability is to ensure that the efforts of individuals are functional, i.e., that they contribute to the attainment of established goals.

In a very real sense, then, accountability permits the professionals in education to be accountable to *themselves*. The process begins with the setting of tangible goals, and it ends with appropriate assessment to determine whether the goals were attained. If the goals are realistic, they should be reached or exceeded. If they are not, there is reason to re-examine both the goals and the methods employed in pursuing them with a view toward making improvements. We feel that this aspect of accountability—which permits the professionals in education to examine their own performance—is the most important of all. Only after the process of teaching is specified to the extent that it can be subject to careful scrutiny can there be truly systematic attempts to improve it.

Of course, there are others who have a stake in accountability. *Parents* deserve an opportunity to appraise the performance of their children and their schools. As it is now, it is very difficult for parents to evaluate any complaints made by their children and by the school critics. Accountability systems that are confined to the basic skill areas will not solve all of the school-community relations problems, but they will be a significant step in the right direction. *Boards of education* can use accountability as a monitoring device to identify and investigate problems and problem areas that interfere with pupil performance. The *children* have the most to gain, and they must be informed about the system—if not specifically about their personal performance—as soon as they are old enough to take an interest. They should understand that accountability is a useful device for improving the performance of all pupils and that it does not exist to stigmatize pupils whose achievement is low.

5. *What does all this have to do with objective-based reading instruction?* At least four basic points from the preceding discussion of accountability are relevant here. First, whether we like it or not, the fact is that the accountability focus is on reading and mathematics. Given the philosophical, political, and technological facts of life when it comes to moving into other areas, the focus is likely to remain where it is for the foreseeable future. Second, one of the major problems to date is that the professional educators have not taken major roles in building many of the accountability programs that have been tried out. Consequently, educators—particularly classroom teachers—have had little to say about many programs for which they are responsible. Third, the criteria for demonstrating accountability must be concrete, but they must also be relative. To expect the performance of pupils with disadvantaged backgrounds to match that of pupils in more advantaged circumstances is not realistic. The goals may be the same in the basic skill areas, but the pacing must be adjusted. Fourth, a system designed to demonstrate accountability can also be the basis for self-evaluation and self-improvement in the schools.

We are convinced that objective-based approaches to reading instruction provide the basis for demonstrating accountability in reading. If the professionals in education will take the initiative in working out the details of such approaches, they can expect certain benefits. First, they will be assured of a voice in setting realistic goals for themselves rather than having the goals imposed by others. Second, they will retain much credibility regarding the need for relative criteria if the goals reflect that need from the start. Third, they will be assured that the system is one that will in fact permit self-improvement through diagnosis and evaluation. The movement toward accountability in education can be a threat or a challenge. It will become the worst kind of threat if it means that the professional educators must take responsibility for goals that are established wholly by others. It can continue to be a challenge if the response is active, positive, and optimistic.

## Behavioral Objectives

Objective-based approaches to reading instruction are built on goals stated in terms of pupil behavior. In current usage, such goals are called *behavioral objectives*. Here, we describe exactly what they are and how to go about writing them; we then examine their benefits and limitations.

## What they are

Educators have always had goals, but until fairly recently those goals have tended to be so broad and general in nature that they have been implicit rather than explicit. The testing and technological movements in education have, however, caused much more attention to be paid to the precise definition of objectives and the outcomes associated with them. Now, there is much agreement that precisely defined objectives are, of necessity, *behavioral* objectives. Such objectives focus on pupil behaviors—the *observable* outcomes of instruction.

Consider two frequently quoted definitions of behavioral objectives. A very concise definition is offered by Montague and Butts (1968, p. 33).

> A behavioral objective is a goal for, or a desired outcome of, learning which is expressed in terms of observable behavior (or performance, if you prefer) of the learner.

A definition stated in terms of three criteria to which the writer of behavioral objectives must comply is offered by Mager (1962).

> *First,* identify the terminal behavior by name; you can specify the kind of behavior that will be accepted as evidence that the learner has achieved the objective.
>
> *Second,* try to define the desired behavior further by describing the important conditions under which the behavior will be expected to occur.
>
> *Third,* specify the criteria of acceptable performance by describing how well the learner must perform to be considered acceptable.*

Each definition calls for a clear statement of what is expected; the latter gets even more specific by putting down where to look for the expected behavior and how to decide when it has been successfully demonstrated.

In another context, Mager (1968, p. vii) lightheartedly stated exactly what good behavioral objectives amount to (and offered a bit of an incentive for using them, to boot):

> To rise from a zero
> To Big Campus Hero,
> To answer these questions you'll strive:
>> Where am I going,
>> How shall I get there, and
>> How will I know I've arrived?

---

* R. F. Mager, *Preparing Instructional Objectives*, Palo Alto, Calif.: Fearon, 1962, p. 12. Reprinted by permission.

And in a much more scholarly vein, Bloom, Hastings, and Madaus (1971) had this to say about Mager's definition:

Gagné (1965, p. 34), summarizing the high degree of specificity described in the work of Mager . . . , breaks a statement of an objective into four basic components. The four are illustrated in this sentence taken from Gagné: "Given two numerals connected by the sign +, the student states orally the name of the number which is the sum of the two." First, the statement contains words denoting the stimulus situation which initiates the performance ("Given two numerals connected by the sign +"). Second, there is an action word or verb which denotes observable behavior ("states"). Third, there is a term denoting the object acted upon (which sometimes is simply implied). Finally, there is a phrase indicating the characteristics of the performance that determines its correctness ("the name of the number which is the sum of the two").*

Lighthearted or scholarly, the consensus is that a good behavioral objective (1) describes desired pupil performance, or *behavior*, (2) identifies competence level, or *criterion* or *minimum level of acceptable performance*, and (3) may specify the conditions of the performance. The last is not always needed, but when applicable a statement of conditions helps to make the intent perfectly clear.

## How to write them

First, remember that a behavioral objective is a goal stated *in behavioral terms*. In the examples that follow, the portion of each objective which describes the desired pupil behavior is underscored:

The child is able to locate points and describe the location of points in relation to a simple street grid.
The child is able to tell when the words in a pair have the same, opposite or simply different meanings.
The child is able to alphabetize words by attending to their first and second letters.

Note that in each objective the behavior is *observable*; that is, it can be observed, checked, and/or recorded. The behavior is, in effect, "point-at-able." Some verbs that denote point-at-able acts are:

| | | |
|---|---|---|
| to state | to write | to demonstrate |
| to recognize | to recite | to compare |
| to predict | to solve | to identify |
| to compute | to match | to discuss |

Such verbs serve to pin down the *behavior* in a behavioral objective.

---

* B. S. Bloom, J. T. Hastings, and G. F. Madaus, *Handbook on Formation and Summative Evaluation of Student Learning*, New York, McGraw-Hill, 1971, pp. 35–36. Reprinted by permission.

Second, a behavioral objective identifies the *expected competence level.* The competence level is double-underlined in the examples that follow:

Given a maximum one-second exposure per word in context, the child is able to recognize all of the words on the Dolch Basic Vocabulary List of 220 words.

The child is able to identify the common—scr, shr, spl, spr, str, thr—three-letter consonant blends in at least 80% of the real and nonsense words containing such blends pronounced by the teacher.

The child is able to focus all previously mastered skills in independent study and/or research.

Some writers refer to competency level as *optimum level, minimum level of acceptable performance,* or simply *criterion.* Competency level has to do with the measurement, evaluation, or description of the observable behavior specified in a behavioral objective. Adjectives and quantity words are used to identify competency levels. (Sometimes a single competency level is established for an entire set of objectives, e.g., 80% of the items correct on each objective-related test. Then, there is no need to identify the level in each objective.)

Third, a behavioral objective *may* specify the conditions of the performance. The statement of conditions is in brackets in each of the examples that follow:

[Given a brief written-oral selection in the active voice], the child responds to questions about detail found in the selection.

[Given axis and coordinate referents], the child is able to locate points and describe the location of points in relation to a simple picture grid.

[Given two real or nonsense words pronounced by the teacher], the child is able to tell when the words begin alike.

A statement of conditions should be included if it helps to clarify the objective by specifying whether certain data, tools, or materials are "given" or "withheld."

Now see if you can write a good behavioral objective. If you can honestly say that your objective has these three (or four) qualities, you are on your way to focusing your own reading instruction!

1. Anyone who reads it can perceive its intent.
2. The expected pupil behavior is described in behavioral terms.
3. A competence level is clearly identified.
4. (This one is optional, depending on the kind of performance required.) The materials, tools, or data that are given or withheld are specified.

If you feel you need some more practice, work through Mager's (1962) programmed book, *Preparing Instructional Objectives.* That book has emerged as the classic how-to-do-it on writing behavioral objectives.

Remember, though, that no matter how skilled you become at the technical aspects of writing them, the objectives you produce will never be any better than the ideas they represent. Good objectives are no substitute for poorly conceived goals. Because they are tools that help us tackle certain jobs in education, they are intrinsically neither good nor bad. They become desirable or not in their application. Consider some of the benefits and limitations of the use of behavioral objectives (Haberman, 1968).

## Benefits

1. *Behavioral objectives set clear purposes for both teachers and pupils.* In Chapter 3 we discussed the need for behavioral objectives when one attempts to organize instruction for the application of sound learning principles. Objectives stated in observable terms specify expectations for both teachers and pupils. They thus facilitate planning and permit teachers and pupils to communicate about the pursuit and attainment of mutually understood objectives. (Review the sections of Chapter 3 that deal with the how-to-do-it of individualizing instruction and the application of learning principles. Note in each instance the need for clearly stated purposes.)

2. *Specific objectives break broad content or curriculum areas into manageable bits.* To say that functional literacy for all pupils is the goal in reading is to say nothing that is useful to a teacher who is responsible for planning instruction. Certainly, the broad objective is a desirable one, but it offers no clues as to how it might appropriately be pursued. Specific, skill-related objectives can serve to outline a curriculum area like reading in terms that lend focus and direction to the instructional process that leads to functional literacy.

3. *The sequence and/or hierarchical arrangement of content can be worked out in terms of objectives.* In order to state behavioral objectives in the first place, their arrangement according to priorities and developmental sequences must be carefully considered. This means that task analyses must be done to identify the essential components of a given curriculum area, logical analyses must be made to fix priorities about what is retained and what is dropped from the curriculum, and developmental analyses must be made to determine what a pupil must know before he is able to tackle subsequent objectives. Once these initial analyses have been completed and the initial objectives have been described, the groundwork is laid for continuous analysis, justification, and improvement of the scope and sequence of objectives in a curriculum area. Teachers can begin to systematically decide which objectives are most important, which are most difficult, which must come first, which can be dropped, which must be modified, etc.

4. *Behavioral objectives facilitate evaluation.* An objective provides the basis for criterion-referenced assessment. That is, each objective describes the expected behavior in observable terms and sets a criterion level for performance. Evaluation, then, becomes self-evident in most cases—the pupil either can perform in the pre-

scribed manner or he cannot. (Remember, though, that to limit evaluation to specific objectives *could* be to stop short of the ultimate goal that is desired. This problem is considered in the discussion of limitations.)

5. *Objectives aid in the organization and selection of instructional materials.* Given behavioral objectives, it is possible to identify materials and procedures that are in line with instructional goals in a much more systematic manner than is usually possible. One procedure that works very well is to develop "resource files" of materials and procedures, with one file for each objective in an area. Since all of the entries in a given file are appropriate for pursuing a given objective, the file amounts to a handy reference, or resource, for locating materials and ideas. When teachers collaborate in building such files, they have many opportunities to examine new materials in a systematic way and to share ideas and experiences. Ready access to a variety of approaches to a given objective enables a teacher to choose the one (or ones) that appears to be most appropriate for a given individual at a given point in time.

6. *Objectives can play a major role in teacher training.* This is true at both the pre-service and in-service levels of training. With an objective-based approach, the focus is on the behavioral expectations we have for pupils. Training, then, can be largely a matter of (1) practicing and becoming expert in putting subject matter into behavioral expectations, and (2) identifying and refining the instructional techniques that will facilitate pupil attainment of objectives. Such an approach makes pupil behaviors the basis for teacher training. This, we feel, is putting the emphasis where it ought to be. Too many so-called competency-based, teacher-training programs flounder because they pay little or no attention to *pupil* competences.

7. *Objectives clarify the role of research and planning in education.* Research in education *can* help us to find the best means for achieving clearly stated goals. It *cannot* answer any basic questions about the direction and purpose of education. An objective-based approach will help us to ask the right questions of the right people. Educators need to establish their own goals and then to ask researchers to help find out how best to reach them.

## Limitations

1. *The process of schooling amounts to much more than mastering content.* Here, we shall resist a strong temptation to go into an extended discussion. Many supporting points could be made, but the truth of the basic point must be obvious to anyone who has ever been a teacher or a pupil in a school. Stephens (1967) has written a whole book about his theory of "spontaneous schooling." Take a look at it if you feel a need to put behavioral objectives into perspective.

2. *Individuals have idiosyncratic ways of organizing content.* Although content can be organized logically, according to the results of multiple analyses and empirical tests, the fact remains that idiosyncratic learning styles and experiences permit

pupils to organize content in many other ways. Some children, for example, learn how to read—to at least decode—with no formal instruction. They "figure it out" without mastering any established sequence of objectives, and they probably would not be able to demonstrate mastery of many of the objectives in such a sequence. To insist that they start over in order to master the sequence would be foolish.

3. *Objectives may cause an overemphasis on skills at the expense of generalizations, interpretations, and applications.* The critics say that an objective-based approach to reading instruction can lead to situations in which children who know the specific skills involved are unable to decode and comprehend when they attempt to read connected text. This can indeed happen if children are not given many opportunities to apply the skills as they acquire them. Successful reading turns out to be much more than the sum of the specific skills involved.

4. *Certain content areas do not lend themselves to a behavioral approach.* We have already stated our belief that certain skill areas, e.g., reading and mathematics, are best suited for an objective-based approach. In a behaviorally oriented curriculum it is unlikely that art would be equally valued with math.

5. *Objectives may be stated with little regard for the realities of the classroom.* A content area can be broken down into its components, and objectives can be stated by experts who have little knowledge of children or teachers or the process of schooling. To proceed in such a manner is to impose limitations that can never be overcome in application.

6. *Unanticipated outcomes may be as important as intended results.* Many writers have taken issue with the idea that the outcomes of education can be predicted in advance. They argue that the dynamics of teacher-pupil interaction may cause changes in direction as a learning sequence progresses. Maguire (1968) was speaking to the point when he wrote that

> if there is any advantage to the teacher over other methods of presentation, it likely lies in the flexibility of the teacher which allows him to take advantage of the unpredictable occurrences in a classroom discussion and turn them into useful learning experiences. Although it does not necessarily follow that the expression of specific objectives preempts the taking advantage of momentary occurrences, what is known about cognitive set makes such preemption seem very unlikely.*

Popham (1969, p. 135), one of the most outspoken proponents of behavioral objectives, acknowledges the possibility of unanticipated outcomes, but he considers the assessability of results at the same time, as shown on the following schema.

---

\* T. O. Maguire, "Value Components of Teachers' Judgments of Educational Objectives," *AV Communications Review* **16**, 1968, p. 68. Reprinted by permission.

|               | Intended results | Unanticipated results |
|---------------|:----------------:|:---------------------:|
| Measurable results | A | B |
| Unassessable results | C | D |

Cell A would be clearly covered by behavioral objectives. The unanticipated out-comes in Cell B should, if they are important, influence any evaluation of an instructional sequence. Cell C would include "expressive" or "open" objectives, which are intended but objectively unassessable outcomes. And Cell D would include out-comes that are both unanticipated and unassessable and therefore of no utility. Popham feels that educators have traditionally relied too heavily on Cells C and D and that optimal instructional planning would find teachers heavily emphasizing Cell A, devoting modest attention to Cell C and being alert to the possible import of Cells B and D" (p. 65).

Perhaps Popham's words amount to a reasonably good summary for a discussion about the benefits and limitations of behavioral objectives, for in effect they suggest that we ought to make use of objectives for what they can do and be alert to what they cannot do. We have seen objectives abused when they are prepared without thought and applied without reason. But we have also seen objectives bring order to curriculum planning and focus to the instruction of individual pupils. We would be reluctant to advocate an objective-based approach to all areas of the curriculum. But we are convinced that an objective-based approach to reading instruction is both sensible and defensible.

## Objective-Based Instruction

Sometimes the distance between a good idea and successful application of the idea is so great that there is no practical way to bridge the gap. Some critics claim that this is the case with behavioral objectives. They insist that the limitations are too pervasive to be dealt with successfully and that an objective-based approach will be heavy-handed, mechanistic, and short-sighted. We recognize the problems, and we readily concede that behavioral objectives *can* be misused and, perhaps, overused. But most of the problems can be solved if we will concentrate on the sensible *use* rather than the excessive *misuse* of behavioral objectives. In this section we deal with some of the practical problems involved in the application of an objective-based approach to instruction.

### "Closed" and "open" objectives

Consider again Popham's analysis of *intended* vs. unanticipated results. Popham's conclusion was that teachers ought to devote most of their attention to Cell A, which includes outcomes that are both intended and assessable, and some of their attention to Cell C, which includes outcomes that are intended but not assessable. Cell A can be adequately handled with standard behavioral objectives; Cell C, however, with its unassessable results, presents something of a problem. Even Popham admits to being perplexed:

> ... that schools must be concerned to some extent with providing activities for which we are as yet unable to assess the outcomes is worthy of consideration. Being perfectly candid, this probem has perplexed me since the day I became interested in thinking about the implications of instructional objectives for educational practice.*

The problem is apparent when one considers an objective-based approach to reading instruction. Word-attack skills, study skills, and even comprehension skills can be handled with standard behavioral objectives, and they fit quite nicely into Cell A. But the skills involved in such areas as self-directed reading, interpretive reading, and creative reading fall into Cell C. In the latter areas we can generally agree on what we want, but we have great difficulty in assessing what we get by way of outcomes.

A solution to the problem appears to be inherent in Eisner's discussions of "open," or "instructional," objectives as contrasted to "closed," or "expressive," objectives. This is what he says about *open* and *closed* objectives;

> To state an objective in terms clear enough to know what it (the terminal behavior) will look like requires that the paramaters of that behavior be characterized in advance. This is possible when one is working with closed concepts or closed objectives. When one is dealing with open objectives, the particular behavior cannot be defined by a preconceived standard; a judgment must be made after the fact. When educational ends are directed toward open objectives, the form and content of the pupil's behavior are identified and assessed after the educational activity concludes.†

And this is how he differentiates, in another paper, between *instructional* objectives—where the focus is upon the attainment of a specific array of behaviors—and *expressive* objectives:

> Expressive objectives differ considerably from instructional objectives. An expressive objective does not specify the behavior the student is able to acquire after having engaged in one or more learning activities. An expressive objective describes an educational encounter: it identifies a situation in which children are

---

* W. J. Popham, E. W. Eisner, H. J. Sullivan, and L. L. Tyler, *Instructional Objectives*, American Educational Research Association Monograph Series on Curriculum Evaluation, Chicago: Rand McNally, 1969, p. 135. Reprinted by permission.
† E. W. Eisner. "Educational Objectives—Help or Hindrance?" *School Review* **75**, 1967, p. 279. Reprinted by permission of the University of Chicago Press.

to work, a problem with which they are to cope, a task they are to engage in—but it does not specify what from that encounter, situation, problem or task they are to learn. An expressive objective presents both the teacher and the student with an invitation to explore, defer or focus on issues that are of peculiar interest or impact to the inquirer. An expressive objective is evocative rather than prescriptive.*

In short, Eisner acknowledges the fact that certain anticipated outcomes can be handled adequately with behavioral objectives, whereas others cannot. He suggests that the latter be handled in a more open-ended manner—that the objectives be *descriptive* rather than *prescriptive*.

The differentiation is sensible, and it makes an objective-based approach to reading instruction more workable than it would be if it were limited strictly to prescriptive behavioral objectives. The more descriptive objectives permit us to focus on important aspects of reading for which we have not yet devised—and perhaps never should—means for anticipating and prescribing outcomes. For some specific examples of closed and open objectives, see Chapter 7 through 10. In Chapters 7, 8, and 9, respectively, we have suggested behavioral objectives—closed objectives—for the areas of word attack, study skills, and comprehension; in Chapter 10 we have suggested open objectives for the areas of self-directed, interpretive, and creative reading.

### Levels of objectives

Krathwohl (1965) has described three levels at which objectives may be stated. First, at the most abstract level, objectives are broad, general statements that specify goals for an entire school unit, e.g., elementary school, middle school, junior high, etc., guide program development, and/or identify courses and areas to be covered. Second, at a more concrete level, objectives, stated in behavioral terms, are appropriate for analyzing general goals into more specific instructional goals. Third, at the most specific level, objectives are so explicit that they prescribe a particular route to the attainment of objectives stated at the second level; they provide the kind of detailed analysis that is required by a programmed approach to instruction.

Objectives at each of the three levels serve a purpose, but the second level is probably most appropriate for use by the teacher in the classroom. (The objectives in Chapters 7, 8, and 9 are stated at level two.) We agree with Maguire, who observed that

the kinds of objectives that the teacher makes use of in his classroom activities are the objectives of Krathwohl's second level ... For classroom use, level-two

---

*    E. W. Eisner, "Instructional and Expressive Objectives: Their Formulation and Use in Curriculum," paper presented at the annual meeting of the American Educational Research Association, Los Angeles, February 1969, p. 20.

objectives are useful for determining the content to be covered in a unit, for selecting experiences to be arranged for students, and for guiding the construction of evaluation instruments.\*

Midlevel objectives, then, serve to establish attainable, observable goals without being so specific as to be prescriptive in nature. Thus, the goals serve as milestones, or check-points, but they permit each teacher considerable flexibility in pursuing them. It is this flexibility that makes an objective-based approach to reading instruction compatible with the individualized/personalized approach advocated in Chapter 3. Goals are clearly established, but the pathways to those goals are worked out in view of the realities of individual differences and available resources.

## Scope of objectives

The discussion here is limited because this is not the place to consider the general matter of scope in the application of behavioral objectives. Yet, the fact is that the matter presents a very real problem, even when we limit our consideration to objective-based reading instruction. The problem is due in part to the ways in which different people define reading. Some, for example, would limit the definition almost entirely to the decoding, or word attack, aspect, whereas others, at the opposite extreme, would go far beyond decoding to include evaluative, interpretive, and creative reading. The former would insist that the only unique thing about "reading" is the decoding of words and that anything beyond that is "thinking," or "reasoning." The latter would argue that the whole matter of helping children to deal with printed matter is the concern of the reading teacher. Perhaps reality lies somewhere in between these views, but one point to be made here is that the definition chosen determines the scope of the related objectives. Another aspect of the problem has to do with the role of behavioral objectives in the total reading program. Whether behavioral objectives are seen as the basis for the entire reading program or for only the skill-development aspect, too, determines the scope of objectives. On the one hand, there would be objectives for all aspects of reading performance; on the other hand, objectives would be limited to the skills that serve as a basis for successful reading, however it is defined.

The main point here is that any objective-based approach to reading instruction can proceed only after some decisions have been made. The process of defining what we mean by "reading" and deciding exactly what we want our objectives to cover can be painful. It forces us to stick our necks out and say what we mean and what we mean to do. Having done that, we are vulnerable to the slings and arrows of every critic who wants to take a shot at us. (Remember, too, that for the most part the critics have stated no objectives and that they have taken no definitive stands, so it is difficult or impossible to shoot back.) Once again we refer you to Chapters

---

\*     T. O. Maquire, "Value Components of Teacher's Judgments of Educational Objectives," *AV Communication Review* **16**, 1968, p. 68–69. Reprinted by permission.

7–10. The scope of the objectives stated there reflect some basic decisions we have made. Specifics about those decisions are given in the final section of this chapter.

## Application of objectives

Up to this point you have had a close look at behavioral objectives. You have at least a textbook knowledge of what they are, what it takes to write them, and some of the problems involved in making use of them. Now, whether you are able to prepare objectives and/or make use of them in ways that are satisfying to you remains to be seen. Whether your experience turns out to be mainly positive or negative will depend to a large extent on your attitude toward objective-based instruction, on your willingness to "roll with the punches" as you put objectives to use, and on your ability to keep the focus of your teaching on the pupils and on the facilitation of learning—not only on the objectives.

The following points are distilled from considerable experience with objective-based instruction. Keep them in mind as you work with behavioral objectives.

1. A behavioral objective can be no better than the idea it represents. Technical perfection in stating an objective is no substitute for the hard work—task analysis, developmental analysis—and common sense—relevant behaviors, realistic criteria—that provide the basis for stating the objective in the first place. Do not be lulled into a false sense of security because you have a list of behavioral objectives. Start with good ones and look for ways to make them better.

2. Do not expect to be able to describe all of your goals as a teacher, or even as a teacher of reading, in terms of behavioral objectives. Open objectives and expressive objectives will continue to serve a worthwhile purpose, but don't feel defensive about having still other goals, particularly in the affective areas. Behavioral objectives are tools. Use them for what they are.

3. Mastery learning is implicit in any objective-based approach to instruction. That is, once defensible, essential objectives have been set, the assumption is that each objective ought to be mastered. The danger is that the demonstration of mastery may become a mechanical process whereby criterion tasks are checked off and then forgotten. Thus, a critical problem with objective-based skill development is how to ensure that skills, once mastered, will be retained so that they can be applied as needed in reading and in further skill development.

We have observed two reasonably effective ways to deal with the problem. First, be certain that each skill has in fact been mastered; look for evidence in both formal testing situations and in informal application. In some instances *overlearning*—that is, repetition *after* the essential learning has been mastered—is desirable. The mastery of essential skills in reading is, in our opinion, such an instance. Second, look for opportunities to reinforce and review, and provide opportunities to apply the skills. Once you know what your objectives *are*, you can make use of them in many situations. If you will provide for overlearning and for follow-up, retention of mastery will not be a serious problem.

4. Look for the pay-off. The goal of objective-based reading-skill development is functional reading ability, the ability to deal with increasingly complex reading tasks both in and out of school. There is some danger with an objective-based approach that so much attention will be paid to the specific skills that the total act of reading will be neglected. This will not happen if many opportunities are provided for each pupil to apply his skills in sustained reading situations. Focus on specific skills to see that the essential ingredients are there, but see to it that all of the skills are brought to bear in tackling real-life reading tasks. In reading, as in many other instances, the whole is greater than the sum of its part. As pointed out in Chapter 3, skill mastery is nothing if it does not lead to functional reading ability.

## Focusing Reading Instruction

Objectives provide a basis for criterion-referenced assessment, the organization of instructional materials and procedures, and the management of individualized instruction. By making it possible to implement the approach to organizing instruction that we described in Chapter 3, these functions make the focusing of instruction workable.

### Criterion-referenced assessment

Criterion-referenced measurement relates an individual's test performance to absolute standards rather than to the performance of others. The latter is norm-referenced assessment, and the most common examples are standardized tests of achievement and of intellectual ability. With a norm-referenced test the individual is compared to some normative group, and the meaningfulness of his score emerges from the comparison. Thus, a score that might place him, say, in the top quartile, at the 80-percentile, in the eighth stanine, or at the fifth-to-sixth-grade level shows how his performance compares to that of others who have taken the same test. With a criterion-referenced test, there is no such comparison with other individuals. Instead, each individual's performance is evaluated in terms of some established criterion, or performance standard. Behavioral objectives establish performance standards and serve as a basis for criterion-referenced assessment.

Advocates of criterion-referenced tests cite a number of limitations of norm-referenced, standardized achievement tests:

1. They have a low degree of overlap with the actual objectives of instruction at any given time and place.

2. Because of this low overlap, they are not useful as aids in planning instruction.

3. They often require skills or aptitudes that may be influenced to only a limited degree by experiences in the classroom.

4. They do not indicate the extent to which individuals or groups have mastered the spectrum of instructional objectives.

5. Due to all of the above, they are not likely to prove very useful in an account-ability context. Furthermore, they invite corruption and dishonesty in such a context, because the cursory sampling in most areas makes "teaching the test" a simple matter.

The main point that is implicit in these limitations is that norm-referenced tests yield little information about individuals' attainment of specific objectives. Of course, they were never meant to yield such information, but the fact is that more often than not, they are treated as if they do. Perhaps this false expectation is truly their most severe limitation, for it causes them to be suspect even when they are appropriately used and properly interpreted. The baby goes out with the bath water. In any event, the point to be made explicit is that an objective-based approach to reading instruction not only makes criterion-referenced assessment possible, it also demands criterion-referenced assessment. We define our goals with behavioral objectives, and we assess each individual's progress with criterion-referenced tests. Diagnosis amounts to determining which objectives have and which have not been mastered by individuals; the focusing on instruction amounts to bringing to bear the materials and procedures that will most efficiently facilitate the attainment of objectives.

Criterion-referenced measures can be used for preassessment—to identify instructional needs and to determine initial placement—or for postassessment—to determine whether skills have been mastered *after* instruction. Such measures may take any one of several forms, depending on the nature of the objective-referent and the situation. The measures may be formal or informal, and they may be written or oral, as shown in the schema that follows. Here, we shall assume that in each instance a behavioral objective is the criterion referent.

|          | Written                 | Oral                 |
|----------|-------------------------|----------------------|
| Formal   | paper-and-pencil tests  | performance tests    |
| Informal | work samples            | teacher observations |

*Paper-and-pencil tests*

The main advantage of formal paper-and-pencil tests is that, as a rule, they are designed for group administration and rapid scoring. They make it possible to test large numbers of children for initial placement, for periodic accountability checks, and for other purposes that involve across-the-board testing. One example of a collection of criterion-referenced paper-and-pencil tests is *The Wisconsin Tests of Reading Skill Development*. The tests are based on behavioral objectives, with one test provided for each objective in the skill-development sequence. The tests are constructed for group administration, and they can be computer-scored. In general, each test is as short as reasonable reliability will permit, which means that the tests are 15 to 20 items long and have reliability coefficients of .80 or better. One of the tests is shown in Fig. 6.1.

NAME _____    DATE _____

# TEST 8
## CONSONANT DIGRAPHS

|  | | | | |
|---|---|---|---|---|
| EXAMPLE | ch Ⓐ<br>ss Ⓑ<br>sh Ⓒ<br>st Ⓓ | 6. | th Ⓐ<br>ch Ⓑ<br>tw Ⓒ<br>tr Ⓓ | 12. | th Ⓐ<br>zz Ⓑ<br>ss Ⓒ<br>sh Ⓓ |

1.    sh Ⓐ
      th Ⓑ
      tr Ⓒ
      ch Ⓓ

7.    th Ⓐ
      st Ⓑ
      zz Ⓒ
      sh Ⓓ

13.   th Ⓐ
      ch Ⓑ
      zh Ⓒ
      st Ⓓ

2.    sh Ⓐ
      th Ⓑ
      sc Ⓒ
      sk Ⓓ

8.    sh Ⓐ
      ch Ⓑ
      sw Ⓒ
      st Ⓓ

14.   ph Ⓐ
      sh Ⓑ
      th Ⓒ
      ch Ⓓ

3.    sh Ⓐ
      tw Ⓑ
      th Ⓒ
      ch Ⓓ

9.    sh Ⓐ
      ch Ⓑ
      ph Ⓒ
      sw Ⓓ

15.   ch Ⓐ
      ss Ⓑ
      st Ⓒ
      sh Ⓓ

4.    th Ⓐ
      ch Ⓑ
      sh Ⓒ
      st Ⓓ

10.   sh Ⓐ
      ch Ⓑ
      th Ⓒ
      st Ⓓ

16.   ck Ⓐ
      th Ⓑ
      ch Ⓒ
      ss Ⓓ

5.    ph Ⓐ
      tt Ⓑ
      th Ⓒ
      sh Ⓓ

11.   ch Ⓐ
      sh Ⓑ
      ss Ⓒ
      st Ⓓ

17.   ss Ⓐ
      sh Ⓑ
      ch Ⓒ
      st Ⓓ

*Fig. 6.1    Criterion-referenced paper-and-pencil test; behavioral objective: given real or nonsense words pronounced by the teacher, the child identifies the letters in the simple two-consonant combinations* sh, ch, th *that result in a single new sound. (*Wisconsin Design for Reading Skill Development, *Madison: Wisconsin Research and Development Center for Cognitive Learning, The University of Wisconsin, 1970. Reprinted by permission.)*

Although paper-and-pencil tests make for efficiency in testing large numbers of children, the fact remains that they have some rather severe limitations. The format is rigidly prescribed by the requirement for computer scoring and, of course, oral responses are excluded. Thus, certain objectives cannot properly be assessed by such tests. Furthermore, we know that some children never respond adequately in formal, paper-and-pencil testing situations; they fail to show what they really can do. Consequently, less rigid, more spontaneous bases for assessment are needed, and performance tests, teacher observations, and work samples can meet the need.

### Performance tests

If you had an objective that called for ability to pronounce phonically regular words, you would need to observe a child's oral responses. A *performance test*, which elicits an oral and/or motor response by assigning a task related directly to the objective, would be useful. You would simply ask the child to read an appropriate list of words. The child's success is determined by teacher judgement, which would be based on the criterion established by the objective.

Note that performance tests are "formal" in our schema. This is because the response is elicited by the teacher; the performance is directed, not spontaneous. But at the same time, the teacher is in a position to provide immediate feedback and to humanize the testing situation. Worthwhile performance testing requires careful planning and preparation, but the price is right, because the information gained is likely to reflect what a child really can do.

### Informal observations

Formal test results can be checked and/or augmented with more informal *teacher observations* and *work-sampling* procedures. Written work can be sampled by focusing briefly on a child as he goes about his daily assignments. Simply make a note when he appears to have difficulty applying the skill or skills being observed at a given time. As always, your behavioral objectives identify the specific behaviors and set the criterion for mastery. Still more informal teacher observations can be made at any time in the school day. Simply select an objective—perhaps on a daily basis— and look for instances in which the relevant behaviors are demonstrated. Such observations will, of course, be most appropriate for checking to see that presumably mastered skills are applied. They are also useful for maintainance and review as well as for initial demonstration of mastery.

### Organization of materials and procedures

There is no lack of variety in the range of materials and procedures available to teach reading skills. To the contrary, materials and suggestions are available in such profusion that teachers are confronted with the problem of how to track down the specific things they need to reach specific goals. We do not need *more* materials for teaching reading, but we do need a way to organize what already exists. Here again, an objective-based approach can serve us well. Once we have agreed on the behavioral objectives we wish to pursue, we have the basis we need to organize existing materials and procedures for easy retrieval.

We have shown the way in which a behavioral objective provides a basis for criterion-referenced assessment by defining the objective in behavioral terms and establishing a criterion for judging mastery-level performance. The behavioral objective serves the same function in the organization of materials and procedures. Once the objective has been stated, it is possible to identify reading passages, workbook exercises, chalkboard activities, games, etc., that are likely to contribute to the development of the criterion behaviors.

Each time a given objective comes up, one could start from scratch, so to speak, and begin to assemble materials and identify procedures that would be relevant in facilitating pupils' attainment of the objective. On the positive side, such a procedure would ensure focused, goal-directed instruction. But on the negative side, there would be much repetition of effort and no systematic try-out of instructional approaches. Far better to begin to organize a filing system whereby relevant materials and procedures are keyed to the objectives of the program. With such an approach, teachers can cooperate in identifying appropriate means for pursuing each objective and can, over a period of time, build up a pool of use-tested ideas for each one.

The mechanics of building such a file can be quite simple. Start a manila folder for each behavioral objective in your program and store the folders in a file. In each folder, then, you can enter notations of textbook page numbers, workbook pages, descriptions of activities, games, etc., as they are identified. You should plan to go through from time to time to weed out any entries that turn out to be not useful or irrelevant. And, if you should come upon good times, you can transfer the whole thing to a computer. Then, once an entry is made you can forget about further filing chores. But remember that only *you* can tell the computer what you want stored.

## Management of individualized instruction

With both assessment and instruction based on behavioral objectives, we have a foundation for well-coordinated diagnosis and instruction. But one thing more is needed to make focused reading instruction run smoothly—a management system that will expedite the systematic grouping and regrouping of pupils as their skill-development needs change. Grouping is required because we have found that the only practical approach to individualization is through differentiated instruction (see Chapter 3). This means carefully focused instruction is provided to individuals when necessary and to groups whenever possible. Examples of how to proceed with the instruction are given in the final chapters of this book. Here, we will consider only the record keeping that is required to make systematic grouping possible.

Reduced to fundamentals, what you will need is a way to keep a running record of which of your objectives have and which have not been mastered by each of your pupils. With this information available, you can identify pupils who need instruction related to a given objective and form groups as required. The record can take any one of several possible forms. We shall describe two, but you may devise a format that is more to your liking.

*Individual folders.*    The record is simply a file folder on which all of your program objectives are keyed. Space is provided next to each objective to indicate (1) when there is evidence of criterion-level performance, and (2) the date and outcome of at least one subsequent recheck. Thus, a folder can be started when a pupil first gets reading instruction and can be continued throughout his elementary school experience.

In addition to its primary function, the record can be useful in a number of other ways:

1. It keeps a statement of all reading objectives constantly before you, the teacher.

2. It provides a basis for communication among teachers and a basis for cross-class or interclassroom grouping.

3. It provides a concrete basis for discussing progress with individual pupils.

4. It can also be the basis for parent-teacher conferences.

*Classroom charts.*    A variation on the individual folder, classroom charts offer the advantage of making it possible to scan the status of a number of pupils at once. Pupil names are listed on the vertical axis of a sheet of paper, and program objectives are listed on the horizontal axis, as shown in Fig. 6.2.

The dates of initial mastery and any subsequent checks are written in the appropriate boxes. Thus, a teacher can quickly scan the chart to spot individuals with gaps in their attainment of objectives and groups with common needs. The chart can be desk-drawer size, or it can be exploded to a wall chart if a public record is desired.

| Word-attack objectives — Level C | | | | | | |
|---|---|---|---|---|---|---|
| Name | 1 | 2 | 3 | 4 | 5 | 6 |
| | | | | | | |
| | | | | | | |
| | | | | | | |
| | | | | | | |

*Fig. 6.2    Classroom chart.*

The individual folders and the classroom charts are the simplest and, because you can make them, the most readily available record forms. Again, if you come upon good times, you can use a computer to keep your pupil profiles. Whatever the format, you need to keep continuous records for each pupil. Adequate record keeping is what makes an objective-based approach to reading instruction workable.

## Overview of Specific Objectives

In the four chapters that follow, we present what we feel are essential objectives in reading. We offer them not as a definitive list to be adopted without modification, but as an example of one attempt to take an objective-based approach to reading instruction. We have already noted some of the characteristics of our objectives in the preceding pages of this chapter. This, then, is a very brief overview of the specific objectives given in Chapters 7–10.

1. "Reading" is broadly defined, with objectives given for word attack (Chapter 7), study skills (Chapter 8), comprehension (Chapter 9), and for self-directed, interpretative, and creative reading (Chapter 10).

2. Closed objectives are given for word attack, study skills, and comprehension, whereas self-directed, interpretive, and creative reading are handled in terms of open objectives.

3. The objectives in each area are clustered at four to seven levels, with each level roughly equivalent to a traditional grade level, as shown in Table 6.1.

**Table 6.1    Objectives by area and by traditional grade level**

| Area | K | 1 | 2 | 3 | 4 | 5 | 6 |
|---|---|---|---|---|---|---|---|
| | | | | Grade | | | |
| Word attack | A | B | C | D | — | — | — |
| Study skills | A | B | C | D | E | F | G |
| Comprehension | A | B | C | D | E | F | G |
| Self-directed reading | A | B | C | D | ← | E | → |
| Interpretative reading | A | B | C | D | ← | E | → |
| Creative reading | A | B | C | D | ← | E | → |

The clusters are tied to grade levels only because we have found that the grade-level referent continues to have meaning for most teachers and in relation to many instructional materials. Once an objective-based approach gets under way, the grade levels should, of course, be ignored, and pupils should move from one cluster to the next in a continuous sequence.

4. Word-attack objectives are limited to the first four clusters, because we feel that the essentials are introduced and taught to the average child by the end of the primary experience. Interpretive and creative-reading objectives are

clustered at Level E to permit and encourage their consideration and refine-
ment in the middle grades.

5. The objectives for word attack, study skills, and comprehension are stated
   at a midlevel of specificity, as discussed in a preceding section of this chapter.

6. All of the objectives given are the result of much discussion, try-out, and compromise. A specific rationale is given for the objectives in each area in the
   appropriate chapter.

7. An 80-percent criterion is assumed for each objective; a specific competence
   level is not given in each one. Thus, the expectation is that the child would get
   80 percent of the items in a paper-and-pencil test or demonstrate adequate
   behaviors 80 percent of the time in observations in order to meet the criterion
   for mastery. Of course the 80-percent criterion is arbitrary; it could be set
   higher or lower, depending on such things as the testing situation and other
   conditions. But 80 percent permits room for error of measurement, while still
   setting reasonably high expectations.

## References

Bloom, B. S., J. T. Hastings, and G. F. Madaus. *Handbook on Formative and Summative
Evaluation of Student Learning*, New York: McGraw-Hill, 1971.

Eisner, E. W. "Educational objectives—help or hindrance?" *School Review* **75** (1967):
250–260.

"Instructional and expressive objectives: their formulation and use in curriculum," a paper
presented at the annual meeting of the American Educational Research Association, Los
Angeles, February 1969.

Gagné, R. M. *The Conditions of Learning*, New York: Holt, Rinehart and Winston, 1965.

Haberman, M. "Behavioral objectives: bandwagon or breakthrough?" *Journal of Teacher
Education* **19** (1968): 91–94.

Krathwohl, D. R. "Stating objectives appropriate for program, for curriculum, and for
instructional materials development," *Journal of Teacher Education* **16** (1965): 83–92.

Mager, R. F. *Developing Attitude Toward Learning*, Palo Alto: Fearon, 1968.

————. *Preparing Instructional Objectives*, Palo Alto: Fearon, 1962.

Maguire, T. O. "Value components of teacher's judgments of educational objectives," *AV
Communications Review* **16** (1968): 63–68.

Montague, E. J., and D. F. Butts. "Behavioral objectives," *The Science Teacher* **35** (1968):
33–35.

Popham, W. J. "Epilogue," in Popham, W. J., E. W. Eisner, H. J. Sullivan, and L. L. Tyler,
*Instructional Objectives*, American Educational Research Association Monograph Series on
Curriculum Evaluation, Chicago: Rand McNally, 1969.

Stephens, J. M. *The Process of Schooling*, New York: Holt, Rinehart and Winston, 1967.

# 7 / Objectives for word attack

Be sure that you have a good understanding of the introduction to objective-based reading instruction in Chapter 6 before you begin to examine the specific objectives in this chapter and the three chapters that follow. Like almost anything else, objectives need to be viewed in context. And remember that we noted a number of special characteristics of these objectives. Keep them in mind as you consider the ways in which you might begin to make use of objectives in your teaching.

## Skills and Objectives for Word Attack

We have clustered word-attack skills at Levels A, B, C, and D, which correspond roughly to traditional Kindergarten and Grades 1, 2, and 3. The clusters serve two purposes. First, they provide an overall sequential arrangement of skill development without dictating the sequential arrangement of specific skills. Thus, for example, the skills at Level C come after the skills at Level B and before the skills at Level D, but there is no implicit sequential arrangement within the levels. This arrangement makes grouping for instruction more workable than would a rigidly prescribed sequence. Second, the clusters make it possible to use a grade-level referent in both making a transition from traditional grades to continuous progress and locating instructional materials. The word-attack skills are limited to four levels because the essentials ought to be introduced and taught to an average child by the end of his primary school experience, but the pacing with an individual pupil must, of course, be adapted to his ability to respond to instruction.

Our procedure in identifying a list of essential word-attack skills was to begin with a well-constructed elementary school curriculum guide for reading. We had two main reasons for making such a start. First, we chose a curriculum guide that is the better scope and sequence statements in use across the nation. that it reflects the substantial agreement among school people as ack skills need to be taught. Second, we felt the statement of a ool curriculum department would reflect the thinking of school personnel regarding the *essential* skills. We assumed that the skills are in line with both practice and expectations in the classrooms; thus, the list had credibility because it came from the "consumer."

Over the course of several years we have had opportunities to work with the list and to revise it in view of the reactions of teachers, reading consultants, and professors of reading education. As it now stands, the list—or the "Outline of Word-Attack Skills," as it is presently arranged—is one that has the consensual support of many teachers after several years' use in the classroom. The outline of skills is the basis for our word-attack objectives; we have written a behavioral objective for each skill.

The objectives, too, are the result of a series of revisions. We have attempted to state them clearly and unambiguously and to keep them usable and in touch with the realities of the classroom. Note again that each objective is stated at a midlevel of specificity that is somewhere between the broad goals set for entire school programs and the highly specific objectives of programmed instruction. Thus, each objective amounts to a *milestone* that represents significant progress toward independence in word attack. Each one can subsume a number of more specific objectives to be determined by a teacher who is aware of the idiosyncrasies of both pupils and resources in a given situation. The objectives set goals without prescribing the specifics of instruction.

Our skills and objectives for word attack amount to a rather traditional phonics approach. We decided to take such an approach because we wanted to reflect the broadest possible base in terms of school practice in teaching the word-attack skills. Modifications would be required to make the skills and objectives fully compatible with certain other approaches, particularly those with a "linguistic" orientation.

Taken together, the word-attack objectives should lead to an ultimate, or terminal objective like the one that follows:

> The student, upon completion of all of the word-attack skills, will be able to independently attack phonically and/or structurally regular words and recognize on sight all the words on the prescribed sight word list. Children of average or above average ability will attain this objective by the end of the fourth year (third grade) in school, while others will attain this objective by the end of the seventh year (sixth grade) in school.

Such an objective is worthwhile and should always be stated when a sequence of objectives is pursued, because it sets expectations for teachers and permits the technical evaluation of the objective-based approach. The broad objective given above will, of course, need to be adapted in terms of your local situation and the characteristics of your pupils. For example, given a suburban school and children with above average ability, the projection might be that 75 percent of pupils would attain the objective by age nine, 90 percent by age ten, and 100 percent by age twelve. On the other hand, the expectations might be rather different in a school in the central city.

In any event, the overall objective of the word-attack objectives is to get pupils to be reasonably independent in decoding words. Ultimate success in decoding will always be heavily dependent on each child's language development. That is, mastery of the word-attack objectives should permit a child to decode the printed words that are in his oral vocabulary. However, there is little value in his being able to tackle words that are infrequent at a given level and/or without meaning in his personal repertoire.

## Outline of Word-Attack Skills

Our list of essential word-attack skills follows. The list is arranged in outline format to indicate the four levels and to show the relationship of certain subskills.

I. Word-Attack

*Level A.* The child:

1. Listens for rhyming elements
   a) Words
   b) Phrases and verses
2 Notices likenesses and differences
   a) Pictures (shapes)
   b) Letters and numbers
   c) Words and phrases
3. Distinguishes colors
4. Listens for initial consonants

*Level B.* The child:

1. Has a basic sight vocabulary
2. Follows left-to-right sequence
3. Has phonic analysis skills
   a) Consonant sounds
      1) Beginning consonant sounds
      2) Ending consonant sounds
   b) Beginning consonant blends
   c) Rhyming elements
   d) Short vowels
   e) Simple consonant digraphs
4. Has structural analysis skills
   a) Compound words

   b) Contractions
   c) Base words and endings
   d) Plurals
   e) Possessive forms

*Level C.* The child:

1. Has an expanded sight vocabulary
2. Has phonic analysis skills
   a) Consonants and their variant sounds
   b) Beginning consonant blends
   c) Vowel sounds
      1) Long vowel sounds
      2) Vowel plus *r*
      3) *a* plus *l*
      4) *a* plus *w*
      5) Dipthongs *oi, oy, ou, ow, ew*
      6) Long and short *oo*
   d) Vowel generalizations
      1) Short vowel generalizations
      2) Silent *e* generalization
      3) Two vowels together generalization
      4) Final vowel generalization
   e) Common consonant digraphs
3. Has structural analysis skills
   a) Base words with prefixes and suffixes
   b) More difficult plural forms
4. Distinguishes among homonyms, synonyms and antonyms
   a) Homonyms
   b) Synonyms and antonyms
5. Has independent and varied word-attack skills
6. Chooses appropriate meaning of multiple meaning words.

*Level D.* The child:

1. Has an expanded sight vocabulary
2. Has phonic analysis skills
   a) Three-letter consonant blends
   b) Simple principles of silent letters
3. Has structural analysis skills
   a) Syllabication
   b) Accent
   c) Unaccented schwa
   d) Possessive forms

## Objectives for Word Attack

Behavioral objectives that parallel the skills in the outline follow. In each instance a standard format is used:

*Skill.* The skill is identified.

*Objective.* The behavioral objective is stated.

*Note.* Any explanatory or supplementary notes are given.

*Assessment.* A criterion-referenced measure of performance is suggested.

The notes provide supplementary information; they are not part of the objective they accompany. We have included examples of each of the criterion-referenced measures already described—paper-and-pencil tests, performance tests, work samples, teacher observations—among the suggested assessments. The examples are given to familiarize you with possible approaches to criterion-referenced assessment rather than to prescribe the measure to be used. Remember that we have established a criterion of 80 percent for all of the objectives.

After the objectives for each level, a brief resumé for the entire level is given. Again, this is supplementary information for your consideration; it is not a part of the objectives.

## Level A

*Skill.* Rhyming elements: words.(1)

*Objective.* Given familiar words pronounced by the teacher, the child indicates which of three words rhymes with a stimulus word *or* tells whether two words do or do not rhyme.

*Note.* "Familiar" words are words in the child's spoken vocabulary.

*Assessment.* Say to the child: "These words rhyme or sound alike: cat-rat; sit-hit; hen-men. Listen to the words I say, and tell me whether they rhyme." Follow this with 10 to 15 pairs of words that are familiar to the child. (Performance test)

*Skill.* Rhyming elements: phrases and verses.(2)

*Objective.* In real or nonsense verses read by the teacher, the child supplies the missing words in a couplet (e.g., The little red hen/Lived in a _____) *or* identifies the rhyming words.

*Assessment.* Read some two-line rhyming verses to the child. Ask him to tell you the rhyming words. (Performance test)

*Skill.* Likenesses and differences: pictures (shapes).(3)

*Objective.* The child identifies shapes that are the same or different in form and/or orientation.

*Assessment.* Give the child a page of pictures (shapes) arranged in rows as in the examples that follow. Have him choose the picture in each row that is the same as (or different from) the target, or first, one. (Paper-and-pencil test)

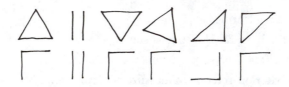

*Skill.* Likenesses and differences: Letters and shapes.(4)

*Objective.* The child selects the letter (upper or lower case) or number in a series that is identical to a key letter or number.

*Note* This objective focused on the visual perception of letters and numbers. Letter names and alphabetical sequence are covered in the objectives for study skills.

*Assessment.* Give the child a page of letters and numbers arranged in rows. Have him pick the letter or number in each row that is the same as the first one. (Paper-and-pencil test)

$$
\begin{array}{llllll}
P & / & B & P & F & C \\
f & / & b & h & l & f \\
6 & / & 9 & 6 & 8 & 5 \\
\end{array}
$$

*Skill.* Likenesses and differences: words and phrases.(5)

*Objective.* The child selects the word or phrase in a series that is identical to a stimulus word or phrase (e.g., *down:* wand, down, bone, find).

*Assessment.* Similar to the paper-and-pencil exercises described for shapes, letters, and numbers

*Skill.* Colors.(6)

*Objective.* The child identifies the colors blue, green, black, yellow, red, orange, white, brown, and purple when named by the teacher.

*Note.* This skill is only tangentially related to early reading. It has become a traditional "readiness" skill probably because it helps children to refine their observation, develop their oral vocabulary, and begin to make arbitrary matches of *name* and *characteristic.*

*Assessment.* Give the Child a page of colored boxes arranged in rows. Have him pick the color you name in each row. (Paper-and-pencil test).

*Skill.*   Initial consonant sounds.(7)

*Objective.*   Given familiar words pronounced by the teacher, the child indicates which of three words begins with the same consonant sound as the target word.

*Note.*   The focus here is on the auditory discrimination involved in identifying identical consonant sounds and on the concept of "like" and "different" as applied to letter sounds. The order in which the consonant sounds are dealt with must be determined by the specific instructional sequence actually employed.

*Assessment.*   Give the child rows of four pictures that represent common objects and name the objects in each row. Have him mark the picture that has a name that begins like the first one. (Paper-and-pencil test)

(Pail)          (Ball)              (Pig)          (Man)

*Resumé for Level A*: The Level A objectives deal almost exclusively with the traditional kindergarten-readiness skills. As such, they have only modest value as prereading skills per se. They have to do more with the *process* of learning to read than with the specifics. See Chapter 5 for a discussion of specific prerequisites to reading.

## Level B

*Skill.*   Sight-word vocabulary.(1)

*Objective.*   Given a maximum one-second exposure per word, the child recognizes selected words from a high-frequency word list.

*Note.*   The specific sight words to be taught at this level will most appropriately be determined in view of the instructional materials that are actually used. We feel that sight words should, first and foremost, be words that appear frequently in the printed materials used by the child; at the same time, however, the words should not be incompatible with whatever approach is being taken at the beginning stages of instruction in word attack.
   A number of sight-word lists exist, and they have been widely used. Yet the limitations they share are that they are only pseudoempirically based, and they are based largely on frequency counts of adult materials. Here, we offer a list that has neither of those limitations. The 500 words on the list (Table 7.1) are the ones that appeared most frequently in a carefully chosen sampling of 840, 875 words used in third-grade materials. You can use the list as a resource in selecting the sight words

**Table 7.1　The Great Atlantic and Pacific Word List**

| Rank | Word | Rank | Word | Rank | Word | Rank | Word | Rank | Word |
|---|---|---|---|---|---|---|---|---|---|
| 1 | the | 26 | one | 51 | them | 76 | could | 101 | where |
| 2 | a | 27 | this | 52 | write | 77 | time | 102 | called |
| 3 | to | 28 | all | 53 | their | 78 | more | 103 | me |
| 4 | and | 29 | had | 54 | words | 79 | down | 104 | went |
| 5 | of | 30 | from | 55 | about | 80 | my | 105 | put |
| 6 | in | 31 | be | 56 | by | 81 | no | 106 | around |
| 7 | you | 32 | can | 57 | like | 82 | go | 107 | new |
| 8 | is | 33 | but | 58 | see | 83 | get | 108 | know |
| 9 | he | 34 | there | 59 | so | 84 | now | 109 | come |
| 10 | it | 35 | not | 60 | if | 85 | long | 110 | who |
| 11 | that | 36 | when | 61 | these | 86 | find | 111 | things |
| 12 | was | 37 | how | 62 | make | 87 | look | 112 | its |
| 13 | on | 38 | were | 63 | into | 88 | made | 113 | came |
| 14 | for | 39 | your | 64 | him | 89 | just | 114 | right |
| 15 | are | 40 | do | 65 | other | 90 | big | 115 | air |
| 16 | they | 41 | each | 66 | word | 91 | very | 116 | sound |
| 17 | I | 42 | will | 67 | would | 92 | back | 117 | think |
| 18 | with | 43 | up | 68 | water | 93 | first | 118 | tell |
| 19 | his | 44 | many | 69 | little | 94 | way | 119 | after |
| 20 | said | 45 | we | 70 | two | 95 | over | 120 | Mr. |
| 21 | at | 46 | then | 71 | has | 96 | too | 121 | man |
| 22 | as | 47 | her | 72 | did | 97 | than | 122 | may |
| 23 | have | 48 | or | 73 | people | 98 | good | 123 | much |
| 24 | she | 49 | out | 74 | an | 99 | use | 124 | does |
| 25 | what | 50 | some | 75 | which | 100 | day | 125 | say |

| | | | | |
|---|---|---|---|---|
| 126 same | 151 name | 176 earth | 201 took | 226 hearts |
| 127 been | 152 mother | 177 last | 202 sentence | 227 side |
| 128 take | 153 asked | 178 men | 203 story | 228 until |
| 129 only | 154 pciture | 179 plants | 204 land | 229 should |
| 130 old | 155 most | 180 read | 205 never | 230 sometimes |
| 131 away | 156 part | 181 left | 206 always | 231 own |
| 132 children | 157 used | 182 hear | 207 sentences | 232 dog |
| 133 help | 158 food | 183 show | 208 play | 233 door |
| 134 looked | 159 saw | 184 end | 209 began | 234 once |
| 135 why | 160 different | 185 don't | 210 give | 235 birds |
| 136 work | 161 live | 186 found | 211 years | 236 days |
| 137 through | 162 well | 187 eat | 212 below | 237 enough |
| 138 here | 163 any | 188 boy | 213 boys | 238 near |
| 139 animals | 164 school | 189 need | 214 also | 239 trees |
| 140 place | 165 even | 190 still | 215 head | 240 kind |
| 141 before | 166 under | 191 keep | 216 grow | 241 oh |
| 142 three | 167 line | 192 together | 217 set | 242 top |
| 143 home | 168 because | 193 sun | 218 paper | 243 didn't |
| 144 house | 169 thought | 194 us | 219 it's | 244 draw |
| 145 again | 170 next | 195 got | 220 morning | 245 letters |
| 146 another | 171 small | 196 Mrs. | 221 I'll | 246 told |
| 147 number | 172 every | 197 great | 222 while | 247 country |
| 148 our | 173 going | 198 father | 223 soon | 248 white |
| 149 must | 174 want | 199 along | 224 let | 249 large |
| 150 off | 175 something | 200 night | 225 hard | 250 I'm |

| Rank | Word | Rank | Word | Rank | Word | Rank | Word | Rank | Word |
|------|------|------|------|------|------|------|------|------|------|
| 251 | year | 276 | knew | 301 | fast | 326 | short | 351 | moon |
| 252 | letter | 277 | often | 302 | (4) | 327 | lived | 352 | song |
| 253 | wanted | 278 | add | 303 | answer | 328 | times | 353 | miles |
| 254 | fish | 279 | better | 304 | best | 329 | turned | 354 | baby |
| 255 | (2) | 280 | room | 305 | light | 330 | stop | 355 | beautiful |
| 256 | car | 281 | such | 306 | red | 331 | family | 356 | girls |
| 257 | city | 282 | vowel | 307 | means | 332 | form | 357 | second |
| 258 | ran | 283 | almost | 308 | hand | 333 | black | 358 | above |
| 259 | page | 284 | ground | 309 | green | 334 | others | 359 | leaves |
| 260 | spelling | 285 | sea | 310 | gave | 335 | those | 360 | girl |
| 261 | (3) | 286 | heard | 311 | across | 336 | am | 361 | sat |
| 262 | world | 287 | try | 312 | yes | 337 | living | 362 | bird |
| 263 | eyes | 288 | ways | 313 | says | 338 | horse | 363 | town |
| 264 | high | 289 | pictures | 314 | learn | 339 | front | 364 | cannot |
| 265 | ever | 290 | money | 315 | can't | 340 | seen | 365 | friends |
| 266 | kinds | 291 | box | 316 | change | 341 | started | 366 | walked |
| 267 | might | 292 | cut | 317 | both | 342 | makes | 367 | fire |
| 268 | four | 293 | thing | 318 | Indians | 343 | ready | 368 | call |
| 269 | few | 294 | far | 319 | sounds | 344 | eggs | 369 | plant |
| 270 | move | 295 | Mother | 320 | turn | 345 | body | 370 | talk |
| 271 | sure | 296 | today | 321 | places | 346 | whole | 371 | that's |
| 272 | (1) | 297 | cold | 322 | warm | 347 | blue | 372 | animal |
| 273 | miss | 298 | inside | 323 | Sam | 348 | stood | 373 | important |
| 274 | feet | 299 | run | 324 | without | 349 | table | 374 | really |
| 275 | tree | 300 | cried | 325 | between | 350 | Jim | 375 | soil |

| # | | # | | # | | # | | # | |
|---|---|---|---|---|---|---|---|---|---|
| 376 | ball | 401 | half | 426 | rain | 451 | order | 476 | carry |
| 377 | hot | 402 | true | 427 | river | 452 | sleep | 477 | slowly |
| 378 | sky | 403 | walk | 428 | garden | 453 | strong | 478 | woman |
| 379 | study | 404 | dark | 429 | Indian | 454 | anything | 479 | hole |
| 380 | ago | 405 | sing | 430 | John | 455 | try | 480 | remember |
| 381 | spell | 406 | summer | 431 | piece | 456 | let's | 481 | ship |
| 382 | looking | 407 | missing | 432 | buy | 457 | snow | 482 | King |
| 383 | stay | 408 | outside | 433 | fine | 458 | tall | 483 | stand |
| 384 | toward | 409 | behind | 434 | nothing | 459 | round | 484 | tiny |
| 385 | feel | 410 | learned | 435 | catch | 460 | Bucky | 485 | friend |
| 386 | young | 411 | open | 436 | everyone | 461 | care | 486 | kept |
| 387 | Bill | 412 | book | 437 | Tom | 462 | hands | 487 | ride |
| 388 | himself | 413 | six | 438 | legs | 463 | names | 488 | Sally |
| 389 | tells | 414 | glass | 439 | A | 464 | store | 489 | tail |
| 390 | fly | 415 | ice | 440 | grass | 465 | Ann | 490 | seeds |
| 391 | (6) | 416 | coming | 441 | Jack | 466 | built | 491 | against |
| 392 | cat | 417 | start | 442 | tried | 467 | ones | 492 | covered |
| 393 | (5) | 418 | ten | 443 | listen | 468 | hit | 493 | wood |
| 394 | hold | 419 | five | 444 | someone | 469 | maybe | 494 | bright |
| 395 | comes | 420 | watch | 445 | happy | 470 | class | 495 | cars |
| 396 | face | 421 | road | 446 | being | 471 | fun | 496 | Father |
| 397 | stopped | 422 | winter | 447 | happened | 472 | street | 497 | game |
| 398 | wind | 423 | milk | 448 | everything | 473 | space | 498 | rest |
| 399 | window | 424 | goes | 449 | gone | 474 | bed | 499 | Eddie |
| 400 | done | 425 | gold | 450 | numbers | 475 | complete | 500 | sets |

W. Otto and R. Chester, "Sight Words for Beginning Readers," *Journal of Educational Research* **65**, 1972, pp. 436—443. Reprinted by permission.

you will teach at Levels B, C, and D. We first presented the list in an article in the *Journal of Educational Research* (Otto and Chester, 1972). See the entire article for a more complete discussion of the list, which we have dubbed "The Great Atlantic and Pacific Word List."

The list is arranged in order of frequency. Braces indicate words with identical frequency rankings. The words with tied rankings are arranged in alphabetical order.

*Assessment.* Make flash cards for the words you wish to teach as sight words. The child should be able to recognize each word with an approximate one-second exposure. (Performance test)

*Skill.* left-to-right sequence.(2)

*Objective.* The child reacts to number or letter stimuli in a left-to-right sequence.

*Assessment.* (1) Give the child a page of numbers and letters arranged in rows and see whether he handles them in a left-to-right sequence. (Paper-and-pencil test) (2) Observe the child as he deals with number-and-letter stimuli in his daily work. By the end of first grade or of the second year in school, the proper sequence should be virtually a habit, with very few inversions. (Teacher observation).

*Skill.* Phonic analysis: beginning consonant sounds.(3)

*Objective.* Given real or nonsense words supplied by the teacher, the child (1) identifies the letter that stands for the initial sound *and* (2) tells whether two words do or do not begin alike; or (3) supplies another word that begins with the same sound.

*Note.* Some teachers object to nonsense words because they feel learning should always be meaningful. But in certain instances nonsense words provide the only pure test of whether an objective has been met. If, for example, you ask a child whether *bat* and *bed* begin alike, you have no way of knowing whether his correct response is based on prior visual knowledge of the words or true knowledge of the sounds. The use of nonsense words eliminates the problem. For similar reasons we recommend the use of nonsense words in a number of instances throughout the list of objectives.

*Assessment.* Pronounce a word and ask the child to think of another word that begins with the same sound. Ask him what letter makes the sound. (Performance test)

*Skill.* Phonic analysis: ending consonant sounds.(4)

*Objective.* Given real or nonsense words pronounced by the teacher, the child (1) identifies the letter that stands for the ending sound *and* (2) tells whether two words do or do not end alike; or (3) supplies another word that ends with the same sound.

*Assessment.* Similar to beginning sounds.

*Skill.* Phonic analysis: beginning consonant blends.(5)

*Objective.* Given real or nonsense words that begin with the consonant blends *pl, gl, tr, fr, sl, br, dr, gr, pr, cr, fl, cl, bl,* the child (1) identifies the two letters that stand for the initial blend in words pronounced by the teacher; *or* (2) identifies words that begin with the same blend as a stimulus word pronounced by the teacher *and* (3) pronounces words that begin with the blends listed above.

*Note.* You may wish also to focus explicitly on such *ending* blends as *It, rn, nd, rl, ck.* If so, add an objective.

*Assessment.* Give the child a page with rows of pictures on it. Ask him to find the picture in each row with the name that begins with the same two sounds as a word you pronounce. (Paper-and-pencil test)

*Skill.* Phonic analysis: rhyming elements.(6)

*Objective.* Given a word, the child (1) selects a rhyming word based on structure (e.g., *man, pan,* and *fan* are from the same word family); *or* (2) supplies a real or nonsense word based on structure.

*Assessment.* Ask the child to tell you words that rhyme with words you say. (Performance test)

*Skill.* Phonic analysis: short vowels.(7)

*Objective.* Given one-syllable words with a single short-vowel sound pronounced by the teacher (e.g., *man, duck, doll*), the child (1) identifies the letter that stands for the vowel sound; *or* (2) reproduces the vowel sound.

*Assessment.* Have the child listen for the vowel sound in words you read to him. Ask him to say the vowel sound and tell you what vowel makes the sound. (Performance test)

*Skill.* Phonic analysis: simple consonant digraphs.(8)

*Objective.* Given real or nonsense words pronounced by the teacher, the child identifies the letters in the simple two-consonant combinations *ch, th, sh, wh* that result in a single new sound.

*Note.* Whether or not the child knows the term *digraph* is of less importance than whether he recognizes that two consonants can combine to make a single sound. So don't get hung up on the terminology. We do feel, though, that having the child learn at least the basic terms will help to expedite future instruction.

*Assessment.* Ask the child to tell you what two consonants go together to make a new sound in words that you pronounce (e.g., *she, teeth, beach, what*).

*Skill.* Structural analysis: compound words.(9)

*Objective.* The child (1) identifies compound words; *or* (2) specifies the elements of a compound word.

*Assessment.* Read some sentences that contain compound words to the child. Ask him to identify the compound word and to name the two words that make it up. (Performance test).

*Skill.* Structural analysis: contractions.(10)

*Objective.* The child identifies simple contractions (e.g., I'm, it's, can't) and uses them correctly in sentences.

*Assessment.* Similar to the exercise for compound words.

*Skill.* Structural analysis: base words and endings.(11)

*Objective.* The child identifies the root word in familiar inflected words (e.g., *jump*ing, *catch*es, *run*s).

*Assessment.* Give the child a list of inflected words. Have him read each word to you and tell you the root word. (Performance test)

*Skill.* Structural analysis: plurals.(12)

*Objective.* The child tells whether familiar words (noun plus *s* or *es*) are singular or plural.

*Assessment.* Give the child a list of words. Ask him to read each word and tell you whether it means "one" or "more than one." (Performance test)

*Skill.* Structural analysis: possessive forms.(13)

*Objective.* The child identifies the possessive forms of nouns used in context.

*Assessment.* Give the child a list of sentences. Ask him to follow as you read each one. Ask him to tell you whether the word underlined tells you that something belongs to someone or not.

> *Resumé for Level B*: The Level B objectives deal with the sight recognition of frequently appearing words, the establishment of left-to-right sequence, and the introduction to basic phonic and word analysis skills. They lay a foundation for the child's ultimate independence in word attack, so they deserve careful attention.

## Level C

*Skill.* Sight vocabulary.(1)

*Objective.* Given a maximum one-second exposure per word, the child recognizes selected words from a high-frequency word list.

*Note.* The objective is stated the same as at Level B. The expectation is that the sight vocabulary will be expanded to include additional high-frequency words from the actual materials used.

*Assessment.*   Same as at Level B.

*Skill.*   Phonic analysis: consonants and their variant sounds.(2)

*Objective.*   Given words containing variant sounds of *s*, *c*, and *g* (e.g., *sit-trees*, *c*ake-*c*ity, *go-giant*), the child indicates whether the italicized letters in given pairs of words have the same or different sounds.

*Note.*   Although the consonants *c*, *g*, *s*, *q*, *d*, *x*, *t*, and *z* have more than one sound, variant sounds of *s*, *c*, and *g* are most common at this level.

*Assessment.*   The best exercise is suggested in the objective.

*Skill.*   Phonic analysis: beginning consonant blends.(3)

*Objective.*   Given real or nonsense words beginning with the consonant blends *st*, *sk*, *sm*, *sp*, *sw*, *sn*, *sc*, the child (1) identifies the two letters that stand for the initial blend in words pronounced by the teacher; *or* (2) identifies words that begin with the same blend as a stimulus word pronounced by the teacher, *and* (3) pronounces words that begin with the blends listed above.

*Note.*   You may wish also to focus on the ending *s*-blends like wa*s*p, fir*s*t, and de*s*k.

*Assessment.*   Pay particular attention to the words with consonant blends as you listen to the child read orally. (Teacher observation)

*Skill.*   Phonic analysis: long vowel sounds.(4)

*Objective.*   The child (1) identifies the letter that stands for the single vowel sound in real or nonsense words pronounced by the teacher (e.g., *nose*, *bribe*, *cheese*, *seat*, *labe*) and indicates whether the sound is long or short; *or* (2) pronounces real or nonsense words with a single vowel sound.

*Assessment.*   Give the child a list of real and nonsense words. Have him read each word aloud, name the vowel sound heard, and tell whether it is long or short. (Performance test.)

*Skill.*   Phonic analysis: vowel plus *r*.(5)

*Objective.*   The child (1) identifies the vowel that is with *r* in real or nonsense words pronounced by the teacher (e.g., darl, der, mur, (form); *or* pronounces words with *r*-controlled vowels (e.g., part, for, hurt, bird).

*Note.*   Because *er*, *ir*, and *ur* have the same sound, *e*, *i*, or *u* is the appropriate response in *er*, *ir*, and *ur* words.

*Assessment.*   Have the child read a list of *r*-controlled vowel words to you. (Performance test)

*Skill.*   Phonic analysis: *a* plus *l*.(6)

*Objective.* The child (1) identifies the letters that stand for the *al* sound in real or nonsense words pronounced by the teacher; *or* (2) pronounces words in which there is an *al* combination (e.g., salt, ball, yall).

*Assessment.* Similar to the exercise for *r*-controlled vowels.

*Skill.* Phonic analysis: *a* plus *w*.(7)

*Objective.* The child (1) identifies the letters that stand for the *aw* sound in real or nonsense words pronounced by the teacher; *or* (2) pronounces words in which there is an *aw* combination (e.g., draw, saw, blaw).

*Note.* The *au* sound is often taught with *aw*, but it is not so common.

*Assessment.* Similar to the exercise for *r*-controlled vowels.

*Skill* Phonic analysis: diphthongs.(8)

*Objective.* Given words containing *oi, oy, ou, ow, ew,* the child (1) identifies the dipthong in nonsense words pronounced by the teacher; *or* (2) pronounces words containing the dipthongs.

*Assessment.* Similar to the exercise for *r*-controlled vowels.

*Skill.* Phonic analysis: long and short *oo*.(9)

*Objective.* The child (1) indicates whether the *oo* in words has the long (e.g., choose) or the short (e.g., book) sound; *or* (2) pronounces words in which there is an *oo* combination.

*Assessment.* Similar to the exercise for *r*-controlled vowels.

*Skill.* Phonic analysis: short vowel generalization.(10)

*Objective.* Given real or nonsense words in which there is a single vowel and a final consonant (e.g., bag, his, cat, gum), the child (1) tells whether the real words are pronounced according to the generalization; *or* (2) pronounces the words giving the vowel its short sound.

*Note.* Children should learn that some familiar sight words are exceptions to this generalization. Note, too, that the generalization *can* hold with multisyllable words where there are syllables with a single vowel and a final consonant.

*Assessment.* Give the child a list of single-syllable words with a single vowel and a final consonant. Be sure all of the words have the short vowel sound (e.g., cat, hat, but, mab) as he pronounces them. After he has pronounced all of them, ask him whether the vowel sound was long or short. Then have him tackle a list of similar words, but with long and short vowel sounds (e.g., fun, cold, will, light, hold, send). (Performance test)

*Skill.* Phonic analysis: silent *e* generalization. (11)

*Objective.* Given real or nonsense words that have two vowels, one of which is a final *e* separated from the first vowel by a consonant (e.g., cake, tube, mape, jome), the child (1) tells whether the real words are pronounced according to the generalization; *or* (2) first attempts pronounciation by making the first vowel long and the final *e* silent.

*Note.* Again, some familiar sight words are exceptions to this generalization (e.g., come, have, prove).

*Assessment.* Similar to the exercise for the short vowel generalization.

*Skill.* Phonic analysis: two vowels together generalization.(2)

*Objective.* Given real or nonsense words that have two consecutive vowels, the child (1) tells whether the real words are pronounced according to the generalization; *or* (2) first attempts pronounciation by making the first vowel long and the second vowel silent.

*Note.* Again, some familiar sight words are exceptions to this generalization (e.g., bread, August).

*Assessment.* Similar to the exercise for the short vowel generalization.

*Skill.* Phonic analysis: final vowel generalization.(13)

*Objective.* Given real or nonsense words in which the only vowel is at the end (e.g., go, she, thi), the child (1) tells whether the words are pronounced according to the generalization; *or* (2) pronounces the words by first giving the vowel its long sound.

*Note.* Some notable exceptions to the generalization are *who* and *do*.

*Assessment.* Similar to the exercise for the short vowel generalization.

*Skill.* Phonic analysis: common consonant digraphs.(14)

*Objective.* Given real or nonsense words pronounced by the teacher, the child identifies the letters in the two-consonant combinations *ch, th, sh, wh, ph, nk, ng, gh, ck* that result in a single new sound.

*Note.* This is an expansion of the Level B objective related to digraphs.

*Assessment.* Similar to the exercise for consonant digraphs at Level B.

*Skill.* Structural analysis: base words with prefixes and suffixes. (15)

*Objective.* The child selects base (root) words with or without affixes that are appropriate to the context.

*Assessment.* Give the child sentences like the following and have him complete each one by adding the correct beginning or ending—if needed—to the word in parentheses. (Performance test)

    \*An unbrella is (_____) on a rainy day. (use)
    \*The teacher is (_____) on the chalkboard. (write)

*Skill.* Structural analysis: more difficult plural forms.(16)

*Objective.* The child tells whether more difficult plural forms (e.g., mice, children, ladies) are singular or plural.

*Assessment.* Similar to the plural forms exercise at Level B.

*Skill.*  Homonyms.(17)

*Objective.* Given a sentence context, the child chooses between homonyms (e.g., Mother bought some *meet/meat* for dinner).

*Assessment.*  Prescribed by the objective.

*Skill.*  Synonyms and antonyms.(18)

*Objective.* The child tells whether words in a pair have the same, opposite, or simply different meanings.

*Assessment.*  Give the child pairs of words like strong/weak, quiet/silent, now/soon and ask him if they mean the *same, opposite,* or just *different* things.

*Skill.*  Independent and varied word attack. (19)

*Objective.* In both self-directed and teacher-directed reading, the child uses a variety of skills (e.g., picture clues, context clues, structural analysis, sound/symbol analysis, comparison of new to known words) in attacking unknown words.

*Assessment.* This objective can best be assessed through the administration of an informal reading inventory—as described first by Betts (1946), Chapter XXI) and since then by Otto and Smith (1970, Chapter V) and many others—because it provides an opportunity to observe applications of the full range of word-attack skills. (Work sample/performance test)

*Skill.*  Multiple-meaning words.(20)

*Objective.* Given a multiple-meaning word in varied contexts, the child chooses the meaning appropriate to a particular context.

*Note.* (1)This objective simply introduces the notion of multiple-meaning words; it does not prescribe the full array of such words. (2) Don't forget the *homographs* like rec´-ord/re-cord´ and ad´-dress/ad-dress´.

*Assessment.* Given sentences like the following, the child reads them and tells you what the underlined words mean. (Performance test or work sample)

*Tim gave the *right* answer to the question.

*Put your name in the top *right* hand corner of the paper.

*Resumé for Level C*: Upon completion of the Level C skills, the child ought to have a substantial sight vocabulary and be able to attack at least one-syllable words with reasonable efficiency. Furthermore, he should be attuned to making systematic attempts to use context and other cues to figure out the meaning of new words that are not in his spoken vocabulary.

## Level D

*Skill.*  Sight vocabulary.(1)

*Objective.*  Given a maximum half-second exposure per word, the child recognizes selected words from a high-frequency word list.

*Note.*  Only the speed of recognition is changed from Level C. The expectation, as at Level C, is that the sight vocabulary will be further expanded to include additional high-frequency words from the actual materials used for instruction and for recreational reading.

*Assessment.*   Same as Level B.

*Skill.*   Phonic analysis: three-letter consonant blends.(2)

*Objective.*   The child identifies the letters in the three-letter blends *scr, shr, spl, str, thr* in real or nonsense words pronounced by the teacher.

*Assessment.*   Pronounce both real and nonsense words with the three-letter blends and ask the child to tell you what the first three letters are. (Performance test)

*Skill.*   Phonic analysis: silent letters.(3)

*Objective.*   Given words containing silent letters (e.g., knife, gnat, write) the child (1) identifies the silent letters; *or* (2) pronounces words containing silent letters.

*Note.*   Silent consonants commonly occur in the following combinations: (k)n, (g)n, (w)r, m(b), (b)t, i(gh), (t)ch.

*Assessment.*   Give the child a list of words with silent letters—know, thumb, witch, sail, read, wrong, sign. Ask him to tell you what letter or letters are silent in each word. (Performance test)

*Skill.*   Structural analysis: syllabication.(4)

*Objective.*   The child divides words into single-vowel sound units by applying syllabication generalizations.

*Note.* The following are the most commonly taught syllabication generalizations. We believe, however, that in reading, the focus ought most appropriately to be on pronunciation units rather than on formal syllabication, so exercise some judgment in assessing performance.

*A one-syllable word is not divided.

*A compound word is divided between the two words.

*A prefix is always divided from its base word.

*A suffix or inflected ending is divided from its base word if the vowel in it is heard. *Bushes* would be divided, but *does* would not.

*If a vowel sound is followed by two consonants, the first syllable usually ends with the first of the two consonants.

*When a consonant comes between two vowels, the consonant is part of the first syllable if the first vowel is short, e.g., palace.

*When a consonant comes between two vowels, the consonant is part of the second syllable if the first vowel is long, e.g., hotel.

*Assessment.* Have the child tell you whether the words in a daily assignment have one or more parts. If more than one part, have him tell you what they are. (Work sample)

*Skill.* Structural analysis: accent.(5)

*Objective.* The child indicates the accented part (syllable) in familiar words, primarily two-syllable ones.

*Assessment.* Similar exercise to that for syllabication.

*Skill.* Structural analysis: unaccented *schwa*.(6)

*Objective.* Given words that he knows, the child specifies the unaccented syllable containing a *schwa*.

*Note.* Although the ability to *identify* the *schwa* has no inherent value, the child who is aware of the existence of a *schwa* sound will be able to deal more successfully with vowel sounds than one who does not.

*Assessment.* As the child tackles unknown words, note whether he uses the *schwa* sound in decoding. (Teacher observation)

*Skill.* Structural analysis: possessive forms.(7)

*Objective.* The child identifies possessive nouns and pronouns used in context.

*Assessment.* Given sentences like the following, ask the child to tell you which of the italicized words tell that something belongs to someone or something. (Performance test)

*The *boys* went to the show with *their* mother.

*The cat hurt *its* paw.

*Resumé for Level D*: Level D adds some final touches to the pupil's repertoire of word-attack skills. Having completed Level D he should have attained the terminal objective of independence in tackling most words in the English language.

## References

Betts, Emmett A. *Foundations of Reading Instruction*, New York: American Book, 1946.

Otto, W. and R. Chester. "Sight words for beginning readers," *Journal of Educational Research* **65** (1972): 435–443.

Otto, W. and R. J. Smith. *Administering the School Reading Program*, Boston: Houghton Mifflin, 1970.

# 8 / Objectives for study skills

By this time you should have a relatively good understanding of what objective-based reading instruction is all about. Also, you should have had an opportunity to examine some specific objectives together with their special characteristics as presented in this text. By examining the objectives in word attack, you have become acquainted with their midlevel of specificity and with some of the ways of assessing them. It is important to keep these things in mind in the discussion of study skills that follows.

## Skills and Objectives for Study Skills

We have clustered study skills in much the same way as we did word attack. The only difference is that the levels of study skills go from A through G (kindergarten through grade six) rather than from A through D, as in word attack. As in word attack, this clustering serves to provide an overall sequential arrangement of skill development without dictating sequential arrangement of specific skills, and it simplifies grade-level reference where materials and traditional grade-level referents are used. Grade-level reference in this program should be considered descriptive rather than prescriptive. Levels A to G are points on a continuum rather than lock steps beyond which the student cannot proceed.

Even though there are seven levels of study skills (K–6), we must realize that some children will master all of the skills much earlier, perhaps as early as at the end of grade four. On the other hand, some will need more than seven years to gain proficiency in all of them. Unlike many of our traditional tasks, which are locked into a particular grade level and particular materials, objectives are independent of both. Objectives can be established and proficiency sought at the level of the student's need, regardless of grade level or materials.

Our procedure for identifying a list of study skills was essentially the same as that used in selecting word-attack skills. We began with a well-constructred elementary school curriculum guide and modified it as research, classroom teachers, and experience dictated. Because the list of skills has been tried out in the schools and has proved successful, we assume that it is both credible and practical.

The skills included in study skills fall mainly into three categories—maps, graphs and tables, and reference skills. The map skills category includes representation, location, and measurement areas covering such skills as interpretation of symbols, use of grids and directions, and function and application of scales. The graphs and tables grouping includes skills involving interpretation of vertical and horizontal picture graphs, bar graphs, circle graphs, and line graphs. Also included are skills involving interpretation of single and multicolumn tables and schedules. The reference category includes location, book skills, library use, reference materials, reading rate and purpose, organizing and evaluating materials, and work habits.

The skills within each of these three categories move from the concrete to the abstract, and the tasks involved are arranged in ascending levels of difficulty. Because of this implicit sequencing, it is wise to make sure that the child has properly mastered the skills at lower levels before introducing him to skills at a higher level. In study skills, as well as in the other skill areas, it is important to have an ultimate, or terminal, objective in mind. As mentioned previously, this overall objective should be tailored to fit the individual situation, since each school is in a real sense unique. With this in mind, we offer the following suggested objective, to be modified as the situation demands:

> Upon completion of the study skills program, the student will be able to use study skills to locate, derive, and interpret information from standard reference sources, as well as from maps, graphs, and tables.

Most children should be able to achieve this objective by the end of elementary school, and nearly all should have done so by the end of middle school. In either case, whether the child reaches mastery by the end of elementary school or by the end of middle school, the key word is *mastery*. When the child achieves mastery, he achieves a certain measure of independence. And this is what the skills program is all about— the independence to apply skills where and when the need arises. As long as the child is handicapped by his lack of appropriate skills, he can never reach his full potential, no matter what grade he is in.

Finally, once you have looked at the specific skills, it will be obvious that they are not bound by content areas. Study skills can and must be applied to a large variety of materials and situations. To attempt to teach these skills in isolation, that is, out of the context in which the child will be using them in his work, is to build a flaw into your program. Skills are best taught by using materials and situations out of which arise specific needs and applications. For instance, what better place could there be to teach maps, graphs, and tables than in social studies and math? What could be a more appropriate way of teaching reference skills than using them in daily classroom activities? By calling them study skills in reading, we do not suggest that they are not appropriately taught in all content areas.

## Outline of Study Skills

Our list of essential study skills follows. The list is arranged in outline format to indicate the seven levels and to show the relationship of certain subskills.

### Level A

1. Describes position of objects
2. Has measurement skills

   a) Describes relative size
   b) Determines relative distance

3. Has beginning work study skills

   a) Follows simple directions
   b) Is able to remember details
   c) Has attention and concentration span suitable for his ability
   d) Has beginning of independent work habits

4. Has basic book-handling skills

5. Is familiar with procedures within library (book table, book corner, learning center, instructional materials center, or media center)*

### Level B

1. Identifies representational relationships
2. Has location skills

   a) Locates objects in relation to other objects
   b) Locates points in relation to a simple picture grid

3. Has measurement skills

   a) Describes relative size
   b) Determines relative distance

4. Interprets picture graphs

5. Interprets single-column tables

6. Refines beginning work-study skills

   a) Follows oral directions given to a group
   b) Follows oral directions given individually
   c) Follows written direction

---

\* *Note:* We have selected "library" as a descriptive term for whatever facilities are available to the child for finding either books or audiovisual learning aids.

7. Begins locational skills (letters and digits)
8. Expands book skills
9. Expands use of the library
10. Uses a picture dictionary for spelling new words
11. Begins to organize materials for his own use

    a) Arranges pictures and words in sequence
    b) Classifies ideas

## Level C

1. Has representation skills

    a) Uses picture symbols to interpret maps
    b) Uses semipictorial symbols to interpret maps
    c) Uses color key to interpret maps

2. Has location skills

    a) Locates points in relation to a simple grid
    b) Indicates cardinal directions on a globe

3. Has measurement skills

    a) Interprets relative size
    b) Expresses relative distance

4. Has graph skills

    a) Picture graphs
    b) Bar graphs

5. Interprets multicolumn tables
6. Shows increasing independence in work
7. Groups and orders words by initial letter
8. Expands book skills
9. Expands use of library
10. Begins to use reference materials
11. Reads to find answers; takes notes
12. Organizes and evaluates materials

    a) Keeps simple reading record
    b) Recognizes organization of ideas in sequential order
    c) Begins to make judgments and draw conclusions

## Level D

1. Has representation skills

    a) Uses a key containing nonpictorial symbols to interpret maps
    b) Uses a color key to interpret maps

2. Has location skills
   a) Locates points on a number-letter grid
   b) Determines cardinal directions on globes, in his environment, and maps

3. Uses scale to determine whole units of distance

4. Has graph skills
   a) Picture graphs
   b) Bar graphs
   c) Circle graphs

5. Interprets multicolumn tables

6. Has independent classroom and research work habits
   a) Follows oral or written directions independently
   b) Begins to do research assignments independently

7. Expands locational skills
   a) Applies basic alphabetizing skills
   b) Uses guide words in encyclopedias and dictionaries
   c) Uses "see" references in encyclopedias

8. Expands book skills
   a) Uses table of contents
   b) Uses glossary
   c) Begins to use indexes
   d) Uses study aids in textbooks

9. Expands use of library

10. Begins to expand use of reference materials

11. Reads to locate information
    a) Begins to adjust reading rate
    b) Uses headings and subheadings

12. Organizes and evaluates materials
    a) Recognizes that printed statements may be fact or opinion
    b) Evaluates relevance of materials
    c) Checks accuracy of statements

**Level E**

1. Uses point and line symbols to interpret maps

2. Has location skills
   a) Applies rectangular grid to earth sphere
   b) Determines intermediate directions on globes, in the environment, and
      on maps

3. Makes limited use of scale to determine distance

4. Has graph skills

    a) Picture graphs
    b) Bar graphs

5. Interprets multicolumn tables

6. Has independent classroom and research work habits

7. Expands locational skills

    a) Uses alphabetical system
    b) Uses guide words and guide letters
    c) Uses alphabet skills related to card catalog

8. Expands book skills

    a) Refines use of indexes
    b) Considers special features of books in selection

9. Extends familiarity with library

10. Expands use of reference materials

    a) Uses dictionaries independently
    b) Consults encyclopedias and atlases
    c) Uses pamphlet files
    d) Uses magazines and newspapers
    e) Uses selected specialized reference books
    f) Uses nonfiction materials as references

11. Adjusts reading rate to:

    a) Difficulty
    b) Purpose

12. Organizes and evaluates materials

    a) Has beginning outlining skills
    b) Makes simple bibliographies
    c) Draws inferences and makes generalizations
    d) Evaluates information in terms of his own experience and/or known facts

**Level F**

1. Uses point, line, and area symbols

2. Has location skills

3. Has measurement skills

    a) Identifies differences among maps drawn to different scales, e.g., 1 inch = 1000 miles, 1 inch = 100 miles, and 1 inch = 50 miles
    b) Makes use of scale to determine distance

4. Has graph skills

    a) Bar graphs
    b) Circle graphs
    c) Line graphs

5. Interprets schedules

6. Has independent classroom and research work habits

7. Increases locational facility

   a) Refines card catalog skills
   b) Refines cross-reference skills

8. Expands book skills

9. Expands facility in using library

10. Expands use of reference materials

    a) Uses dictionaries for pronunciation
    b) Uses "see also" direction
    c) Uses *Subject Index to Children's Magazines*

11. Adjusts reading rate to:

    a) Difficulty
    b) Purpose

12. Organizes and evaluates materials

    a) Makes notes of main ideas and supporting facts
    b) Summarizes materials

## Level G

1. Has representation skills

   a) Identifies likenesses and differences between two or more areas
   b) Synthesizes information about an area

2. Uses meridians and parallels to determine directions on any projection

3. Has measurement skills

   a) Locates the same point or cell on various projections
   b) Uses inset maps to determine relative size of areas

4. Has graph skills

   a) Bar graphs
   b) Line graphs

5. Interprets schedules

6. Has independent classroom and research work habits

7. Refines book skills

8. Increases facility in using library

   a) Uses all information on catalog cards
   b) Increases understanding of Dewey system

9. Expands use of reference materials: current periodical indexes

10. Adjusts reading rate to:

    a) Difficulty
    b) Purpose

11. Organizes and evaluates materials
    a) Gains skill in note taking
    b) Makes formal outlines

## Level A

*Skill.*   Describes positions of objects.(1)

*Objective.*   The Child is able to describe or respond to descriptions of the positions of objects in his environment in relation to himself by using the following terms: up-down, on, between, near (beside), behind-in front of (front-back), below-above (over-under).

*Skill.*   Describes relative size.(2)

*Objective.*   The child is able to use descriptive terms (e.g., bigger-smaller, taller-shorter, lower-higher) to express comparisons of size of objects in his environment.

*Skill.*   Determines relative distance.(3)

*Objective.*   The child is able to use descriptive terms (e.g., closer-farther, long way-short way) to express comparisons of distance in his environment.

*Note.*   The three skills above can best be assessed through informal play or game-type situations. Guessing games or adapted play activities such as Simons Says would be very appropriate here.

*Skill.*   Follows simple directions.(4)

*Objective.*   The child is able to perform the actions in simple one- and two-stage directions, e.g., "Mark an X in the middle of your paper," "Please come and take one of these boxes of paper shapes to your work area."

*Assessment.*   Assessment of this activity is adequately illustrated in the objective; however, it should be noted that formal assessment is generally not necessary. This information is usually available from teacher observation.

*Skill.*   Is able to remember details.(5)

*Objective.*   The child is able to remember sufficient details: (1) from an oral presentation, i.e., story, show-and-tell, to respond to specific questions, e.g., four questions about specific facts based on a 100-word presentation; and/or (2) from an event he is describing to give an intelligible account of what happened.

*Assessment.*   Read to the individual child or group of children a short selection (approximately 100 words) and ask a child four or five who, what, where, when, why, and how questions. You may also get a measure of the child's ability to remember detail by asking him to tell the story in his own words.

*Skill.*   Has attention and concentration scan suitable for his ability.(6)

*Objective.*   The child is able to demonstrate active participation in classroom listening situations. (The child attends to an oral presentation and responds appropriately, i.e., follows directions, reacts with relevant questions, and/or contributions.)

*Note.*   Assessment is best carried out over a span of time during which the child can be observed in a variety of situations and his behavior compared to that of his age/grade group.

*Skill.*   Has beginning of independent work habits.(7)

*Objective.*   The child shows independence in his assigned work by: (1) asking questions that are necessary for clarification of the task, (2) not asking attention-seeking questions once the task is clear, (3) keeping the necessary tools, i.e., pencil, paper, crayons, scissors, etc., at hand, (4) accepting responsibility for completion of quality of work, and (5) pacing himself to complete a task acceptably in the allotted time.

*Note.*   The preceding objective must be assessed by observing the child over a period of time. Special note should be made of the child who does neat work, but only at the expense of extended, painstaking effort.

*Skill.*   Has basic book-handling skills.(8)

*Objective.*   The child demonstrates basic book skills by: (1) selecting books appropriate to his interests and ability level, (2) handling books reasonably (i.e., right-side-up, from front to back), and (3) referring to books by their main character or subject (e.g., "The book about the butterflies").

*Skill.*   Is familiar with procedures within the library (book table, book corner, etc).(9)

*Objective.*   The child (1) locates groups of books appropriate to his needs, and (2) is able to check books in and out.

*Note.*   Assessment of the two preceding objectives is obviously best carried out by day-to-day observation by the teacher. However, the fact that these skills are considered important in the training of the child should be taken as further emphasis that the child should be given regularly scheduled time in the library.

## Level B

*Skill.*   Identifies representational relationships.(1)

*Objective.*   The child is able to place three-dimensional representations of objects to reflect their actual locations in the environment, e.g., place blocks that represent houses on a large floor map, build models in a sand box.

*Assessment.* The example in the objective seems adequate for explaining how this skill might be assessed.

*Skill.* Locates objects in relation to other objects.(2)

*Objective.* The child is able to describe or respond to descriptions of the positions of objects and representations of objects in relation to other objects and representations in the following terms: right-left, up-down, on, between, near (beside), behind-in front of (back-front), below-above (over-under).

*Assessment.* Give the child a picture (e.g., a landscape) and have him put an X on the object you describe, e.g., put an X on the tree to the right of the house; put an X on the bird on top of the gate; put an X on the flower behind the walk etc.

*Skill.* Locates points in relation to a simple picture grid.(3)

*Objective.* Given axis and coordinate referents the child is able to locate points and describe the location of points in relation to a simple picture grid.

*Assessment.* Give the child a simple picture grid (perhaps 3″ × 3″) and ask him to locate an object within the grid by naming the row or column or both.

*Skill.* Describes relative size.(4)

*Objective.* The child is able to use descriptive terms (e.g., bigger-smaller, taller-shorter, lower-higher) to express comparisons of size of representations of objects (e.g., scale models, pictures).

*Assessment.* Give the child a work sheet containing pictures of objects which are alike except for size. Have him locate different objects such as the largest, smallest, tallest, shortest, etc. This exercise can also be accomplished with three-dimensional objects.

*Skill.* Determines relative distance.(5)

*Objective.* The child is able to use descriptive terms (e.g., closer-farther, long way-short way) to express comparisons of distance in representations of objects (e.g., sand box, pictures).

*Assessment.* Give the child a worksheet containing a picture of objects in some sort of order or arrangement (a furnished room, for example). Ask him to put an X on the chair closest to the door, the table closest to the window, the stool closest to the wall, etc.

*Skill.* Interprets picture graphs.(6)

*Objective.* Given a simple vertical picture graph in which each symbol represents a single object and there are no more than three to five columns of pictures, the child is able to determine the purpose of the graph, compare relative amounts, and extract information directly from the graph.

*Assessment.*  Give the child a simple vertical picture graph in which each symbol represents a single object. Ask him to tell you what the graph represents (e.g., school absences for one week). Have him tell you on which day there were the most absences, on which day there were the fewest, etc. Ask him to tell you the number of absences on Tuesday, Friday, etc.,

*Skill.* Interprets single-column tables.(7)

*Objective.*  Given a single-column table containing three to five rows, the child is able to determine the purpose of the table, locate a particular cell within the table, and use the table to compare relative amounts.

*Assessment.*  Give the child a single-column table containing three to five rows. Ask him to look at the title of the table, its contents, etc., and tell you the purpose of the table, (e.g., the table may contain the number and types of toys owned by John). Ask him to indicate how many wagons John had, how many toy trucks, how many rubber balls, etc. Then ask him which toy John had the largest number of, the fewest of, etc.

*Skill.*   Follows oral directions given to a group.(8)

*Objective.*  The child is able to follow two-stage oral directions when the directions are administered to a group, i.e., ten or more pupils, of which the child is a part.

*Skill.*   Follows oral directions given individually.(9)

*Objective.*  The child is able to perform the actions in two-stage directions that require some judgment when the directions are given directly to him.

*Note.*  The two preceding objectives can best be assessed by observing the child's performance over a period of time, for contrived situations are likely not only to have an aura of contrivance, but also to be of too short duration to be very meaningful. Special note should be made of the child who responds adequately with individual attention but not in a group or, conversely, who can take cues from the group and proceed satisfactorily but breaks down when left to himself.

*Skill.*   Follows written directions.(10)

*Objective.*  The child is able to follow a series of three to four brief written directions.

*Assessment.*   Assessment of this exercise is best observed by having the child manipulate three-dimensional objects or exhibit some physical behavior (lifting arm, crossing legs, touching eye, etc.) according to a specific sequence of written directions.

*Skill.*  Begins locational skills (letters and digits).(11)

*Objective.* The child is able to: (1) indicate the correct symbol when letters and digits are presented orally, and (2) match capital and other allographs of one letter.

*Assessment.* (1) Give the child a worksheet containing several rows of letters and digits. Ask him to locate in row one the digit or letter you pronounce. (2) Give the child a worksheet containing capital letters and other allographs of one letter and ask him to draw connecting lines between the symbols which belong together.

*Skill.* Expands book skills.(12)

*Objective.* The child demonstrates expanded book skills by: (1) continuing to select appropriate books, (2) beginning to identify books by their titles, and (3) using the table of contents in textbooks.

*Skill.*    Expands use of the library.(13)

*Objective.*   The child demonstrates expanded use of the library by: (1) using more materials, such as picture dictionaries, (2) asking for help in finding books about a specific subject, (3) continuing to observe local rules, and (4) attempting to apply other skills, e.g., the child may try to locate a book in the card catalog by title, etc.

*Note.*   The two preceding objectives can best be assessed by observing the child's performance over an extended period of time. Contrived situations for assessing these skills are both awkward and generally ineffective.

*Skill.*    Uses a picture dictionary for spelling new words.(14)

*Objective.*   The child is sufficiently familiar with a picture dictionary to check the spelling of words he uses in writing.

*Assessment.*   Ask the child to use the picture dictionary to locate the spelling of words which you pronounce orally.

*Skill.*   Arranges pictures and words in sequence.(15)

*Objective.*    The child can recreate the sequence of a story or event by arranging pictures or by arranging key words in order (e.g., *The Three Bears*: "hot—bears walk—Goldilocks—breakfast—chairs—beds—bears come home").

*Assessment.*   Give the child the pictures from a comic strip which have been cut into individual blocks and mixed in order. Have him put the story together into its proper sequence.

*Skill.*   Classifies ideas.(16)

*Objective.*   Given five ideas or facts, the child is able to determine which are relevant to a given topic.

*Assessment.*   Give the child a topic (hobbies, for example) and five ideas or facts (e.g., collecting stamps, making a scrapbook, going to the market, brushing your teeth, making model cars) and have him indicate which are related to the topic.

**Level C**

*Skill.* Uses picture symbols (e.g., 🏠 🌳) to interpret maps.(1)

*Objective.* The child is able to use realistic pictures to derive information from maps.

*Assessment.* Give the child a worksheet containing a diagram or simple map. Use pictures (realistic) to indicate various objects on the map. Ask the child to locate certain points on the map (e.g., the path). Ask other questions such as: "What is near the house?" "What is the girl walking toward?"

*Skill.* Uses semipictorial symbols (e.g., ⌂ ⌂) to interpret maps.(2)

*Objective.* The child is able to use semipictorial symbols which are explained in a key (legend) to derive information from maps.

*Assessment.* Give the child a simple map containing a key. Ask him to use the key (semipictorial symbols) to locate certain objects in the picture. Ask him to locate such things as the symbol on the map which represents a boat, the symbol which represents a stream, the symbol which represents a lake, etc. Ask him what specific symbols on the map mean.

*Skill.* Uses color key to interpret maps.(3)

*Objective.* The child is able to use distinct colors (e.g., brown, red, yellow, and blue) which are explained in a key to derive qualitative information from different maps, e.g., blue may denote water, grocery stores, or parks on different maps.

*Assessment.* Give the child a map containing objects color coded according to a key. Ask him to use the color key to locate various objects and points on the map.

*Skill.* Locates points in relation to a simple grid.(4)

*Objective.* The child is able to locate points and describe the location of points in relation to a simple street grid.

*Assessment.* Give the child a worksheet containing a simple street grid. Ask him to locate particular points on the grid by using street names, e.g., "Put an X at the corner where Oak and Elm come together; put an X where Pine street goes into Spruce Street," etc. You might also add other dimensions by putting objects into the picture and asking questions about them, e.g., "Jim lives at the corner of Maple and Spruce. Which house on the map belongs to Jim?"

*Skill.* Indicates cardinal directions on a globe.(5)

*Objective.* The child is able to indicate on a globe: (1) north and south with reference to the North Pole, South Pole, and equator; and (2) east and west with reference to north-south.

*Assessment.* Assessment of this skill is obvious from the description of the skill. Assessment should be carried out on an individual basis.

*Skill.* Interprets relative size.(6)

*Objective.* The child is able to interpret the relative size of areas in semipictorial maps, e.g., lakes, parks, forests.

*Assessment.* Give the child two semipictorial maps drawn to the same scale and ask him to answer questions requiring decisions about measurement and size. By naming the maps (e.g., East Town–West Town), you may ask more specific questions; e.g., "Which town contains the largest building?" "Which town has the most parks?" "Which town has the least number of buildings?" etc.

*Skill.* Expresses relative distance.(7)

*Objective.* The child is able to use familiar nonstandard units of measurement (e.g., blocks, houses) to express distance and comparisons of distance on semi-pictorial maps.

*Assessment.* Give the child a semipictorial map laid out with blocks, streets, houses, etc., and ask him questions about distances from point to point, e.g., "How many blocks does Jack live from the Post Office?" "How many houses are there between Elm Street and Maple Street?"

*Skill.* Picture graphs.(8)

*Objective.* Give horizontal picture graph in which each symbol represents more than one unit (i.e., 2 to 10), the child is able to: (1) determine the purpose; (2) compare relative amounts, (3) extract directly; and (4) determine differences between numbers extracted.

*Assessment.* Give the child a horizontal picture graph in which each object represents more than one unit; (e.g., each symbol equals two model cars). Have him use the symbols to compute answers to questions requiring the translation, addition, and subtraction of numbers represented by symbols. He should be able to note the purpose of the graph and make direct comparisons of both symbols and amounts represented by symbols.

*Skill.* Bar graphs.(9)

*Objective.* Give a vertical bar graph which has one group of bars and a small interval on the coordinate (i.e., 2 to 10), the child is able to: (1) determine the purpose, (2) compare relative amounts, and (3) extract directly.

*Assessment.* Give the child a bar graph which has one group of bars and a small interval on the coordinate (i.e., 2 to 10). Have the child determine the purpose of the graph by examining its title and contents. Then have him compare relative amounts (e.g., most-least, taller-shorter, etc.) and determine the exact amount represented by each.

*Skill.*   Interprets multicolumn tables.(10)

*Objective.*   Given a simple, multicolumn table with from two to four rows and columns, the child is able to: (1) determine the purpose, (2) locate a cell, (3) compare relative amounts in a single dimension, and (4) determine relationships among cells.

*Assessment.*   Give the child a simple, multicolumn table with from two to four rows and columns. After you have had him determine the purpose of the table, ask him to locate a particular cell (e.g., "How many marbles does Jim have?"). Then ask questions which require him to compare two or three cells (e.g., "Who has the most marbles? Who has the fewest?"). When he can accomplish this satisfactorily, ask him questions which require him to compute exact differences in two cells (e.g., "How many more marbles does Jack have than Jim?").

*Skill.*   Shows increasing independence in work.(11)

*Objective.*   The child shows independence and acceptance of responsibility by: (1) asking the questions required to clarify a task, (2) keeping the materials required to complete a task available and organized, (3) showing an awareness of a standard for general quality in assigned work, and (4) pacing himself to complete assigned tasks in the time allotted (30 minutes).

*Note.*   Assessment of this objective can best be carried out over an extended period of time during which the child can be observed in a variety of situations and his behavior compared to that of his age/grade group.

*Skill.*   Groups and orders words by initial letters.(12)

*Objective.*   The child is able to: (1) group words by their initial letters, (2) order words by their initial letter, and (3) choose appropriate encyclopedia volumes by letter (e.g., "Look in the *E* volume for information about elephants").

*Assessment.*   Information in the objective gives adequate explanation for the assessment of this skill.

*Skill.*   Expands book skill.(13)

*Objective.*   The child demonstrates expanded book skills by: (1) identifying books by their titles, (2) finding the title page in a book, (3) associating authors with books, (4) finding the author's name on the title page, (5) locating the table of contents in a book, and (6) locating the index in a book.

*Assessment.*   Much of the assessment of this skill can be done through classroom observation. However, more specific information can be gained by asking the child to locate the author's name on the title page, locate the table of contents, index, etc. By having him describe several books he has read and asking him their titles, you can surmise whether he is using titles to identify books.

*Skill.*   Expands use of library.(14)

*Objective.*   The child is able to: (1) find easy books for independent reading, (2) locate fiction books by the author's last name, (3) locate nonfiction books, encyclopedias, and dictionaries, and (4) ask for assistance in using the card catalog.

*Assessment.*   Assessment of the child's ability to find easy books for independent reading is best done by observing the books he selects for reading. Other parts of the objective can be assessed through direct questions and/or specific tasks described in the objective.

*Skill.*   Begins to use reference materials.(15)

*Objective.*   The child is able to: (1) select pictures appropriate to a given topic from a picture file, (2) differentiate in his use of encyclopedias and dictionaries, (3) use encyclopedias for browsing, and (4) use some nonfiction materials as authoritative sources.

*Assessment.*   As in a number of the preceding skills, extended classroom observation is the best means of assessing this skill. However, a more direct way can be devised by assigning the child a topic for an oral report and observing his selection and use of materials.

*Skill.*   Reads to find answers; takes notes.(16)

*Objective.*   The child is able to read for answers to direct questions, take simple notes to answer the questions, and use the notes to answer the questions at a later time (2–3 days).

*Assessment.*   Assessment of this objective can be carried out by giving the child four or five direct questions which require him to read for answers. Ask him to make notes which he will later use to answer the questions. Two or three days later, ask him to answer the questions, using only his notes. Although the questions should be simple, they should be complicated enough to require the use of notes rather than memory.

*Skill.*   Keeps simple reading record.(17)

*Objective.*   The child lists the titles of books consulted about a given topic.

*Assessment.*   Rather than assigning a topic and asking the child to list the titles of books consulted, it is more appropriate to examine his work on various projects over an extended period of time to see if he is performing in this manner.

*Skill.*   Recognizes organization of ideas in sequential order.(18)

*Objective.* The child is able to recognize sequential relationships among two or three ideas.

*Assessment.* Give the child several unordered steps in a sequential operation (e.g., brushing the teeth or dressing) and ask him to order them.

*Skill.* Begins to make judgments and draw conclusions.(19)

*Objective.* Given facts, the child is able to respond correctly to questions requiring that he make judgments and draw conclusions on the basis of the facts presented.

*Assessment.* Give the child two or three related facts on the basis of which he can draw a conclusion. Since children sometimes come up with unorthodox conclusions, it is well to ask them why they believe a particular answer is true. If the child can support his answer reasonably, it is well to accept it.

## Level D

*Skill.* Uses a key containing nonpictorial symbols to interpret maps.(1)

*Objective.* The child is able to use a key containing nonpictorial symbols (e.g., lines, dots) to derive information from maps.

*Assessment.* Give the child a map containing nonpictorial symbols such as dots representing cities, lines representing roads, wavy lines representing streams, etc. Give him a key to use in interpreting the symbols. Then ask him to use the map and key to answer relevant questions, e.g., "How many cities are there in Jones County?" "Would the most direct route from city *A* to city *B* be by water or by highway?"

*Skill.* Uses a color key to interpret maps.(2)

*Objective.* The child is able to use a color key (in which colors identify classes and no more than three shades of any color identify subclasses) to derive information from maps, e.g., the child reports that there are two areas of marshland (light blue) and one area of swamp (dark blue).

*Assessment.* Give the child a map and key in which colors have been used to represent various classes and subclasses (something similar to a topographical map would be appropriate). Instruct him to use the key to interpret information on the map and to answer relevant questions about comparisons of areas (e.g., sea level, altitude, size, vegetation, etc.).

*Skill.* Locates points on a number-letter grid.(3)

*Objective.* The child is able to locate points and describe the location of points on a number-letter grid.

*Assessment.* Give the child a grid in which rows are labeled by numbers and columns are labeled by letters. Ask him to locate specific cells by interpreting row and column descriptors. Ask him to answer other questions which require him to locate and describe the location by using row and column designations.

*Skill.* Determines cardinal directions on globes, in his environment, and on map.(4)

*Objective.* The child is able to: (1) determine cardinal directions to describe relative location of two points on globes, in his environment, and on maps, and (2) relate the location of points on gloves and maps to the location of points in the environment, e.g., the child matches objects pictured on a map with objects in his environment to determine direction.

*Assessment.* Give the child a map and a key indicating the directions N, S, E, and W. Ask him questions which require the use of cardinal directions, e.g., "What city is directly east of city A?" "Is city D east, west, north, or south of city X?" "Toward what city would you be going if you leave city B and go south?"

*Skill.* Uses scale to determine whole units of distance.(5)

*Objective.* The child is able to use a scale bar referent or verbal referent (i.e., 1 inch = X standard units of measure) to compare and determine distances between points one or more referent units apart when one referent unit equals one standard unit of measure, e.g.,

$$1 \text{ inch} = 1 \text{ mile}, 0\underline{\hspace{4cm}}1,$$
$$\text{miles}$$

and one referent unit apart when one referent unit equals more than one standard unit of measure (e.g., 1 inch = 20 miles).

*Assessment.* Give the child several maps, each containing a separate scale bar referent (e.g., 1 inch = 1 mile, 1 inch = 1 foot, 1 inch = 20 yards, etc.). Then ask him to use the appropriate scale bar to answer questions which require him to compute and/or compare distances between various points.

*Skill.* Has picture graph skills.(6)

*Objective.* Given a picture graph in which each symbol represents more than one unit (e.g., 2, 10, 20), the child is able to: (1) determine the purpose, (2) compare relative amounts, (3) extract directly, (4) determine differences between numbers extracted, and (5) make a summary statement (summarize all of the data presented, e.g., from a graph showing the number of ships built in various countries, the child concludes that one country is the major source of production).

*Assessment.* Assessment of this skill is the same as assessment of skill C(8) except for the addition here of the summarizing statement explained in the objective.

*Skill.* Has bar graph skills.(7)

*Objective.* Given a horizontal or vertical bar graph which has one group of bars and a small interval (e.g., 2, 10, 20), the child is able to determine the purpose, compare relative amounts, extract directly, determine differences between numbers extracted, and make a summary statement.

*Assessment.* Assessment of this skill is the same as assessment of skill C(9) except for the addition here of the comparison (by addition and/or subtraction) of exact amounts represented by given horizontal and vertical bars and the addition of a summarizing statement as described in D(6).

*Skill.* Has circle graph skills.(8)

*Objective.* Given a circle graph with from two to four divisions, the child is able to determine the purpose and compare relative amounts.

*Assessment.* Give the child a circle graph containing two to four labeled divisions. Ask him questions which require him to make judgments about relative amounts represented by the divisions. Ask questions based on the comparison of amounts represented by various divisions.

*Skill.* Interprets multicolumn tables.(9)

*Objective.* Given a multicolumn table with from five to eight rows and columns, familiar units for denominate numbers (explained in a key), and/or totals included for each column and row, the child is able to determine the purpose, locate a cell, compare relative amounts in a single dimension, determine relationships among cells, and make a summary statement.

*Assessment.* Give the child a multicolumn table and key similar to that described in the objective. After he has determined the purpose of the table, ask him to locate a particular cell. Then ask him questions which require him to compare relative amounts both in the single dimension and in multiplicative relationships, e.g., "Which batter got the most hits in the 1970 season?" "Which player got three times as many hits as Brown in the 1967 season?" Then ask the child questions which require him to summarize information, as in D(6).

*Skill.* Follows oral or written directions independently.(10)

*Objective.* The child is able to remember and follow a series of directions in sequence, and generalize from directions for one task to a similar task.

*Skill.* Begins to do research assignments independently.(11)

*Objective.* The child shows independence or acceptance of responsibility by working independently on assigned projects and pacing himself to complete long-term tasks in the time allotted (one week).

*Assessment.* Assessment of the two preceding objectives can best be carried out over an extended period of time during which the child can be observed in a variety of situations. Classroom performance, work assignments, and special projects should all be taken into consideration when evaluating these skills.

*Skill.*   Applies basic alphabetizing skills.(12)

*Objective.*   The child is able to alphabetize words by first and second letters, and locate target words in dictionaries and encyclopedias.

*Assessment.*   Put a list of words in random order of alphabetization on the board. Ask the child to list them alphabetically on his paper. The rest of the objective is self-explanitory.

*Skill.*   Uses guide words in encyclopedias and dictionaries.(13)

*Objective.*   The child is able to locate the appropriate alphabetical section of a reference book for a given topic or target word by attending to the alphabetic sequence of guide words.

*Assessment.*   Although it is possible to devise an artificial situation for assessing this skill in a group, assessment is best done on an individual basis. An effective and direct method can be accomplished by simply giving the child a topic or word to locate and then observing if he attends to topic or guide words.

*Skill.*   Uses "*see*" references in encyclopedias.(14)

*Objective.*   The child locates the topic referred in response to a "*see*" reference (e.g., having located "Plain Indians. See Indian, American," the child locates the topic referred).

*Assessment.*   Give the child a list of topics, some of which are listed under topic reference and some under "*see*" reference, and have the child locate the specific pages in the books containing the information.

*Skill.*   Uses table of contents.(15)

*Objective.*   The child refers to the table of contents to determine if a book is relevant to his specific purpose (e.g., interest, research topic) and/or locate a particular chapter or section in a book.

*Assessment.*   Ask the child to answer a number of specific questions by referring to the table of contents, e.g., "On what page does Chapter 7 begin?" "Which chapter would probably give you the most information about green plants?"

*Skill.*   Uses glossary.(16)

*Objective.*   The child locates and uses the glossary in a book, rather than a dictionary, to look up the meaning(s) of words as they are used in the context of the book (i.e., he finds new meanings for familiar words and unfamiliar words as they are used in a given context or subject area).

*Assessment.*   Although it is quite simple to assess this skill by giving the child a list of words and having him look them up in the glossary, the value of such an assessment is limited. The skill is much more realistically assessed through classroom observation over an extended period of time during which you see if he uses the skill.

*Skill.*   Begins to use indexes.(17)

*Objective.*   Having identified a general topic, the child uses the indexes of books to locate information about the topic.

*Assessment.*   A measure of the child's ability to find information in an index can be easily assessed by asking him questions about information found there. However, assessment of whether he actually uses indexes should be determined over an extended period of classroom observation.

*Skill.*   Uses study aids in textbooks.(18)

*Objective.*   The child finds and uses such study aids as boldface type, italics, and/or marginal notes in using textbooks.

*Assessment.*   This skill is assessed through classroom observation over an extended period of time. The lack of this skill is more readily observed than the presence of it. This is especially true concerning marginal notes. Another approach to getting at one aspect of this skill is to have the child explain the significance of boldface type, italics, and marginal notes.

*Skill.*   Expands use of library.(19)

*Objective.*   The child is able to locate magazines and some nonfiction books relevant to his interests and assigned work, and continues to attempt higher-level skills such as using the card catalog with the assistance of the librarian.

*Skill.*   Begins to expand use of reference materials.(20)

*Objective.*   The child will independently seek additional reference sources: (1) if the first source consulted does not give sufficient information, and/or (2) pursue interest aroused by initial stimulation, e.g., having found a picture of an igloo in the dictionary, the child consults the encyclopedia to learn about the construction of igloos.

*Note.*   Encyclopedias are considered an important beginning reference material. Teachers should check that they are being used to check facts and as a beginning source rather than as sources for complete reports, verbatim from encyclopedias.

*Assessment.*   Assessment of the two preceding skills can best be accomplished over an extended period of time during which the child can be observed in a variety of situations. The key word here is independence. Can he work effectively and efficiently on his own?

*Skill.*   Begins to adjust reading rate.(21)

*Objective.*   The child skims materials at a rapid rate when seeking to verify or locate specific information, e.g., a date, a name.

*Assessment.*   Assessment of this skill should be carried out several times over an extended period of time to see if rate increases. The interval between questions should be short enough to force the child to skim rather than to read for answers.

*Skill.*   Uses headings and subheadings.(22)

*Objective.*   Having located a topic in a reference book, the child uses the organization of the material to search efficiently for target information.

*Assessment.*   Give the child a topic and a list of subtopics stated as paragraph headings. Have him select the paragraphs on the basis of the paragraph headings which will most probably contain information for answering specifically stated questions.

*Skill.*   Recognizes that printed statements may be fact or opinion.(23)

*Objective.*   The child is able to make a considered decision as to whether given statements represent fact or opinion.

*Assessment.*   Ask the child to make a considered decision as to whether given statements represent fact or opinion. Then ask him to defend his decision by explaining his reason for making it.

*Skill.*   Evaluates relevance of materials.(24)

*Objective.*   Given an assigned list of topics, the child is able to choose from among available sources those that are likely to include relevant information on specific topics.

*Assessment.*   Give the child a specific topic and a list of sources containing information about a variety of topics. Ask the child to select from the list those sources which would probably be most relevant to his own topic.

*Skill.*   Checks accuracy of statements.(25)

*Objective.*   The child is able to identify discrepancies between simple factual data from two sources (e.g., number of parks in a city).

*Note.*   When children identify these discrepancies through classroom research, they should then be directed to discover *why* two sources provided different answers; e.g., it is their error in note-taking; is one source out of date; are the graphs, tables, etc., consulted labeled differently?

*Assessment.*   Give the child two factual data sheets which contain discrepancies in agreement (e.g., figures from two separate years, 1962 and 1972). Have him locate discrepancies and explain why they exist. (The number of parks in the city may have increased between 1962 and 1972.)

## Level E

*Skill.* Uses point and line symbols to interpret maps.(1)

*Objective.* The child is able to use point and line symbols (e.g., circle of different sizes, lines of different widths) to derive qualitative and quantitative information from maps, *e.g.*, the child identifies the largest city on a map as the one represented by the largest circle.

*Assessment.* Give the child a map and key which have been designed to give qualitative information through circle size, thickness of lines, etc. Ask questions which require the identification, interpretation, and comparison of qualitative and quantitative information indicated on the map and explained by the key.

*Skill.* Applies rectangular grid to earth's sphere.(2)

*Objective.* The child is able to use lines of latitude as referents for describing general locations (e.g., north of equator) and lines of longitude as referents for describing general locations (e.g., west of Prime Meridian).

*Assessment.* Give the child a map of the earth's sphere containing lines of latitude and longitude. Ask questions which require the use of referent descriptions (e.g., north of the equator, west of the Prime Meridian, etc.).

*Skill.* Determines intermediate directions on globes, in the environment, and on maps.(3)

*Objective.* The child is able to determine intermediate directions to describe relative location to two points on globes, in his environment, and on maps, and to relate the location of points on globes and maps to the location of points in the environment, e.g., the child matches objects pictured on a map with objects in his environment to determine direction.

*Assessment.* Give the child a map or globe and ask him to describe the relative location of two points by using intermediate directions, e.g., "Point A is northwest of point B. City X is southeast of city Y. If you travel northwest from city W, you will go toward city T."

*Skill.* Makes limited use of scale to determine distance.(4)

*Objective.* The child is able to use a scale bar referent or verbal referent (e.g., 1 inch = X standard units of measure) to compare and determine distances between points one or more referent units apart when one referent unit equals two or more standard units of measure, e.g., when 1 inch = 3 miles, the child concludes that 3 inches = 9 miles.

*Assessment.* Give the child several maps, each containing a separate scale bar referent with one referent unit equaling two or more standard units of measure (e.g.,

1 inch = X number of standard units). Ask him questions about the separate maps which require him to compute and compare distances using the various scales.

*Skill.*   Has picture graph skills.(5)

*Objective.*   Given a picture graph in which each symbol represents more than one unit (e.g., 2, 10, 20) and half-symbols are used, the child is able to: (1) determine the purpose, (2) compare relative amounts, (3) extract directly, (4) extract by interpolating, (5) determine differences between numbers extracted, (6) make a summary statement, and (7) make projections and relate information.

*Assessment.*   Give the child a picture graph containing symbols and half-symbols. After he has determined the purpose of the graph, ask him questions which require him to compare relative amounts, sum rows and/or columns, and interpret partial symbols. Then ask questions which require him to compare specific differences through addition and substraction of row and/or column sums. Next, have him formulate summary statements or answer questions about summary statements similar to those in D(6). Finally, have him state probable trends based on information given in the graph.

*Skill.*   Has bar graph skills.(6)

*Objective.*   Given a horizontal or vertical bar graph which has one group of bars and a small interval (e.g., 10, 20) the child is able to: (1) determine the purpose, (2) compare relative amounts, (3) extract directly, (4) extract by interpolating, (5) determine differences between numbers extracted, (6) make a summary statement, and (7) make projections and relate information.

*Assessment.*   Give the child a horizontal or vertical bar graph which has one group of bars and a small interval. After the child has determined the purpose of the graph, ask him questions about the comparison of relative amounts. Ask questions which require him to note the line to which a particular bar comes and answer by giving the number beside the line. Also check to see if he can accurately estimate the amount represented by a bar which ends between the lines. Finally, have him formulate summary statements or answer questions about summary statements similar to those in D(6), and have him formulate probable trends based on information given in the graph.

*Skill.*   Interprets multicolumn tables.(7)

*Objective.*   Given a complex multicolumn table with denominate numbers (explained in a key or the title) and/or totals included for each column and row, the child is able to: (1) determine the purpose, (2) locate a cell, (3) compare relative amounts in a single dimension, (4) determine relationships among cells, (5) make summary statements, and (6) make projections and relate information.

*Assessment.*    Assessment of this skill is the same as assessment of D(9), except for the addition here of the formulation of statements of probable outcomes or trends based on information given in the table.

*Skill.*    Has independent classroom and research work habits.(8)

*Objective.*    The child is able to focus all previously mastered study skills in independent study and/or research.

*Note.*    The child should demonstrate ability to direct his own independent inquiry, e.g., pursue special interests related to assigned tasks, and to initiate independent projects. Assessment of this skill is done through classroom observation over an extended period of time.

*Skill.*    Utilizes alphabetical system.(9)

*Objective.*    The child is able to alphabetize words.

*Assessment.*    Put a list of randomly ordered words on the board and ask the child to list them alphabetically on his paper.

*Skill.*    Uses guide words and guide letters.(10)

*Objective.*    Given (1) the guide words and page numbers from three to six pages in a reference book, the child is able to specify the page on which specific words could be found, and/or (2) the guide letters and drawer numbers of a card catalog, the child is able to specify the drawer in which specific words, names, or topics could be found.

*Assessment.*    Give the child a list of six to twelve guide words selected from a reference source and ordered sequentially. Give him a second list of topic words randomly ordered. Have him fit the topic words into their proper places among the guide words. For example, *gagster* would be listed between *gadget* and *gall*, and *gallant* would be listed between *gall* and *gambir*. The second part of the objective can best be assessed by actually having the child locate specific topics in a card catalog.

*Skill.*    Uses alphabet skills related to card catalog.(11)

*Objective.*    For locating information in the card catalog, the child (1) uses guide cards in the drawers to locate his target word quickly, and (2) ignores initial articles.

*Assessment.*    As in the case of E(10), this can be done most effectively by having the child locate specific topics or target words.

*Skill.*    Refines use of indexes.(12)

*Objective.*    Having identified or been given a general topic, the child uses the indexes of books or the index volume of an encyclopedia to locate specific information about subtopics, e.g., SPACE, Space travel: development of flight plan, history of.

*Assessment.* Give the child a general topic and have him use indexes of books or the index volume of an encyclopedia to locate specific subtopics under which he might find further information. Have him list the subtopics and their sources.

*Skill.* Considers special features of books in selection.(13)

*Objective.* The child examines books to judge their relevance to his purposes.

*Note.* The child considers such questions as: Does the book include relevant pictures, maps, graphs, tools, etc.? Does a general text include information on a given topic?

*Assessment.* Although informal observation is your best source of information here, you might contrive a situation whereby you give the child a topic and a list of books. You could then ask him to list the books which are relevant and explain why he rejected the others.

*Skill.* Extends familiarity with library.(14)

*Objective.* The child is able to (1) locate and identify author, subject, and title cards in the card catalog, and (2) use them to locate books and other materials.

*Note.* Included among other materials are such things as games, film strips, films, records, photographic equipment, etc., which may be found in a well-stocked library. In the present context, emphasis is placed on books.

*Assessment.* Assessment of this skill is best accomplished by giving the child a task which requires him to locate and use author, subject, and title cards to locate books and other materials.

*Skill.* Uses dictionaries independently.(15)

*Objective.* The child uses dictionaries to check the spelling and/or meaning of words as needed.

*Note.* The emphasis here is on independent use of the dictionary. Assessment of this skill is best carried out through observation of the child's work habits and work sheets. Does he actually seek help from the dictionary at an independent level?

*Skill.* Consults encyclopedias and atlases.(16)

*Objective.* The child locates (1) information on one topical heading in more than one encyclopedia by adapting his locational skills to the idiosyncrasies of each set (e.g., some have individual volume indexes, some have no indexes, some have a multivolume index), and (2) maps in atlases.

*Skill.* Uses pamphlet files.(17)

*Objective.* The child routinely includes the pamphlet file in a check for material available on a subject.

*Skill.* Uses magazines and newspapers.(18)

*Objective.* The child selects magazines and newspapers as sources of current, topical information.

*Note.* Skills E(16), E(17), and E(18) are self-explanatory. Assessment is best accomplished through classroom observation. Skills 17 and 18 can be evaluated partially through examining the child's list of sources associated with various work projects. However, observation of the child in action is your best source of information.

*Skill.* Uses selected specialized reference books.(19)

*Objective.* The child selects (1) *World Almanac* and/or *Information Please Almanac*, or (2) *Junior Book of Authors*, or (3) a dictionary, or (4) an encyclopedia, or (5) an atlas, or (6) a nonfiction book, whichever is most appropriate to answer specific questions.

*Note.* The child should select the *World Almanac* to find demographic information and dates, a dictionary for word meaning, an encyclopedia for general background, *Junior Book of Authors* for biographical information about a children's author, etc.

*Assessment.* Give the child a list of specialized reference books such as those described in the objective. Then give him a list of questions requiring specialized information (e.g., demographic, bibliographic, dates, etc.) and ask him to list probable sources from which he might learn the answers to the questions.

*Skill.* Uses nonfiction materials as references.(20)

*Objective.* The child chooses nonfiction books and materials not formally designated "Reference" when appropriate.

*Assessment.* Assessment of this skill can be done by examining the sources that the child listed for various projects. It can also be carried out by a process similar to that in skill E(19). In this case, you will need books with which the child is familiar or which have descriptive titles.

*Skill.* Adjusts reading rate to difficulty.(21)

*Objective.* The child adjusts his reading rate appropriately as reading materials become more or less difficult as purposes change. For example, the child reads a given type of material, e.g., science material, written at his independent reading level of difficulty at a more rapid rate (greater number of words per minute) than similar material written at his instructional level of reading difficulty.

*Assessment.* Once the child's independent and instructional rates of reading have been established, assessment of this skill is easy. Assessment can be carried out by simply timing the child's reading rate on various types of material.

*Skill.* Adjusts reading rate to purpose.(22)

*Objective.* The child skims materials at a rapid rate when seeking to verify or locate specific information; he reads material at a slower (but still rapid) rate when seeking an overview or general idea about content; and he scans material at a relatively slow rate when his purpose is to master or locate to verify and recall factual information.

*Assessment.* Give the child several selections of about the same length and readability level. After establishing a specific purpose for a selection, have the child read it. By varying the purpose of the selections and by timing the child's reading time, you should be able to get an estimate of whether or not he is modifying his speed in accordance with the task.

*Skill.* Has beginning outlining skills.(23)

*Objective.* Given the major points in a formal outline, the child is able to select and fill in second-order points from well-organized paragraphs written at his instructional level of difficulty, e.g.,

I. Birds are alike in many ways.
   A.
   B.
   C.

II. A bird's feathers are useful.
   A.
   B.
   C.

*Skill.* Makes simple bibliographies.(24)

*Objective.* The child lists books he has consulted by author and title.

*Note.* Both of the objectives above are self-explanitory.

*Skill.* Draws inferences and makes generalizations.(25)

*Objective.* Given facts, the child is able to respond correctly to questions requiring that he make inferences and generalizations on the basis of the facts presented.

*Assessment.* The key words here are *infer on the basis of facts.* Assessment should measure the child's ability to infer from the facts given in the selection being studied. For instance, he might infer that it's winter because there's snow on the ground and children are sledding. He should not be able to answer questions by finding the answer stated in the selection. Equally true, he should not be able to answer questions on the basis of his past experience.

*Skill.* Evaluates information in terms of his own experience and/or known facts.(26)

*Objective.* The child relates new information to his personal experiences and/or known facts and evaluates both new information and the past experiences and knowledge in terms of the relationship.

*Note.* Assessment of this objective is most realistically based on observations over a period of time. One basis for assessment would be observations of reactions to commercial advertisements of products with which the child is familiar. The child should be able to not only criticize in terms of his personal experience, but also reevaluate his past observations in light of new information, e.g., note when a product has been inappropriately used, recognize unrealistic expectations.

## Level F

*Skill.* Uses point, line, and area symbols.(1)

*Objective.* The child is able to use point, line, and area symbols to derive qualitative and quantitative information from maps.

*Assessment.* Give the child a map (possibly a road map) which contains point, line and area symbols, and a key. Ask questions which require the identification, interpretation, and comparison of qualitative and quantative information indicated on the map and explained in the key, e.g., "Which highway in the northern half of state X is under construction?" "What is the highway number for the scenic route from point Y to point Z?" "How many gold mines are located in C county?" "Name two state parks in state X where camping is allowed."

*Skill.* Has location skills.(2)

*Objective.* The child is able to use lines of latitude and longitude to locate points on a map or globe, e.g., New York City is 40° north latitude and 74° west longitude.

*Assessment.* Give the child a map or globe containing lines of latitude and longitude. Ask him to locate several points or places by giving their longitude and latitude. Then ask him to name the place found at the longitude and latitude lines you give.

*Skill.* Identifies differences among maps drawn to different scales.(3)

*Objective.* The child is able to identify differences (amount of detail) among maps of the same area drawn to different scales, e.g., 1 inch = 1000 miles, 1 inch = 100 miles, and 1 inch = 50 miles.

*Assessment.* Give the child three maps of the same area, each drawn to a separate scale, e.g., 1 inch = 50 miles, 1 inch = 100 miles, and 1 inch = 1000 miles. Have the child explain the difference in detail among the three maps. Ask questions which require him to use the various maps to locate answers.

*Skill.* Makes use of scale to determine distance.(4)

*Objective.* The child is able to use a scale bar referent or verbal referent (i.e., 1 inch = X standard units of measure) to compare and determine distances between points that are combinations of fractional and whole referent units apart when one referent unit equals two or more standard units of measure. For example, when 1 inch = 10 miles, the child concludes that $2\frac{1}{2}$ inches = 25 miles.

*Assessment.* Give the child a map having a scale bar referent of 1 = X number of standard units of measure (e.g., 1 = 10 miles). Ask him questions which require him to compute and compare differences between various points. Require him to compute the fractional units as well as the whole units. For example, 1 inch = 10 miles; therefore $2\frac{1}{2}$ inches = 25 miles.

*Skill.* Has bar graph skills.(5)

*Objective.* Given a horizontal or vertical bar graph which has two groups of bars, the child is able to: (1) determine the purpose, (2) compare relative amounts, (3) extract directly, (4) extract by interpolating, (5) determine differences between numbers extracted, (6) make a summary statement, and (7) make projections and relate information.

*Assessment.* Assessment of this skill is exactly the same as the assessment of skill E(6). The only difference lies in the fact that here there are two groups of bars instead of one.

*Skill.* Has circle graph skills.(6)

*Objective.* Given a circle graph with four or more divisions, the child is able to: (1) determine the purpose, (2) compare relative amounts, (3) extract directly, and (4) make a summary statement.

*Assessment.* Give the child a circle graph divided into four or more sections. After he has determined the purpose of the graph, have him compare relative amounts within the circle (e.g., more money for food than for clothes,) and have him give exact amounts listed in various sections (e.g., 45% for taxes, 20% for food, 10% for entertainment). Then have him formulate a summary statement similar to that given in D(6).

*Skill.* Has line graph skills.(7)

*Objective.* Given a single line, noncumulative line graph, the child is able to: (1) determine the purpose, (2) compare relative amounts, (3) extract directly, (4) extract by interpolating, (5) determine differences between numbers extracted, (6) make a summary statement, and (7) make projections and relate information.

*Assessment.* Give the child a single line, noncumulative line graph. After he has determined the purpose of the graph, have him compare relative amounts represented by the line at different points on the graph. Ask questions which require him to determine the amounts represented at various points with respect to both axis and coordinate references. Then have him state differences between numbers extracted, e.g., More peaches were sold in June 1969 than in June 1970. Finally, have him formulate a summary statement similar to that in D(6) and make projections on the basis of the graph.

*Skill.*   Interprets schedules.(8)

*Objective.*   Given a simple schedule (e.g., boat, bus) the child is able to: (1) determine the purpose, (2) locate a cell, (3) compare relative amounts in a single dimension, (4) determine relationship among cells, and (5) make a summary statement.

*Assessment.*   Give the child a simple schedule and ask him to determine its purpose. Then ask him to locate a particular cell, e.g., "What time does Bus 17 leave for Chicago?" Next, ask him questions which require him to make comparisons; for instance, "Which bus line makes the most trips a day to New York?" Ask other questions which require him to examine the differences or multiplicative relationships among two or more cells, e.g., "Which bus line makes twice as many trips to Seattle per day as any other line?" Finally, have him formulate summary statements based on given situations; e.g., from a schedule have him select a carrier and a departure time required to get him to a designated place at a designated time.

*Skill.*   Has independent classroom and research work habits.(9)

*Objective.*   The child is able to focus all previously mastered study skills in independent study and/or research.

*Note.*   The objective is the same as at Level E. The child's ability to direct his work independently should, of course, increase from level to level.

*Skill.*   Refines card catalog skills.(10)

*Objective.*   The child is able to locate target card quickly by applying these filing rules: (1) names beginning with either Mac or Mc are filed together as if all were spelled m-a-c; (2) if a word has been abbreviated, as Mr., it is filed as if it were spelled out; and (3) if numbers are used, they are filed as if they were spelled out.

*Assessment.*   Using the filing rules stated in the objective, select a list of names and titles from the card catalog in your school. Put the names and titles in random order and have the child order them according to which would come first, second, third, etc., in the card catalog.

*Skill.*   Refines cross-references skills.(11)

*Objective.*   The child applies the cross-references skill in D(14) to all types of reference books.

*Assessment.*   Assessment of this skill is explained in the objective.

*Skill.*   Expands book skills.(12)

*Objective.*   The child consults the bibliography of a subject book to help him locate other materials of interest and/or uses the special study aids in textbooks (glossaries, appendixes) to help master factual information.

*Assessment.*   One way of assessing this skill is by giving the child a list of the various parts of his text book (index, glossary, bibliography, etc.) and having him discuss what type of information he would get from each part. Obviously, the most straight-forward procedure is through classroom observation. You can observe whether he turns to these sources for help and note whether the sources are reflected in his written work.

*Skill.*   Expands facility in using library.(13)

*Objective.*   The child is able to locate any book or material by its call number and/or many subject areas by using the ten major groupings of the Dewey Decimal System (000 General Works, 100– Philosophy, 200– Religion, 300– Social Science, 400– Language, 500– Pure Science, 600– Technology, 700– Art, 800– Literature, 900– History).

*Assessment.*   The best way of assessing this skill is by giving the child the call numbers for several books of various kinds and having him locate them. By observing his behavior, you can easily determine if he has mastered this skill. The second part of the skill can be assessed by giving the child a list of call numbers and asking him to determine in which subject area each book can be found.

*Skill.*   Uses dictionaries for pronunciation.(14)

*Objective.*   The child is able to use the diacritical marking in a dictionary to interpret the pronunciation of unfamiliar words, e.g., Charybdis, escutcheon, imbroglio, spiegleisen.

*Assessment.*   Give the child a list of unfamiliar words and ask him to look up their pronunciations in a dictionary. Then have the child pronounce the words by using information derived from the dictionary.

*Skill.*   Uses "*see also*" directions.(15)

*Objective.*   Given a "*see also*" direction, the child locates the referred topic to find supplementary information.

*Assessment.*   This skill is assessed in the same way as skill D(14).

*Skill.*   Uses *Subject Index to Children's Magazines.*(16)

*Objective.*   The child searches for current information in the subject index and/or tries to relocate specific articles read previously.

*Assessment.* This skill can be assessed by assigning the child a topic to research. By selecting a topic of current interest, you can devise a situation calling for a search among current sources of information. You can then quickly assess his capabilities by observing him in action.

*Skill.* Adjusts reading rate to difficulty.(17)

*Objective.* The child adjusts his reading rate appropriately as reading materials become more or less difficult as purposes change. For example, the child reads a given type of material, e.g., science material, written at his independent reading level of difficulty at a more rapid rate ( greater number of words per minute) than similar material written at his instructional level of reading difficulty.

*Note.* Directions for the assessment of this skill can be found by looking at skill E(21).

*Skill.* Adjusts reading rate to purpose.(18)

*Objective.* The child skims materials at a rapid rate when seeking to verify or locate specific information; he reads material at a slower (but still rapid) rate when seeking an overview or general idea about content; and he scans material at a relatively slow rate when his purpose is to master or locate to verify and recall factual information.

*Note.* The objective is the same as at Level E. The difficulty of selections would, of course, increase from level to level. Directions for assessing this skill can be found by looking at Skill E(22).

*Skill.* Makes notes of main ideas and supporting facts.(19)

*Objective.* The child is able to identify main ideas and supporting facts in a selection and make notes in his own words.

*Assessment.* Assessment of this skill can be accomplished by assigning a specific selection to be read by the child. Then ask him to identify and write down in outline form the main ideas and supporting facts.

*Skill.* Summarizes materials.(20)

*Objective.* The child is able to write concise summaries, e.g., identify major issues or main points of view expressed, of expository materials.

*Assessment.* Give the child a selection and after he has read it, ask him to identify and summarize in X number of words the major issues or main points of view expressed.

## Level G

*Skill.* Identifies likenesses and differences between two or more areas.(1)

*Objective.* The child is able to make comparisons of geographic areas in terms of topographic, climatic, political, and demographic information provided on maps.

*Assessment.* Give the child a map on which various types of geographical information have been designated (i.e., topographical, climatic, political, and demographic). Ask questions which require comparisons of geographic areas in terms of the descriptors mentioned, e.g., "Which country has the most rainfall per year?" "Which states have the highest percentages of Indians?" "Which country has the largest number of mountain ranges?"

*Skill.* Synthesizes information about an area.(2)

*Objective.* The child is able to use a variety of maps (e.g., topographic, climatic, political, and demographic) or a given area to determine specific characteristics. For example, the child infers that since a particular area has an average rainfall, gently rolling hills, and moderate climate, the occupations of the inhabitants may be mostly farm-oriented.

*Assessment.* Using the same maps as used in G(1), ask the child to make inferences based on the information given.

*Skill.* Uses meridians and parallels to determine directions on any projection.(3)

*Objective.* The child is able to use meridians and parallels to determine directions on any projection. For example, on an elliptical projection with the Prime Meridian at the center, the child traces the meridian from a given point to the pole to show north or south.

*Assessment.* Give the child several projections of the earth's sphere on which meridians and parallels are clearly marked. Ask him to use the meridians and parallels to determine directions. For example, give the child a diagram projecting the earth from the North Pole and ask him to determine which of several points labeled A, B, C, and D, are northeast of point X.

*Skill.* Locates the same point or cell on various projections.(4)

*Objective.* The child is able to locate the same point or cell on various projections, e.g., polar, Mercator.

*Assessment.* Give the child maps similar to those in G(3). Ask him to locate a particular point on three different projections.

*Skill.* Uses inset maps to determine relative size of areas.(5)

*Objective.* The child is able to determine the relative size of two or more areas drawn to different scales by comparing the inset maps, which are drawn to the same scale. For example, the child determines that even though his maps of Rhode Island and Texas are the same size, Texas is indeed larger, since the area outlined on the inset map (which is of the United States) is much larger than that area outlined for Rhode Island.

*Assessment.* Give the child two or three maps drawn to different scales but containing inset maps drawn to the same scale. Ask him questions which require computation and comprehension of sizes based on the inset maps. For example, give him maps of three states drawn to different scales, but each containing an inset of the United States drawn to the same scale. Since the darkened area in each inset represents the size of the state, he should be able to compare sizes of land areas.

*Skill.*   Has bar graph skills.(6)

*Objective.*   Given a horizontal or vertical bar graph which has three or four groups of bars, the child is able to: (1) determine the purpose, (2) compare relative amounts, (3) extract directly, (4) extract by interpolating, (5) determine differences between numbers extracted, (6) make a summary statement, and (7) make projections and relate information.

*Assessment.*   Assessment of this skill is exactly the same as assessment of E(6). The only difference is that here, there are three or four groups of bars instead of one.

*Skill.*   Has line graph skills.(7)

*Objective.*   Given a single or multiline cumulative or noncumulative line graph, the child is able to: (1) determine the purpose, (2) compare relative amounts, (3) extract directly, (4) extract by interpolating, (5) determine differences between numbers extracted, (6) make a summary statement, and (7) make projections and relate information.

*Assessment.*   Assessment of this skill is the same as assessment of Skill F(7). The only difference is that here, there are both multiline and single line cumulative and noncumulative line graphs.

*Skill.*   Interprets schedules.(8)

*Objective.*   Given any schedule, the child is able to: (1) determine the purpose, (2) locate a cell, (3) compare relative amounts in a single dimension, (4) determine relationship among cells, and (5) make a summary statement.

*Assessment.*   Assessment of this skill is exactly the same as assessment of Skill F(8). The difference in the two skills lies in the fact that here, you use a variety of schedules at more sophisticated levels of difficulty.

*Skill.*   Has independent classroom and research work habits.(9)

*Objective.*   The child is able to both focus all skills developed to this point on one problem and apply all relevant skills in all subject matter areas.

*Assessment.*   This skill is best assessed through classroom observation over an extended period of time. It may sometimes be advisable to confer with other teachers. This is especially advisable when the child attends content-area classes outside his homeroom.

*Skill.*   Refines book skills.(10)

*Objective.*   The child is familiar with some reference books and their idiosyncratic organization (e.g., indexes are usually found in the back of a book, but the index of the *World Almanac* is in the front).

*Assessment.*   This skill may be assessed by listing reference books with known idiosyncratic organizations and having the child explain their idiosyncracies.

*Skill.*   Uses all information on catalog cards.(11)

*Objective.*   The child uses the information given on a catalog card—date of publication, publisher, number of illustrations, type of illustrations—to decide if the book or other material is appropriate for his purpose.

*Assessment.*    Give the child a specific topic and a number of facsimilie catalog cards. Ask the child to determine if certain books or pieces of material contain information appropriate to his topic by examining the information on the cards. For best assessment, you should ask him what information on the card led him to select or reject each specific item.

*Skill.*   Increases understanding of Dewey decimal system.(12)

*Objective.*   The child is able to locate numbers for sections more specific than the ten major groupings as his interests become more specialized (i.e., 391– costumes, 394– holidays, 520– astronomy, 540– chemistry, 597– fishes, 796– sports, 92 or B– biography, 917– travel in North America (information about states), 970– Indians, 973– American history).

*Assessment.*   Give the child the names of some specific sections as listed in the Dewey decimal system (astronomy, chemistry, sports, biography, etc.) and have him use reference books to determine their specific numbers.

*Skill.*   Expands use of reference materials: current periodical indexes.(13)

*Objective.*   The child uses the *Subject Index to Children's Magazines* for locating materials in children's magazines and the *Abridged Reader's Guide* for locating material in general adult magazines.

*Assessment.*  One way of assessing this skill is by giving the child a list of topics to look up in the *Subject Index to Children's Magazines* and the *Abridged Reader's Guide.* However, the best assessment is accomplished by examining the child's research habits and class reports to see if he refers to these works as sources of information.

*Skill.*  Adjusts reading rate to difficulty.(14)

*Objective.*  The child adjusts his reading rate appropriately as reading materials become more or less difficult as purposes change. For example, the child reads a given type of material, e.g., science material, written at his independent reading level of difficulty at a more rapid rate (greater number of words per minute) than similar material written at his instructional level of reading difficulty.

*Note.*  Directions for assessment of this skill can be found by looking at Skill E(21).

*Skill.*  Adjusts reading rate to purpose.(15)

*Objective.*  The child skims materials at a rapid rate when seeking to verify or locate specific information; he reads material at a slower (but still rapid) rate when seeking an overview or general idea regarding content; and he scans material at a relatively slow rate when his purpose is to master or locate to verify and recall factual information.

*Note.*  The objective is the same as Levels E and F. The difficulty of selections would, of course, increase from level to level. Directions for assessment of this skill can be found by looking at Skill E(22).

*Skill.*  Gains skill in note taking.(16)

*Objective.*  The child is able to take notes from varied sources in a form that is useful to him; this permits him to retrieve information as needed.

*Assessment.*  One way of assessing this skill is to require the child to use only his notes to answer questions about a topic he has been researching. Another way is to have him hand in samples of his notes for examination from time to time.

*Skill.*  Makes formal outlines.(17)

*Objective.*  Given selections written at his instructional level of difficulty, the child is able to select and order main points in a formal outline (e.g., I.A.1.).

*Assessment.*  Assessment of this skill is explained adequately in the objective.

# 9 / Objectives for comprehension

So far, we have examined the objectives in word attack and study skills. By now you should be well aware of the special characteristics of objectives as presented in this text, as well as the specific idiosyncrasies of each skill area. Although all of the areas have commonality in that they are all skill-centered, statements of objectives and methods of assessment must, by their very nature, be modified to meet skill dimensions. It is important to keep this in mind while examining the area of comprehension.

## Skills and Objectives for Comprehension

Comprehension skills have been clustered in the same ways as study skills, that is, they run A through G (K–6). Similarly, as in the other skill areas, this clustering serves to provide an overall sequential arrangement of skill development without dictating sequential arrangement of specific skills. We emphasize again that grade-level reference in this approach should be considered as descriptive rather than prescriptive. Assessment and instruction should be dictated by need and ability rather than by theoretical grade level.

Our procedure for identifying a list of comprehension skills was similar to that used in identifying skills in our other areas. By beginning with a well-constructed elementary curriculum guide and modifying it as research, classroom teachers, and experience dictated, we have been able to devise a list which has consensual, historical, and limited empirical support. This is not to imply that everyone agrees with our particular approach. Comprehension is an especially controversial area in education, and there are many knowledgeable educators who prefer other approaches. However, in light of present research and our own experience, the approach presented here appears to have two important advantages over most others. First, it s on the needs and abilities of individuals. Second, it presents an organized, ...atic approach to assessment and instruction which is oriented toward the ...dual. In the final analysis, these seem to be the most important issues involved in comprehension.

Before going on to discuss specific skills and objectives in comprehension, it seems wise to first consider some of the dimensions of the area. Unlike those in word attack and study skills, the skills in comprehension are of a more nebulous nature, and their dimensions are not always discrete. In the sense that a child must decode "reading material" before he can read it with comprehension, the relationship between comprehension and word attack is a dependent one. Furthermore, we recognize that this dependent relationship extends in the other direction in that the most useful aid to successful decoding is the understanding of what is being decoded. As we have mentioned previously, children will have less difficulty in learning to decode words which are part of their listening and speaking vocabularies than words which are foreign to them.

In addition to being aware of the relationship between comprehension and word attack, you should also be aware of the relationship between comprehension and thinking. If a student cannot comprehend spoken language, why should we call his inability to comprehend written material a reading problem? If he cannot draw conclusions about information presented orally, is it legitimate to say that he has a reading problem because he cannot do the same thing with written material? In other words, we need to ask, "Is it a reading-comprehension problem, or is it a comprehension problem?" The difference between the two types of problems is no small one.

A further relationship to be examined is that of reading comprehension to intelligence and mental growth. We have said before that there will be times when you will have to wait for the child's mental growth to catch up with his needs. This is especially true in reading comprehension. Since reading comprehension must, by its very nature, be preceded by the ability to handle successfully a number of fairly mental operations, there may be times when you will have to wait until the child is ready. Since these mental operations range from the less difficult to more sophisticated types of mental analysis, you will want to modify your instruction and expectations to meet the needs of the child where he is.

You should also be aware of the fact that a child may not mature in all areas of development at the same rate. Although a child may be advanced in decoding words and in vocabulary, he may still not be able to successfully cope with materials which require abstract reasoning and inferential thinking. On the other hand, he may be able to handle the mental operations in comprehension, but may be deficient in vocabulary and word-attack skills. And then, of course, he may be adequate in both reasoning and decoding, but simply may not have the skills to get it together in reading comprehension. In other words, successful reading comprehension depends on the integration of many factors, all of which are important.

Traditionally, comprehension skills have been divided into two groups: those skills dealing with specifically stated information and those skills requiring inference. Both skill classifications, literal and inferential, are represented in our skills list. ✳ The skills list is organized by type as well as by level. The main categories are: (1) main idea, (2) sequence, (3) reading for detail, (4) affixes (semantics of), (5) use of context, and (6) reasoning.

*Main idea.*   This category deals primarily with the student's ability to infer the main thought or central idea expressed in the information given. It begins by asking the child to merely identify the main topic of a picture. It continues by having the child identify topics from listening and finally, by having him read for the main idea of an extended selection.

*Sequence.*   This skill is handled in a more or less traditional manner. Students are required to perform specific tasks which indicate whether they can properly sequence pictures, words, sentences, events, etc.

*Reading for detail.*   Reading for detail is not handled in the traditional manner. Rather we have tried to deal with not only the child's ability to read for specific information, but also with some of the various syntactical structures with which he must deal if he is to understand that information. Among the things we have included in this area are active and passive voice, interpretation of negatives, and interpretations of complicated sentence structures.

*Affixes.*   The skills in this area center on the student's ability to interpret suffixes and prefixes as they relate to vocabulary development. The emphasis here is toward semantics, i.e., how the affixes change or modify the meaning of words. The difference in affix skills in word attack and in comprehension is largely a matter of focus rather than content. In word attack, the focus is mainly on structure.

*Context clues.*   The emphasis here is on the use of contextual aids in determining the meaning of unknown or unfamiliar words. Also emphasized is the use of context in deriving unfamiliar meanings for words which occur frequently in everyday language. The affix skills and the use of context clues constitute the major skills associated with vocabulary development.

*Reasoning.*   This category is by far the most difficult in comprehension. It includes synthesizing information, inferring outcomes, recognizing cause-effect relationships, inductive and deductive reasoning, and applying principles to new situations. As explained earlier in this chapter, it is closely associated with thinking and reasoning. The child is required to perform a variety of mental operations ranging in difficulty from simple classification to semisophisticated reasoning. Both literal and inferential skills are represented in the strand.

   One further word about comprehension. The objectives for this area encourage, if not demand, convergent thinking. Although this is an extremely important aspect of comprehension, you should not overlook the development of divergent thinking. To some extent, this is carried out in Chapter 10. However, a simple modification of many of the comprehension objectives stated in this chapter might also be helpful. For instance, in predicting outcomes, you might establish a situation and ask different children to predict the outcome. There may be several possible outcomes. By asking the children to establish their rationale for their particular answer, you can soon determine whether they are making logical inferences.

A second example of how comprehension objectives can be used to examine divergent thinking may be drawn from cause-effect. Establish a causal situation and ask the children to predict several possible effects and explain their answers. Similarly, you may give them a principle and ask them to give several examples of where the principle is applicable. In either of these cases, there may be several different answers, all of which are correct.

## Outline of Comprehension Skills

Our list of comprehension skills follows. You should remember, however, that this list has been designed to complement the total reading skill development program that we are presenting. You will find that many of the skills traditionally listed under comprehension, have been listed here under our areas of study skills, self-directed, interpretive, and creative reading.

### Level A

1. Identifies a topic: pictures
2. Determines sequence: first or last event
3. Uses logical reasoning: synthesizes information
4. Uses logical reasoning: predicts outcomes

### Level B

1. Identifies a topic: paragraphs
2. Determines sequence: event before and after
3. Uses logical reasoning: sythesizes information
4. Uses logical reasoning: predicts outcomes
5. Reads for details

### Level C

1. Identifies a topic: paragraphs
2. Determines sequence: event before and after
3. Uses logical reasoning: determines cause-effect relationships
4. Reads for details

## Level D

1. Identifies a topic sentence
2. Determines sequence: explicit and implicit relationships
3. Uses logical reasoning: determines cause-effect relationships
4. Uses logical reasoning: reasons from a premise
5. Reads for details: interprets negative sentences
6. Reads for details: interprets sentences with right-branching
7. Reads for details: interprets sentences written in passive voice
8. Uses context clues: unfamiliar words

## Level E

1. Identifies a main idea: paragraphs
2. Determines sequence: implicit relationships
3. Uses logical reasoning: reasons syllogistically
4. Uses logical reasoning: reasons inductively
5. Reads for details: interprets sentences with one centrally embedded part
6. Reads for details: interprets negative passive sentences
7. Uses context clues: unfamiliar words
8. Determines the meaning of prefixes

## Level F

1. Identifies a main idea: two paragraphs
2. Determines sequence: orders events along a time line
3. Uses logical reasoning: applies a premise
4. Reads for details: interprets sentences with one centrally embedded part combined with right-branching
5. Uses context clues: unfamiliar words
6. Determines the meaning of suffixes

## Level G

1. Identifies a main-idea statement: extended passage
2. Determines sequential relationships between events from separate passages
3. Uses logical reasoning: reasons syllogistically
4. Uses logical reasoning: applies a premise
5. Uses context clues: obscure meaning of familiar words
6. Determines the meaning of prefixes

## Level A

*Skill.*  Identifies a topic: pictures (1)

*Objective.*  The child identifies the topic of a picture.

*Assessment.*  Assessment of this skill is best carried out on an individual basis. Remember, at this level you may expect answers to be rather gross or general. A scene depicting a child with a book might evoke such answers as "playing school," "reading," "looking at pictures," etc. Be prepared to accept diverse responses if the child can justify his answer.

*Skill.*  Determines sequence: first or last event.(2)

*Objective.*  After hearing a story, the child selects the one of four pictures that depict the first or last event in the story.

*Assessment.*  Although the objective is self-explanatory, it seems wise to emphasize a couple of points. First, for small children, the sequential relationships should be obvious. Second, the story should not be so long that it taxes the memory load for a child of this age.

*Skill.*  Uses logical reasoning: synthesizes information.(3)

*Objective.*  The child selects the one picture that depicts the two-event activity described in an oral sentence.

*Assessment.*  Repeat for the child a sentence containing two events. Such a sentence might be: "Father put on his hat and put a newspaper in his coat pocket." Show the child several pictures depicting various versions of the events in the sentence, e.g., father with a newspaper in his pocket but no hat, father with a hat but no newspaper, mother with a hat and newspaper, etc. Ask the child to select the one picture that shows what the picture says.

*Skill.*  Uses logical reasoning: predicts outcomes.(4)

*Objective.*  The child selects the one picture that depicts the outcome of a two-event activity described in an oral sentence.

*Assessment.*  For formal assessment of this skill, you might repeat for the child a sentence containing a two-step activity and ask him to predict the next step. For example, you might say, "*John put on his bathing suit and went outside to the swimming pool.* Which picture tells you what happened next?" You may then show several pictures depicting John in a bathing suit playing in the pool, John wearing his clothes while playing in the pool, John in his bathing suit riding a bicycle, etc.

A much simpler method of assessment can be carried out informally by repeating the stimulus sentence for the child and asking him to tell you what he thinks happened next. If in this situation the child gives you a divergent answer, i.e., one you had not expected, you should make sure he can justify it reasonably.

## Level B

*Skill.*   Identifies a topic: paragraphs.(1)

*Objective.*   The child identifies the topic of a written-oral selection, i.e., a written selection which the child scans silently while the teacher reads it aloud.

*Assessment.*   After you have identified an appropriate paragraph, you will want to read it to the child, even though it may be written at a low vocabulary level. You must take every precaution to prevent the decoding task from being a handicap. Also, if you assess this skill with a formal paper-and-pencil test, e.g., multiple-choice, you must insure that none of your incorrect answer choices can be construed as correct. If time permits, informal, individual, assessment which requires the child to generate and justify his answers is best.

*Skill.*   Determines sequence: event before and after.(2)

*Objective.*   After hearing a story, the child selects the one of three pictures that depicts the event occurring immediately before or after another event pictured in the story.

*Assessment.*   Assessment of this objective is obvious from the description given in the objective. It is suggested that you use pictures in order to keep the task from becoming too complicated for the reader at this level. Using the story of the *Three Little Pigs* as an example, you might show a picture of the wolf climbing down the chimney. You might then ask the child to choose from three pictures (which you have previously shown the child while telling the story) the one that shows what happened next in the story.

*Skill.*   Uses logical reasoning: synthesizes information.(3)

*Objective.*   The child selects the one picture that depicts the three-event activity described in an oral sentence.

*Assessment.*   Assessment for this skill is exactly the same as that described in skill A(3) except that here, a modification is made for a three-event activity.

*Skill.*   Uses logical reasoning: predicts outcomes.(4)

*Objective*:   The child selects the one picture that depicts the outcome of a three-event activity described in an oral sentence.

*Assessment.*   Assessment for this skill is exactly the same as that described in skill A(4) with the exception that here, a modification is made for a three-event activity.

*Skill.*   Reads for details.(5)

*Objective.*   The child answers questions about detail found in a written-oral selection containing sentences written in the active voice.

*Assessment.* This is the most elementary level of questioning for detail. The information should be presented in the active voice, i.e., the subject does the acting rather than is acted on, as is the case in the passive voice. Assessment of this skill can be carried out by using almost any type of material written at the child's listening level. The objective is to see if he can note significant details in a selection read to him. At this level, it is not necessary to question him about obscure or insignificant facts. Gross detail is sufficient. Assessment of this skill can be formal or informal. However, if you do use a paper-and-pencil-type test, you should take care to see that the student isn't confounded by the test operation.

## Level C

*Skill.* Identifies a topic: paragraphs.(1)

*Objective.* The child identifies the topic of a written selection.

*Assessment.* Assessment of this skill is exactly the same as that described in B(1) with the exception that at this level, the child must read the material himself. Materials must be carefully selected in order to ensure that the results are not confounded by the decoding task. You should also remember that your primary objective here is to see if the child can identify the topic. You are not asking him to recount or summarize the story. As is the case in skill B(1), informal individual assessment can be very effective; however, at Level C a formal paper-and-pencil test is appropriate for group administration.

*Skill.* Determines sequence: event before or after.(2)

*Objective.* After hearing a story, the child selects the one of three statements that describes the event occurring immediately before or after another event described in a statement taken from the story.

*Assessment.* Assessment of this skill is exactly the same as that described in skill B(2) with the exception that at this level, the child must work with written material. As in other skills at this level, you should minimize the decoding task. You should also be careful to select stories with clearly defined sequential relationships.

*Skill.* Uses logical reasoning: determines cause-effect relationships.(3)

*Objective.* The child selects the one statement that is a logical cause for an effect stated in a stimulus sentence.

*Assessment.* Assessment of this skill is obvious from examining the objective. However, we cannot overemphasize the importance of selecting good assessment items. At this level, cause-effect relationships should be straightforward and, as far as possible, uncluttered with insignificant detail. Also, care should be taken to select items based on experiences common to the students in your classroom. A child growing up in the city may not understand the relationship between the fact that

Mr. Jones sold his cow yesterday and the fact that he has no milk today. However, such an item might be very meaningful for some rural children.

*Skill.* Reads for details.(4)

*Objective.* The child answers questions about details found in paragraphs containing sentences written in the active voice.

*Assessment.* This skill is assessed in the same way as skill B(5) with the exception that at this level, the child is responsible for the decoding task.

## Level D

*Skill.* Identifies a topic sentence.(1)

*Objective.* The child identifies the topic sentence of a paragraph.

*Assessment.* Assessment of this skill is rather straightforward. You may begin by giving the child several paragraphs written at his reading level. His task is to underline the topic sentence in each paragraph. Care should be taken to see that each paragraph does indeed contain a topic sentence and that the topic sentences do not all fall at the same place in all paragraphs, i.e., that some are found near the beginning, some near the middle, and some near the end.

*Skill.* Determines sequence: explicit and implicit relationships.(2)

*Objective.* Given one to four sentences which have explicit and implicit sequential relationships, the child determines the order of events.

*Note.* Explicit sequential relationships are identified by specific cue words (e.g., next, finally). Implicit sequential relationships are inferred from the meaning conveyed in the passage content.

*Assessment.* To assess this skill, you must locate or develop passages that contain a sequence of events made up of both explicit and implicit relationships. Once the passage has been identified, you may use any of a number of ways of assessing the child's ability to determine sequence. Multiple-choice or short-answer questions are very appropriate. However, one of the easiest methods of assessing this skill is illustrated below.

*Directions* (for the child)

Read the selection carefully. Next, read the list of events below the passage and put them in their proper order. You may do this by marking a *1* in front of the event that occurred first, *2* in front of the event that occurred second, etc.

*Passage*

Early in December the tree farmer marks certain of his trees with white tags. These tagged trees are later cut and loaded onto large trucks. The trucks take the trees to Christmas tree lots. At the lots, each tree is measured and then priced according to its size.

*Events to be ordered sequentially*

> trees are cut
>
> tree are loaded onto trucks
>
> trees are marked
>
> trees are measured
>
> trees are taken to city
>
> trees are priced

*Skill.*   Uses logical reasoning: determines cause-effect relationships.(3)

*Objective.*   The child determines whether the relationship between two statements is cause-effect.

*Assessment.*   Assessment of this skill is straightforward and direct. Give the child a list containing several pairs of statements. Ask him to identify those pairs which have a cause-effect relationship. Such a list might contain items like the following:

1. John has brown hair.
   He is a good reader.
2. Jill forgot to turn off the faucet in the bathtub.
   The tub overflowed.
3. The boy picked up a hot pan.
   He was burned.
4. My friend lives in Alaska.
   He is in the fifth grade.

Care should be taken to make sure that the relationships which are not cause-effect are not misleading. For instance, given the item: "Jim has a new game. He has been sick," the child might construe this as a cause-effect relationship. When in doubt, ask the child.

*Skill.*   Uses logical reasoning: reasons from a premise.(4)

*Objective.*   Given two to four sentences containing one premise, the child answers a question based on that premise.

*Assessment.*   The premise in this objective merely indicates a statement of fact. However, the child should be able to derive the answer on the basis of the premise given. Examples of a format appropriate for assessing this skill are given below:

*Format I*

Roger lives several blocks from his school. He usually walks to school and takes the bus only when it rains. This morning Roger took the bus to school. What was the weather like this morning?

1. It was sunny.
2. It was rainy.
3. It was hot.
4. It was windy.

### Format II

Roger lives several blocks from his school. He usually walks to school and takes the bus only when it rains. This morning the weather was clear and sunny. How did Roger get to school?
(Let the child generate his own answer.)

*Skill.*  Reads for details: interprets negative sentences.(5)

*Objective.*  The child determines whether negative or positive statements based on information taken from a selection are true or false.

*Assessment.*  To assess this skill, you must locate or develop paragraphs containing sentences stated in the negative, or which contain negatives such as *no, not, never*. You must then develop true and false statements which reflect the inverse of positive or negative sentences given in the selection, i.e., positive statements stated in the negative and negative statements stated in the positive. An example of this follows.

### Selection

Bill enjoyed working in his father's store. He swept the floors, dusted shelves, and washed windows. He was never in the way, and he was always helpful. His father often said that he could not get along without Bill's help. Bill didn't mind hard work, and he had no better way to spend his extra time.

### True-False statements

1. Bill wasn't always helpful.
2. Bill's father was glad to have his help.
3. Bill didn't enjoy working in the store.
4. Bill was always in the way.
5. Bill wanted to spend his extra time working at the store.

*Skill.*  Reads for details: interprets sentences with right-branching.(6)

*Objective.*  The child answers questions about details found in a paragraph containing sentences with right-branching.

*Assessment.*  Right-branching in this objective refers to sentences that end with a dependent clause. To assess this skill, you must first locate or develop passages containing a number of sentences ending in dependent clauses. You may then use such techniques as true-false questions, open-ended questions, or questions requiring multiple-choice answers to assess the child's ability. The example which follows is one way of assessing this skill.

*Passage*

There was no ball game on Wednesday because of the rain. Bob and Joe were very disappointed, since they had already made plans to go to the game. However, Wednesday turned out to be a good day in spite of the weather. Bob's uncle came for a visit. He was one of the ball players who could not play because the game had been cancelled. They spent the afternoon talking about baseball.

*Questions*

1. Which statement below best completes this senetence: *The baseball game was not played*

   a) because Bob's uncle came for a visit.
   b) since the boys had made plans to go to the game.
   c) in spite of the rain.
   d) because of the weather.

2. Which statement below best completes this sentence: *Wednesday turned out to be a good day*

   a) because the boys had made plans to go to the game.
   b) in spite of the weather.
   c) because the game was cancelled.
   d) because it rained.

*Skill.*   Reads for details: interprets sentences written in passive voice.(7)

*Objective.*   The child determines whether restatements of information taken from sentences written in the passive and active voices are true or false.

*Assessment.*   To assess this skill, you will need to locate or develop paragraphs that contain sentences written in both the passive and active voices. You may then use true-false, multiple-choice, or open-ended questions to examine the child's understanding of the content. One example, using the true-false format, is given below.

*Directions*   (for the child)

Read the passage and decide whether the statements below are true or false.

*Passage*

The Jonesville team was practicing baseball. Jim wanted to be the pitcher. He threw the ball to Sam. Sam was supposed to hit the ball. Instead, he was hit by it. Sam was not hurt, but he asked for a new pitcher. Billy was chosen to be the new pitcher.

*True-False statements*

1. Sam hit the ball.

2. The ball was thrown by Jim.

3. Billy chose the new pitcher for the team.

4. The ball hit Sam.

*Skill.* Uses context clues: unfamiliar words.(8)

*Objective.* The child determines the meaning of an unfamiliar word in context by using the following devices: cause and effect, direct description, contrast.

*Assessment.* To assess this skill, you must locate or develop several sentences containing context clues which help unlock the meaning of key words. You must then substitute nonsense words for the key words so that the child uses only context clues to unlock their meaning. Nonsense words are quite appropriate here, since the child may know the meaning of any real word without having to use context clues. Below are examples of types of questions you may wish to use in assessing this skill.

> *Cause effect*
>
> Because Robert had lived for some time in Germany and always went back there for vacation, his friends thought he was *Zurlyan*. Zurlyan means _____ .
>
> *Direct description*
>
> Hanna always danced with beautiful grace and perfect balance. She was a *megdt* dancer. megdt means _____ .
>
> *Contrast*
>
> Richard usually eats his dessert last. However, it looked so good today, he decided to eat it *gesmn*. gesmn means _____ .

## Level E

*Skill.* Identifies a main idea: paragraphs.(1)

*Objective.* The child identifies a statement of a main idea of a paragraph with no topic sentence.

*Assessment.* To assess this skill, you must locate or develop paragraphs which have no topic sentences. You should then prepare several statements from which the child can choose the one that is the best expression of the main idea of the stimulus paragraph. Your distractors, i.e., incorrect statements of the main idea, should be as carefully constructed as your correct statement. You should make sure that they contain information about the paragraph expressed either too generally or too specifically to be correct. Below is one example of a format which lends itself to this type assessment.

*Directions*    (for the child)

Read the passage carefully. Then look at the statements below. Decide which statement is the best expression of the main idea for the passage.

*Passage*

Susan wanted to go to summer camp. In order to do this, she needed to earn money. She worked in her father's store every Saturday. She did odd jobs for her mother at home. She even worked as a baby-sitter for her neighbor. She put all of the money she earned in a bank. By summer, she had enough money to go to camp.

*Statements of main ideas*

Susan works in a store.

Susan goes to camp.

Susan wants to go to camp.

Susan earns money to go to camp.

*Skill.*   Determines sequence: implicit relationships.(2)

*Objective.* The child determines the order of events from scrambled statements which together make a story with implicit sequential relationships.

*Assessment.*  As previously explained, implicit relationships are those inferred from information given in the content, but not necessarily cued by particular key words such as *next, finally,* etc. To assess this skill, you must begin by locating or developing a series of statements which have implicit relationships. The statements are listed in random order, and the child's task is to order them correctly. The example below illustrates how this might be done.

*Directions*    (for the child)

In the spaces to the left of the statements below, place the numbers 1 through 7 to indicate the order in which the events would have occurred. The statement describing what happened first will be number *1*.

*Randomly ordered statements*

The water rushed down the hillside into the river below.

Helicopters and boats came in to rescue the people.

By midmorning the rain was coming down in torrents.

The streets began filling with water.

The damage left by the flood was terrible.

At dawn the sky began to grow dark.

The river overflowed into the town.

*Skill.*   Uses logical reasoning: reasons syllogistically.(3)

*Objective.* Given the premise that A renders B, B renders C, and C renders D, presented both in and out of order, the child concludes that A renders C and/or D, and/or B renders D.

*Assessment.* At first glance, this skill looks both obscure and highly sophisticated. In fact, however, the skill constitutes no more than very elementary logic, something very essential to understanding relationships. It entails both careful reading and thoughtful consideration of facts, two factors necessary for comprehension.

To assess this skill, you will probably have to develop your own materials. In doing this, you should first consider the main parts of your syllogism. For example, you might begin with something like this: (1) all dolphins are mammals; (2) all mammals are animals; (3) all animals require oxygen for life.

After determining the relationships you wish to examine, you should develop a selection incorporating the information. In doing this, you will want to include some extraneous material in order to keep your syllogism from being too obvious. Below is an example illustrating how you might test the syllogism previously given.

*Directions*   (for the child)

Read the following selection and decide whether the statements below it are true or false. Put a T beside those statements that are true and an F beside those that are false.

*Selection*

Roger and Bill went to the zoo. They saw some dolphins. They read a sign which said that dolphins are mammals. They already knew that mammals are animals. And of course, everyone knows that animals require oxygen for life.

*True-False statements*

1. all dolphins are animals.
2. all animals are mammals
3. all mammals require oxygen for life
4. all mammals are dolphins

*Skill.*   Uses logical reasoning: reasons inductively.(4).

*Objective.*   The child infers a general premise from a selection in which specific pieces of information supporting that general premise are given.

*Assessment.*   As in other skills in this category, you will probably have to develop your own assessment materials. Excellent resources for building your materials are easily found in content-area texts such as those used for science and social studies. To assess this skill you should first determine the general premise that you wish the children to reach. An example of such a premise might be that *hot air is lighter than cold air*. You should then decide which specific pieces of information you wish to use in leading the children to this conclusion. Below is one example illustrating how this skill might be tested.

*Directions*   (for the child)

Read the paragraph and answer the question on the basis of the information given.

*Selection*

Long ago, men discovered that by filling a large balloon with hot air, they could fly. They soon discovered, however, that when the air inside the balloon cooled off, the balloon began to come down.

*Question*

On the basis of the information in the paragraph, we may conclude that:

1. cool air is lighter than hot air

2. cool air and hot air weigh the same

3. hot air is lighter than cool air

4. hot air is heavier than cool air

*Alternative question*

On the basis of the information in the paragraph, what conclusions might we come to concerning the weights of hot and cool air?

*Skill.*   Reads for details: interprets sentences with one centrally embedded part.(5)

*Objective.*   The child answers questions about details found in a paragraph containing sentences with one centrally embedded part.

*Note.*   An embedded part is defined here as a phrase or clause interjected between the subject and verb in a sentence.

*Assessment.*   To assess this skill, you must locate or develop paragraphs containing sentences with centrally embedded parts. For example, *Jack, coming in out of the cold, went directly to the stove*, contains an embedded part. The words, *went directly to the stove*, break up the relationship between the subject and verb. After you have identified your stimulus selection, you must then generate questions to test the sentences with embedded parts. You may use any of a number of formats, such as true-false, multiple-choice, or open-ended questions. Below is an example illustrating how true-false questions might be used to assess this skill.

*Directions*   (for the child)

Read the selection and then mark the statements true or false according to the information given in the selection.

*Selection*

Winter came suddenly to the valley that year. Jack, coming in out of the cold, went directly to the stove. Jack, better known as Biff to his friends, rubbed his hands vigorously. He didn't like winter. Winter, with its long cold nights and short days, meant staying inside and wearing heavy clothes. Jack didn't even like to wear shoes, much less boots, coats, caps, and gloves. Yes, thought Jack sadly, it's going to be a long winter.

*True-False statements*

1. Jack went directly to the stove when he came inside.
2. Biff's friends usually referred to him as Jack.
3. Jack thought of winter as being a time of long days and short nights.
4. Jack, thinking it was going to be a long winter, was sad.

*Skill.*   Reads for details: interprets negative passive sentences.(6)

*Objective.*   The child determines whether restatements of information taken from sentences written in the negative-passive and negative-active voices are true or false.

*Assessment.*   To assess this skill, you must locate or develop paragraphs containing sentences in both the negative-passive and negative-active voices. *Bill was not asked by Bob and Alan to go fishing*, is an example of a sentence stated in the negative-passive voice. Stated in the negative-active voice, and using the same information, the sentence reads, *Bob and Alan did not ask Bill to go fishing*. After you have identified your stimulus paragraphs, you must develop statements to test comprehension of information in negative-passive and negative-active sentences. As we have mentioned previously, assessment can be carried out by using any of a number of test formats. Below is an example using true-false questions.

*Directions*   (for the child)

Read the selection and then mark the statements true or false according to the information given in the selection.

*Selection*

Bill was not asked by Bob and Alan to go fishing, because he was sick. He felt bad and went to his room. He decided to work on his fishing tackel. He picked up his tackel box, but the lid could not be opened. He wanted to ask his father for help, but his father could not be found. Bill was glad he had stayed home. He could not have used his fishing tackel if he had gone fishing.

*True-False statements*

1. Bill did not ask Bob and Alan to go fishing.
2. Bill's fishing tackel could have been used if he had gone fishing.
3. Bob and Alan asked Bill to go fishing.
4. Bill's father could not find him.
5. Bill could not open the lid on his tackel box.

*Skill.*   Uses context clues: unfamiliar words.(7)

*Objective.* The child determines the meaning of an unfamiliar word in context by using the following devices: cause and effect; contrast.

*Assessment.* Assessment of this skill may take exactly the same format as that used with skill D(8). The major differences between skills D(8) and E(7) is that direct description is dropped and the level of vocabulary is increased. At this level, you will probably want to put more emphasis on adjectives and adverbs, since they appear to be more difficult to determine by use of context clues.

*Skill.* Determines the meaning of prefixes.(8)

*Objective.* When used with a known word in context, the child determines the meaning of the prefixes: *anti-, bi-, dis-, fore-, in-, mid-, mis-, mono-, non-, post-, pre-, re-, semi-, sub-, super-, uni-.*

*Note.* The selection of prefixes for this level was arbitrary. The decision to include these particular ones was based on consultations with classroom teachers and examination of the frequency of occurrence of prefixes in instructional materials.

*Assessment.* Assessment of this skill is relatively easy and straightforward. However, care should be taken to see that assessment is based on the use of the prefix plus the root word in context. Two ways of assessing this skill are illustrated below.

> *Example I*
> *Directions* (for the child)
> Read the sentence and fill in the blank with the correct word from the list given.
>
> 1. Because the meat was _____, Bob did not have to slice it.
>    a) precut
>    b) recut
>    c) uncut
>    d) miscut
>
> 2. Bill called his new wagon a _____ because it had only two wheels.
>    a) monowheeler
>    b) biwheeler
>    c) uniwheeler
>    d) triwheeler
>
> *Example II*
> *Directions* (for the child)
> Finish each sentence by identifying the statement which best completes it.
>
> 1. Because the meat was *precut*, Bob
>    a) did not have to slice it.
>    b) did not have to cook it.
>    c) did not have to butter it.
>    d) did not have to eat it.

2. Bill called his new wagon a *biwheeler* because
   a) it had two wheels.
   b) it had five wheels.
   c) it had one wheel.
   d) it had three wheels.

## Level F

*Skill.*  Identifies a main idea: two paragraphs.(1)

*Objective.*  The child identifies a statement of a main idea of two paragraphs.

*Assessment.*  To assess this skill, you must locate or develop paragraphs which are linked together by a common main idea. Content-area materials are good sources for paragraphs of this type. You must then prepare several statements from which the child can choose the best expression of the main idea for the two-paragraph selection. For distractors, you may wish to use the main idea of the first paragraph, the main idea of the second paragraph, or several statements about some specific pieces of information in the selection. The correct answer should be broad enough to cut across both paragraphs.

*Skill.*  Determines sequence: orders events along a time line.(2)

*Objectives.*  The child places events with implicit sequential relationships in correct sequence on a time line.

*Assessment.*  To assess this skill, you must locate or develop selections which contain events with implicit sequential relationships. You must then prepare a series of randomly ordered statements which describe the events in the story. The child's task is to place the events in proper sequence on a time line. Below is an example of how this might be carried out.

### Directions  (to the child)

Read the selection and the list of events given below it. Notice that each event is identified by a letter. Write the letter of each event in one of the circles on the time line which indicates when that event occurred.

### Selection

The hikers were safe at last. When they left the cabin yesterday, no one would have believed that they would have such an experience. Fortunately for them, the rescue squad had been notified that they had not shown up at the appointed time. When they weren't discovered along the main trail, everyone knew that the hikers were lost. The first clue to their whereabouts was a piece of material torn from one of the hiker's shirts. Using this information, the rescue team was able to concentrate its efforts in that area and soon discover the boys.

Time line

    a. rescue squad is notified
    b. hikers leave main trail
    c. hikers don't show up at appointed time
    d. hikers leave home
    e. hikers are discovered by rescue team
    f. first clue is found

*Skill.* Uses logical reasoning: application of a premise.(3)

*Objective.* Given a premise, the child uses that premise to answer questions about a hypothetical situation.

*Assessment.* To assess this skill, you must locate or develop a number of premises which the child can understand. Social studies and science texts will probably be your best sources for information of this type. You must next develop hypothetical situations appropriate for testing the child's ability to apply the premises. The examples below will help to illustrate how this might be done.

    *Directions*   (to the child)

    Given the premise that water expands when it freezes, which of the following is most likely to be true?

    1. A bucket containing 12 inches of ice will have more than 12 inches of water when the ice melts.

    2. A bucket containing 12 inches of ice will have less than 12 inches of water when the ice melts.

    3. A bucket containing 12 inches of ice will have exactly 12 inches of water when the ice melts.

    4. The question cannot be answered on the basis of the premise.

    Given the premise that warm air rises, which of the following is likely to be true.

    1. In a gymnasium, the seats in row 40 will be cooler than those in row 3.

    2. In a gymnasium, the seats in row 40 will be warmer than those in row 3.

    3. In a gymnasium, the seats in row 40 and row 3 will be equally cool.

    4. The question cannot be answered on the basis of the premise.

*Skill.* Reads for details: one centrally embedded part combined with right-branching.(4)

*Objective.* The child answers questions about details found in a paragraph containing sentences with one centrally embedded part combined with right-branching.

*Note.*  In this context, right-branching is operationally defined as a dependent clause ending a sentence.

*Assessment.*  Assessment of this skill can be carried out in the same way as suggested for skills D(6) and E(5). The difference in the skill at this level is that we have combined center-embedded parts with right-branching. The example below illustrates one way by which this skill may be assessed.

### *Directions*  (for the child)

Read the selection and then mark the statements true or false according to the information given in the selection.

### *Selection*

Bill Phillips, the center for the Midvale team, walked slowly down the street, deep in thought about tomorrow's game. His team, currently the league leader, was playing Rockville for the state championship. He wondered who would win the title. Bill, although he had never seen the Rockville team play, knew that they were no pushover when it comes to basketball.

### *True-False statements*

1. Rockville was currently the league leader.
2. Bill was center for the Midvale football team.
3. The state championship is to be played tomorrow.
4. The center for the Midvale team was deep in thought as he walked down the street.

*Skill.*  Uses context clues: unfamiliar words.(5)

*Objective.*  The child determines the meaning of an unfamiliar word in context by using the device of direct description.

*Assessment.*  For an explanation of how to assess this skill and some possible formats for carrying it out, refer to skill D(8). The important thing to remember is that the child should be able to unlock the unknown words by using only context clues. At this level, you should concentrate on nouns and verbs, as well as continue to concentrate on adverbs. These seem to be the most difficult words for children to infer through use of context clues.

*Skill.*  Determines the meaning of suffixes.(6)

*Objective.*  When used with a known word in context, the child determines the meaning of the suffixes: *-able, -an, -ee, -eer, -en, -er, -ess, -fy, -hood, -ist, -itis, -less, -let, -or, -ward.*

*Note.*  The selection of suffixes for this level was arbitrary. The decision to include these particular ones was based on consulations with classroom teachers and examination of the frequency of occurrence of suffixes in instructional materials.

*Assessment.*   Assessment of this skill is much like assessment of prefixes at E(8). As in the case of prefixes, care should be taken to see that assessment is based on the use of root words plus suffix in context. The two examples below suggest possible formats for assessing this skill.

*Example I*

*Directions*   (for the child)

Read the sentence and fill in the blanks with the correct word from the list given.

1. After the _____ finished taking up the tickets, she put them in her ticket pouch.

    a) stewardess
    b) steward
    c) stewarder
    d) stewardor

*Example II*

*Directions*   (for the child)

Finish each sentence by identifying the statement which best completes it.

1. After the stewardess finished taking up the tickets

    a) she put them in her ticket pouch.
    b) he put them in his ticket pouch.
    c) they put them in their ticket pouches.
    d) it put them in its ticket pouch.

## Level G

*Skill.*   Identifies a main idea statement: extended passage.(1)

*Objective.*   The child identifies the main idea of a 1000–1200-word passage.

*Assessment.*   Assessment of this skill is obvious from the objective. The important thing to remember here is that this is the point at which the child should be able to read a short story, chapter, or extended selection and come up with the main idea. The 1000–1200 word length is entirely arbitrary and should be modified according to the content, organization, and purpose of the material.

*Skill.*   Determines sequential relationships between events from separate passages.(2)

*Objective.*   Given two brief passages about simultaneous events, the child relates the sequence of events in one passage to the sequence of events in the other passage.

*Note.*   The focus of this skill is on the ordering of sequential events through integration of information from separate passages.

*Assessment.*  To assess this skill, you must locate or create passages which parallel each other in the type of sequential relationship. Using both implicit and explicit clues found in the content, the child should be able to integrate the facts and events into a sequential strand. Formats for assessment may vary. For instance, you may ask the child to combine the events from the paragraphs into one sequential list, you may ask him to place the events on parallel time lines, or you may simply ask questions about the effect of events in one paragraph on parallel events in the other paragraph. Below is an example of one way to assess this skill.

*Selection*

All through January and February, the Continental troops reinforced their fortifications. The attack by the British army seemed imminent. Now that March and April had passed with no sign of the enemy, the troops were beginning to get restless. In addition, their supplies were exhausted. They had received no reinforcements or materials for many weeks, and they were hungry and discouraged. The patrols they had sent out in May had brought back information that the enemy was still encamped only a few miles away. "Why hadn't they attacked?" was the question in everyone's mind.

Meanwhile, the British were having problems of their own. The offensive planned for late winter had to be postponed because so many of the troops were sick with pneumonia and no reinforcements were available. The artillery which was supposed to have arrived for the spring offensive was bogged down in the mud a hundred miles to the south. Although they had successfully cut off the supplies to the Continental troops in April, they found themselves in little better condition than their enemy. The May offensive to the east had taken almost half of their troops. The remaining soldiers were poorly trained and inexperienced.

The British force knew that it was only a matter of time before they became the defenders rather than the attackers.

*Directions*    (for the child)

Below is a list of events experienced by the Continental army. In the space to the right of each event, list what was happening to the British at that same time.

1. Continental troops reinforce            1. _____
   fortifications.                            _____

2. Continental troops expect spring        2. _____
   offensive.                                 _____

3. Continental troops hungry and           3. _____
   discouraged.                               _____

4. Continental army sends out              4. _____
   patrols.                                   _____

*Skill.*  Uses logical reasoning: reasons syllogistically.(3)

*Objective.* Given the premise that A renders B, B renders C, C renders D, and D renders E, the child concludes that A renders C, D, or E; B renders D or E; and C renders E.

*Assessment.* Syllogistic reasoning at this level is merely an extension of skill E(3). As mentioned previously, you will probably have to develop your own materials for assessment. Remember, the content isn't really important here. The important thing is to see that the child has the ability to reason syllogistically. Because of this, you must be extremely careful to make sure that your assessment materials are carefully constructed. You might begin with something like this.

> Natu is a Najas.
> Najas are mountain people.
> Mountain people are poor.
> Poor people never travel.

You should then integrate this information into a logical paragraph containing sufficient extraneous material to keep the child from focusing on the syllogism. The following paragraph illustrates how the material above may be expanded into such a paragraph.

> While traveling last summer, I met a boy named Natu. Natu is a member of the Najas tribe. This tribe is one of those living in the mountains of Maru. Maru has many rich citizens, and only the poor live in the mountains. These poor often have barely enough to eat. I could only have met Natu by going to his home, since the poor of that country never travel beyond their villages.

Below are some true-false statements you might use to assess this paragraph.

1. All Najas are mountain people.
2. All Maruvians are poor.
3. Najas tribesmen never travel.
4. Natu is poor.
5. All poor people are Najas.
6. All Najas are poor.
7. None of the Maruvians ever travel.
8. All mountain people are Najas.

*Skill.* Uses logical reasoning: application of a premise.(4)

*Objective.* Given a premise and a hypothetical situation, the child uses the premise to answer a question about the situation.

*Assessment.* To assess this skill, you will probably have to develop your own materials. You should begin by listing a number of premises around which you plan to build your assessment exercises. You should then develop a number of statements about the premise, some of which describe situations exemplifying it and some of which do not. At this level, the focus of the skill is on the ability to recognize an instance of a premise or principle. The example below should help to explain this further.

*Directions*    (for the child)

Read the paragraph and answer the question on the basis of the information given in that paragraph.

*Selection*

The law of supply and demand suggests that the value of an item depends on its availability. Consequently, the less of a commodity that exists, the more valuable it is.

*Question*

Which of the statements below is an instance of the law of supply and demand.

1. Diamonds are valuable because there are a lot of them.
2. Apples will probably cost more this year because the late frost damaged most of the apple crop.
3. Imported cars will probably become more expensive because more are being shipped into the country.
4. The Teron company manufactures nine different lines of products.

*Skill.*    Uses context clues: obscure meaning of familiar words.(5)

*Objective.*    The child determines the obscure meaning of a familiar word in context by using the following devices: cause and effect, direct description, contrast.

*Assessment.*    To assess this skill, you must begin by locating familiar words with obscure meanings. Using these words, you must then develop sentences, the content of which contains context clues for determining obscure meanings of the words selected. The examples below are intended to illustrate one type of format for assessment.

*Directions*    (for the child)

Read the selection. Note that one word is underlined. From the four definitions listed below the selection, choose the one most appropriate for the underlined word as used here.

*Cause-effect*

Because the coach wanted the problem between the two players to come to a head, he called a meeting with them.

1. the top part of the human body where the eyes, ears, and mouth are
2. the top part of anything: head of a pin, a cabbage, a crane, a drum, a barrel

3. to be in the front of: the head of a line

4. crisis; conclusion

*Direct description*

Australia has many unusual animals. For instance, it is the <u>home</u> of the kangaroo.

1. the place where a person or family lives; one's own house

2. place where one can rest and be safe

3. place where a thing is especially common

4. place where people who are homeless, poor, old, sick, etc., may live.

*Contrast*

The Captain did not want to force the man to stay with the ship. Rather, he chose to place his <u>suit</u> before him and let him make his own decision about the matter.

1. set of clothes, armor, etc. A man's suit consists of a coat, trousers, and sometimes a vest.

2. case in law court

3. make suitable; make fit

4. request; asking

*Skill.*  Determines the meaning of prefixes.(6)

*Objective.*  When used with a known word in context, the child determines the meaning of the prefixes: *ante-, counter-, de-, en-, inter-, intra-, mal-, trans-.*

*Assessment.*  For assessment of this skill, see skill E(8). The assessment exercises are the same, only the prefixes change.

# 10 / Self-directed, interpretive, and creative reading

## Introduction

Up to this point, we have been discussing skills which, for the most part, center on a convergent type of thinking. That is to say, in word attack, study skills, and comprehension, we have been proceeding on the assumption that there are certain behaviors which successful readers must exhibit and that these behaviors are somewhat similar for all children. This does not mean that all children go through the same steps or sequences in arriving at particular levels of proficiency in individual skills; however, it does suggest that the final behaviors are somewhat similar. For example, when you ask a child to produce the sound of a specific vowel within the context of a specific word, there is a correct answer; his answer can be correct or incorrect on the basis of an objective criterion. Similarly, when we ask the child to find the intersection of specific lines of latitude and longitude, or when we ask him to state the main idea of a paragraph, there are acceptable and unacceptable answers which may be objectively determined. All children are expected to come up with the same or very similar answers.

This convergence of thinking does not apply in the areas of self-directed, interpretive, and creative reading. Rather, divergent thinking is more likely to occur, especially in the areas of interpretive and creative reading. When we ask children to interpret information and respond creatively in various situations, we are primarily interested in observing the processes rather than the outcomes. Divergent thinking is not only to be expected, it is to be encouraged. Granted, there are areas of convergence within divergent processes as, for instance, in the case of distinguishing propaganda from factually supported information. However, once the child recognizes that certain information is fact or propaganda, he may interpret that information in any of a number of different ways. Whereas you may expect all of your students to judge whether certain information is fact or exaggeration on the basis of specific criteria, you cannot expect them all to come up with the same interpretation.

In addition to the fact that self-directed, interpretive, and creative reading emphasize, for the most part, divergent rather than convergent thinking, there are other reasons for grouping these three areas together. Some of these reasons are as follows:

1. In self-directed, interpretive, and creative reading, the term *skill* takes on a somewhat different meaning. Its usual meaning is expanded to include descriptive attributes of a successful reader. Furthermore, skills in this area are at times somewhat indicative of a combination of motivation and ability. For example, although we can teach the child the skills to work independently, it does not necessarily follow that he will do so. Or to further illustrate, although we cannot teach the child to enjoy reading, we can establish situations which provide maximum positive reinforcement. In both of these instances, we hope that positive reinforcement will generate positive results. In these and similar instances, assessment takes the form of observing whether the child manifests the desired attributes, thus reflecting the underlying skills.

2. In the areas of self-directed, interpretive, and creative reading, assessment must be made almost entirely on the basis of individual performance. Assessment takes on a broader meaning. The basis for judgment is no longer rightness and wrongness; rather, it is appropriateness. Given the child's total dimension, the situation, and the circumstances, is his behavior appropriate? If you interpret this to mean that the teacher must make a lot of subjective decisions, you're right. But on the other hand, who is better qualified to make these decisions than a professionally trained educator?

3. Assessment in self-directed, interpretive, and creative reading must be based on classroom observation over an extended period of time in a variety of situations. Although contrived situations for purposes of assessment may be developed in some instances, you will generally get a more realistic measure of the child's performance by observing him in real-life situations. Does he read with expression when reading aloud in a group or class situations? Does he rely on the dictionary for help with spelling in project work and homework written assignments? Do you have to pressure him into participating in classroom dramatics and choral reading? Questions such as these are not answered on the basis of one day's performance.

4. In self-directed, interpretive, and creative reading, differences in levels of sophistication may be a matter of personal growth and maturation rather than specific skill development. Consequently, each child's performance should be judged in relation to that of his peer group. Even though a child has mastered the prerequisite decoding skills to read the words in a paragraph, and even though he may be able to respond to questions literal in nature, he may not have matured to the

level of handling abstract thinking. In some cases, further development must wait for further maturation. Although this is true to some extent in all areas of skill development, it is especially true in the areas discussed in this chapter.

5. The relationship of self-directed, interpretive, and creative reading to word attack, study skills, and comprehension is complementary rather than parallel. It would be inappropriate to expect a child to interpret material he cannot decode. Similarly, we cannot expect him to react creatively to material he cannot comprehend. Although it is true that at the lowest levels some of the skills in self-directed, interpretive, and creative reading are only tangentially related to decoding, in most instances this is not the case. Generally speaking, the child will have to have some level of proficiency in word attack, study skills, and comprehension before he can successfully perform in self-directed, interpretive, and creative reading.

As in the case of the other skill areas, the self-directed, interpretive, and creative reading skills included here have consensual, historical, and limited empirical support. This skills list, actually a revision and extension of several earlier lists, represents input from educators, classrooms teachers, and field-test results. However, determining the appropriateness of specific skills for specific situations must, in the final analysis, rest with the individual teacher. It is the classroom teacher who must decide what is appropriate not only for her class, but also for each child. To try to proceed otherwise not only frustrates the teacher, but also does great injustice to the child.

## Self-directed Reading

As the name implies, the skills in the area of self-directed reading are directed toward those activities in which the child takes the initiative. In this area the child must move beyond the level of application. For instance, he may be taught by skill A(1) to care for books properly, but whether or not he does this depends on his own initiative. He may be taught the skills associated with fluency in oral reading, as in C(1), but whether or not he practices them without specific direction to do so depends entirely on him.

Because self-directed reading emphasizes the application rather than the acquisition of skills, assessment in this area becomes largely a matter of observation and teacher judgment. The fact that the child does or does not use certain skills should cause you to modify your instruction accordingly. Classroom performance which doesn't reflect these skills may suggest to you that he either doesn't have them or that he isn't properly motivated to use them.

Although the skills within self-directed reading are not arranged sequentially, the levels of skill introduction are similar in difficulty to those in word attack, study skills, and comprehension. On the other hand, because these skills are accumulative, open-ended, and cyclic in nature, movement from level to level is more a matter of emphasis than of mastery. Once you have introduced the child to a skill at a particular level, you should continue to monitor, reinforce, and refine it through all subsequent levels. For example, once the child has been introduced to skills at levels A and B and has shown a satisfactory level of performance for his grade level, he is ready for skills at level C. While you will now give special emphasis to skills at level C, you will continue to observe his performance in skills at levels A and B to see that regression doesn't set in. From time to time you may become aware of the fact that a particular child cannot apply skills introduced at a lower level to materials used at his present level of instruction. Observing this, you will want to reteach the skill at a higher level of sophistication.

In examining the skills list, you will immediately notice that the skill levels run only through level E. This does not mean that the teaching of skills should stop here; it simply means that the skills listed at level E are to receive major focus at higher levels, i.e., throughout the elementary grades. You will, of course, modify your expectations about acceptable levels of performance and apply them to more sophisticated materials. However, the skills will be essentially the same.

Let us emphasize again that the skills list presented here is offered only as a prototype. You may wish to add to this list or subdivide some of the skills within it. On the other hand, you may find that some of the skills listed are inappropriate for your situation. You alone must determine which ones are appropriate for your unique set of circumstances.

## Interpretive Reading

Interpretive reading is sometimes considered as an aspect of comprehension. Indeed, there are good arguments for such an approach. Here, however, it has been separated mainly for purposes of organization and assessment rather than for theoretical considerations. As mentioned earlier, interpretive reading is likely to be characterized by divergent rather than convergent thinking. Consequently, it seems more legitimate to assess it through observation and daily class performance than through contrived performance tasks. Because such factors as personality traits, character traits, and background experience vary widely among children, assessment should be modified to take these things into consideration.

It should also be pointed out that interpretive reading involves such factors as intelligence, maturity, and socioeconomic background. These factors become especially important when we ask the child to go beyond the literal level of comprehension. For example, character traits which appear admirable to one level of society may appear less admirable to another. That which is humorous to a secure child may be treatening to a less secure one. The abstract thinking involved in making judgments and determining motives may be stimulating to one child, whereas another child in the same grade may find it frustrating. To fail to recognize the unique needs and abilities of each child is tragic; to attempt to push children into the same mold for instruction and assessment is unforgivable.

As in the case of self-directed reading, interpretive reading skills are accumulative, open-ended, and cyclic in nature. The sequential arrangement by level denotes to some extent levels of difficulty; however, it primarily indicates emphasis. By concentrating on specific skills at specific levels, you may systematically move the child through the skills in interpretive reading. By continuously monitoring all previous skills, you have a systematic way of maintaining an awareness of his level of performance (strengths and weaknesses).

Again, in interpretive reading, as in self-directed reading, level E skills are to be emphasized at the upper levels of elementary school. Indeed, several of the skills are quite appropriate for junior high school. The content will become more sophisticated and the expectation should be modified, but the skills remain essentially the same. To cease emphasizing them in the early elementary grades would be tragic, indeed.

## Creative Reading

The creative-reading skills are probably the most neglected skills in reading. Usually, little or no systematic effort is made to develop this aspect of reading. And yet, to neglect these skills is to neglect one important aspect of the total child. Through self-expression and dramatization, the child is able to find outlets for his feelings and emotions which are both creative and productive. Further, he learns to appreciate the self-expression and creativity of others.

Granted, the skills in creative reading are noticeably different from what we usually conceive of as reading skills. The fact that they're different doesn't necessarily mean that they're less important. For instance, the skills in the other areas generally relate to decoding, understanding, and interpreting the creative efforts of others, whereas in creative reading the child should have the opportunity to be creative himself. However, too often we take the creativeness out of creativity. When we ask a child to interpret a passage or story, the nature of our questions often defines the dimensions of his answers. From the time of the child's first experience with us, we continue to influence him by our particular set of expectations. At times we even go so far as to tell him to be creative and then chastize him because his creativity doesn't fit into our expectations!

In creative reading the child must be free to express his own individuality. There are, of course, ways in which we can aid him with the techniques, but to prescribe exactly how the task must be done detracts from the child's expression of creativity. For example, we may explain to the child the rhythm, punctuation, rhyme scheme, etc., of a piece of poetry or prose. However, once he understands these things, he should be free to incorporate his expression of that poem or piece of prose according to his own perception and interpretation. To take another example, we can describe a character in a play and explain his character traits, but the child should be free to express his interpretation of that character. One child may present the villain as a man of violent passion, while another may find him cold and aloof. This difference arises because of the impressions children bring to the situation. To attempt to prescribe conformity is to destroy creativity.

Besides aiding the child in his ability to express himself through reading, the creative-reading skills help him to be a well-rounded individual. By learning to express the feelings of others, shy and withdrawn children can learn to better express their own feelings. Participation in choral readings, dramatics, and play therapy can help the child to gain self-confidence and self-respect. Above all other things, it can give him a chance to succeed, and every child deserves that.

## Self-directed, Interpretive, and Creative Reading Skills

The skills presented in the following pages are suggested as prototype lists. You may wish to modify the lists to suit your own situation. No matter what list you use, we recommend that you use one which the other teachers in your school will find acceptable. By having consensual agreement among teachers, you can systematically move the child through the various skills and levels with maximum benefit to him and minimum reorganization for you.

The suggestions for monitoring (listed below each skill) suggest those attributes and behaviors to which you should give attention. Remember that before a child can exhibit a behavior, he must be given an opportunity to do so. For the most part, these opportunities will develop through daily classroom activities. However, if such opportunities do not occur in your program in its present structure, you may wish to modify your program and instruction to include them.

### Assessment of self-directed, interpretive, and creative reading

Although skills in self-directed, interpretive, and creative reading are not assessed by formal paper-and-pencil or performance tests, they are no less important than those skills which are so tested. Assessment in these areas should be both regular and systematic. An unorganized, hit-or-miss type of classroom observation approach is little better than none at all. It is important that you be aware of not only the specific behaviors indicating the presence or absence of particular skills, but also each child's proficiency in each skill. Without some sort of systematic, organized approach, this is impossible. And if you are unaware of the child's needs, you will not be able to modify your instruction to meet them.

There are several ways in which you might organize your program of observation and assessment. You will, of course, want to develop one which fits your particular situation. However, you may wish to consider the following example as one type of approach.

On a 6″ × 8″ index card, list the skills from an area by level. Beside each skill, put four or five blanks, depending on the number of times you wish to monitor that skill during the year. Next, determine the marking scale you wish to use for determining your observations. You may wish to use one similar to that listed below.

*1 = never.*   This means that you observe that the child never exhibits the behaviors associated with a particular skill. This can mean that he doesn't possess the skill or skill prerequisites. It can also mean that he simply hasn't been motivated to use it.

*2 = seldom.*   Even though the child seldom exhibits behaviors which indicate that he has a skill, we may assume that if he uses it at all, he has the skill prerequisites. In this case, you will want to modify your instruction to give him more opportunities and motivation for using the skill.

*3 = occasionally.*   The fact that the child uses a skill only occasionally usually suggests that he has the skill prerequisites but lacks opportunity or motivation to put them to use. A rating of 3 may reflect more about the method of instruction and the types of material used than about the child.

*4 = rather frequently.*   Rather frequent usage of a skill indicates that the child has incorporated it into his learning sequence.

*5 = very frequently.*   Very frequently is a relative term dependent to a large extent on the skill. Frequent usage of one skill may mean daily usage, whereas for another skill it may mean that the skill is used only a couple of times a week. In either case, "very frequently" usually means that the child doesn't need further help with that particular skill at that particular level.

*Note.*   This rating scale must be altered to something like: (1) very poor, (2) poor, (3) fair, (4) good, (5) very good in order to apply to creative reading skills.

Your monitoring card may look something like that shown in Fig. 10.1. When you monitor a child in a particular skill, you record the date and score on his skill card, as shown in Fig. 10.1. By having such a record, you are always aware of the skills the child can handle satisfactorily and is using regularly. When you observe that a child is not using a skill, you may check to see if he has the prerequisites. You may also wish to reanalyse your instruction and materials to see if he has had opportunities to use it. This system is both a handy aid for you to keep up with the pupil's skill levels and a way to help you organize your instruction in a systematic manner. Whether you choose to develop a monitoring system similar to the one discussed here or one entirely different, an organized and systematic approach to observation is essential.

Name: *Mary Smith*   Grade: *2*   Skill area *Interpretive Reading*

| | | | | | |
|---|---|---|---|---|---|
| A.1 | Reacts to pictures | A.1 | 9/6 (5) | 12/6 (5) | |
| A.2 | Story interest | A.2 | 9/8 (4) | 12/6 (5) | |
| A.3 | Mood of poems | A.3 | 9/15 (3) | 11/12 (4) | |
| B.1 | Sees humor | B.1 | 9/15 (3) | 11/15 (4) | |
| B.2 | Reads with expression | B.2 | 9/15 (2) | 10/30 (3) | |
| B.3 | Empathizes | B.3 | 9/12 (3) | 11/6 (4) | |
| C.1 | Character traits | C.1 | 9/15 (1) | 10/22 (2) | |
| C.2 | Story plots | C.2 | 9/12 (3) | 11/12 (4) | |
| D.1 | Motives of characters | D.1 | 9/12 (3) | 11/17 (4) | |
| D.2 | Story backgrounds | D.2 | 9/15 (2) | 1/15 (3) | |
| etc. | | | | | |

*Fig. 10.1   A sample monitoring card.*

## Self-directed reading skills

*Level A*

*Skill 1.*   Cares for books properly. Observe whether the child:

1. carries books properly
2. turns pages carefully
3. keeps books clean

*Skill 2.*   Applies knowledge of sequence within book. Observe whether the child:

1. holds book right side up
2. turns pages from front of book to back
3. looks at left-hand page before right-hand page

*Skill 3.*   Shows initiative in selecting picture books. Observe whether the child:

1. selects a book of interest to him
2. takes time to select carefully
3. considers several books before making his selection
4. asks for guidance when needed

*Level B*

*Skill 1.* Begins to apply independent word-study skills. Observe whether the child:

1. sounds out unfamiliar words as he reads
2. uses context to unlock unfamiliar words

*Skill 2.* Begins to do recreational reading. Observe whether the child:

1. selects reading as a free-time activity
2. engages voluntarily in recreational reading

*Skill 3.* Begins to select suitable reading materials independently. Observe whether the child:

1. selects material suitable to his ability
2. selects reading material with only occasional guidance from an adult
3. looks at several books before making his selection

*Level C*

*Skill 1.* Finds answers to questions independently. Observe whether the child:

1. finds answers to questions posed by others
2. finds answers to questions posed by himself
3. acts independently in his search for answers

*Skill 2.* Locates sources of information independently. Observe whether the child:

1. finds encyclopedia, dictionary, atlas, etc.
2. finds reference books independently
3. locates varied sources of information independently

*Skill 3.* Develops increasing oral fluency. Observe whether the child:

1. reads orally in a fluent and smooth manner
2. reads a 100-word selection at his independent reading level orally with less than five self-corrected errors

*Level D*

*Skill 1.* Develops varied purposes for selecting material. Observe whether the child:

1. reads for recreation from various fiction categories such as fantasy, mystery, family life, etc.
2. reads books from various nonfiction categories such as biography, sports, science, history, etc., for enjoyment
3. selects books for information related to projects he is doing

*Skill 2.* Begins to do independent research assignments. Observe whether the child:

1. completes research assignments
2. does research independently
3. seeks guidance when necessary

*Skill 3.* Applies reading skills to subject-matter areas. Observe whether the child:

1. reads for main ideas in all subject areas
2. grasps the organization of what is read in a variety of materials
3. applies word-attack skills in learning vocabulary for each subject area

*Level E*

*Skill 1.* Applies word study skills in conducting independent research. Observe whether the child:

1. collects research independently
2. collects information in a form usable for later reference
3. uses bibliography as guide to materials
4. makes own list of sources in research work

*Skill 2.* Enjoys reading and reads widely. Observe whether the child:

1. shows interest in building a private library
2. usually has a book which he is currently reading for enjoyment
3. reads fiction books from various categories for enjoyment
4. reads nonfiction books from various categories for enjoyment
5. cherishes and rereads favorite books and stories
6. reads to learn how to do something

*Skill 3.* Keeps a brief record of his library book reading. Observe to see whether the child records books read without being prodded to do so.

*Skill 4.* Enjoys sharing his reading experiences with others. Observe whether the child:

1. initiates conversations about books he has read
2. voluntarily gives oral book reports to a group
3. discusses at home books that he is reading

**Interpretive-reading skills**

*Level A*

*Skill 1.* Reacts to pictures and relates to own experience. Observe whether the child:

1. talks about pictures during discussion
2. recalls events similar to those pictured
3. expresses himself well verbally
4. understands ordinary concepts
5. demonstrates understanding of pictures through drawings, story telling, pantomimes, or by answering questions

*Skill 2.* Shows interest in stories read. Observe whether the child:

1. listens attentively to stories
2. reacts appropriately to story (evidenced by facial expressions and comments)
3. requests rereading of favorite stories
4. voluntarily draws pictures of characters and events from stories he likes
5. spontaneously suggests projects related to a story

*Skill 3.* Begins to react to and enjoy mood of poems and stories. Observe whether the child:

1. reacts to mood of literature (e.g., the child covers face when hearing a scary episode in a Halloween story)
2. demonstrates understanding of mood through creative dramatics
3. reflects enjoyment by repeating phrases, words, and rhythms from poems and stories heard
4. requests retelling of stories and poems he has enjoyed

*Level B*

*Skill 1.* Sees humor in situations. Observe whether the child:

1. enjoys humorous stories and poems read to him (as indicated by facial expressions, laughter, comments)
2. enjoys humor in poems and stories read independently (as indicated by expressions, laughter, comments)
3. selects humorous incidents in stories and draws pictures about them
4. sees humor in situations (indicated as he shares amusing anecdotes with others)
5. creates amusing stories or poems alone or cooperatively with a group

*Skill 2.* Reads orally with expression. Observe whether the child:

1. reads orally in meaningful phrases
2. drops his voice at the end of a sentence
3. indicates questions by his tone of voice
4. reads exclamatory remarks with excitement and emphasis

*Skill 3.* Empathizes with characters. Observe whether the child:

1. tells how he thinks specific characters felt about events in the story
2. gives possible reasons for the characters' behavior in particular situations
3. draws parallels between characters in stories and people in real life
4. relates to characters by dramatizing the character's role

### Level C

*Skill 1.* Identifies character traits. Observe whether the child:

1. uses clues given in a story to create a picture of a character
2. uses information given to demonstrate character traits in dramatizations
3. draws a parallel between traits in storybook people and real people

*Skill 2.* Begins to make judgments about story plots. Observe whether the child:

1. judges the sequence of a story as logical
2. judges whether the ending of the story is reasonable
3. judges whether a story is truth or fiction

### Level D

*Skill 1.* Recognizes reactions and motives of characters. Observe whether the child:

1. gives reasons for a character's behavior
2. shows originality through dramatization in his interpretation of a character's feelings and behavior
3. communicates clearly a character's feelings about events
4. recognizes a character's reactions by relating his own reactions to similar circumstances

*Skill 2.* Relates to stories set in backgrounds different from his own. Observe whether the child:

1. constructs settings based on clues given in a story
2. expands verbally on ideas given in the story about time, place, and characters
3. distinguishes between ideas common to his experience and those unfamiliar to him
4. compares the way people live in different cultural settings

### Level E

*Skill 1.* Relates isolated incidents to the central idea of a story. Observe whether the child:

1. identifies the characteristics of an incident which make it relevant to the central idea of a story

2. relates preceding and subsequent events in the story

3. cites statements in the story which serve as bases for his judgment of what incidents are most important

4. defends his ideas about the story by relating them to the development and conclusion of the story

*Skill 2.* Understands character roles. Observe whether the child:

1. identifies attributes of characters and relates these traits to the roles played in the story

2. tells the importance of a character to the story

3. tells how the character's actions influenced the outcome of the story

4. interprets character roles through dramatizations

*Skill 3.* Forms and reacts to sensory images. Observe whether the child:

1. gives detailed descriptions of suggested sights, smells, etc.

2. compares descriptions of sights, smells, etc., with familiar sensations, objects and experiences

3. conveys his images of a story through art, dramatics, writing and discussion activities

*Skill 4.* Identifies and reacts to tone and mood. Observe whether the child:

1. discerns tone and mood of written language

2. explains how the tone and mood are created through the use of carefully selected words and phrases

3. recognizes the author's intent from the tone and mood of the story

4. interprets creatively the tone and mood of a selection

*Skill 5.* Recognizes and analyzes subtle emotional reactions and motives of characters. Observe whether the child:

1. portrays his interpretations of a character's feelings through dramatizations

2. communicates clearly his understanding of a character's motives for behaving in a certain way

*Skill 6.* Interprets and appreciates types of language (figurative, idiomatic, and picturesque dialectical). Observe whether the child:

1. appreciates various types of language (e.g., dialectical, idiomatic, or figurative)

2. recognizes figurative language and understands its implied meaning

3. explains the relationship between an expression used and the object or idea being described

*Skill 7.*   Senses subtle humor and pathos. Observe whether the child:

1. describes his emotional reactions to characters and situations in stories read
2. identifies the qualities in characters and incidents which made them humorous or aroused feelings of sympathy
3. explains how the emotive qualities of the characters and incidents contributed to the total meaning of the story

*Skill 8.*   Begins to identify elements of style. Observe whether the child:

1. recognizes that an author writes from a particular point of view
2. recognizes that an author's style depends on his choice of words and way of using them

*Skill 9.*   Begins to identify the author's purpose in writing. Observe whether the child:

1. recognizes that authors have different purposes for writing
2. identifies the author's purpose in a piece of writing

*Skill 10.*   Begins to evaluate and react to ideas in light of the author's purpose. Observe whether the child:

1. examines facts and ideas in evaluating an author's presentation
2. uses the time and place of the story as one way to help him identify the author's purpose
3. evaluates the total selection in light of the purpose for which it was written

**Creative reading skills**

*Level A*

*Skill 1.*   Participates in dramatizations based on stories heard. Observe the child's ability to:

1. dramatize his understanding of how others think and feel
2. use voice effectively in expressing his conception of storybook characters
3. be his unique self in creative dramatic play
4. evaluate a dramatization for ways it can be improved

*Skill 2.*   Reflects mood in use of voice in retelling stories and rhymes. Observe the child's ability to:

1. change pitch and tone of voice in characterizations
2. vary voice in retelling stories
3. reflect mood of a story in his voice as he tells a story or rhyme

*Level B*

*Skill 1.* Enjoys rhythm in words of poems and stories. Observe the child's ability to:

1. tap or clap the rhythm of words in poems or stories
2. recite poems or riddles, using rhythm as he does so
3. respond spontaneously to rhythm where encountered

*Skill 2.* Interprets ideas and stories through discussions, dramatizations, drawings, etc. Observe the child's ability to:

1. make inferences about characters' feelings and events which preceded those in the story
2. make predictions about possible story endings and consequences following the ending
3. draw conclusions about why certain events happened and how they could have been different
4. relate the story situations to similar real-life experiences

*Skill 3.* Participates in group problem-solving activities based on reading. Observe the child's ability to:

1. contribute ideas to group planning sessions
2. agree to take part in an activity even when it is not his first choice
3. cooperate in making group decisions
4. complete well his portion of the work
5. help others who need it

*Skill 4.* Participates in development of adaptations of stories read. Observe the child's ability to:

1. contribute to a class-written adaptation of a story
2. think in new ways about known relationships
3. be an independent thinker

*Level C*

*Skill 1.* Uses voice intonation creatively in oral reading. Observe the child's ability to:

1. use voice creatively in oral reading
2. vary pitch, inflection, and stress of voice effectively as he reads aloud
3. project his own interpretations of the story through his voice intonation

*Skill 2.* Interprets and acts out stories read. Observe the child's ability to:

1. freely contribute his ideas about a story to class discussion
2. express himself well verbally in acting out a play
3. engage in independent thinking as he interprets stories and characters

*Level D*

*Skill 1.* Creates own plays based on stories read. Observe the child's ability to:

1. write a play that tells a story
2. write a play that is understandable to an audience
3. be creative in giving his interpretations about a character or situation

*Skill 2.* Projects to new situations knowledge of character traits and situations encountered in reading. Observe the child's ability to:

1. understand a story character
2. relate to situations encountered in stories
3. project knowledge of characters to new situations
4. project knowledge of situations from stories to new settings

*Level E*

*Skill 1.* Participates in and enjoys choral reading activities. Observe the child's ability to:

1. enunciate words clearly in choral reading
2. breathe properly while participating in choral reading
3. maintain good tone quality of voice in choral reading

*Skill 2.* Effectively evokes mood and emotional impact in retelling stories read. Observe the child's ability to:

1. be enthusiastic in telling a story
2. tell a story in his own words
3. use facial expressions and gestures to indicate character's feelings
4. vary the timing of words to emphasize words or phrases in the story

*Skill 3.* Expresses in artistic media ideas gained from reading. Observe the child's ability to:

1. experiment, using different artistic media
2. express ideas in art work
3. spontaneously engage in uses of artistic media as means of self-expression

# 11 / Organizing learning situations for individual differences

As educators face the 1980s, they must act to correct the lip-service that has been given to *individual differences*. Today, most schools are still locked into the grade-level concept of education. This concept implies that when a child enters a grade, be it first, third, or tenth, he is expected to perform the tasks prescribed by the texts or instructional media for that grade. He will pass or fail in accordance with his mastery of the content. In some instances, the pupil may get adjusted reading instruction in a small-group setting to meet his special reading needs, but the rest of his instruction that requires reading will usually be in grade-level content materials in a large-group setting.

If you believe the maxim that *success breeds success* and *failure breeds failure*, you can see that many pupils are being forced into failure by our educational system. Certainly, any approach that would alter the present lock-step system and provide instructional alternatives that would help in meeting the unique individual needs of our students would be more humanistic than our more conventional approach that insures failure and boredom for many students. Our students deserve the best education we can give them if they are to have the diversity of skill and abilities needed to meet the society they will build.

Reading is an important means for gaining skills, knowledge, attitudes, and values, but pupils differ greatly in their ability to deal with reading tasks. In this chapter we consider the matter of individual differences in reading and ways to deal with them.

## Causes of Individual Differences

We all recognize the fact that children are different in many ways. The causes of these differences are not discrete and isolated factors that can be studied under a microscope; rather, they are enmeshed and interwoven into the life pattern of each learner. Each year of a child's life adds to his uniqueness as a learner, and this makes the teacher's job of identifying the child's special instructional needs more difficult.

## Experiences

*Out-of-school experiences.* Pupils become unique individuals largely due to the type and richness of the everyday experiences they encounter. Experiences form the basis for all our concepts. Research has indicated that a home environment that provides books, magazines, trips, excursions, good language patterns, parents who read, and other activities that require learning involvement tends to produce better readers. A child also develops his early self-concept from his home and community interactions. Experiences that build healthy egos and self-respect tend to make the complicated learning-reading process a little easier.

*School experiences.* Varied and wide educational experiences also affect the learner. The more restricted and rigid the reading or learning program, the more difficulty the learner will experience in the whole learning process. Overcrowded classes, lack of variety in materials and approaches, being forced into a lock-step approach, and many other current educational practices may tend to limit the teacher in adjusting to individual differences. Such practices affect the learner, the teacher, and the learning atmosphere in a negative manner.

The teacher brings a special type of educational experience to the learner. Each teacher's abilities and knowledge of individual pupils do much to determine the richness and variety of educational experiences her whole class faces. In considering any approach that will meet the intructional needs of individuals, a teacher must:

1. understand what she is to teach;
2. know how to teach it in many and varied ways;
3. know how to assess and evalute her effectiveness in helping children learn.
4. know how to diversify as students' understandings and learning pace spread wider and wider apart.

## Inherent differences within the student

In addition to his unique experiences, the child must cope with the biological traits and tendencies he inherits. Although it is difficult or impossible to separate biological from environmental factors, the fact remains that certain things we do in a particular way relate back to our biological heritage.

*Ability factors.* Educators and psychologists have many definitions for ability, but all recognize ability as an important factor in reading and learning. Inherited ability is important because it helps us to:

1. *organize* internally the incoming experiences we face daily;
2. *adapt* to our surroundings or external circumstances; and

3. *assimilate* and *use* our experiences to meet and cope with new situations and circumstances.

An individual's ability is determined by his biological endowments and his experiences within his environment. If reading is concerned with *bringing* our knowledge and abilities *to* printed symbols, then our ability to both cope with and use symbols and to profit from experiences are necessary. The reader cannot take meaning from the symbols if he does not first have some understanding of the content he is to read.

Ability will not cause problems in reading *unless it is ignored or taken for granted*. So long as the teacher tries to meet individual learning needs, applies reasonable methodology, and uses proper instructional materials and procedures, the pupil's overall ability to learn is unlikely to be a problem.

*Learning rate.*   Each child has his own learning rate. This rate varies in accordance with the pupil's health, interest, ability, prior knowledge of prerequisite skills, and the meaningfulness of the material he is expected to learn. In order to learn, a slower-paced pupil usually needs more concrete and varied experiences than does the child with a quicker pace. And since each student's pace fluctuates, a teacher must make frequent assessments in order to keep abreast of a pupil's present pace. There are plateaus when a teacher may feel a child is not learning, but these resting places appear to be a normal phenomenon which should be accepted.

Obviously, a pupil with limited mental ability might require a program with a slower pace, while the brighter child can move at a more rapid pace toward meeting educational goals. However, it is very difficult to assess some children, and generalizations fail to hold as you face the individual pupil. Some children, for example, are late bloomers, and as such tend to confuse the matter of learning rates. Most often, late bloomers are boys who appear to be slow learners in the first few grades, but their difficulties tend to dissipate by the end of fourth grade. The main point to be made is that it is best to make no wide generalizations about rate and to just accept the fact that differences do exist and must be considered in teaching.

*Fluctuation factors.*   A teacher cannot count on students' being consistent in their interest, readiness and motivation to learn, drive, attentiveness, and many other individual traits and qualities that affect reading. The student is simply not always ready for new learning tasks. From time to time, home distractions, personal problems, peer relationships, personal tastes and interest, and experiential requirements of the new materials may work in direct opposition to the new learning activity.

For example, consider the case of Billy, a third grader. It was apparent he was not learning and was slowly drifting away from the class with daydreaming and window-watching. A visit with his mother appeared to indicate that nothing was wrong at home. And the teacher's soul-searching produced no reason why this bright little boy was being lost. One day he left home to meet the school bus, but he did not arrive at school. He was later located by the visiting teacher and his mother. He was hiding in his closet. His mother physically carried him to the teacher, although he managed to get in a few good bites and kicks before the door closed to block his last escape route. A conference with his mother later that afternoon indicated that the home was a battle ground for two warring parents. The father was continually leaving home after long, verbal battles Billy could not escape hearing. He was simply frightened by the fact that if Daddy could leave him, Mom could do the same thing.

No significant difference in learning occurred for Billy until his grandmother moved in and promised she would always be waiting for him at home—that he would not be left alone. Billy's "dragons" were so large that he spent all his time fighting them. He had no time to waste on his books. His case was extreme, but we don't always know what particular "dragons" are affecting the interest and imagination of our students. We have to do such a good job of motivating that we make the pupils want to come with us and learn.

As a teacher, you therefore need "a bag of tricks" to help you shift gears quickly when you see that you are losing your students' interest. You need a stock of practical and concrete materials that will involve your students mentally and physically in their learning tasks. You need to be very sure that you don't ignore readiness factors or the understanding level of the individual pupil as you attempt to move forward in instruction. Taking time to build interest, to develop background experiences, to build curiosity with leading questions, and to get the child on your side may help in solving many minor learning-reading problems.

### Diagnosis—The First Step

A first step in any instructional program is to locate the specific needs that must be met in order to get started. Through an understanding of what is needed, the teacher can set up work goals for individuals, small groups, paired learners, or large groups.

### Differences among pupils

Differences among pupils are more obvious than those within a single pupil. Locating brighter and more responsive pupils or slower students is a daily task of the teacher. Her daily assignments and weekly reviews are continual reminders that Mary cannot spell and that John's oral reading is very poor. However, these are only generalizations and will not be of much help to her because they don't go to the heart of Mary's or John's problems.

If Mary is to overcome her spelling problem, her errors and error patterns must be located, and the missing skills and/or abilities must be dealt with soundly. Maybe Mary has poor visual memory or a high-frequency hearing loss that limits her spelling ability. Maybe she has not learned special family spelling patterns. Diagnostic teaching is a necessity, and both daily work and weekly reviews should be used in assessment to tell us what the students are learning and how well they are using their skills.

A first consideration for the teacher is to determine the various instructional levels with which she must cope. The instructional level is usually considered to be the highest level at which a pupil can work independently in his reading materials without frustration. You can establish your own norms, but according to two widely accepted norms, the child should be able to comprehend 75 percent of what is read and easily decode 95 percent of the words. Identifying the students' general instructional levels will help you collect materials for instruction and the class library. Two other levels of functioning to be considered are the student's independent and frustration levels. The frustration level is reached when the vocabulary load, conceptual load, and/or skill demands exceed the student's skills and understanding. The result is that the child meets frustration and failure. By contrast, the independent level is where the child can function without aid. A safe generalization is that the child's independent level is about one year below his instructional level.

As mentioned in Chapter 3, locating specific skill needs for the class is a little more difficult. Educators have yet to agree on a universal set of skills or the level at which they should be taught. Therefore, there is no test or diagnostic device that can be used to locate all of a student's specific skill needs. Nonetheless, a list of basic skills is necessary to good instruction. Daily work sheets and teacher-made survey tests of specific skill areas should be used to locate the skills the students need. Specific suggestions for doing this are given in Chapters 7, 8, and 9. After the teacher has determined through testing what skills need to be developed, she should gather teaching materials and make charts to indicate graphically the scope of her problems. She should also find ways to indicate when a skill, having been learned, can be applied in new settings.

## Differences within a single pupil

These differences are the most difficult to assess. A student is like a stone wall that has been built by several workmen. Each worker has his own way of placing stones, and the wall is a composite of all the strengths and weaknesses of the workmen who helped construct it. As each successive layer of stones is set, mortar is used to hide the gaps and cover places where the stones don't quite meet. The wall is finished; it appears to be solid enough to withstand any problem. But rains and chipmunks manage to locate the weaknesses. The wall is undermined and, depending on the stress placed on it, is weakened or falls down. So, too, the pupil has all the weaknesses of his "gaps." And the more gaps he has, the more likely it is that he will have problems when educational stress is too great.

Teacher-made assessment forms can be used to locate weaknesses, and daily observations can be used to evaluate the validity of the test results. Remember that a passing score on a work sheet may not indicate that all the difficulties involved within a learning problem have been solved. On the other hand, one or two errors is not sufficient evidence that a problem exists. But *error patterns* can indicate both a gap in learning and the causes of a problem.

### Using different kinds of assessment

Screening of the student's visual and auditory acuity and perception should be a part of any educational assessment. In the first grade, these factors should be a prerequisite to instruction. Beyond the first grade, pupils should be given periodic reviews of vision and hearing to assure the teacher that sensory disabilities are not interfering with learning.

No one way of assessing skills or instructional needs is satisfactory by itself. A combination of approaches should be employed to assure both the teacher and the learner that the diagnosis is correct. Children fluctuate daily, and their long-term responses to worksheets, reviews, and tests are a more valid form of assessment. Remember that your assessment of a specific problem is only as valid as the student's responsiveness to the form of evaluation you use on the day of testing.

*Standardized tests.*   The most commonly used survey devices are standardized tests which yield grade-placement scores. In some instances, these tests offer a type of checklist to locate skill weaknesses. Generally, standardized tests of reading measure factual comprehension and vocabulary. The major purpose of the survey is to locate achieving and nonachieving readers. The grade placement or equivalent scores such tests yield are usually considered frustration scores, because they represent the level at which the student cannot handle the material independently. Grade-placement scores are seldom valid for making decisions about the individual. Since most standardized tests do not account for measurement error, the results are suspect. Many educators are therefore reconsidering the usefulness of such devices for making any individual or teaching decision.

*Intelligence tests.*   The results of this form of standardized survey are as susceptible to error as are the results from standardized reading tests. In addition they have been shown to be inadequate with certain groups. Remember that intelligence measures are only one indicator of a child's ability to learn. Some school systems have dropped intelligence tests entirely or have limited the availability of the test results to teachers because misuse of data can sometimes cause problems for both teachers and learners.

*Informal inventories.*   These tests can be constructed to locate general levels of functioning. In some instances, *informal group inventories* are used to determine instructional levels through the overall assessment of basic reading functioning. The student is at the instructional level if he can function independently with at least 75 percent comprehension and 95 percent accuracy in decoding. An instructional level of $3^2$, for example, means that a student can function with materials that are about equal in difficulty to graded materials for the middle third grade. Yet this is an oversimplification. The graded materials used in an informal inventory usually cannot be compared directly to materials in the content areas, where the materials tend to be more difficult because of the heavy vocabulary load. Thus, the general level of functioning indicated by an informal inventory indicates only an approximate starting point for instruction.

*Specific task assessment.*   Locating a class's general skill needs is a good place to start. The teacher could put several skill worksheets together to make a general skill review, then branch out to individual assessments. In this way no child would necessarily have the same set of worksheets or assessment forms after the first test. Particular care can be taken to locate specific skill deficiencies by using assessment devices such as those suggested in Chapters 7, 8, and 9. A record of skill acquisition, growth, and further needs can then be kept for lesson planning. The record form shown in Fig. 11.1 is a record card used by the Wisconsin Design for Reading-Skill Development. To use the record, the teacher merely punches out the hole by each skill to indicate mastery.

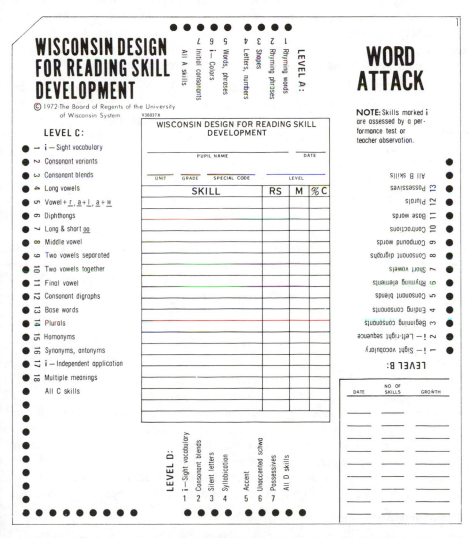

*Fig. 11.1   Skill-development record.* (Wisconsin Design for Reading Skill Development, *Madison: Wisconsin Research and Development Center for Cognitive Learning, The University of Wisconsin, 1970. Reprinted by permission.*)

Bear in mind, though, that a skill is never wholly learned at any one specific time. A child needs time to refine a skill through continuing stages until it is stored internally, ready to be used in another context next time. So before a skill can be considered mastered, the child should be able to apply it in a new setting. Too often, for example, young students can give the sounds for the letters in isolation, but cannot use these same sounds and knowledge when attacking a new word.

*Daily work.*    One of the most valid types of assessment can be made with a student's daily work. Noting errors and error patterns will lead you to a better understanding of what specific problems need to be corrected. You should be more concerned with the meaning of a student's errors than with his overall score. Pupil work samples kept in a cumulative folder will provide a continual skill assessment, as well as a time-sequence evaluation of his progress in skill development.

*Observation.*    This is the proof of the pudding and may be the best form of assessment. Observation helps prove when we have chosen wisely for the student and whether our instructional choice really fits the learner. Watching a student perform over a period of time will give you a good record of growth. But don't rely on your memory to record your observation; make objective, anecdotal comments in his folder.

Observation is an essential form of assessment when changing from one instructional method to another. But you can't always predict what type of educational change will occur with a new method. Observation is the quickest indication that a change is "negative or positive." This determination can later be tested more adequately with more objective measures. If you are changing from an analytical approach in phonics instruction to material which uses a synthetic approach, keep a close eye on the student's reaction or lack of reaction to the material. This will help insure that the material fits the needs and the learning style of the individual.

## Classroom Management

Good teaching can happen in a variety of settings, but for most of us, organization helps. In trying to focus instruction on specific needs, you will need to structure different types of learning settings. Consider the classroom as a small, structured community set up to meet the educational needs of individual members. Each member is free to pursue his own special needs and is encouraged to contribute to the whole learning atmosphere. Each student progresses at his own pace rather than being held back by slower-paced students or rushed by faster-paced students.

In setting up such an environment, you will need to understand such factors as: (1) physical setting, (2) pupil management, and (3) skill-development management.

### The physical setting

Traditional classroom settings are characterized by four or five straight rows of desks. There might be a reading circle and a library table to meet some individual needs, but there is little else in such settings to aid and encourage free movement or active involvement in the learning environment. Indeed, quite often the setting is structured to limit movement and to discourage any form of communication. Figure 11.2 depicts the traditional class setting. Note how closely it resembles a military formation.

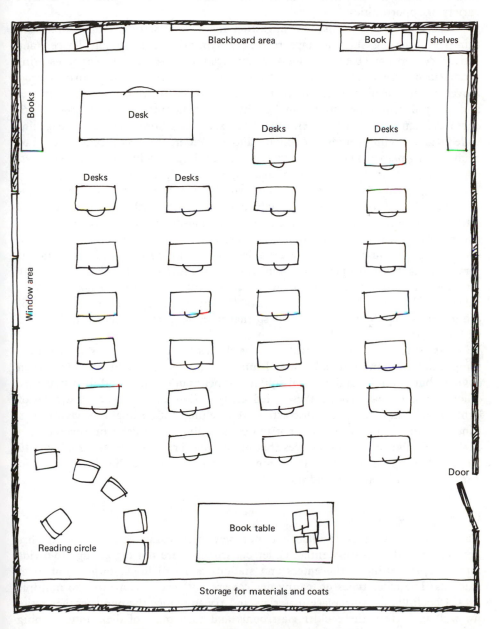

*Fig. 11.2    Traditional classroom setting.*

### Seating for involvement

Simply rearranging desks will not necessarily change teaching practices, but a freer classroom setting serves as a constant reminder that you are attempting to cope with individual needs. Class settings should offer the teacher and the learner a variety of opportunities.

Figure 11.3 represents one suggestion for a freer setting. Notice that such things as listening stations, tape recorders, typewriters, projection devices, and activity centers have been added to the more traditional setting. Tables and seating arrangements are spread out across a room, and rows are eliminated to encourage movement and involvement. A teacher does not necessarily need all of these activities and materials within her classroom, but she can aim her instruction to those experiences she can meet at any given time. For example, a library center, a magazine collection, a reading center, an activity and art center, and a skill center would be good starting places. A borrowed typewriter, places for individual work, rug samples, and reading pillows for the reading area might also help initially.

In structuring a new setting in which you can function, consider ease of movement and the ability to move quickly from one place to another. In the traditional setting, movement is usually limited to an up-and-down-the-row pattern. When two people meet in the middle of a row, there is a need for accommodation. Often, such a meeting causes friction. Being able to move easily from station to station is very important in an open classroom. Avoid congestion where all centers empty into one common area. Avoid narrow aisles and centers that are too close together. Always work to see that the students establish standards of behavior and set procedures in manipulation of materials so that a learning atmosphere is maintained within the space.

Make sure you remove hazards such as electric cords in pathways. Such simple things can lead to injured children and ruined audio-visual equipment. It may seem obvious, but place the audio-visual equipment near outlets first, and then structure other learning areas around these fixed centers. Consider windows as sources of light or irritating glare, or a distraction. A listening station might survive near a window if the outside forces are not too entertaining. Consider workspace near a chalkboard, and remove all devices that might interfere with a clear visual path to the board. Keep all shelves in the center of the room to waist height so that you can easily see over and around them.

### Centers and stations

The concept of centers of interest is not new to education, but the concept has not yet reached its full potential. Older classrooms were not big enough to divide into an open setting with centers and stations and still house large numbers of students. The older types of seating devices are not readily converted to multiple uses. Hopefully, as we replace materials and try to reduce the pupil-teacher ratio, we will restructure these older classrooms and turn more of them into learning laboratories.

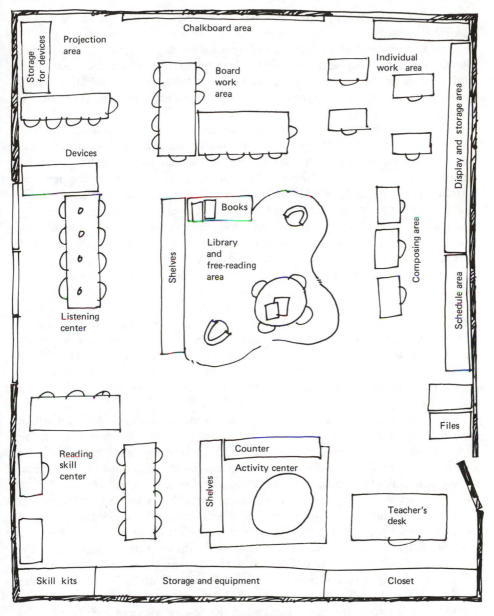

*Fig. 11.3   Possible classroom setting.*

A *library center* and an area for *free reading* are almost essential to an open class setting and differentiation of instruction. These centers help by giving the students free access to a variety of reading materials and serve as a resource for research and work-study skills. The skills we teach are valuable only if the student wants to read to gain knowledge from printed materials. A place to read close to the library area is also desirable.

Some children like to read in different positions and settings. As adults, we do not necessarily read only while sitting up straight. Getting rug samples, pillows, and comfortable chairs or rocking chairs might be equally as satisfactory as the table shown in Fig. 11.3 for the reading area. The informality might even help the young readers.

The library center should receive a continual flow of books from the larger school library in order to keep the students interested. Plan on three or four books per pupil in order to offer a wide range of books for free selection. The school librarian is a good source of help in locating interesting books for the age group within a class and in locating a variety of differing reading levels to assure weaker and stronger students a selection at their reading level.

Advanced technology has now produced the *listening station*. Multiple headphones enable a few students to listen to recorded materials without disturbing the rest of the class. A wide range of materials is available in the form of tapes and records. You can find tapes with worksheets to teach auditory discrimination; records and tapes for story telling; tape-recorded stories to follow along with a book; advanced tapes and worksheets for listening skills; and tapes for advanced work in study skills. Do not overlook the possibility of making your own tapes for a group or single child where special needs arise. The individual tape might be a real help for the dependent nonreader. The teacher could carefully program a longer period of work for this student, and by playing both sides of the tape, the child would be able to work independently without the constant need for special instruction.

A *composing center* with typewriters is also a good tool for individualized instruction. The typewriter has proved useful in many applications in the regular classroom. It is an instructional device that is well worth its cost. For work with a reluctant or nonreader, the typewriter can be used to increase his visual span and awareness of words as individual units. Children do not mind practice so much when they can type their lessons. And typing is a particular boon to the student whose handwriting is almost unreadable. The typewriter is also an excellent device for reinforcing the language-experience technique and for producing class books and newspapers.

An *activity* and *art center* gives students the opportunity to apply what they are learning. Making visual devices, exhibits, dioramas, or even whipping up a simple recipe might be a logical outcome of special skill development. One student might easily avoid following directions until he is given a model to construct or a package mix of fudge to make. Remember the reward value of having a tangible outcome you can keep or eat. Art materials, construction devices, and boxes of odds and ends should offer the child space and adventure to apply what he has learned. Activity cards stressing specific skill outcomes might be constructed by the teacher to offer a more structured experience at the center. Books of "how to" activities are an excellent means of making reading and learning meaningful.

*Science* and *content centers* provide many opportunities for children to read and use their reading skills. Such centers are a natural for teaching work-study and research skills. Science centers usually have a high degree of motivation in their favor.

A *projection center* is now a classroom reality. Many new projection devices can be used without darkening the whole room. One such machine is the super 8-mm projector with single-concept films. These films usually come in cartridges that snap easily into the small projectors and can be used by the students without darkening the room. In most instances there is no sound involved, just a visual experience. Such films are an excellent starting point for written work or storytelling.

Projectors with self-contained rear screens are also available in small or medium sizes to encourage the use of filmed materials such as filmstrips and slides in small groups or by individuals. There are several companies specializing in skill-type filmstrips to aid in word-recognition development. Content materials are also plentiful.

The overhead projector is another excellent teaching device that is now available in most schools and many individual classes. It can be used to teach or to display work. Some companies are making materials for skill teaching, and one very interesting one has been developed around map-reading skills. This device is readily adaptable to teacher-made teaching devices.

A *reading-skill center* is an essential station for focused instruction. The teacher can begin to collect old and new workbooks, tear them up, and rearrange them according to specific skills. By using plastic sheets and new instructions, consumable materials can be converted into more permanent teaching tools. Commercial kits are also available for specific areas of skill development. The teacher should gather her equipment and materials, organize them, revise them, and then use them in teaching. Ways to organize the center for more effective instruction will become evident as the materials are used. Don't start off with a format that cannot be changed. Reorganization of the skill center should include planning by both teacher and pupils so that the best way will be found to set up the center for all participants.

*Individual carrels* are a must in a freer setting. The space set aside for individual work allows the student some privacy from groups coming and going to work stations. A special quiet place to work should be a privilege. Such settings should never be used as a punishment, for their effectiveness will be thereby destroyed. If it is necessary to isolate a pupil, try to do it in such a way that no center gets a stigma as a "punishment center."

Any type of center that adds to the overall learning of the pupils and helps the teacher to meet individual needs is an acceptable one. Do not discount commercial packages in setting up a center, but do not depend entirely on them. Packaged material will not accommodate all the learning styles you will encounter. You may find it necessary to change the instructions, find more materials to strengthen one skill area, or in extreme cases you may have to totally remove a whole area of packaged materials. Creativity is the key to building good centers.

*Material arrangement and storage*

No one setting can be described that will meet the needs of every teacher. Class size, room construction, availability of materials, the nature of the learners, school rules, and your own style of teaching will determine how you use materials, arrange the class setting, and meet students' needs. Nonetheless, it is obvious that a wide range of materials is involved in an open learning setting. Whenever possible, store materials close to the place where they will be used. Moving large objects from place to place might disturb students or, worse yet, cause damage or injury. In considering the placement of a device that must be moved, the safety of students and equipment must have first priority. Furthermore, there may be school rules limiting the use of audio-visual equipment. In some instances, insurance policies may stipulate that all A-V materials be returned to a closet for safekeeping. Thus, setting up fixed centers may be more difficult, but it is not impossible. In such cases, consider tables with rollers to facilitate movement and relieve lifting.

In considering material storage, the teacher should plan for collecting, organizing, and storing pamphlets, clippings, texts, trade books, newspapers, brochures, puzzles, games, work-type exercises, puppets, felt boards, picture files, commercial materials, teacher-made materials, pupil-made materials, A-V equipment, and odds and ends. Consider the weight, height, availability, usage, movement, and closeness to the teaching center.

**Pupil management plan**

To individualize instruction, you must physically structure the class so that each student is actively involved in a worthwhile task. It is important that both you and your students know three things: what to do, how to do it, and when. As the teacher, you should direct each student to his own work station, and then see that he moves ahead in his studies to the next station at the proper time. If all this sounds like an "Excedrin headache," remember that good planning can help to make things run smoothly.

*Overall plans*

*Visual aids* help to make organization easier. As a first step, you might set up four or five centers so that students have the opportunity to do independent work. The chart in Fig. 11.4 shows five centers, with a sixth area for students' individual work spaces. Below the large chart, there is a hook for each child's name tag. At each work center, the number of hooks equals the capacity of the station. During the first few weeks, you might want to structure all the center assignments to make sure that each individual has a complete understanding of the centers and how each works.

In order to move to a different center, a student would go to the large chart and remove his name tag, refer to his lesson plans, replace his tag in the new position, and go to his new work station. In some instances, there might be a green tag to indicate a free choice—the chance to use any station where space is available. You will have to establish class rules on the use of the chart and arbitrate conflicting

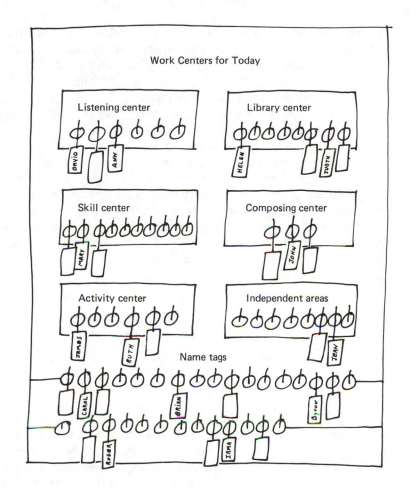

*Fig. 11.4     Classroom organization chart.*

free choices. A large chart like that on Fig. 11.4 serves as a guide for the students and a checkpoint for the teacher. Standing at the chart, you can determine the location of each student. If anyone is out of place, it is easy to see what he is doing and to redirect his activity, if necessary. Remember that Fig. 11.4 is only one suggestion. Develop your own chart to fit your own classroom and needs.

*Individual plans*

Set up your own student records and planning procedures, depending on the way you teach and the types of students you are teaching. You can store information in notebooks, card files, index folders, or a computer card to develop complete records which are easy to maintain, locate, and understand.

You may need two sets of files—a master file for yourself with assessment forms and cumulative data for long-range plans and information storage, and a student file for short-term plans and daily or weekly work schedules. Each student should maintain his own folder, keeping it in order and storing it at the end of each day. Store all folders in a central file near the large planning chart. In the cumulative file, you might keep a class information sheet indicating each student's name, age, standardized test data, general comments on interests, progress, and the nature of any reading or learning problems. Assessment sheets for the present grade and a check list of reading skills are helpful for periodic checks on a student's progress.

Each student needs to thoroughly understand his schedule during lab periods in order to minimize confusion or unnecessary movement. Perhaps he will work at two or three stations during a lab period, with an additional period for free reading or a learning game aimed at reinforcing specific skills. Having the work folders and your large plan chart together will help the students move ahead with their instruction without unnecessary movement about the room.

A student's daily plan might be as follows:

1. Listening station: Work Sheet 5b (listening for details) Tape 5b

2. Activity center card 15: (diorama—classification of animals)

3. Group activities: Teacher (introduction to diagraphs)
   (work sheets—Lab 4)
   (work sheets 28 and 29)

4. Individual work: follow-up on work sheets for Lab 4

5. Library center: free choice today

Each lesson depends on the student's ability to function independently. For Mary, a nonreader, a cassette recorder and work sheets might be provided. The lesson cassette would include step-by-step instructions for working through the materials, going to the listening center, listening again to the cassette for instructions, going to an assigned student for help with rhymes, listening to the cassette, and so on until the work period has ended.

With careful planning, you can create a variety of environments conducive to learning. Your students could work in pairs, groups, or individually to accommodate various learning needs. You will also need to consider the smoothest transition from individual to group settings or vice versa. For example, if you have gathered a new group around the listening station, you can't wait for one student to finish his work sheets or another to finish her diorama. But you can probably overcome this organizational problem by thoroughly acquainting your students with the "how and why" of what they are doing.

A large motivation factor in the learning lab is having all the children work toward a personally meaningful educational goal. The students, therefore, should help you plan their lab periods. This approach helps to eliminate potential idleness by offering the students a relatively free environment in which to learn and work.

**Management of skill development**

After you have selected a list of skills, you will need to collect instructional aids. The aids in this section may not be new to you, but the terminology has been updated to reflect current usage.

*Learning packages*

A major development for the lab classroom is the increased emphasis on packaged learning materials which aid teachers and students in individualized instruction. Ideally, a pupil moves through the package at his own pace. Although other students might also be using the same materials, each student works independently.

Many of the presently available packaged materials, however, do *not* offer: (1) carefully defined objectives; (2) reasonable and well-though-out methodology; and (3) alternative and varied learning routes for deviant learners. To avoid problems that may result from these omissions, you should carefully study commercially prepared material and perhaps evaluate its effectiveness on a few students before using it as a general teaching device.

One program, under careful study by the Learning Development Center of the University of Pittsburg, is called Individually Prescribed Instruction (IPI). This program is aimed at specific objectives and includes diagnostic devices, teaching material, and prescribed methodology in an attempt to meet the diverse individual needs within the classroom. The subject matter within the program is not limited solely to reading. At the Wisconsin Research and Development Center for Cognitive Learning (University of Wisconsin-Madison), the concept of Individually Guided Education (IGE) is being developed and carefully researched. Again, the focus is on differentiation of instruction to meet individual needs. IGE differs from IPI in a number of ways, but perhaps the most important difference is the stress placed on the productive role of the teacher in IGE. The reading component in IGE is the Wisconsin Design for Reading Skill Development.

There are also programs under development to assist teachers in preparing their own material for individualized instruction. For example, the Unipac concept, developed by the staff of IDEA Materials Center in Anaheim, California, has the teacher define and describe a single concept or skill she plans to teach. She lists specific objectives for the Unipac, structures the best learning route or routes she can plan for her students, and either collects and/or constructs the materials needed to execute her teaching plan. Part of each Unipac is a pretest and a posttest to indicate the need to learn the skill and the effectiveness of the Unipac in developing the concept. The Unipac concept is geared to the student working independently through the learning route prescribed by the teacher, but it does not necessarily exclude help from the teacher when needed.

Other types of *learning packages* are similar to the Unipac, but broader in scope. Whereas Unipac teaches one small skill or single concept, the *learning package* might contain a broader concept. You might build a Unipac around the circle, as a sphere, and its relationships to objects we use, whereas you would make a *learning package* to develop the larger concept of shapes. In the *learning package* you might include such shapes as the square, the rectangle, the diamond, and the triangle. Both the Unipac and the *learning package* aim at teaching the content in a logical, sequential order. Both also stress independent work, but the scope of the *learning package* is broader.

### Learning sequences

The skill of critically evaluating the author's intent or bias is not isolated from the skills of factual recall, inference, or main idea. Skills are developmental and tend to benefit from a sequential form of presentation. There is no universally accepted set of skills; thus, there is no standard sequence to follow to ensure that all skills are taught at the proper time.

In the area of structural analysis, it would appear that adding such endings as *ing*, *es*, *ed*, or *s* should be taught prior to suffixes such as *ful*, *tion*, or *ly*. In teaching comprehension, it would be wise to have students master concrete concepts before developing these ideas into more abstract concepts. Similarly, in constructing an instructional program, the sequence of skill development needs to be considered. Scope-and-sequence charts from several types of reading materials may help you to establish the best sequence of skill development to use in your classroom or school.

Skills are not isolated; they vary and covary. The *tion* and the *ity* suffixes do not simply exist on their own, waiting to be developed independently. Each must be added to a word, and each is made up of specific letters in a set order. Both have sound patterns that are exact, although not necessarily the sum of all the letter sounds that make up the pattern. Each suffix has a specific meaning when added to a base word, and each can change the use of the base word within the sentence pattern. Each skill, therefore, needs to be developed in varying contexts so that the use, sound, and meaning can be applied in a new setting. Although one of these might not lead to an understanding of the other, the concept of using suffixes might strengthen the student's learning of each skill at the time it is introduced by the instructor. The point here is that you must have some reasonable sequence in mind as you work toward focused reading instruction.

### Grids and patterns

Some type of chart is helpful for indicating specific skills and their level of introduction. The computer card (see Fig. 11.1) for the Wisconsin Design is a type of skill-development grid that can be incorporated into a folder as a cumulative record which shows growth and development in the word-attack skill areas. It can show which skills need to be further developed. Another skill development gird that could be dittoed and expanded is suggested in Table 11.1. Such a pattern can be developed for any level or skill area. The grid or pattern concept represents a method of focusing on what needs to be taught, as well as a way to visualize the scope of the instructional program. The grid or pattern can give you a comprehensive overview of what has been done and what still needs to be accomplished.

**Table 11.1 Individual skill grid**

Name: _____

## Identifying data

### Letter-sound associations

**Consonants (single)**

| | | |
|---|---|---|
| b ___ | k ___ | v ___ |
| c ___ (hard) | l ___ | w ___ |
| c ___ (soft) | m ___ | x ___ |
| d ___ | n ___ | y ___ |
| f ___ | p ___ | z ___ |
| g ___ (hard) | q ___ | |
| g ___ (soft) | r ___ | |
| h ___ | s ___ | |
| j ___ | t ___ | |

**Consonant digraphs**

| | |
|---|---|
| ch ___ | th ___ (thumb) |
| sh ___ | th ___ (the) |
| wh ___ | wr ___ |
| ph ___ | wn ___ |
| kn ___ | ck ___ |

**Consonant blends**

| | | |
|---|---|---|
| sl ___ | cr ___ | sk ___ |
| pl ___ | fr ___ | st ___ |
| bl ___ | tr ___ | sc ___ |
| fl ___ | gr ___ | sm ___ |
| cl ___ | pr ___ | sn ___ |
| gl ___ | dr ___ | sp ___ |
| | br ___ | sw ___ |

### Structural elements

**Inflected endings**

| | | |
|---|---|---|
| s ___ | es ___ | 's ___ |
| ed ___ | er ___ | s' ___ |
| ing ___ | est ___ | |

**Derived endings**

| | |
|---|---|
| er ___ | en ___ |

**Prefixes**

| | | |
|---|---|---|
| ex ___ | im ___ | com ___ |
| de ___ | en ___ | dis ___ |
| ab ___ | be ___ | sub ___ |
| ad ___ | a ___ | pre ___ |
| re ___ | un ___ | pro ___ |
| in ___ | | |

**Suffixes**

| | | |
|---|---|---|
| able ___ | ant ___ | al ___ |
| ance ___ | ary ___ | en ___ |
| hood ___ | ful ___ | ly ___ |
| less ___ | ion ___ | |
| ness ___ | like ___ | |

**Rules**

dropping final e ___
changing y to i ___

Continue skill listings.

### Comprehension

**Comprehension skills**

symbol-meaning relationship ___
punctuation ___
phrasing ___
following directions ___

**Factual recall**

specific recall of terms ___
recall of dates ___
location of information ___
main idea ___

**Organization**

sequence ___
cause-effect ___
part-whole ___
time ___
place ___
general-specific ___
class ___
size ___
number ___

**Inference**

outcomes ___
relationships ___
actions ___

Continue skill listings.

*This type of chart should be continued to include all skills.

## Scheduling the Learning Period

The goal of scheduling the learning period is to have all students actively involved in learning. This means that some will be working simultaneously in skill materials, books, kits, or with mechanical devices and audio-visual equipment. It would be difficult to set up a program so that each pupil worked by himself all day long. Such a program might be equally difficult for the students in that they enjoy sharing and talking. You should strive for a balance—having them do certain things independently, and using group settings for the sharing of common experiences and the development of new skills.

Consider what time of day you plan to work on reading. Sometimes reading instruction is scheduled for a period of about an hour in the early part of the day. In the classroom setting where labs and stations are set up, you can individualize other content areas in order to move instruction continuously forward without encountering different rates of learning and functioning, which cause problems. When scheduling is done properly, no discrete period for reading instruction is necessary. A student simply moves into his next set of assignments without waiting or interruptions.

Another possibility is to have a block of time for language arts. This is when you teach reading, writing, spelling, listening, and language skills in an interrelated manner. This procedure of language experience is a good way to tie various subject matters together loosely; you can then build up a backlog of specific skill packets in each instructional area to help you teach all the skills necessary within a particular level. This way, you can use the larger skill areas to reinforce individual skills in each subarea. Spelling skills, for example, correspond to many word-recognition skills, and developing listening skills helps develop reading-comprehension skills.

## Grouping Techniques

Historically, educational or instructional groups have been formed to achieve homogeneity on the basis of some criterion. A first-grade class usually has been formed on the basis of the students' age—five or six years old. It has been assumed that children of the same age are sufficiently alike to form an educational group. In some instances students have been grouped on the basis of an ability or a result on a readiness test. Classes were formed by putting high scorers in one class, low scorers in a second group, and middle scorers in a third group. Such groupings are based on the concept that low scorers are similar in either achievement or ability and will benefit by being clustered for adjusted instruction. Breaking the class into reading groups on the basis of performance is still another pattern which has been used frequently.

Yet no matter how students have been grouped for instruction, it is generally overlooked that each member of the group remains an individual entity. For all the grouping and regrouping, no adequate method has been found which clusters children, yet eliminates the multitude of differences within the group.

How long a group should continue to function is another problem faced by educators. Many of us like to put things into neat little places with appropriate titles to help us define our problems; but students do not fit into neat little packages you can label and pigeonhole. Too often, groups have been allowed to continue long after they have served whatever useful purpose they may have had originally. Grouping by ability is a prime example of such an inflexible pattern. Consider the "late bloomer" who gets misplaced in a slower-moving, basic group. More often than not, once such a child is placed in that basic group, he is left to languish there forever. Eventually, without challenging content or instruction, he becomes what he was mistaken to be—slow.

Grouping should be attempted only to meet a specific need or to pursue a specific goal. Too often, this injunction is overlooked in the classroom. To identify a group without clearly defining its purpose is to suggest that by putting "like" learners together, we can teach to their similarities, thereby cutting down on our own planning time. We have talked a good game about students being different, but our practices have fallen far short of our talk. Groups should be formed only to meet valid educational goals. To group for any other purpose is to neglect our responsibility to deal with students as individual human beings.

## Flexible patterns

Flexibility is probably the key to all effective and efficient grouping. The first step in creating a flexible pattern is to have short-term goals. In reading, the goal should be a specific need that has to be met. When that need is met, the group should be disbanded. Don't label a child in September and leave him in that group until June. If you have three reading groups—red birds, blue birds, and robins, for example— there is really no goal other than teaching reading while moving through a body of materials set up in some sequential and developmental manner. By applying a set of materials with an inherent philosophical bias to a whole group of red birds, you lose the learner's special needs in the process. At times, learners may become unequally yoked as instruction changes them, and a group may need to be reorganized even before its goal has been met.

No set size can be established for an ideal group, because the group size must be related to the set goal. The nature of the learners within the group is also a consideration, as some children do not work well together. Factors to be considered in flexible grouping are the rate, or pace, of each learner's achievement, social maturity, specific strengths and weaknesses, the size of the group in relation to the available space and learning setting, and the ability of the leader to help the group reach its goal.

*Grouping patterns*

*Group dynamics.*   Because the group itself can be an active teacher, the truly active group has particular advantages over a singular learning experience. In a functioning group the members pool their knowledge, compare ideas, and use their collective strengths and knowledge to help solve a problem or meet their specific goals. They share strengths to help individuals overcome their weaknesses.

In a lab setting, for example, you will have students working independently, working together harmoniously, interacting in all types of small-group activities without you, and reacting meaningfully to large-group activities while still being guided toward meaningful ends. Using group techniques properly will enhance total group cohesiveness and aid in building a whole-class learning setting. In some instances the group can be structured to provide success experiences and to enhance prestige by getting jobs done well. In other instances students' leadership qualities can be developed. Often, teachers cannot be with each group, and the students have to depend on themselves to reach specific goals. This also encourages students to become independent learners and frees the teacher from the responsibility of being a mother hen to all her students for the entire day.

Now, a word about what an active group setting is not:

1. It is not a situation in which every student opens the same book to the same page, reads ten pages, and answers five questions.

2. It is not a lecture in which the teacher carries the entire burden of instruction and the students remain passive.

3. It is not five or ten students sitting in a reading circle, chirping their own one or two paragraphs from the book in turn.

4. It is not a static setting which lacks interaction among the leader and the learners.

Figure 11.5 illustrates the four types of instruction you should plan for structuring a lab setting. Note that the three overlapping outer circles require the use of groups to accommodate the individual work. You cannot separate work of this nature into neat little segments. As a skill to be developed, reading spills over into all areas of learning in which we must translate the printed code. Reading skills spread out over the whole, broad content area, helping learning occur and enriching all the learning experiences.

*Small groups.*   The concept of the small group is quite different from the traditional pattern of large classrooms. It rests on the basic idea of interaction between learners and between learners and teacher. The individual members of the group have a chance for interaction and involvement. The student who is reluctant to face embarrassment in the large group setting can be encouraged to open up in the safety of the small group.

Small groups offer unlimited potential for developing skills in critical reading and thinking. If specific skill development were the goal, the teacher could initially

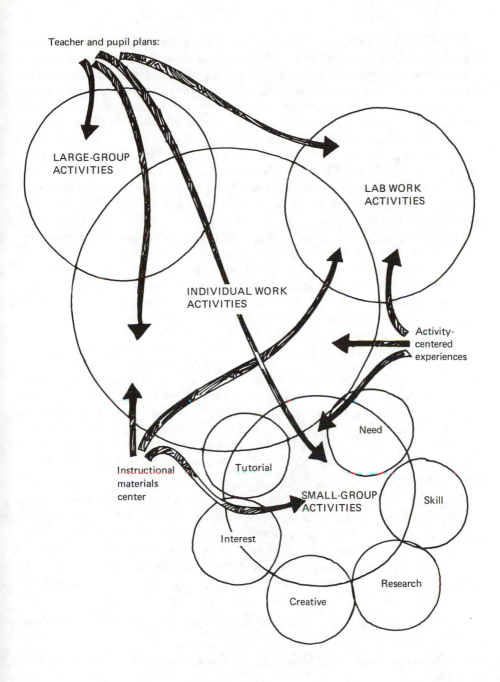

*Fig.* 11.5 *Individualizing instruction.*

take a more active role, then continue guiding the group in a more passive way as the students learned the skill and began to carry on independently. Even in a limited space, physical movement and involvement can be introduced into the learning activity, helping you identify those children having trouble with the new concept.

An example of this type of teaching is developing the concept of dropping the silent *e* from such words as *love*, *like*, and *move* prior to adding the inflected ending of *ing*. The students could be given large letters and then asked to form the words in front of the group. When the teacher called the word, each child with the appropriate letter would take his place. When she called for the inflected ending to be added, the *ing* group would "bump" the silent *e* if he failed to remember to leave willingly. Watching this in a class setting, students quickly learn that the silent *e* must leave as fast as possible.

Some extremely small groups being used in today's classrooms include only a student and a student who acts as teacher or leader. A more capable class member may be paired with a student having trouble with a particular skill. When the student has difficulty following instructions, attacking new words, or following through with an assignment, he may go to his leader for help. Such leaders need to understand initially that the helping student cannot do the work for his needful pal; the helping student should only aid and guide.

Another possibility is to have an older student come from the classroom at a set time each day to help, under the teacher's guidance, a less advanced student. Two types of older student helpers are being used with some advantages. One is the older student who is having no trouble with his own work and who comes to teach when he is not putting his own work in jeopardy. A second type of older aide might be a fifth grader who is reading well in, say, third-grade materials and comes to help a third grader who is reading at the lowest second-grade level. In such settings the two students help each other, but the older one gets a boost for his ego from helping another child.

*Large groups.* Whereas small groups lend themselves to making learning more personal, large groups tend to make this less a reality. As the size of the group grows, there is less contact between the leader and other group members. In most instances the leader must take most of the responsibility for what is presented. She must also make some accommodation for interaction with the group and feedback about what its members are learning. Large- or total-group instruction probably works best when:

1. You wish to introduce a new concept or present a demonstration to advance common understanding;

2. A group meeting is used to discuss class rules, work periods, or other common interests;

3. Audio-visual materials are presented;

4. A motivation session is held to introduce a new unit;

5. The teacher and class join in reading choric responses;

6. Group presentations are made to conclude a unit of work;

7. A test is given for some type of assessment; or

8. Entertainment is used to lighten the load of the students.

*Types of Groups.* A *need group* is commonly used in classrooms. For example, if six students are having trouble classifying concrete objects by their usage, the teacher can have these students work together until they finally grasp the main idea involved. The group members might change. As soon as some students understand the new concept, they could be sent back to work on individual reinforcement materials. Those having trouble should receive more and more teacher aid until they master the concept.

Due to the involvement of a classroom aide, an older student, para-professional, a specialist, or a parent volunteer—all working under the teacher's guidance, *tutorial groups* are becoming more common in the classroom. Such groups usually have long-range goals, since more than one or two specific skill deficiencies may be involved. The lesser trained paraprofessional or volunteer will need your help in setting up lesson plans. Thus, if you have a student who needs tactile and kinesthetic reinforcement in order to master sight words, you can help the aide to master the teaching technique and supervise her work with the student each day.

*Research* and *interest groups* are appropriate when the group members share a desire to learn a certain thing. The teacher usually selects the topic to be studied in the research group, whereas the students usually set their own goals in the interest group.

## A Systems Approach to Material Management

Today, there is an almost limitless variety of printed materials and multimedia devices available for reading instruction. Yet in many instances, adjustment and organization of these materials is necessary so that they can be presented systematically in order to meet specific objectives. Keep in mind the fact that a great many of the materials presently available were published after the federal government appropriated funds for schools to purchase special materials and equipment for deviant groups of learners. Some publishers and authors rushed into production, and the resulting materials and devices did not receive the professional research and careful review they really needed. Consequently, many of these materials must be used with care and must be adapt for use in any given setting.

### Strategies for meeting individual needs

Hopefully, educators are beyond the point of opening a standard text, starting with page one, and continuing through the body of materials to the last page. The main goal of such an approach seems to be the students' parroting of information from the text as a sign of learning. It tends to limit teachers and discourage learners. Basically, such an approach asserts that the authors, no matter how far removed from the learners, know what is best for the students to learn. This is not to say that our educational texts are bad, but rather that they should not be the ultimate source for what and how to teach. As instructors grow in their ability to teach toward a specifically stated objective, they depend less and less on *The Text* as an ultimate source, using it more as a resource and a reference.

*Adapting commercial materials*

As already mentioned, we are currently faced with a plethora of commercially prepared materials and devices designed to help us teach students to read. The classic instructional material in reading instruction is the basal reader, graded material organized to develop reading skills within a sequence of such materials. The teacher's manual for the basal reader usually stresses initial readiness, the development of basic reading and thinking skills, and suggestions for enrichment. The manual offers a resource for teaching needed skills in a developmental, sequential manner. The basal reader was never structured to be a complete reading program, however, though it has tended to become the "whole show" in too many school systems.

Since no two series represent the same philosophy of reading, there has always been a variety of approaches from which to choose. Most companies stress the group setting for presenting the materials within the overall package. Many of the major companies publishing these materials do revise their programs regularly in light of new research into reading; therefore, there is a continuing presentation of basal materials. In some instances, different types of materials are being added to the basal curriculum to offer students enriched learning experiences.

Each set of basal materials has its own scope and sequence chart of skill development, making it difficult to switch from one series to another. To use these materials in teaching specific objectives, a teacher must have a separate chart to show where a skill is developed in each of the materials available to her. She needs to be able to look at the appropriate chart to see that the material includes specific pages which will help her teach, for example, the skill of adding the inflected ending, *es* to nouns. Table 11.2 presents a prototype chart which should help in organizing skills. It also provides a method for visually locating the specific material needed to teach a specific skill.

Because of the need to classify all the available sources, the type of organization shown in Table 11.2 takes time to construct. The job is particularly time-consuming if a single teacher must do it on her own. Therefore, it would be wise for a school system to assume the major responsibility for correlating and organizing the instructional materials available to its teachers. Teacher participation in the process, though, would probably be very important to the subsequent use of such materials. Scheduling work days when groups of teachers work with sets of materials, locating skills and ways to reinforce them, will help build a skill-reinforcement manual for all the system's teachers.

**Table 11.2    Locational guide for skill materials**

|  | Basal | Workbooks | Kits | Visual aids |
|---|---|---|---|---|
| Skill stated in | Name of book | Name of workbook | Name of kit | Type of visual aid |
| behavioral terms | Publisher | Publisher | Publisher | Name of particular aid |
|  | Level | Page | Package | Publisher |
|  | Page | Location ↓ | Card | Location ↓ |
| Skills found in adopted sequence | Location ↓ | ↓ | Location ↓ | ↓ |
| Skill | ↓ | ↓ | ↓ | ↓ |

Many workbook-type materials are available for teaching phonic and word-recognition skills. Many school systems object, however, to ordering such materials because: (1) too often they have been misused as "busy work" to keep some children occupied while other groups within a class are actively learning; and (2) they are consumable and can be costly over a long period of time. Both objections can be overcome by changing these materials from the workbook form into learning kits, collections of reusable work sheets. By ordering two copies of each book, a teacher can take the workbooks apart in order to classify and assemble the pages according to specific skill areas. These pages can be placed in heavy-duty plastic folders so that they can be used for instruction without being consumed. Individual pages can sometimes be mounted on cardboard and stored in files. In most cases the teacher will have to rewrite some pages or add instructions so that they can be used independently of other material. As a child has need for instruction in a specific skill, the teacher will have revised work sheets ready to help her reinforce learning needs. Several types of workbook materials could be combined to expand the learning kit and to offer a variety of materials for skill development and reinforcement.

*Teacher-made and student-made materials*

There is an increasing emphasis on having teachers prepare materials for instructional purposes. This is a legitimate approach, because the teacher really knows her students better than do authors who are not with her children. No producer of instructional materials can know what your students are like—their strengths, weaknesses, and peculiar likes and tastes in reading. While a teacher is learning to meet her student's needs, she often tends to depend on commercial materials. But as she grows in her teaching ability and builds her own "bag of tricks," she will be able to produce her own materials whenever she realizes that the commercial ones are not appropriate to some of her student's needs. As you branch out and start making your own materials, try to save them. Over a period of time you can organize them for easy retrieval, because you will undoubtedly want to use them again and again as similar special needs arise each year.

Among the materials you can create and accumulate are:

1. *Goofy cards.* These are devices built around pictures or printed materials from newspapers and magazines. Thinking and research are the two basic skills needed to develop these materials. The major emphasis is on the student functioning independently, with the learning activity becoming the involvement. The title of these cards sets the flavor, indicating that they are not weighty educational tasks to be attacked as one would a lesson in math or science. Each card should involve thinking, research, and an activity which actively involves the student in learning. Activities should be simple, e.g., making a puppet, planning things to put into a suitcase for a trip to the moon, or finding out why a train takes 18 hours to go 10 miles in Nepal. There must be a stimulus picture and/or caption, or a paragraph from printed materials. Figure 11.6 depicts a sample of a goofy card.

2. *Indexed moments.* These cards offer the student a chance to have fun for a few minutes within the work period. Such cards can be given any nonsensical name you might choose, but they should focus five or ten minutes of the student's time on activities that aid in relaxation. Several companies produce minipuzzles that might be a legitimate pursuit for a few minutes. Good comic books might be used, or the student might enjoy the chance to create a poem about the teacher at her worst.

The stores are full of ideas to aid in structuring such enterprises. Miniature puzzles, dice with letters, stickers with slang or common expressions, silly crossword puzzles, and many other such items can be used to construct cards with which the students can legitimately relax after completing their assigned work. Creativity is the key word to developing such activities.

3. *Games.* Don't discount your own creative ability for making original educational games or for making commercial games more functional as educational reinforcers. Take a checkerboard and paste duplicate sight words in each black square. Two students can play by conventional rules, but they have to call out the word before jumping into each new block. By leaving some black squares blank, the initial games will be less difficult for the students, giving them some free jumps in case sight words are a problem for the students. Several boards might be made, graduating from easy boards to progressively harder ones. Skills could range from sight words and sound knowledge to classification knowledge.

# Bad News: No-See-Ems Are Plentiful

It is my irritating duty to inform campers that the no-see-ems are so thick that you can see 'em.

No-see-ems?

Why these are little insects who, in singular form, are unworthy of mention. However, when a no-see-em gangs up with the rest of the gang—like a million of his relations—a camper best be on his guard.

Actually, it is difficult to see one no-see-em. When a no-see-em brings his relatives and they position themselves between you and the sky all you see are tiny dark dots which zip and blip against the heavenly background.

A covy of no-see-ems attack different campers in different ways. Personally, I always get it in the hair. Did you ever have a herd of no-see-ems run through your hair barefoot? It

**BOB HARRELL Camping Editor**

is hard for me to explain the effect except to confess that their presence in my hair drives me up the wall or tree if the former is unavailable. The feeling of a million no-see-ems roaming the thin and graying wilderness of one's natural and uppermost covering is compared to a slight electrical shock supplemented with feather-tickling sensations.

Answer the following questions:

1. What type of insects could be identified as "no-see-ems"?

2. What words does the author use to describe the attack on his hair by a host of "no-see-ems"?

3. Write words to describe how you would feel if a host of "no-see-ems" attacked your:
   a) ears
   b) eyes
   c) back
   d) hands

4. If you were camping, how would you protect yourself from "no-see-ems" when you went to sleep?

5. Why do you think the author used the term "no-see-em" rather than the insects name?

6. Write a discussion of a group of "no-see-ems" who are planning an attack on the blonde, curly hair of a lady camper.

7. Draw a picture of a "no-see-em."

*Fig. 11.6    Goofy card.*

Student-made materials are a "coming event" in education. Encouraging students to become authors helps them in all of the language art skills. Classroom newspapers, a library shelf for student-made books, and a game corner for games they create by themselves will encourage their participation in developing educationally valid materials. Many schools are getting new materials which both teachers and students can use to create good learning tools, develop new visual aids, and involve the students in learning. The use of the camera for developing visual experiences has been most interesting for students. In some instances, they have made their own films to describe events or to introduce concepts that are to be learned.

An excellent way to develop books for reluctant readers is to have an older group of students make their own books for specific groups of reluctant readers. A fifth-or sixth-grade class might be encouraged to make books for the second or third grade. Science and mystery stories are always in demand as interesting learning tools. Both groups of students, older and younger, gain from such an experience. One group is encouraged and assisted in developing writing skills, and the other group gains from having new and interesting stories to read. Suggest titles such as "The Ghostly Dog," "The Sneaky Raccoon," "Billy Seed," or "Sam the Tired Bee" to get the students started. You'll find they will take the ball and run with it.

In one class, for example, some boys decided to write a story about a seed. They planted lima beans in dirt and placed beans between glass on moist paper to study the way in which the bean developed. The illustrations depicted what they had learned about the seed's growth. The illustrations also developed the roles of the clouds, sun, air, and soil in relationship to the emerging Billy Seed. The only problem that emerged during this work was the day the newly bound book was to be presented to the second-grade class. The boys wanted to keep it. It had become an important part of them. Making two copies might be wise!

*Content and presentation-controlled materials*

Some materials are made so that they cannot be easily adapted for specific learners. The content or manner of presentation is built into the material; adapting it would undo the intent of the material. The *Programmed Reading Series*, published by McGraw-Hill, is an example (Fig. 11.7). In this material the reader does open the book at page one, continuing through the book to the end of the final page. This particular set of materials is built on the assumption that it: has multiple easy steps, requires a response from the student for each frame, gives immediate knowledge of results, and, offers many repetitions to assure success. The publishers of these and similar materials claim that they allow the individual to work at his own pace. This is true, but some of your quicker learners may not need so much repetition, and some slow learners may need more.

Other instructional packages exist and may be useful for students who need such careful programming. One very interesting approach to this type of presentation is the Talking-Typewriter, developed by O. K. Moore. The instructional program

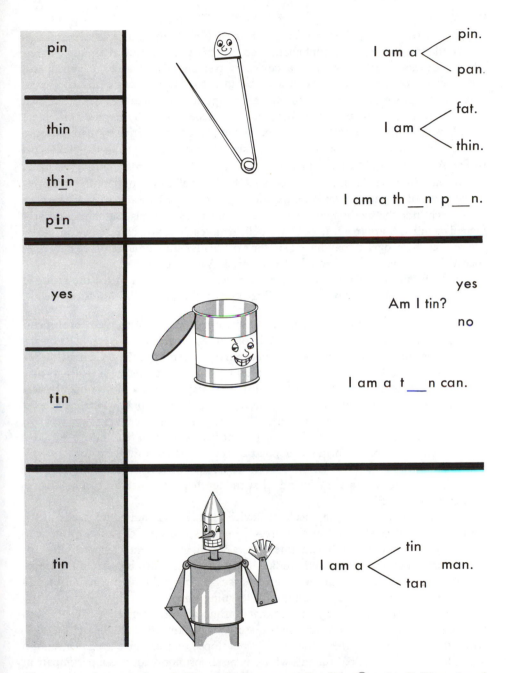

| | | |
|---|---|---|
| pin | | I am a — pin. / pan. |
| thin | | I am — fat. / thin. |
| th_i_n | | I am a th__n p__n. |
| p_i_n | | |
| yes | | yes / Am I tin? / no |
| tin | | I am a t___n can. |
| tin | | I am a — tin / tan man. |

*Fig. 11.7    A sample from Sullivan.* (Programmed Reading, © *1963, Sullivan Associates Buchanan, Cynthia Dee, Book 1, p. 24. Reprinted by permission.*)

for the Talking-Typewriter is very highly structured and follows a set sequence. The child first learns the alphabet, then words, sentences, and finally stories. The motivational effect of such a device is tremendous. If a child typed c-a-t, the machine replies "cat" to reinforce the idea that the letters equal the word. The student is simply "plugged in" to the program and moves forward at his own pace. He seeks help if he has trouble, and the teacher stands by to guide or restart him. Unfortunately, the cost of the system is considered prohibitive by many schools.

If such a locked-in approach is to be used, the methodology and the child must be carefully matched. Don't put a bright, quick child into a program that has many repetitions. Similarly, a slow child doesn't function well in a program that lacks frequent repetitions and regular reinforcement. Since you will be able to adjust neither the content nor the methodology with such controlled materials, watch the students to make sure the approach is working well. As a teacher, you should be constantly aware that the program may have gaps for a particular student and that he may need special help as he moves through the material. Again, controlled material assumes that the content and the approach are adequate for all learners or for the group of learners identified as its target group. Regrettably, this generalization is erroneous.

*Content materials.*   Content materials represent a special type of problem for students having difficulty with reading. The body of content materials is presented by the development of new concepts and new vocabulary. Therefore, the child may have to master anywhere from 20 to 50 new words in a lesson before he is ready to cope with the material and to fully understand it. This may present a substantial problem for some students, as these materials tend to develop ideas quickly, without respect to students' learning rates or their need for adequate reinforcement. As a teacher, you should recognize this and adjust such materials when you feel the content load is too high. Readability formulas applied to these materials indicate that a single book can contain as much as three years difference in lesson readability. Such a large discrepancy in content demands that the teacher make necessary adjustments as they are required.

The unit approach is an excellent device for meeting individual needs in the content areas. Basically, the unit approach involves breaking the total group into smaller groups for research and interaction. Each group takes responsibility for certain areas of the content and studies it. The teacher helps by setting the learning objectives, identifying the work groups, suggesting culminating activities, and guiding the development of a meaningful learning unit.

The advantage of this approach is that it offers a viable alternative to everyone's having the same text. This means that the teacher can introduce high-interest, low-vocabulary materials in the subjects to be developed and can give special attention to readers who need help. Students who may be almost nonreaders can participate in the construction of materials for class presentation and learn from the group while everyone works on the project. The emphasis on visual aids in their final reports to the class insures meaningful understanding among the slower learners.

## Curriculum adjustment

It must be clear that an overstructured, rigid curriculum can only hamper a student's reading progress. Ask yourself: Do all learners need the exact same experiences and knowledge to function in our society? When we set up rigid performance standards to be met by a certain time, we are saying that—regardless of a student's learning problems, his experiences or lack of them, his ability to function and learn in new material, or his pace of learning, he must digest a certain amount of material. Is this a reasonable expectation?

Let's be reasonable in setting up educational goals for instruction. Let's be flexible in structuring goals that are within the capacity of the individual learner. If the child with an IQ of 70 is reading at the sixth-grade level by the time he graduates from high school, he has succeeded. But in order to succeed, all the printed materials he uses will have to have been adjusted so that they are not beyond his ability to achieve—from the first grade through the twelfth. On the other hand, if a pupil with an IQ of 140 is functioning only at grade level, we have failed. He, too, needs a special curriculum adjusted to his personal needs.

Every curriculum should be geared to the pace of the individual learner. We can determine certain skills that make a good reader, then structure specific experiences to enhance the development of these skills. We do not have to say that these skills must be learned by a certain year in the student's educational experience. But setting up a logical, orderly, sequence for introducing skills is necessary. Finding alternative ways to develop these skills for various types of learners is also vital.

Beyond adjusting the timing for introducing reading skills, some adjustment will also be required in content materials, based on the varying rates at which reading skills and abilities emerge in individual students. Students having difficulty with reading will need all their reading materials, even content materials, adjusted to their own levels of functioning. Similarly, students who are well advanced in their reading skills will profit from advanced materials. The ideal situation is a class in which each student moves forward, at his own pace, in material which he can comfortably handle but which also presents him with a motivational challenge.

## Conclusions

Every teacher should strive to create a learning atmosphere that encourages learning. The lab setting is one approach that will help you teach individuals within a group. Each student is different and deserves to have his learning experiences matched to his individual needs. As a teacher, you have a challenging and important task in assessing needs, gathering and organizing materials, creating a meaningful learning setting, and diversifying instructions for each unique individual assigned to you. No one should ever make light of the dedicated teacher's contribution. Her task is great, but so is her reward: seeing children enjoy learning and profiting by her efforts.

# 12 / Individualization by objective

You will encounter a wide variety of reading abilities among your students. This variety makes it imperative that you teach the individuals within your class rather than the class as a whole. Individuals—not groups—absorb, learn, and respond, and each person learns most readily the things that he feels are personally meaningful and useful. Remember that reading skills alone don't automatically lead to adequate reading behavior; they aid and reinforce appropriate behavior. When you teach reading skills, try to remove all the obstacles that will block progress. And always keep an eye on the larger goal—the involved, responsive, interested reader.

As a teacher, you are responsible for stimulating the reading growth of your students. To do this, you must know:

1. the essential reading skills
2. ways to assess skill knowledge in individual or group settings
3. symptoms of gaps in skill development that may block further development
4. materials that aid in the development of essential skills in a variety of ways
5. methods and approaches to both teach and reinforce skill development
6. devices, games, and activities to aid in skill application
7. motivational techniques to interest and guide learners in reading activities.

## Methodology

Virtually every approach to the teaching of reading involves a special method or combination of specific learning methods designed to help the student learn through reading. In choosing any approach, you should consider the individual's style of learning. For example, a student with either a high-frequency hearing loss or a deviant speech pattern will have sound-production problems with certain letter sounds. Therefore, if you stress a synthetic phonics approach, you may encourage failure. A better approach might be to teach either visual analysis of word structure or perception of the word as a whole recognition unit.

It is obvious that you need to spend time observing students working with materials selected for their instruction. You may be tempted to assume that each student will move ahead easily to new materials. For many, however, failure occurs because the material conflicts with the student's individual style, mode of learning, or physical deficiencies.

## Analytic and synthetic controversy

For some time, educators have tried to reach a decision on the best way to teach word-analysis skills. Throughout the history of reading, the many reforms have stressed the value of the analytic approach over the synthetic—or vice versa. It is not really a question of which is the best approach. The question is: "Which is best for the student, and what can he gain from either/or a combination of both?"

*Synthetic methods* begin with smaller, pronounceable elements—letters or letter patterns—and build up to the whole word or the larger recognition units. In the word *cat*, for example, the student would attack this word synthetically in a letter-by-letter manner: *k-a-t = cat* or *kuh-a-tuh* = cat. This approach can be compared with induction. The main distinction is that with induction, one moves from meaningful parts to the whole; in the synthetic approach, however, the individual parts don't have implicit meaning. The *alphabetical* or *rugged phonic* approaches are examples of the synthetic approach.

*Analytic methods* of teaching reading stress the larger units—words, phrases, or sentences—at first. Thus, the student starts with a meaningful whole and then goes back to an analysis of the parts if he needs to. Because the analytic approach starts with whole words, some critics have jumped to the conclusion that it amounts to a *look-say* method that involves no phonics or "sounding." Such a conclusion is short-sighted, because the approach moves very quickly to the phonic analysis of words.

You should be thoroughly familiar with both methods of developing skills. Some materials combine both analytic and synthetic methods to help the student analyze and synthesize words at the same time. Both sets of reading skills help the student develop a variety of ways to unlock new words in reading. Both have strengths and weaknesses in dealing with various problems. In synthetic approaches you must be sure to stress meaningful interpretation of the materials and some form of meaningful application. Since the individual parts don't have inherent meaning, the student may focus on just decoding the printed symbols—word calling. In the analytic approach the student may not have the ability to meet the continual demands for analyzing and finding the facts that support a major structure.

Determine whether to use the analytic or synthetic approach by:

1. studying the approach thoroughly
2. determining its style or method
3. assessing its strengths and weaknesses in relation to a specific student's needs
4. adjusting the approach to the student's needs and learning style
5. adjusting the materials when they are needed for successful reading for each student.

## Basic approaches

There are many materials and approaches designed to augment your reading-skills program. The recent proliferation of reading materials is phenomenal. Rather than just the few materials available to teachers a few years ago, you have a wide variety to choose from in determining the most appropriate materials for your students' needs.

### The basal reader

Herrick (1961) says that a basal program "is a set of reading materials designed to develop important reading skills, to cover all the important kinds of reading, and to provide for some overall plan of development." Since this approach is the one most widely used in public school, you were probably taught with one also. Since it has been a major contributor to reading instruction, you should become fully aware of its nature and scope. Basal readers may have changed since you used them. They are broader now, with audio-visual devices added to the basic instructional approach.

When you use basal readers, don't assume that you have all the materials needed to teach *all* students equally well. You will continually have to add materials for your slow-learning and deviant learners. Another problem develops from the assumption that once a student completes a basal reader, he is automatically ready to move on to the next text in the series. The student's growth rate should be carefully and continuously assessed before he is introduced to any new material.

### Language experience

This stimulus approach deals with experiencing and recording thoughts in print. Dechant (1970) indicates that language experience dates back some 60 years and has always focused on student interest and stressed reading for meaning. The *experience chart* was an early development in this approach. Initially, however, this approach did not stress organized sequential development of a variety of reading-language skills. Rather, the emphasis was on the student's experiences.

You may remember taking an "observation" walk around your school with your teacher. As you walked, she helped you focus your attention on the objects you passed. When you returned to the room, the whole class shared in dictating a class story which your teacher charted and illustrated to reuse in reinforcing new vocabulary and sentence structure. She was using the experience-chart approach.

L.E.I.R., or Language Experiences in Reading (Encyclopaedia Britannica Press, 1965), is a similar approach which systematically structures 20 basic reading-language elements. The student is encouraged to explore, investigate, think, create, pose learning problems or tasks, propose solutions, and develop his own reading materials. The whole approach stresses involvement and commitment to one's self as a learner and as an author.

The basis for the L.E.I.R. theory is:

> "A child learns . . .
> that which he thinks about,
>           he can say . . .
> that which he says can be written by his teacher
>           or by himself . . .
> and . . . which is written can be read
>           by himself and by others."

There are many other approaches to language experience. Texts and commercially devised packages are available which reinforce the close relationship of language and reading. But most of them don't have as highly an organized and structured skill program as does L.E.I.R.

### Phonemic-linguistic systems

Linguistics is the study of our oral language. When a reading system or program claims to be linguistic, it basically stresses the function of reading as a special language skill. The major emphasis in such an approach is decoding—changing print into oral language. Technically, language experience is a linguistic approach, since it stresses the structure of each student's oral language patterns. Holt, Rhinehart and Winston's *Sounds of Language Series* is also linguistic, since it stresses the sounds, melody, and structure of oral language. However, when we see the word *linguistics* as describing a reading approach, it is usually used to indicate a phonemic approach. A phoneme is the smallest unit of speech that distinguishes one utterance from another. The phonemic approach is based on using the small units to attack words in a systematic way.

*Let's Read*, by Barnhart and Bloomfield, is one example of a phonemic-linguistic approach. The materials focus on the consistent sound patterns in our language. The system rests on three major points:

1. Language is basically an oral process.
2. Our language is based on an alphabetic code system that can be broken.
3. Consistent and systematic patterns reoccur in our language that can aid in the decoding process.

Linguists who espouse the phonemic approach simply believe that because of the consistency within our language, you can teach a child to call words easily and thereby break the reading code. They equate word-calling (decoding) with reading.

Two examples of the phonemic-linguistic approach follow:

> *at* Nat is the cat.
> Nat, the cat, is fat.
> Nat, the fat cat, has a hat.
> Nat's hat is black.
> The fat cat's hat is black.

> *an* Dan has a can.
> The can is tan.
> Dan has a tan can.
> The tan can is Dan's.

This type of approach offers a high degree of consistency for a student who may need help learning sounds or may need repetition to help him retain information. The main problem is that the emphasis on decoding doesn't help the student understand the meaning of the phrase. The student is also restricted to reading "jingle-like" stories. So, if you choose to use a linguistic-phonemic approach, remember to reinforce meaning. Other examples of linguistic-phonemic approaches are the SRA *Basic Reading* Series, Benziger's *The Linguistic Readers*, and *Programmed Reading*.

*Individualized reading*

In the late 1950s, many educators emphasized the need for an individualized approach to reading. They wanted the student to be able to select his own reading materials and to stop wasting time taking part in round-robin reading practices in the reading circle. Individualized reading rests on the student's: (1) seeking his own materials, (2) selecting his own reading materials, (3) self-pacing as he moves through the materials, and (4) self-evaluation of his reading progress.

You can entice your students to read if you offer a wide variety of materials and stimulating activities. In addition to the basal reader, you can expose them to trade books, magazines, comic books, mysteries, joke books, references, and fictional and nonfictional materials. In addition to having conferences with individual students for checking on progress and special skill needs, you may also wish to plan group sessions when you see that a number of students share a need. However, planning conferences is only part of your responsibility. You will also have to gather new materials, encourage, diagnose, and keep adequate records of growth and needs. You are the backbone and motivator of the program.

It is obvious that the independent and advanced student will thrive under this individualized approach if he is taught the necessary skills in spelling and language sessions. But you must be able to recognize deviant reading behavior readily and adjust this approach so that a dependent learner has greater contact with you. Otherwise, the student with the greatest needs might be left behind.

*Other approaches*

There are many other materials designed for individual reading needs. Perhaps the most interesting are the skill programs based on behavioral objectives. The *Wisconsin Design for Reading Skill Development*, for example, is an organized approach for building subskills in reading. The literature accompanying this approach, published by the Wisconsin Research and Development Center for Cognitive Learning, says that, "Skill development is best facilitated when teachers direct learning experiences according to their pupils' characteristics and needs." The *Design* stresses local participation in correlating and organizing the system's own materials to implement the instructional program. The *Design's* organizational materials consist of a rationale, set of guidelines, teacher's planning guides, resource files, and tests for specific skill assessment. The *Design* is coupled with Individually Guided Education, (IGE), a "system for formulating and carrying out instructional programs for individual children in which planned variations are made in what each child learns, how rapidly he learns, and how he goes about learning" (*Wisconsin Design*). Basic skill areas developed are word attack, study skills, comprehension, self-directed reading, interpretive reading, and creative reading.

The *Design's* program is also quite economical, since it incorporates your presently available materials. You have guidelines for organizing your materials by specific objectives for a more direct attack on specific skill weaknesses.

Other programs are discussed in Chapter 13 and include many approaches that can be adapted for classroom use with deviant learners. These approaches are valid in the classroom when a student has a special need for them. Such methods are the Fernald-Keller method, the Cruckshank approach, the Lehtinen approach, the Kephart approach, the Gillingham approach, i/t/a, "words in color," and programmed reading.

## Eclecticism

Using the eclectic approach, you choose a variety of teaching materials. You do not view any one approach as "the way" to teach reading; rather, you select the best materials and approaches from several sources to broaden the base of your reading program. Electicism gives you an opportunity to assess your knowledge and your teaching skills. You can select those packages with which you are comfortable and then slowly add to your repertoire as you gain experience and confidence teaching reading. Thus, your overall program becomes more flexible, broader, and better equipped to handle the instructional needs of all your students. You have a greater opportunity to adjust to special learning needs, and you have a variety of ways to develop and reinforce skill development. For example, you might combine language experience, the *Wisconsin Design*, and basal readers into a logical approach that could be managed rather easily. However, any combination is valid, as long as it fits the needs of your pupils and you are able to manage the various elements.

## Considerations that Aid Learning

Let the strengths and needs of your students guide your teaching, whatever your approach. Develop your own creativity so that you can make an activity more reasonable, interesting, or understandable, thereby enhancing its acceptance, usefulness, and application in a new setting.

### Prerequisites and previous experiences

Any time you teach a student, be sure he has all the understandings and skills he needs to handle a new concept. A major reason for diagnostic teaching is to establish a clear indication of strengths and needs prior to instruction. Structuring devices to evaluate skill knowledge is not too difficult and constitutes time well spent.

When you are developing *concepts* that underlie a skill such as figurative language, you must be careful to understand the *wall of verbalism* so characteristic of today's young students. All of the stimulations offered through the audiovisual media expose the students to a wide vocabulary and a great variety of experiences. Therefore, they have more sophisticated, grown-up words to express their thoughts. Often, they can anticipate the response you *want* to hear and answer accordingly, without really understanding the skills you are trying to develop. Often, your students chirp their answers, receive their rewarding "good" or "that's right," and completely miss the point of the lesson because of their ability to hide their ignorance behind correct verbage.

### *Sequence of skill development*

Another part of the readiness concept is that skills are presented in sequence so that they are acquired developmentally. In order to insure this, you need to structure your teaching schedule so that easier concepts precede broader ones, enabling your students to develop a framework for understanding their materials. There won't be a problem if you are teaching the inflected forms of *s, ing,* or *ed,* as none of these seems to depend on the others for development. You can choose which one you will teach first. If you are teaching figurative-language skills, though, your students will need a specific range of vocabulary and inferential skills to help them understand figures of speech. Or, if you are developing deviant vowel sounds and have not taught the basic short and long ones, your students might have trouble recognizing the long and short from the deviant sounds, which need a special category of their own. When individual skills are so interrelated that one is dependent on the prior knowledge of another, their teaching must proceed in a given order to assure success.

### Concrete objectives leading to abstract objectives

Too often, we expect our students to function at our level of understanding without our years of experience. We tend to teach at our level of functioning without going to the student's level of comprehension. A basic mistake is to assume that a student understands a new concept or skill at the abstract level. In the fifth grade, for example, many students are introduced to American history with such terms as democracy, freedom, rights, justice, etc., used extensively. Little effort is made to really develop any basic explanation of these words. Therefore, students often learn to just mimic or verbalize in order to appear knowledgeable.

A major part of any lesson is to find the lowest level of understanding, teach first at this level, and then build up to the more abstract level. Some typical learners, slow learners, and experience-deprived students never achieve a higher level of abstract application, because they don't have the skills. However, it is still important to reach these students, and this can be done only by working with them at a level at which they can function.

**Visual reinforcement**

Finding ways to help a student hold a visual image in his mind's eye is an aid to learning. Most young learners have difficulty in "seeing" time in the correct dimension and proportion. Such words as era, century, year, eon, and other "time" words confuse students when they try to interpret them. Their 40-year-old teacher seems ancient, and they often ask her how things were in the "old days." The *time line* has proved an excellent device for putting time into visual perspective to help students develop time in proportion to blocks. The same type of reinforcement is needed with work you expect students to overlearn. You should try to develop visual clues to put skills into patterns they can easily remember.

Some teachers use configuration clues to help a student remember the shape of a particular word. Developing "clue words" for sounds of short vowels is also used. A chart with pictures of an apple, an egg, an Indian, an octupus, and an umbrella will visually remind students of the short vowel sounds. Since these pictures all have the sound in the initial position, there is less confusion in matching the sounds. When the student forgets, he can refer to the chart. Eventually, he internalizes these symbols and no longer needs the chart for reference.

Using numbers within written materials as clues to understanding sequence is an excellent device for helping students visualize the order in which things happen. A recipe is a good technique for teaching numbering and reinforcing sequence. Using pictures to reinforce classification skills is also a good way to help students visualize central concepts.

When students have a low level of understanding, you can promote learning by developing new concepts with visual devices. Using games with visual clues to aid learning and to reinforce skills is also acceptable. All of these devices reduce the limitations of regular classrooms and the textbooks and involve students in learning. For instance, it is difficult for all students to fully comprehend such things as the presence of bacterial life in our drinking water. With a projection microscope, however, the whole class can take part in the same experience. You will know the nature of visual experience your students have had, and you can build on that experience to clarify concepts.

By using visual devices to stimulate learning, you can broaden, enrich, and reinforce learning. You therefore have an opportunity to go beyond the limitations of textbooks by illustrating and expanding ideas through pictures, visuals, and projection devices. If you are describing the specific color "blue," for instance, your words are almost ineffectual without a visual illustration.

## Teaching Specific Objectives

This section in no way tries to develop the many skills discussed in the previous chapters. Rather, this chapter deals with selected skills to acquaint you with a variety of considerations connected to skill development. Basically, you need to know:

1. what is involved in the final development of a skill
2. what prior knowledge affects successful development and attainment of any new skill
3. how to transfer the new learning to any situation where it will help the learner function more easily through reading
4. how to develop a reader who has a variety of skills which enable him to work in any area where reading is a task.

### Developing likenesses and differences

*1. Level A*

*Skill.* Likenesses and differences: words and phrases.

*Objective.* The child selects the word or phrase in a series that is identical to a stimulus word or phrase (e.g., *down*: wand, down, bone, find).

The desired outcomes of this task are numerous: the clear visual intake of the symbols; visual discrimination of the likenesses and differences within the symbol groups; awareness of symbols as units; and visual memory of discrete symbol patterns. At the initial stage of word-symbol discrimination, meaning is not necessarily involved. This will be added as the child attempts to unlock new words or learns by sight methods. Therefore, experiences relating to word meaning are not a serious consideration in the initial teaching of this skill. However, the child must be able to understand the letters of the alphabet and their particular characteristics. For many children, the letters *b, d, p, q, g*, and *j* or *h, n, m*, and *r* may need further clarification before they can develop the skill in word or phrase setting.

*Assessment.* For initial testing, you should use three types of discriminations to determine the child's level of functioning:

1. gross (wet-mother) or (cow-butter) (wet mother wet)
2. medial (butter-cattle) or (mother-catcher) (butter cattle cattle)

3. fine (want-went) or (there-three) (want want went)

You could also use nonsense words and come to the same understanding about a child's ability to match word shapes. For example:

1. gross (zit-plutm) or (maw-loftu) (zit zit plutm)
2. medial (motlu-nalto) or (potry-gitcy) (motlu nalto nalto)
3. fine (zop-zap) or (luv-lov) (zop zop zap)

Another consideration in developing discriminations is the use of capital and lower-case letters. Lower-case letters offer a wider variety of shapes than do block-type capital letters. You could start with capital-letter words and progress to lower-case words if a student needs a longer period of training. Initially, you might want to limit discriminations to two or three letter units and move on to longer ones as the student is able to handle them.

Because of the diverse abilities among the students, various exercises should be developed for teaching letter patterns. You are then able to teach the student at the level at which he is able to match symbols. Color-coding certain letter patterns (color clues), sandpaper letters (tactile-kinesthetic reinforcement), copying work on the board (kinesthetic reinforcement), and games are legitimate exercises to help the student master the understanding of word shapes. The variety and frequency of these exercises is the key to developing these skills.

When the student demonstrates that he can handle word-matching, you can add phrases. Here is a possible order:

1. command—go home, get out, stay there (two words)

          go home:   get out   get away   go home

2. adjective + noun—black cat, blue hat, little dog (two words)

          black cat:   blue hat   blue dress   bad balloon

3. prepositional phrase—on the can, in the bag, under the chair (three words)

          in the bag:   on the hag   in the car   in the bag

4. subject—the old man, the cold cat, the cool day (three words)

          the cold cat:   the cold cat   the old bat   the cool ant

You should start with simple two-word clusters and move gradually to more involved discriminations aimed at increasing visual intake and expanding visual memory. Technically, meaning is not involved in this exercise, just matching similar visual patterns. However, the child must come to recognize the word and then the cluster of words as a pattern to remember. Hopefully, this understanding will carry over when definitions are taught.

To stimulate visual memory, you might give the student five symbols to remember, then have him locate them in order in clusters of printed symbols. This form of application helps you determine the student's ability to match specific word shapes set in with other distracting word shapes. For example, you might have the student remember the words:

cat   dog   go   in   out   now

The child would then be asked to locate these words in the cluster that follows:

the   meow   cat   under   on   dog

to   no   go   at   tip   in   see

play   our   out   not   cow   now

Another form of application is to make a set of cards with two cards for each word and a few single words as distractors. Put these cards in a jar or box; the child can empty the contents and match up pairs. Depending on how difficult you want the game to be, you can use either close or gross discriminations.

## 2. Level A

*Skill.*   Initial consonant sounds.

*Objective.*   Given familiar words pronounced by the teacher, the child indicates which of three words begins with the same consonant as the target word.

This skill extends the concept of likenesses and differences to letter sounds and auditory discrimination. The focus is on discriminination of identical initial consonant sounds. In the assessment of this skill, it is suggested that the teacher use pictures to reinforce the words as they are presented. Developing the skill will depend on the following preliminary skills:

1. adequate and correct sound knowledge

2. adequate experiences with concrete concepts

3. experiences with pictorial presentation of concrete concepts

4. ability to associate a word with a picture that represents the same meaning.

When teaching any sound skill you should screen the students to make sure that their auditory perception of the sounds involved is adequate. Some students come from culturally different groups and may have certain lacks or deviant sound productions which will need to be considered. You may need to provide extended periods of readiness or to seek an alternative approach to develop this skill at the visual level.

Technically, there is a slight difference in the sound of *d* in *day, dig, dust, dot,* and *deck.* The position of the mouth in making the consonant-vowel sound accounts for the slight deviation. It might be best, therefore, to develop new consonant sound with the same vowel sound following it to ensure consistency and to rule out as much dissimilarity as possible. For children with sound confusions or for slow learners, this is essential.

Initially, for example, you might teach the *m* sound. Begin with some clue to the sound, such as the Campbell Soup song:

> "Mmmmmmmmmm, mmmmmmmmmmm, good,
> Mmmmmmmmmm, mmmmmmmmmmm, good,
> That's what Campbell's soups are,
> Mmmmmmmmmm, mmmmmmmmmmm, good."

Then take pairs of words to compare with the song. You would call two words and the students would see if the words both matched the *m* sound in the song. In the pair of words, *man* and *tan*, the teaching would go about like this:

> Mmmmmmmmmm, mmmmmmmmmmm, *man*
> Mmmmmmmmmm, mmmmmmmmmmm, *tan*

The child should be able to hear that while *man* started correctly, *tan* did not. You would then follow up with such pairs as man-map, mouth-mouse, moon-tap, and mug-monkey. The use of pictures could be added to reinforce the meaningfulness of the concepts you were using to discriminate sounds.

In introducing an initial consonant sound, it is not wise to stress the *uh* sound as is often done (e.g., mmm*uh* for the *m* sound). Developing the *m* sound in relation to some known word with its own vowel sound will not add to the confusion of removing the added *uh* sound in real words, i.e., map is not *muh-ă-puh*. To pronounce *map* correctly, you need only the sounds indicated by the letters. If you teach the extra vowel sound, the child will have to find some way to eliminate it in order to sound the vowel correctly.

After the student has developed initial awareness of a sound, give him groups of words with pictures to match. Start with two similar and one dissimilar word/ sounds and add more as the child becomes more proficient. You will have to choose the words and pictures in view of the teaching materials you are using to be sure that you introduce the consonant sounds in proper order. Take care to be sensitive to the range of subtle differences in pronounciation that different people bring to the same words.

As to conceptual loads represented by the pictures used, remember that certain words (like pail, which is used in the assessment suggested in Chapter 7) may not be in the child's understanding vocabulary. He may recognize a picture and understand the use of it, but he might be thinking *bucket* when the target word is *pail*. When you call his *bucket* a *pail*, he may not respond to the task appropriately.

Pail is also a homonym for *pale*. The child may have this association with the sound and be confused by the task. Some picture clues that are confusing for many children are:

> rat-*m*ouse        *p*lane-*j*et-*a*irplane
> *r*abbit-*b*unny       *b*oat-*sh*ip

Notice that the initial consonants are quite different and could cause confusion for the learner if his concept did not match the teacher's intent. Although the child may know the core concept, he may need the exact signal for the concept in order to respond appropriately. Therefore the progression for skill development related to the objective might be to develop letter sounds initially, then sound clues with pictures, pictures matched with other pictures, and finally printed words, using the initial consonant as a basis for discrimination.

## Sight words

*1. Level B*

*Skill.*  Sight-word vocabulary.

*Objective.*  Given a maximum one-second exposure per word, the child recognizes selected words from a high-frequency word list.

Sight words represent a problem for many children because most of the words tend to be abstract. Often, their shapes are very similar, and if they are overlooked while reading, the reader will still grasp the meaning of the sentence within the acceptable boundary of understanding. Your teaching objective is to have the student recognize these words quickly and consistently while reading so that they won't become stumbling blocks. In other words, you want your student to *overlearn* these words, i.e., when he sees them, he responds to them automatically, without hesitation. You must be concerned with a quick visual intake, a visual memory of a set word shape, perceptual correctness, and a meaningful response to the symbol.

A major problem with the *overlearning* that will permit quick recognition is that it requires continual repetition. If the skill is developed in isolated drill, the reader may not be able to transfer the word to new situations. Many approaches have been developed in an effort to help students with this problem. No single approach has proved more successful than any other, but many authorities suggest that sight words should be developed in a sentence or phrase, or in a picture context so that meaning will be emphasized. Simply drilling words from a list by flashing them, by writing them over and over, or by whatever means you might employ will not assure their correct usage in reading. And of course, proper application is your final goal—the ability to transfer a skill from one situation to another.

Configuration, or word shape, is often suggested as a clue to visual memory of a word. Notice the configuration patterns in some of the first 100 words of the Great Atlantic and Pacific Word List shown at the top of the next page.

Obviously, these shapes are too much alike to use configuration as a clue in teaching them. In fact, some words on the list are so close in configuration that they actually cause recognition problems. Some of the most commonly confused pairs are: want-went, there-where, was-saw, on-no, there-three.

If you plan to use configuration, eliminate as much confusion as you can by selecting words that have different shapes. Contrast in visual teaching is very helpful whenever you introduce a new skill requiring discrimination.

Since meaning clues are very important in developing sight words, these words should be taught in context. Such words as *there, here, was, were* and *it* have to be

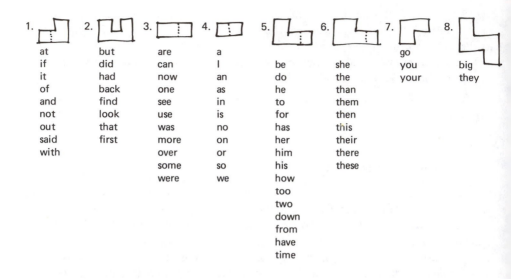

| 1. | 2. | 3. | 4. | 5. | 6. | 7. | 8. |
|----|----|----|----|----|----|----|----|
| at | but | are | a | be | she | go | big |
| if | did | can | I | do | the | you | they |
| it | had | now | an | he | than | your | |
| of | back | one | as | to | them | | |
| and | find | see | in | for | then | | |
| not | look | use | is | has | this | | |
| out | that | was | no | her | their | | |
| said | first | more | on | him | there | | |
| with | | over | or | his | these | | |
| | | some | so | how | | | |
| | | were | we | too | | | |
| | | | | two | | | |
| | | | | down | | | |
| | | | | from | | | |
| | | | | have | | | |
| | | | | time | | | |

learned within the language base in which they will be used. Their meaning is derived basically from the surrounding words in which they will be used. Flash-phrase cards to develop these words are just as simple to make as are flash-word cards. Also helpful in developing past recognition of these words are teaching initial consonants, using color clues on initial letters or vowels that are causing difficulty, labeling items in the classroom, and using family words. The use of language-experience techniques, which encourage a student to use these words in his own sentences, is also a good technique for developing sight words.

Games are also good devices for reinforcing and practicing skills. Take an old checker board and convert it into a sight-word game by typing a pair of words and gluing them to the board so that both players can read them from each side of the board. The game is played as it normally is, but in order to jump into a square, the player must call out the word and use it in a sentence. If a player cannot call a word, he must find out what the word is and miss a turn. Making easy boards and more difficult ones will offer your students progressive steps in developing new sight words. As a student masters an easy board, he can play with a more difficult set of words.

Making picture-word cards is a game a child can play by himself. Take a picture of common objects and print a matching word for each picture. Mix the word and picture cards and let the child match them up. Paint patterns on the back of the cards so that the child can check himself to see if he is right (○, +, □).

### Development of endings

*1. Level B*

*Skill.*   Phonic analysis: rhyming elements.

*Objective.* Give a word, the child either selects a rhyming word based on structure (e.g., man, pan, and fan are from the same family) or supplies a real or nonsense word based on structure.

Rhyming involves the ability to both hear the sounds of speech and discriminate between the likenesses and differences. For example, given the words *cat, sat,* and *cot,* the child can hear that *cat* and *sat* sound alike and that *cot* is different. Visually, he can also see that the structure of *cat* and *sat* is more alike than either *cot* and *cat* or *sat* and *cot.*

Initially, this skill should be taught at the aural-oral level, since both hearing and sound production are involved in discrimination and so you can respond quickly to pupils who are having trouble. If a student can't hear the sound discriminations, you should quickly switch him to the family word (phonemic) approach or another approach where sound discrimination is not so vital. Family-word techniques teach similar skills at the visual level. Both approaches do stress consistencies of certain visual patterns, which might help students who are having problems with sounds.

You can develop a unipac for rhyming by using a cassette tape recorder with pictures. If you want to introduce a student to independent learning, you can collect pictures of things that sound alike, e.g., cat and rat, and tape a lesson on a cassette. Earphones offer a lot of support for anyone with poor hearing, because they can block out distracting noises. They are also fascinating to a youngster.

A matter of concern for teaching any approach dependent on sound is that not all students in this country have the same speech characteristics or sound patterns. For example, if you were teaching rhyming to southern children and you chose *hen, ten, men* and *pen,* they would rhyme with each other; but they would also rhyme with *tin, pin,* and *fin.* Many southern children do not make a distinction in the short *e* or short *i* sounds in some words. Some New England children would have a similar problem with the *aw* pattern in *saw.* Also, in many parts of the country, there are special sound patterns which need consideration whenever you use a standard phonics program. If you use activity books from basal materials, be sure to adjust the answer sheets according to local speech patterns. Many workbooks use pictures to teach these skills, so make sure the students understand the pictures and the concepts represented by the symbols.

The sequential steps for developing rhyming are: aural intake, oral production, visual clue to aural reception and oral production, and visual patterns as sound units that rhyme (at, ike, ump). When the students have mastered the aural and oral steps, you can add visual reinforcement of family words and homonyms to help refine rhyming understandings.

### 2. Level B

*Skill.* Structural analysis: plurals.

*Objective.* The child tells whether familiar words (nouns plus *s* or *es*) are singular or plural.

Structural analysis involves identifying roots and affixes added to a word in order to use it in a new or special way. It is through unit identification that you teach the relationship of affix to the root word. Here, you are dealing with four basic skills:

1. visual identification of the root
2. visual identification of the inflected endings *s* and *es*
3. sifting between inflectional units as plural or verb form
4. recognition of *s* and *es* in words as the plural form.

The objective of this skill implies that the student's visual memory of the root form and the inflectional *es* and *s* should be overlearned. Major emphasis is placed on developing meaning while affixes and roots are developed. Oral production of the sound is also an integral part of the objective.

A major consideration while teaching *s* and *es* as plural forms is that they also function with verb in a confusing and contrasting way. For instance:

The boy*s* run. (plural noun; verb unchanged)

The boy run*s*. (singular noun; verb takes *s*)

The match*es* catch fire. (plural noun; verb unchanged)

The match catch*es* fire. (singular noun; verb takes *es*)

When added to a verb, the *s* and *es* correspond inversely with the noun forms of *s* and *es*. In each example, the verb can also be made into a noun by changing its place and emphasis in the sentence:

*run* (noun) The boy hit four home runs.
      (verb) The boy *runs* quickly.

*catch* (noun) He made three good *catches* and put the runners out.
        (verb) He *catches* pop-ups easily.

In teaching the skill of plurals through inflectional endings, stress the fact that you are working with nouns. If a pupil refers to the verb relationship, draw him back to the noun relationship. Your more capable students might quickly become aware of the confusion and be led out of it correctly. For slower students, however, or those having difficulty with the concept, it is best to stress noun + inflectional endings and leave the verb form alone while teaching the plural skill.

Since *s* and *es* combine with the noun to form a plural relationship, meaning must be stressed from the beginning. Discussions showing singular and then plural objects—perhaps using concrete objects, visuals, or workbooks,—will reinforce the concept.

While teaching the concept at the aural level, it is quite easy to slip into the oral production of the new sounds. The *s* and *es* sounds at the ends of nouns tend to take on the *z* sound of *s* and an *ez* sound for *es*.

car—kär                    church—chərch
cars—kärz                  churches—chərchez

The study of visual units follows an awareness of aural-oral skills and the emphasis on meaning. Start with the singular root and continue developing the skill until the child recognizes patterns where the simple *s* is added or consonant patterns which indicate that *es* should be added. You must also stress generalizations for making plurals with some words that end in *y* or *f*. These letters may indicate a change or special handling of the root to accommodate the ending. You may also have to touch lightly on exceptions, e.g., ox, for which neither *es* nor *s* forms the plural of the word.

If you wish to structure an individual approach or a unipac for the *s* and *es* plural forms, you could easily adapt the use of pictures, tape recorder, or Language Master to replace your personal involvement in the aural-oral presentation. With such an approach, meaning would still be emphasized as visuals stress the plural or singular form. Tape cards of the Language Master are a sample of what could be done. Here is a sample with tape cards:

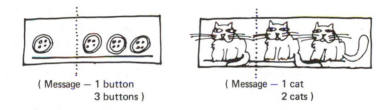

( Message — 1 button              ( Message — 1 cat
        3 buttons )                       2 cats )

On a second set of cards, you might remove the visual symbols and print just the word symbols. The student tries to say the words; he then listens to the taped message to see if his response is the same as the recorded one. The number clue is given only in the recorded message.

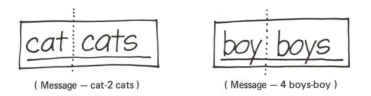

( Message — cat-2 cats )          ( Message — 4 boys-boy )

Work sheets without sound reinforcement could also be used easily to help reinforce the skill and develop the rules by which either the *s* or the *es* is used.

Most students who have good command of language patterns have a well-established concept of the plural form. For students who haven't established hearing or pronouncing the plural forms, you must carefully help them develop these skills.

One word of caution is necessary. Many black children leave off the endings of words. In some instances, they understand the concept of plural, but have never fully developed this skill at the oral level. At the oral level they may read, "the boy are runnin'." Although they see "the boys" and they often conceptualize the idea that more than one is involved, they still say "boy." This is a part of their characteristic speech patterns.

### 3. Level C

*Skill.*   Structural analysis: base words with prefixes and suffixes.

*Objective.*   The child selects base words with or without affixes that are appropriate.

A root, or base, word is simply the group of letters that represent a central thought. To this base word, both prefixes or suffixes, or inflectional and derived endings can be added. A basic understanding for developing this skill is to recognize the core word in whatever form it appears as an ammended word. For example, in the word *unsatisfactorily*, the student must recognize the core idea as *satisfactory* by ruling out the prefix (*un*), the suffix (*ly*), and converting the *i* back to a *y* to reconstruct *satisfactory*. The student learns about roots as he learns about inflected endings and how they affect the core word, and he should also have learned how to handle *e* and *y* at the end of words when adding inflected forms. Such concepts will probably need to be reinforced as you develop the new skills of adding prefixes and suffixes.

Initially, you should teach root location with affixes which don't visually change the root word. Start with prefixes, because they are the most consistent in not changing a root form. As the student masters the concept of adding new parts to words to change the meaning and use of the word, you can slowly introduce words that call for structural change in order to create new words. You should always progress from the base word to the new word and show the changes that occur and use exercises that contrast the new with the old so that the student gets a clear visual picture of the skill involved. Some examples follow:

| Prefixes with no root change | Suffixes with no root change | Suffixes with a root change |
|---|---|---|
| pre*war* | *suggest*ion | *colony*—*colon*ies |
| sub*basement* | *settl*ement | *hungry*—hungrily |
| a*typical* | *casual*ly | *ready*—readiness |
| im*perfect* | *assist*ant | *ease*—easily |
| non*stop* | *grow*th | *love*—lovable |

Although your main goal is root identification, your students must also know that the meanings of words change when you add an affix. Most prefixes completely alter the meaning of the core word. Such words as *a*typical, *non*stop, *im*perfect, *il*logical, and *in*complete are opposite in meaning from the original root word. Another function you must consider is that some suffixes change the use of the word within the sentence. For example, *ment* can change a verb to a noun: settle: settlement, govern: government, and preach: preachment are typical. The suffix *ly* changes the word to either an adverb or adjective, e.g., "a love*ly* day" (adjective) or "she behaved bad*ly*" (adverb).

In teaching these skills, you must consider your students' experience and orientation and develop these skills within a context that will be pertinent to them. For example, if you are teaching *pre* and *post* as time concepts, your students must understand the words used as core concepts. You could add these prefixes to such words as war, construction, revolution, and industrialization and have your students use them in their spoken and written language. Unless you encourage the use of these new words, they become limited to the context in which they are taught. If you take the time to teach concepts like *pre* and *post*, develop them thoroughly enough so that your students will be able to apply the information to new situations. Plan to use writing and oral exercises so that the students practice these skills until they are sure of them and will incorporate them into their skill base. In building your materials to help teach this skill independently, materials such as the ones mentioned in endings and plurals are good devices for developing unipacs for skill instruction.

## Developing consonant sounds

*1. Level B*

*Skill 1.*  Phonic analysis: simple consonant digraphs.

*Objective.*  Given real or nonsense words pronounced by the teacher, the child identifies the letters in the simple two-consonant combinations *ch, th, sh, wh* that result in a single new sound.

The consonant digraphs *ch, th, sh,* and *wh* are basically consonant combinations that make one sound that doesn't resemble either of the two sounds indicated by the letters in the combination. Actually, *ch* has four sounds, *th* and *wh* each have two sounds, and *sh* has one sound. They are as follows:

|  |  |
|---|---|
| ch = ch in *ch*urch | th = th in *th*e |
| j in spina*ch* | th in *th*imble |
| sh in *ch*ef | |
| | wh = wh in *wh*en |
| k in *ch*orus | |
| | h in *wh*ole |
| sh = sh in *sh*ip | |

Since the objective involves sound skills, you need to initially develop these consonant patterns in an aural-oral setting. Your student should be able to discriminate the differences in the digraph sounds and produce them if necessary in an oral setting. You can approach the skill visually through pictures and workbook exercises, using visual devices to evoke sound identification.

For many children, it's wise to develop only one digraph sound at a time, helping the student master one concept before moving on to the next pattern. Since *sh* is the most consistent, develop it first. It you want to program the student's work, you could construct a unipac, using a Language Master or cassette tape recorder to give the student the needed practice in both hearing and sound production. Visuals could be incorporated so that the student could attack new words with the *sh* sound without having to read symbols. Words and sentences that reinforce the skill in context would help the student master the visual task. Games and activities with other students also give the student a chance to utilize his new skills in a new learning setting and reinforce correct learning.

When teaching the *ch* sound, take the major sound and structure all initial materials so that one sound is heard consistently. Use the following sequence in teaching: sound emphasis through visual clues to words. Follow a similar pattern with *th* and *wh*. If you develop *sh* and then *ch*, it's wise to contrast these two sounds in familiar words or with pictures to make sure that the student can distinguish between the two. After developing *wh* and *th*, you could compare and contrast these in a similar way. As a final activity, you might use all the digraph patterns in an exercise which required discrimination of likenesses or differences or matching of patterns on the basis of identical digraph patterns.

### 2. Level C

*Skill.*   Phonic analysis: consonants and their variant sounds.

*Objective.*   Given words containing variant sounds of *s*, *c*, and *g* (e.g., *s*it: tree*s*, *c*ake: *c*ity, *g*o: *g*iant), the child indicates whether the italicized letters in given pairs of words have the same or a different sound.

In order to recognize that these sounds are different, a student must have developed a basic understanding of the various consonant sounds. In this task, you are trying to capitalize on this basic knowledge to lead the student into visual patterns that indicate deviant sound patterns for these letters. The deviant patterns are:

| c | s | g |
|---|---|---|
| s: *c*ent | s: *s*aw | g: *g*oat |
| k: *c*up | z: a*s* | j: *g*em |
| sh: o*c*ean | sh: *s*ugar | zh: gara*g*e |

Your basic concern is to distinguish between the hard and soft sounds of the *c* and the *g*. The *c* basically has no sound of its own, but borrows its soft sound from the *s* and its hard sound from the *k*. *G* maintains its own sound for its hard sound and borrows the soft sound from the *j*. Here is a basic generalization that can be developed at the visual level: *c* or *g* followed by *e*, *i*, or *y*, generally have their soft sounds; *c* or *g* followed by *a*, *o*, or *u*, *c*, or *g* have their hard sounds.

This skill is primarily one of sound discrimination based on visual letter patterns. Initially, you should be sure that the student has developed the ability to distinguish between the *s* and *k* sounds when dealing with *c*, and the *j* and *g* sounds when seeing the letter *g*. Many students may already have this understanding and are ready for the visual generalization. However, if a student still needs aural-oral discrimination of these letter-sounds, you should construct teaching activities that help discrimination at this level. Pictures and recorded devices are other ways of providing a longer period of sound awareness and study.

Authorities do not agree on the best way to develop a generalization when a logical generalization can be derived from the skills and elements involved. Some authorities believe that the child should reach the generalization by adding all the parts or clues together to state the likenesses and then the rule—induction. Others feel that you should tell the child the rule and let him find examples to prove the generalization—deduction. Whichever alternative you choose, keep one point in mind: no generalization is valid unless the child can use it meaningfully.

Another consideration is the students' learning style. Some students learn better through induction and should be taught in that manner. Parroting a rule or general-ization is useless unless the student is comfortable with its application. The catchy little generalization "When two little vowels go for a walk, the first little vowel does nothing but talk" proves faulty, according to studies that show that it is applicable less than 50 percent of the time. Such a rule has little usefulness in attacking unknown word patterns. Make sure that when you teach the *c* and *g* generalization, you couch it in terms that will enable your students to use the information as a key to unlocking new pronunciations.

Visual teaching should start with the letter *c*, which has two distinct sounds you can attack one at a time. Begin with the *k* sound of *c*, as it is most consistent in word structure. Start with words like:

|   | 1. | 2. | 3. |
|---|----|----|----|
|   | cat | cap | cab* |
|   | cot* | cop | cob* |
|   | cut | cup | cub* |

To assure students that you are dealing with real concepts and not nonsense words, you may need to explain the words with an asterisk. Each cluster of words does, however, offer visual consistency, because the only changing pattern is the vowel. The vowel is the visual part that determines the pronunciation of the *c*, so its role should be emphasized.

For developing the *s* sound of *c*, visual consistency, as above, is not possible unless you use nonsense words. Here are some possibilities for using real words:

|   | 1. | 2. | 3. |
|---|----|----|----|
|   | cent | cider* | cycle |
|   | cell | cinder* | cyclone* |
|   | cedar* | cigar | cypress* |

Again, you should make sure that all the words are within the students' vocabulary understandings. For the *g* generalization, you should develop the same understand-ings about the vowel groups that influence the sound of the *g* you use in a new word.

To check a student's success in learning the *c* and *g* generalization at both the visual and oral level, you could use the following nonsense words to see if the student can transfer his skill to a new area:

|  | *c* |  | *g* |  |
|---|---|---|---|---|
| cas | cis |  | goz | gez |
| ces | cos |  | giz | gaz |
| cus | cys |  | guz | gyz |

As indicated above, the *s* has a *z* sound and a *sh* sound, the *c* has a *sh* sound, and the *g* has a *zh* sound. The deviant sounds of these letters do not conform to any visual clue. When teaching the deviant sounds, therefore, you must develop the specific skill in relation to words in which it occurs. Often, these words and their special sounds are internalized as a part of our speaking vocabulary. The greatest difficulty occurs when the student is asked to make comparisons or to develop them in writing. The point at which the student needs help with an understanding of this kind is when it should be developed.

For teaching the consistent patterns of *g* or *c*, you could develop unipacs for each skill and program much of the visual analysis so that each student works independently. Workbook sheets, written exercises which you devise, visuals, and recording devices all help in programming independent learning activities.

**Developing word meanings**

*1. Level C*

*Skill.*   Synonyms and antonyms.

*Objective.*   The child tells whether words in a pair have the same, opposite, or simply different meanings.

Our basic concern in developing antonyms and synonyms is helping students recognize the similarities and differences in word relationships. Another major consideration for developing any skill involving definitions is that a student's experiences must be congruent with the demands of the new skill or understanding. A background filled with a variety of experiences acts as a strong support for new skills and concepts. A third element involved in the recognition of synonyms and antonyms is the ability to use the context or pictures to find words that can be substituted in either of these two ways.

Initially, you might start with words of greatest contrast so that the student will not be concerned with close discriminations in meaning. Antonyms with simple concepts such as *up* and *down*, *in* and *out*, *off* and *on*, *black* and *white*, or *good* and *bad* are usually within the student's conceptual system. These words and their relationship can be manipulated easily within the classroom. Words describing emotions are good for role-playing and pantomiming and can add physical involvement to learning. The Great Atlantic and Pacific Word List (Chapter 7) is also a good source for antonyms. Some examples from this list are:

| | | |
|---|---|---|
| old—new | no—yes | last—first |
| before—after | over—under | father—mother |
| work—play | small—large | boy—girl |
| in—out | good—bad | end—begin |
| little—big | day—night | warm—cool |
| up—down | off—on | right—wrong |

As with many skills involving meaning comparisons or conceptual development, your best teaching approach for antonyms is to use discussions or contextual materials. Start by having the students discuss the new concept and supply their own pairs of words from reading materials. When the opposite concept is fully developed, you can then give them workbook sheets and independent work to help reinforce the skills. Garrison (1970) has developed activities she calls the *shiftables*—gamelike reinforcing techniques which shift from one skill to another. A game wheel is a good example of a way to stimulate interest in learning either synonyms or antonyms. *A* represents a card with the name of the skill being developed. The *B* slots are one set of words to be matched with the *C* words mounted on clothes pins. The student simply connects the correct *B* and *C* words in relation to the skill being developed. You keep shifting and adding new words until the student has learned the number of concepts you want him to learn.

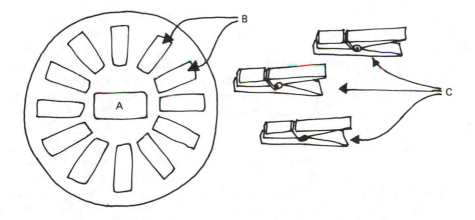

Synonyms are a little more difficult to teach if the child has not had a variety of experiences to help him develop a broad vocabulary. With synonyms, you are dealing with shades of meaning that can sometimes be confusing and misleading. The mystery box pictured here is one method for introducing synonyms. Its purpose is to stimulate senses and word power. Cut a hole out of one side of the box and attach a cloth over the hole to keep eager eyes from peeking inside. Then, put in such objects as peeled grapes, cooked macaroni, a powder puff, or sandpaper and have the students feel the object and describe how the object feels. You and your students record the answers and classify the ones which can replace one another. The students then write sentences trying to use their various new words.

Another good way to get students to use a variety of similar words is to ask them to describe characters in their reading materials. List the suggestions and classify them by similarities. When the students have finished the activity, assign them the task of finding more words that describe a person or character in a story and let them bring back their new words to discuss with the group.

Other types of activities you could use place you in a teaching position. For example, you could call out such words as angry, scared, beautiful, worrywart, hard, or scratchy; have the students record their first thoughts, and then compare all the responses. As you compare the students' answers, you can develop shades of meaning that characterize words similar, though not identical, in meaning. For example, the child might respond with the word "cool" when you say "cold." It is true that cool and cold are similar, but they are not synonyms. Helping a child find a new word to replace "cool" will enable him to build a concept of extreme or mild in relationship to temperature.

You can also construct your own paragraphs that use context as a clue to new words. The mature reader most often uses context to hazzard guesses about new words and their meanings. The teaching of context skills is a natural support for developing synonyms.

Your active teaching of new words encourages a student to broaden his understandings. Show a short film or the action part of a story without sound to encourage discussion and development of words with similar meaning that describe the film. Use discussion as a means of bringing out various words and concepts while you record the responses for further discussions. Remember that descriptive written or oral language will always help a student build new words into his workable vocabulary. Written context should not be overlooked as an excellent form of reinforcement for tasks that require a student to utilize a skill in a new setting.

Develop a unipac to make sure you cover all important aspects of the skills involved in antonyms and synonyms. Don't forget, however, that with skills requiring an understanding of meanings, a great part of active learning comes through discussion and the exchange of ideas with others.

Discussion will not only clear up misconceptions, it will also help develop ideas and concepts needed in the readiness part of a new learning setting.

*2. Level C*

*Skill.*   Multiple-meaning words.

*Objective.*   Given a multiple-meaning word in varied contexts, the child chooses the meaning appropriate to a particular context.

The basic skill involved is the ability to use context to derive a specific meaning for a polysemantic word. The prerequisites are experience with various meanings of the word and the ability to use clues within the context to identify the meaning intended. The word *bill* and *pop* are examples of the behavior involved.

### bill

*Bill* is my friend. (name)
A duck's *bill* is orange. (beak)
Pay the *bill* quickly. (amount due)
The *bill* passed the Congress easily. (legislation)
A *bill* is deadly sharp. (weapon)
We looked on the *bill* to see what was playing. (poster)
Dad gave me a *bill* to pay the check. (money)

### pop

She drank her *pop*. (drink)
The bag broke with a loud *pop*. (noise)
What idea will *pop* into your head next? (insight or caprice)
I will *pop* into bed quickly. (move quickly and lightly)
We will *pop* corn tonight. (explode)
We went to the *pop* concert. (music, usually popular)
The ball was a *pop*-up. (high fly ball)
My *pop* is a great guy (father)
The gun will *pop* off if you are not careful. (shoot or fire)
Will he *pop* the question tonight? (propose)
If you don't slow down, my eyes will *pop* out of their sockets. (protrude)

Basically, this is an organizing and thought-gathering task: you organize your clues, sift your experiences, and derive the meaning intended. This skill can be developed through direct teaching exercises or by specific tasks. The major objectives of such tasks are to:

1. build adequate background experiences to develop the concepts involved in the polysemantic uses.
2. offer a set of materials that will help teach the skills
3. offer a setting where application leads to mastery.

As you can see from the "bill and pop" examples, there are no visual clues to suggest which meaning is intended in each of the applications, i.e., the spelling of the word remains constant. With some polysemantic words, a difference in pronunciation reflects a difference in meaning, but this isn't true with the examples given here. *Record* is an example of different sounds used to apply different meanings:

record: I have a *record* player. (rek-ərd)
record: I'll *record* the sale on my tablet. (ri-kord)

Start teaching multimeaning words by using concepts within the child's workable vocabulary and equal to his level of sophistication. Be careful that the wall of verbalism doesn't deceive you as to the student's true understanding of the new concept, i.e., watch out for the student who verbalizes by rote. Use pictures or visual reinforcement initially, and try to develop specific meanings prior to more abstract meanings.

Direct teaching in a small group is perhaps the ideal introduction for this skill. In this way, you get direct feedback on success or failure in the initial steps of the task. Many workbook exercises can be used for making a unipac to help teach or reinforce this skill on an individual basis. These sheets, however, tend to develop concepts too rapidly, without adequate time for digestion or adequate reinforcement. It is wise to use some of the ideas in these workbooks, but you should adjust each one so that a single concept is developed initially.

Figure 12.1 is an initial worksheet that tries to teach and reinforce the multimeaning concept with visual aides. The world's surrounding context and the related pictures are important in developing a specific meaning. Context can also be used to stress the accuracy of the student's response. After the child can read, groups of sentences could be constructed with emphasis placed on context for deriving meaning clues. In the sentences below, the context clues suggest the exact meaning of *run*:

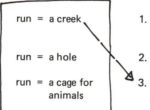

run = a creek

run = a hole

run = a cage for
      animals

1. They kept Kiku in a fenced *run* to protect her from speeding cars.

2. Mother had a *run* in her stocking.

3. The boys went fishing in Bull *Run.*

You will find an abundance of polysemantic words in textual materials related to the grade-level content you are teaching. By locating and studying new polysemantic concepts in materials before the students actually reach that point in their books, you will strengthen your students' grasp of the new materials. Basically, you will be reinforcing and ensuring success in handling content while teaching a needed vocabulary skill.

If you want to include listening activities, you could make tape cards for such words as *record* to emphasize the different sounds related to a specific word and its specific meaning. For slower-learning children, you might want to develop a cassette tape with pictures to allow longer aural-oral reinforcement.

## Comprehension

*1. Level B*

A. Read the following sentences.

1. Drink your *pop*.

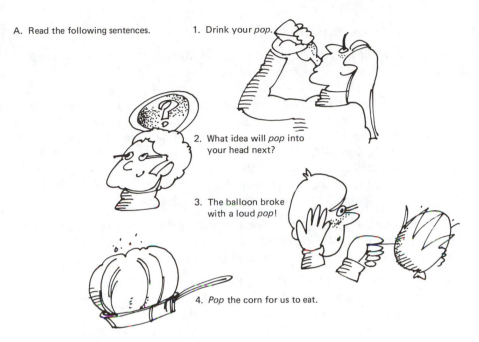

2. What idea will *pop* into your head next?

3. The balloon broke with a loud *pop*!

4. *Pop* the corn for us to eat.

B. Look up *pop* in your dictionary. Write sentences using pop to match the following pictures.

a.

b.

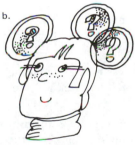

c.

d.

*Fig. 12.1    Worksheet for* pop.

*Skill.*   Reads for detail.

*Objective.*   The child answers questions about details found in a written-oral selection contained in a sentence written in the active voice.

Basically, this skill implies an understanding and recall of specific facts. If a student is asked to name the pitcher in a ball game, he has to remember the facts in the story well enough to respond. If he has to read the story to answer, he is not recalling; he is only locating information rather than using memory or retention skills. The child must focus his attention and concentrate on the incoming data in order to recall it; he may *not* listen passively and then go back and locate what he needs to know in the written materials.

As defined by *Webster's Dictionary* (1966), the active voice is:

Asserting that the person or thing represented by the grammatical subject performs the action represented by the verb (*hits* in "he hits the ball" and *shone* in "the sun shone" are)—contrasted with middle and passive.

In the active voice, the subject performs the action represented by the verb. The relationship is clear as to *who* did *what*, and there are no confusing syntactical relationships to disguise the subject and verb. In the following sentences, you can compare the structure of the active and passive voices and readily see the potential problems in understanding the actual content of the sentence.

1. (Passive)   The man was attacked by the bull.
   (Active)    The bull attacked the man.

2. (Passive)   Sue was hit by the falling brick.
   (Active)    The falling brick hit Sue.

3. (Passive)   The insects were killed by the toxic spray.
   (Active)    The toxic spray killed the insects.

When you select materials for teaching recall, be sure to use simple, straightforward sentences without any confusing sentence structure. Short, clear segments help in teaching the basic skill by eliminating a confusing number of facts and involved relationships. When you begin teaching recall, let your student know that you will ask him a question at the end of a passage, based on information he's about to read. In this way, you let the student know what's expected of him, and you motivate him to *focus* his attention on the material. Do not ask the specific question before the student reads the selection; to do so would eliminate the possibility of recall, and the student would merely locate one answer he knew he was to look for. It is also possible that he would not read and organize the whole selection, but read only as far as necessary to find the answer to your particular question.

A major factor in developing factual recall is reinforcement through correct answers. Factual recall is tedious and requires both focused attention and concentration. The student, knowing he must answer questions, tends to read more slowly or to reread to organize the data for recall. Mentally, he works to organize the *meaningful* facts of the selection so that they will be useful in answering questions. Since success breeds success in this activity, it is wise to let a student know quickly whether he is correct or not. Obviously, if a student reads a selection and answers a question one day and does not receive feedback until the next day or so, he will have forgotten the whole purpose of the exercise. He will then have to go back and reconstruct the activity and try to remember why he answered as he did several days previously. There is also much greater personal gratification in receiving quick feedback. If you are right, you are excited about your success and anxious to repeat it. If you are wrong, immediate feedback facilitates your capacity to learn from the error and correct it.

This comprehension skill—recall—would be ideal for development in a Learning Activity Package (LAP). You could develop *unipacs* based on facts about persons, actions, picture clues, feelings, and any other type of relationship you thought important. Each *unipac* should contain materials pertinent to the basic skill you are developing. You can gather this material by simply cutting out sections of old books and magazines.

Other useful materials for teaching students to isolate events within textual materials are pictures, outlines, directions, multiple-choice questions, and charts of events and actions. Another possibility for helping the student is teaching the words *who, what, when,* and *where* as special function or clue words for determining answers. For example, *who* indicates that you are looking for a person within an answer, whereas *where* indicates a place.

## 2. Level C

*Skill.*    Determining sequence: event before or after.

*Objective.*    After hearing a story, the child selects one of three statements that describes the event occurring immediately before or after another event described in a statement taken from the story.

The skill of determining sequence involves the recognition of basic and essential facts and the ability to organize them into a logical order. The student must have the skill of factual recall established to some degree in his reading habits before he approaches this skill. The major additional element in recognizing sequence is the ability to organize incoming data in a meaningful manner. Organization requires the following abilities:

1. perception of essential whole-part relationships
2. understanding of cause-effect relationships
3. integration of experiences with printed or received data
4. anticipation of logical relationships and outcomes
5. memory, focused attention, and concentration.

Experiences build a supportive framework for helping a student sift essential data from nonessential, perceiving part-whole relationships, and anticipating reasonable or logical relationships and outcomes. If a child lacks the supportive elements of broad experiences, you will have to build basic understandings before undertaking these lesson activities.

Your major instructional task is to build devices that help the student organize the incoming data in a set form. First, the student must know how you expect him to organize the incoming data. You must clearly state specific goals and give clear instructions about the type of organization you expect. As mentioned before, visual clues are excellent aids for integrating facts in some meaningful manner. Initially, you might carefully select materials that have illustrative clues built into them. In the *Three Little Pigs*, for instance, the terms *first*, *second*, and *third* suggest a number clue. Visually, you could present the numbers with pictures of different pigs. You might also depict their building materials—straw, sticks, and bricks—to visually reinforce the concepts of weakness and strength. The story of *Goldilocks* progresses as the little girl moves from room to room in the house. Here, your visual clues might be the items she comes in contact with—chairs, bowls, and beds. Finding strong visual clues helps the student organize the data in a logical, sequential order.

Telling the student what to read or listen for or giving him visual clues as he reads will establish references for organizing the data. Such statements as "Look for the building materials the little pigs used," or "Think about the things the Witch did to entice Snow White to eat the poisioned apple" will focus the student's attention on those points you consider most important. Without telling the student the exact question, you focus his attention on those particular parts you want him to concentrate on or retain.

In teaching this skill of determining sequence, you have to develop the concepts of *before* and *after* as they relate to story events. Perhaps *after* is the simpler of the two concepts as the clue to organization because of the logical consequences or the "cause and effect" relationships. When you ask what happened to Snow White after she ate the poisioned apple, the normal experiences of your student will probably cause him to reply that Snow White got sick or died. The logical consequence may have helped the student organize the data in a meaningful way. However, when you ask what happened *before* Snow White ate the apple, the student has to concentrate on a set of particular facts in order to organize the information. There are many events that could lead up to eating something that is harmful, without any clues to aid in setting up a logical attack. In helping the student organize the data, you might ask him to listen for the event that led up to Snow White's eating the apple and then for what happened after she ate it. In this way, you have not put special emphasis on the *before* events, but the student knows that he is to listen particularly for this series of events.

As in factual recall, the key element to developing this skill is the student's memory. If the student is unable to answer a question, use location of information and discussion to help clarify the points missed and discuss the point fully before going on to the next item in the sequence.

Some additional teaching aids for strengthening the *before* and *after* concepts are:

1. visual clues
2. outlining elements in time sequence
3. studying cause-effect relationships
4. working with essential and nonessential items within a selection as a clue to sequence
5. presenting sentences in scrambled order for rearranging
6. developing short stories without endings or beginnings to develop anticipation of order.

It might be best to develop this skill in small groups until you are sure that the students understand the concept. When the students are ready, you could have a unipac for each *before* and *after* relationship. The students could also work independently with some form of quick feedback to help them pinpoint weaknesses. Again, a cassette recorder with short recorded passages and questions is an excellent teaching device. The students listen to the passage, answer questions, get a correction sheet, and then relisten to the story to find the correct answers. Multiple-choice questions are particularly helpful to students having trouble with the concept, because they have a limited range of choices from which to choose an answer. Cannibalized or disected sections of books can be cut and mounted for the students to place in order. Start with a sequence of three events, with one section pasted permanently on a board. The students read the two remaining selections and place them logically either *before* or *after* the fixed item.

## 3. Level C

*Skill.* Identifies a topic sentence: paragraph.

*Objective.* The child identifies a topic sentence from a written selection.

The topic sentence states the main thought of a paragraph or large, written unit. Usually, it is placed near the beginning of a selection to focus attention on the major thought within the paragraph. The basic ability involved in identifying the topic sentence is organization. The student must be able to understand and retain facts, sift essential and nonessential facts, grasp basic from subordinate relationships, and understand the core concept of the passage.

This is a formidable task for the young learner, and many fail to grasp the skill adequately. You might introduce this skill to a small group so that you can screen out those students having the most difficulty learning. When a student demonstrates that he is handling the task well, you can let him work independently with individual work sheets, printed materials, or unipacs you have constructed. The important thing to remember when you teach this skill is to carefully select paragraphs with a clear, strong topic sentence. Not all paragraphs have topic sentences, however. The author may have used a lead sentence to cover several paragraphs,

An important part of dental care is a regular check-up with your dentist. It is also very important to regulate the amount of high-sugar foods that you eat. Finally, as they say on television, brush after every meal.

(This paragraph contains no topic sentence. All details point to one main topic, which is unexpressed. The student can write a topic sentence for this type of paragraph.)

*The early settler's diet consisted mainly of wild game.* The New England woods abounded with deer and all varieties of wild birds. Many times, the colonist's tables bore squirrel and raccoon, as well.

We have found excellent performance and high gasoline mileage with our car. The finish is of excellent quality and just sparkles without a waxing. *As far as we are concerned, our 1932 Buzzard is the best automobile on the road.*

We have found one fact to be very true. *Being "owned" by a Siamese cat is a wonderful thing.* They're loving and independent; clean and playful; and insist on sleeping on your lap when you're trying to read a newspaper.

*A political convention can be very confusing.* All of the lights, signs, balloons, and noise make one wonder what is going on. One thing is certain, however. *It is truly the democratic way of selecting the "People's Choice."*

*Fig. 12.2    The topic sentence. (A. V. Olson,* Developing Reading Activities, Grades 7–12. *A part of the Superintendent's Research and Educational Development Program, sponsored by the Georgia State Department of Education, College of Education, The University of Georgia, 1964, p. 27. Reprinted by permission.)*

so the one you select may be only a supporting paragraph for a main idea stated earlier.

A visual device discussed by Olson (1964) is presented in Fig. 12.2. Notice that the geometric shapes emphasize the location of the topic sentence. Perhaps the most basic pattern at the level of this skill is the inverted triangle ▽. This pattern might be fully developed as an initial, introductory step to this skill.

This skill lends itself to open discussions in which the students express their ideas and you give immediate feedback to their responses. The best approach for encouraging individual participation is to have each student read a paragraph and answer questions individually. The answers can then be discussed with the entire group. Initially, you might use multiple-choice answers to structure and limit the responses. Later on, use free-response answers to help you diagnose problem areas for each student. One of the most popular exercises for helping students identify the main idea of a passage is that of giving old stories a new name or title. The titles of the old, familiar stories—*Little Red Riding Hood, The Three Little Pigs, Snow White,* or *Goldilocks and the Three Bears*—are weak; they do not give any sort of clue about the story's message, as do the titles *Gone With the Wind, The Silent*

*Spring*, or *The Hideous Strength*. Renaming weak titles and "capsuling" a story's content are excellent devices to help students understand main-idea skills.

Skimming materials quickly to get an overall impression of the story is also an excellent technique for helping students identify the general flavor of an article or paragraph. Visually outlining on the board a paragraph showing the main thought and supportive sentences will help the students recognize sentence organization as a key to determining the topic sentence. Using this method, you can help the student separate essential statements from supportive and subordinate aspects of the paragraph. All these exercises prepare students to function well on their own.

Another approach is to give the students a paragraph in which the introductory statement is left out and have each student write a new topic sentence or select one from a list of alternatives. The student would thus be using the supporting sentences to help him choose a lead sentence that summarized and emphasized the supporting factors. Similarly, you might look for book selections containing several paragraphs about a similar topic. Cut the topic sentence out of each paragraph and paste the remaining parts of a cardboard sheet. Then put the topic sentences in an envelope on the back of the cardboard sheet. The student reads the paragraph and then tries to match the correct sentence with the correct paragraph.

Additional ways to reinforce and develop this skills are to use heading, subheadings, number and letter clues, signals and guide words, and marginal notes.

## Developing study skills

*1. Level A*

*Skill.* Following simple directions.

*Objective.* The child is able to perform the actions in simple one- and two-stage direction(s), e.g., "Mark an X in the middle of your paper." "Please come and take one of these boxes of paper shapes to your work area."

This skill demands that the reader:

1. understand and recall the relevant facts
2. remember the order of the directions
3. organize his facts, their sequence, and follow sequentially the action requested.

From the time a student enters school until the day he leaves, he is expected to follow instructions. He usually meets the same expectations at home or in any meeting he attends. Following instructions is not really a new skill for most students. The key to this skill is *organization*. The ability to follow instructions requires integrative skills in which a student sifts and sorts tasks, organizes an attack on the goal, and then carries through to a conclusion or a logical cutoff point.

At first, following directions is an aural activity that should be mastered at the *A level* of skill development. Carrying out a two- and then three-step set of instructions is a good starting point. For example, you could play a game called "1–2–3." First divide the class into two teams. Place cards with the numbers 1, 2, and 3 in a container. As each team member takes his turn, he draws a number, and the teacher gives him instructions that coincide with the number he has drawn. For example, a teacher might tell a student drawing the number 3: (1) "Go to the board and get a small piece of chalk; (2) put the chalk in the blue box on my desk; (3) then go and turn out the lights." The student must do each task in the proper order to gain a point for his team. Such a group activity encourages active listening and student involvement in learning and doing. The students will become involved and react vocally when a team member goes astray. Since students often try to give verbal clues, your rules should state that a point doesn't count if any clues are given by teammates.

As you move into the visual emphasis and involvement phase of following directions, try such activities as following directions for making fudge or objects students can take home—birdhouses, models, or projects. County personnel in one school system wrote a guide for firing clay, with each step carefully charted for the students to read. The teacher is encouraged to stay out of the whole process unless she detects a safety hazard. The students, from second grade up, fire their own pots without special gauges or devices. The class is divided into groups, with each group having a special area of responsibility. As one group finishes a step in the process, a new group takes over. Each time clay is fired, the groups shift responsibilities. The final result, personal pottery, serves as a bonus and reward for making the instructions work correctly.

Toys, puppets, or games are equally rewarding as instructional teaching devices. If you buy any commercially prepared models, check the instructions carefully for their completeness and relevance to your learners. Rewrite them if you feel the task can't be completed without extra help from you or an aide. Worksheets and activities can also be used to reinforce this skill. Another exercise is a set of simple written directions within the student's reading ability. An example follows.

#### Following Directions

1. Draw five stars.
2. Color the first two blue.
3. Color the last one red.
4. Leave the third one alone.
5. Make the fourth one striped.
6. Get the answer sheet and see how well you did.

Students having trouble with reading can learn to follow directions by listening to a cassette recording. The student listens to the instructions, follows them, and then replays the recording to check his progress and/or success.

A unipac is also a helpful device for developing this skill. Start with easy directions and lead to more difficult ones. A major point to keep in mind if you do build a unipac is to keep your language within the ranges of the student's independent functioning level. You can make the tasks progressively harder, but you must keep the instructions easy enough so that they do not block success.

Another possibility for developing this skill is a set of fun-type "goofy cards." Activities that encourage a student to follow a given order while having fun might strengthen his attentiveness in other settings.

### 2. Level C

*Skill.*  Begins to make judgments and draw conclusions.

*Objective.*  Given facts, the child is able to respond correctly to questions requiring that he make judgments and draw conclusions on the basis of the facts presented.

The skills involved in drawing a conclusion are:

1. recognizing and remembering relevant facts
2. organizing the facts around a central, or core, idea
3. deducting a logical outcome beyond the stated facts
4. involving personal beliefs and values.

When you make a judgment based on a conclusion, you involve norming. This process demands that you: (1) personally identify with the content, and (2) norm the data, i.e., apply your own value system of goodness, badness, or reasonableness to the given facts. The reason this skill presents such a problem for many learners and teachers is that higher levels of thinking, valuing, and norming are egocentric in nature. We value and receive information on the basis of our experiences and our affective response to incoming data. Therefore, in considering a student's response to a question requiring a conclusion or evaluation, you must consider his background knowledge, experiences, and values.

When a student responds to an evaluative question, his answer is "correct" if it is logical in light of the data presented. Even though the answer may not please you, it may be correct within its own frame of reference. Perhaps this is one reason why so many teachers shy away from questions involving advanced thinking and evaluation, i.e., the teacher must be completely open. And teachers are fearful that their students may evaluate them negatively. Teachers are often told not to discuss politics or religion, for example, probably because most of us have developed such strong, personal beliefs on these subjects. But if students are expected to develop certain comprehension skills, they must be allowed to respond openly and freely without feeling "put down" by their teacher or peers. Basically, a student's response should be judged solely on his logical handling of facts and his personal involvement.

The skills involved in forming judgments need thorough discussion. Therefore, it's vital to have an open setting in which students share common reading experiences to compare and contrast their answers with others. Students need the experience of hearing others respond to facts and questions. When you plan one of these sessions, use short, structured paragraphs with a specific purpose. Ask the students to answer a question requiring evaluation. You might have the students write down their answers so that they can't alter their viewpoint if someone they admire and respect takes an opposite position. You can use their written answers to reexamine the thinking that created a student's answer. You can ask the student to recall all of the factors that helped him draw his conclusion or judgment. When a student is failing to get facts or is functioning from a divergent value system, peer interaction can be used to help him determine where he breaks down or diverges. Such a setting can also be used to teach respect for each other's value system and each person's right to think differently in view of his experiences.

What kind of material do you start with to invoke value judgments and conclusions? Characterizations are one of the easiest approaches to developing these skills. All of us tend to identify with the characters in a story either positively or negatively—deciding that a character is good or bad on the basis of his actions. In other words, one draws some conclusion about them and makes value judgments about their behavior in the story. For example, you probably decided long ago that the wolf in the *Three Little Pigs* was a pretty bad character—mean, blood thirsty, and sneaky. You may think of the first two little pigs as lazy and shiftless, oblivious to potential dangers and interested only in playing all the time. The third little pig, on the other hand, is good, intelligent, wise, and industrious—he planned wisely for the future. Where did you get such ideas about these characters? You were taught these values by those who used the story to indoctrinate you with the concept that industry pays. In essence, you reacted "correctly" to the stereotypes within our culture. You applied the values of good and bad to the principal characters in the story.

Consider for a moment. What did the wolf do that a normal wolf shouldn't by looking for food because he was hungry? You'll have to admit that it is pretty normal behavior for a wolf! Lions, tigers, panthers, and other carnivorous animals hunt their prey. Why do you condemn a wolf for doing what is natural for him? In fact, the two frivolous little pigs acted pretty normally for pigs—they enjoyed themselves. Most pigs wallow in mud, sleep, eat, and sometimes frolic a bit. In all honesty, the only animal that acted peculiarly is the third little pig, whom we treat as the hero of the story. He took on human characteristics valued by the society in which he was born. He served as the hero because he was a reminder of certain admirable traits. In some versions of the story, the wolf eats the two worthless, poor, little pigs, and the implication is that they got what they deserved.

Developing such concepts around stories can help students learn to evaluate actions and determine their own values. Goldilocks is an excellent example; uninvited, she entered a home, ate the food, destroyed the furniture, and messed up the beds. Today, she would not be considered inquisitive, alert, and overly interested. Her actions would be judged according to your own terms of destructiveness if she acted similarly in your home.

Start with some traditional stories or fairy tales and really analyze what the characters did and why they acted as they did. Discuss and explore different viewpoints and see if the students change their points of view. The classic book *Charlotte's Web* would be an excellent book to read and discuss. Most youngsters and their teachers do not respond positively to spiders. But the story about Charlotte and her attempts to save Wilbur, the pig, from the slaughter house will capture the sympathy of even the most ardent spider hater. Templeton, the rat, on the other hand, will repel most of the young listeners. Such characterizations will help the students form conclusions and evaluations.

The concept films provide common experience and a basis for discussing reactions. Playing a film without sound and just watching the characters is an excellent initial lesson for describing characters. After the students make some judgments, replay the film with sound so that the students can evaluate their reactions.

Work sheets with short, appropriate paragraphs from texts or the news media and well-stated questions could be used for individual attacks on this skill. If you give the students multiple-choice answers, you will be able to program or limit their reactions. You might also have envelopes on the back of a work sheet with responses similar to the ones in Fig. 12.3 to reinforce their thinking patterns.

Another possibility is a cassette tape recorder with instructions to stop and record the answers. Then, a discussion follows as to which alternatives will and will not work. The main weakness in an individual attack on this skill is that the students do not get a chance to compare and contrast their answers with others, and their thinking might remain rather narrow. There is also less opportunity for a student to receive adequate reinforcement for his responses.

Fig. 12.3    Sample work sheet for teaching children to make judgments and draw conclusions.

*3. Level D*

*Skill.*  Begins to use indexes.

*Objective.*  Having identified a general topic, the child uses the indexes of books to locate information about a topic.

This locational skill has the following prerequisites:

1. knowledge of the nature and location of an index
2. knowledge and use of the alphabet as a locational device
3. knowledge of spelling patterns or attack skills as aids to location
4. categorization skills in identifying alternatives
5. cross-reference patterns and subheading skills.

If you want to look up *"How to use an index,"* for example, first locate the particular type of book with the appropriate information, then locate the index itself and find the letter *I* and all subheadings under it. Scan the *I* column and try to find the entry for *index*; there isn't one. Next, consider the category under which *index* might fall. Since it is a part of a book, look up *book* to see if it is discussed there. Under the subheading "parts of," you find the word *index*. Since there is a cross-reference to *study skills*, you go back to the letter *s* and locate the topic of *study skills*. Under this heading you find *index* with specific pages. You have then located your information. A student can break down at any point along this research line, but most students have trouble finding an alternate category where a concept is cross-listed or indexed.

When you teach the skill of location, you must develop categorization as an additional aid to finding information. Having the skill of categorization indicates that the learner has sufficient knowledge of the data to enable him to switch from topic to topic until he finds the exact subject he is looking for. The skill should be developed either before or during the use of the index.

You can build the necessary teaching and reinforcing exercises around social studies and science materials used in your classroom. At first, use multiple-choice questions as a clue to location. For example:

Find the pages where the nature of spears is discussed:

a. 192–194    b. 76
c. 104    d. not listed

In this way, you have limited all the entries on spears, and the student must locate the correct pages by using the alternatives as clues. Here's a second type of question:

Under which of the following headings would you find spears?
Give the page numbers.

a. wars    b. rituals
c. weapons    d. customs

Each of these alternatives has a logical connection with spears, but the student must choose the most probable one and then check his answer to see if he is correct. Multiple-choice questions can thus be used to structure responses and strengthen the concept of categorization.

This cluster of interrelated skills can be developed easily on an individual basis. You might have the students use filmstrips or programmed work sheets. You can develop each skill logically by using transparency overlays with an overhead projector. Use a tape recorder for instructions to aid the child as he uses the visuals. Color overlays will emphasize each skill as it is added, helping the child visualize the task in a more concrete way. Exercises where the student has to use the index to locate information can be easily constructed to lead to application. Having the students locate their lessons through the use of the index would also help emphasize its role in finding in formation.

## Summary

Reading skills require close scrutiny and thought to aid their development. Careful study of the learning task, its requirements, and the nature of the individual learner is necessary to help students in learning reading skills. You must teach basic skills in a meaningful way to aid the student in transferring his skill to the reading activity. You must not overlook the larger goal—the reader who enjoys reading!

## References

Dechant, E. V. *Improving the Teaching of Reading*, Englewood Cliffs, New Jersey: Prentice-Hall, 1970.

Garrison, E. L. *Individualized Reading—Self-Paced Activities*, Danville, New York: Instructor Publications, 1970.

Herrick, V. E. "Basal reading instruction," in *Development in and Through Reading* (Sixtieth Yearbook of the National Society of Education, Part I), Chicago: University of Chicago Press, 1961.

*Language Experiences in Reading*. Chicago: Encyclopedia Britannica Press. 1965.

Olson, A. V. *Developing Reading Activities, Grades 7–12*, A Part of the Superintendent's Research and Educational Development Program, Sponsored by Georgia State Department of Education, College of Education. The University of Georgia, 1964.

*The Wisconsin Design for Reading Skill Development*. Wisconsin Research and Development Center for Cognitive Learning, Minneapolis: National Computery Systems, 1970.

# 13 / Meeting special needs

## Introduction

Educators have long known that certain students have great difficulty learning. So often teachers feel thwarted by the continuous failure of these children to meet the standards set for the more typical students. Many special teaching approaches have been devised for them, but it is well known that there is no single solution for all the problems. No panacea exists. If you label a child and treat him with a set prescription, you are doing what educators have been doing wrong for years—writing group prescriptions to solve individual problems.

Attempts to diagnose and label students appear to come from medical influence. In dealing with a learning problem, remember that the symptoms are not always clear and concise and that learning tests may not be valid or reliable. Many of the "hows" and "whys" of learning and reading are still unknown or merely postulated, and therefore a clear diagnosis and an accurate prescription may be very difficult. The deviant learner may have problems which are personal, physical, neurological, emotional, or educational. These factors may affect the student singularly, or they may be intermingled. The accuracy of the diagnosis and the validity of the adjusted teaching program will depend on the training and the insight of the teacher or clinician who evaluates the student's learning problem.

In making "educated guesses" about special educational problems, some professionals use a variety of labels, e.g., dyslexia, alexia, strephosymbolia, neurological dysfunction, developmental lags, which continue to confound the problem. In effect, these terms tend to isolate the student from the teacher who must deal with him. Since few clinical personnel have taught in a classroom, they do not appreciate all of the educational and noneducational tasks a teacher has to perform. As a result, the specialist tries to correct the cause, while the teacher tries to cope with the resulting consequences of the learning problem. Sometimes these two paths do not run

297

parallel; they diverge and crisscross, causing even more difficulties for the individual learner.

As a teacher, you are in no way released from your responsibility to educate students with learning problems. You have the same responsibility to them as to the other children in your class. So as you try to develop a workable relationship with clinical personnel, you should respect their viewpoint. You should then use your own training and good sense in adapting their suggestions to your classroom. This responsibility to be well informed about deviant learners includes knowledge about:

1. how to help locate and screen them through systematic observations of patterns of behavior
2. the nature of the specific types of learning problem
3. the various approaches and methodologies that can be used to adjust instruction in order to teach the children effectively
4. where to find help with problems.

This chapter will give you an overview of three major types of learning problems you may encounter in your classroom. But remember that much of what is said will be at a general level and thus may not apply to a single child in your classes. Children with reading problems are individuals. All are different, and a broad understanding may help you face a child's reading problem with empathy rather than with frustration.

## Severe Learning Disabilities and Disorders

Many children have the ability to learn, but they resist conventional instruction. Their presence in the traditional classroom creates difficulty because adjusted instruction is often discouraged by school policies such as grouping, promotion, and grade-level standards. If classrooms and the curriculum are going to meet individual needs, there must be a greater emphasis on preparing teachers to meet the instructional needs of *all* their students. Teachers must be retrained in material and methodology adjustment so that they can handle the recognized needs of their problem learners.

## Nomenclature

Many clinically and medically oriented specialists use words like brain damage, brain dysfunction, neurological disorganization, neurological or developmental lags, deviant sensory impairments, strephosymbolia, chemical imbalance, genetic defects, dyslexia, alexia, and so on. All these terms imply medical diagnosis of some nature in conjunction with reading instruction. Ultimately, you—as the teacher—must effect the cure. It is more advantageous for you to regard any child having difficulty with reading as one who needs your help and understanding in overcoming his problems with symbol translation rather than typing the child with medical terms. You should, however, be familiar with some of the commonly used terms.

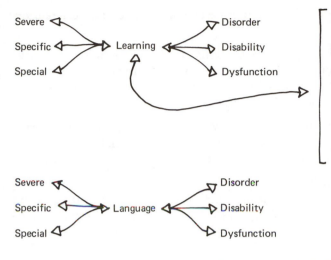

*Fig. 13.1    Translations of* S.L.D.

### S.L.D.

These initials are often used to describe a reading problem and are a compromise between the medical and the educational groups concerned with reading difficulties. The various translations of these are shown in Fig. 13.1. No matter which terms you use, you are indicating that a child has trouble with learning and reading. These terms, by themselves, do not suggest a medical problem and may therefore be more suited to the school setting. A term such as S.L.D. may serve as an "umbrella" for a number of learning problems.

What exactly does S.L.D. mean? This is hard to determine, because it is used by so many different specialists in different ways. You might be wise to use these terms in the following ways:

1. disorder—those cases in which brain damage has been proved

2. dysfunction—those cases in which disruptive brain and neurological processes are strongly suspected

3. disability—those cases in which no damage to the brain or nervous system is suspected, but the child is not functioning according to his apparent ability

4. learning—those processes that combine hereditary and environmental aspects in conjunction with the ability to receive, store, assimilate, and recall symbols in light of the demands of present learning situations

5. language—those processes that relate to retaining and using verbal symbols meaningfully

6. specific and special—those cases in which a problem can be pinpointed

7. severe—those cases in which a problem is extreme and needs special remedial care.

In further discussions, the terms disorder, dysfunction, and disability will be used with these meanings to define the two major groups of disabled readers—those suspected of having either neurological or brain involvements (dysfunction) and those without such involvements (disabilities).

*Dyslexia.*   This is a medical term that originally described a reading disability related to brain damage. Today, it describes almost any reading problem, because different people change its meaning slightly to suit their definitions. Kaluger and Kolson (1969), for example, define dyslexia as:

> Partial inability to read, or to understand what one reads silently or aloud. Condition is usually, but now always, associated with brain impairment. (Some authors refer to genetic dyslexia, affective dyslexia, experiential dyslexia, congenital dyslexia, etc.)*

Harris (1970) reinforces this definition when he says that dyslexia is:

> A term that unfortunately has been used in a variety of ways, . . . it is a broad and vague term equivalent to reading retardation, since it means defective reading.†

Since dyslexia has become a catch-all term, you should be prepared to explain your point of view if you use it. If you are describing a child, you should explain what you see as the major educational implications. In any case, you might say that the use of this term indicates a severe reading-learning problem and may also include brain damage.

*Minimal brain dysfunction or minimal cerebral dysfunction.*   These terms describe chronic brain syndromes, indicating that reading will be extremely difficult. The U. S. Department of Health, Education, and Welfare's definition for minimal brain dysfunction (MBD), as discussed by Clements (1969), follows:

> The term "minimal brain dysfunction" refers . . . to children of near average, average, or above average general intelligence with certain learning or behavioral disabilities ranging from mild to severe, which are associated with deviations of function of the central nervous system. These deviations may manifest themselves by various combinations of impairment in perception, conceptualization, language, memory and control of attention, impulse, or motor function.‡

---

*    G. Kaluger and C. J. Kolson, *Reading and Learning Disabilities*, Columbus, Ohio: Charles E. Merrill, 1969, p. 427.
†    A. J. Harris, *How to Increase Reading Ability*, New York: David McKay, 1970, p. 11.
‡    S. D. Clements, "Minimal Brain Dysfunction in Children," N.I.N.B.D. Monograph No. 3, Washington: U.S. Department of Health, Education and Welfare, 1966, p. 9.

*Educational terms*

Reading educators have long used their own terms for their students' reading problems. The classifications that follow are probably the best terms for classroom use:

*Disabled reader.*   This term can be applied to a student who is performing below his ability as measured by some test of general intelligence. Some educators stress the point that a certain arbitrary discrepancy must exist between achievement and potential. At one time, a two-year discrepancy was suggested as a lag sufficient to be considered a disability. Today, however, we recognize that a child in first grade with a lag of even six months may experience enough difficulty to affect his personal/academic development.

*Retarded reader.*   A student whose achievement is significantly below his grade placement may be called a retarded reader. This term indicates defective reading, but does not limit the consequences that can develop from the use of it. Use of the term retardation has led to an erroneous connotation that implies that the child has mental slowness. This is not the case.

*Slow learner.*   This term denotes a student who functions significantly below his grade-level requirements in reading activities, but functions satisfactorily in relationship to his ability. He does what he can, but you should not expect him to reach the norms set for grade-level achievement.

*Reluctant reader.*   A student who *can* perform up to grade level but often does not is called a reluctant reader. This student is usually erratic in his performance and does well in those subject areas he enjoys. When motivated, he achieves; when he is not motivated, he is usually called "lazy" by his teacher because of his erratic performance.

These terms are the most significant of all the labels given to children with problems in reading. As indicated, a name alone does not amount to a means for approaching the problem. The labels used by the medical and educational professions are ambiguous, and they often add to the problem of dealing with children who are experiencing difficulty.

The following discussion is aimed at the educational aspects of the problem. The medical considerations indicated above should not limit the teacher's creativity in meeting the educational needs of her special students.

## Severe reading-learning problems

Severe learning-reading problems usually result when the student is blocked from further educational progress because of his inability to cope with reading tasks. Such students are usually capable of learning to read, but they do not.

*Symptoms*

Symptoms are significant behaviors exhibited by your disability cases; collectively, they amount to a definition of the reading problem. No universal set of symptoms adequately characterizes disability cases. One symptom that most authorities acknowledge is that the student must be capable of doing better in *all* his work related to reading. He may have trouble with word-attack skills, comprehension, and/or motivation to read. He may also have unacceptable emotional responses because of continual failure in class. Two behavior patterns may emerge: *one*, acting out aggressions, or *two*, retreating inwardly from reality. Often, the student gives up or says he does not care about reading. Most often, problem readers are boys who become aware of their continued failure and react to the frustration. Students who fall into this circular trap of failure, frustration, and pressure have average or better intelligence, and they react negatively to the knowledge that they are failing.

## Soft signs

The term *soft sign* describes deviant behaviors that indicate neurological involvement in the reading problem. Whereas symptoms offer clues to the nature of a reading problem, soft signs are behaviors that suggest neurological involvements which may not be related to reading in the strictest sense. Clinically and medically oriented professionals believe that these signs indicate impaired brain functioning and therefore affect reading in a direct or tangential manner. Some tests evaluate such behaviors as synkinesis (mirror movements), adiadochikinesis (hand turnover), graphesthesia (letter tracing on skin), simultagnosia (simultaneous touch test), and many others. A word of caution: All soft signs may be emotionally based. They may indicate dysfunction in the learning process *or* emotional reactions. Thus, they must be interpreted with extreme care.

The *hyperkinetic syndrome* is a term gaining more and more acceptance to explain a severe disorder with the following signs: extreme overactivity, continuous movement, poor organizational ability, spasmodic performance levels, restlessness, distractibility, short attention span, perseveration, impulsiveness, variability or lability of moods, disobedience, poor coordination, and some tendencies toward aggression. In some instances, the following soft signs are also obvious: poor perception of body image, lack of spatial orientation, confused directionality, poor integrative abilities with symbols, aphasia, speech disorders, and generally poor receptive ability.

## Ego involvement

Obviously, a student experiencing failure and frustration will have ego problems. You, for example, would not pursue a task for ten years if you experienced continual failure. Eventually, you would quit, because failure is not a pleasant personal experience. But a student with a disability or disorder in reading has little choice; the law says he must attend school until he is sixteen. Coleman (1964), discussing a person's frame of reference and ego, noted that:

> it provides his only basis for evaluating new experiences and coping with the world. As a consequence, he tends to defend his existing assumptions—particularly those concerning the adequacy of worth of self.

Feelings of insecurity may have widely differing effects on behavior, but typically they lead to a restriction in activities, to fearfulness and apprehension, and to failure to participate fully in one's world. As a consequence, the individual is denied many enrichment and growth experiences.*

Coleman indicates that when an individual faces too many stress situations, they may affect his achievement negatively. The person exhibits a downward progression in activity level and goal-setting when his frame of reference or ego suffers devaluation from failure and frustration. On the other hand, when a person has successful experiences to bolster his ego, failure is not as traumatic as it is for the student who has almost continuous pressure and failure in the learning situation.

*Educational career*

The success or failure of the classroom experiences for disability or disorder cases often depends on the teacher and the philosophy of the school system. When a conscious effort is made to adjust to their needs and to help them, such students fare better than when they are in situations without such provisions. When these students are expected to follow norms established for the typical grade-level students, they do not thrive. When they are compared to their peers and continuously come out on the short end of the measuring stick, they tend to react negatively to both the teacher and the learning situation.

The students in both the disability and the disorder groups have similar problems. First, children in both groups have problems with learning to read. Second, their reactions to failure may further handicap their learning to read. Third, they have common needs for success and healthy egos.

## Adjusting to the consequences of the handicaps

The teacher and the school administrator have the opportunity to meet the needs of the disability and disorder groups. First, they must be open to change in several areas of the school—curriculum, study materials, the schedule, and the personnel, if necessary. The willingness to change indicates that the total staff is both "tuned in" and "turned on" to finding solutions for the problem learners. Second, the teachers must at least have a broad understanding of the types of problems they face, knowledge of new materials and methodology, skills in manipulating the learning situations, and knowledge of special services that can be contacted for help when a problem student stops and stalls. Third, the teacher must set reasonable, attainable goals for these students to reduce the stress situations that retard their reading progress. Finally, the student's parents must, if possible, be involved to make sure that they reinforce the student's success experiences. Pressure that is either too intense or of the wrong nature should be discouraged. The child needs plenty of support to overcome his educational problems and the resulting problems with his ego.

---

\*    J. D. Coleman, *Abnormal Psychology and Modern Life*, Chicago: Scott, Foresman, 1964, pp. 63, 72. Reprinted by permission.

You should keep the following suggestions in mind when working with problem students:

1. *Base your instruction on adequate diagnosis.* Diagnosis is the important first step that indicates students' needs. Diagnosis should be specific enough for you to know where to start and how to follow the initial instructional steps. Consistent retesting and evaluation can help you determine the proper sequence of learning for a particular student as you plan his further instruction. In fact, many educators suggest that all teaching should be diagnostically oriented—test, teach, retest, reteach. All work a student does should be considered as an indication of what is and what is not being learned. This way, every worksheet becomes an evaluative device, and the error patterns you detect can indicate further instructional needs.

2. *Teach to a student's specific needs.* Too often, global approaches used in reading instruction fail to meet special needs. Instruction should be broken down into small, meaningful parts so that your student is not overwhelmed with too much information at one time. This approach reinforces successful learning.

3. *Use materials that are interesting and that ensure success.* Remember that learning must be personally meaningful and interesting. Since failure and frustration create strong negative reactions among problem students, you should use only materials that build self-confidence in reading. In many instances, you may have to make your own materials or radically adjust existing ones.

4. *Appeal to the student's strengths and touch only lightly on his weaknesses.* In working with a disabled reader, you might tend to be overwhelmed by the extent of the weaknesses that must be overcome. Thus, in your eagerness to help, you attack all his weaknesses at once. It is wiser to discover what the student does well and build success and his self-confidence by concentrating on these areas first. Then, as the student gains self-esteem, you can introduce one small weak area into his instructional program. Approach another weak area after he has mastered the first. The successes that you have helped him build in the first part of his study program will enable him to confront weaknesses with new feelings of self-confidence.

5. *Reading is a developmental, orderly, organized process and should be taught in just this manner.* Many reading skills tend to progress from the easier to more complex ones. The easier skills combine to form more complex behaviors in the competent reader. With good planning and organization, a wide range of skills can be taught in an orderly, logical manner. There is no single list of reading skills that should be followed universally, but there are many well-developed lists that a teacher can follow. Too often, when students change schools, they also change from one reading series or approach to another in which the order of skills is different. This means that many students may not develop many needed skills in a logical sequence.

6. *The teacher should terminate instruction on a specific skill only after the student is able to apply the skill in several different situations.* Regrettably, instruction is usually stopped short of application. Teachers mistakenly consider grades on

classroom tests sufficient evidence of understanding and ability. They should go much farther, demanding that the student apply the knowledge in a new setting.

Educators use the term *overlearning* to describe an act of immediate response that has been practiced enough to be automatic when the appropriate stimulus is presented. In a sense, the student needs just such a command of reading skills. He needs skills that work quickly to help him attack new words, see fallacies, scan information for propaganda, etc. However, rather than just an immediate response, the student needs skills that transfer quickly to a variety of situations. This ability is best developed by teaching each new skill, then offering follow-through with materials designed to insure the usefulness of the new skill.

7. *The student who has a reading disability or a reading disorder needs good teachers.* Good teaching means meeting students' individual learning needs in such a way that the students learn actively and enjoy learning. The teacher identifies her students' needs and continues to adjust instruction until she sees that each child is making progress. She may use simplified or even remedial techniques, but she should sift and sort the methods and materials until she finds what is best for the individual student. This, of course, requires a well-trained teacher. There is a mistaken belief that students with learning disabilities or disorders need special approaches that may be beyond the scope of the classroom teacher's competencies. It is true that most problem readers need adjusted instruction that meets their special needs and their own particular pace of learning. Understanding that the results of instruction with disabled readers may be different from the results we can expect from more typical learners, the wise teacher is flexible in setting goals for her different pupils. If she can combine her perception of the disabled reader's problem with empathy for his needs and realistic flexibility in her expectation, the classroom teacher can almost always give these special students real and meaningful help.

8. *The school system should be responsible for re-educating its own teachers to help meet the special needs of their deviant learning groups.* If we are going to succeed with our "hard to teach" students, many teachers will have to be taught to adjust existing materials and traditional learning settings to accommodate the widely varying needs of individual students. Still other teachers need to be re-educated in methodology, materials, and newer types of learning settings designed to accommodate individual differences. The school system that does accept this responsibility for teacher re-education will usually develop an overall, enlightened policy aimed at meeting the needs of deviant learners. Such a school usually fosters an understanding attitude toward the reading disabilities and disorders that affect students' abilities in other subject areas. Such students are not looked down upon as problems, but are generally regarded as challengers to the best that teachers can give. However, when a school system fails in its responsibility to give help to re-educate its teachers, the individual instructor must rely on her own resources and abilities, through self-education or schooling, to help her meet special learning needs within her class.

In summary, a positive approach designed to meet individual instructional needs is vital to overcoming practices that tend to harm students who have serious learning problems. It is necessary to adjust both instructional practices and the curriculum to meet the needs of these students. An empathetic teacher who recognizes symptoms and possible emotional overlays can help break the deviant learner's cycle of frustration and failure, thereby actually helping him turn his failures into successes.

## Disadvantaged Learners

Early childhood experiences have a strong influence on a student's ability to learn to read after he enters school. If a child's early environment lacked challenges related to certain specific skills and offered limited physical activities, the student will usually have language difficulties, experiential lags, and sometimes negative attitudes toward reading or school.

The term "disadvantaged" has been used synonymously with many ideas, but most often it is used to describe inner-city or rural black children. This is an unfortunate misuse. The term should be used to describe *any* child who is educationally disabled because the first five years of his life have not equipped him to handle the educational tasks expected of him. A "disadvantaged" environment is any home or institution where a child fails to get proper nourishment, rest, educational stimulation, language interaction, and a variety of experiences. Such a situation might exist among inner-city or rural children, migrant children, mountain children, or any children from economically depressed areas. It might also exist among upper- or middle-class children who are neglected or turned over to "others" to be cared for in the absence of their parents. The outcome might be described as educational disorientation or educational retardation. Basically, these children are immature or retarded in skill development and in the attitudes necessary for reading.

### Nature

If a child's early experiences or basic needs are neglected, many interrelated abilities may also be affected. Such neglect can impair the child's ability to learn both in and out of school. Poor nutritional habits, for example, cause deficiencies which affect the whole physical response to learning. A child who is hungry or sleepy will not respond in the same manner as a well-fed and rested child. An undernourished child will not be able to exert much energy over a sustained period, nor will he be able to resist illness and remain in school during the critical early grades. Furthermore, if early symptoms of physical problems are not attended to, they can hinder the child's ability to read and learn. Vision, hearing, and speech impairments must be evaluated and corrected if students are to overcome them.

Within the complex of abilities related to early childhood experiences, are the subareas of language, concept development, perception, learning style, learning rate, and intelligence. Most young children develop and expand these areas through their early contacts with the world. However, disadvantaged children seldom go out of their own neighborhoods. They are therefore restricted to the stimulation of their immediate surroundings and do not have the benefits of a wide variety of experiences. If the language of their parents is limited or of a nonstandard dialect, the children are unable to develop the language skills that would enable them to express reactions to their experiences. Some educators believe that such children lack even the language skills necessary to communicate with those around them. This is not true. More often than not, they can communicate reasonably well within their own communities, even though their ability to think abstractly may be limited.

Language deficits, communication deficits, experiential lags, lower intellectual measures, and a host of related factors lead to educational problems. The two primary concerns for reading are language and experiences.

### Language problems

According to Figurel (1970):

> The language of disadvantaged children reflects all the deficits and limitations of environment ... If a disadvantaged child has innate capacity for language and he has shown that he can acquire language very rapidly, why is it so difficult for him to learn to read since reading is a facet of language? One would suspect that reading requires knowledge of standard English patterns, which are not very well known by the disadvantaged.*

Thus, although a disadvantaged student has his own language, he is expected to function in a second language. Whereas the second language may be similar, it is generally more structured and demanding. The first problem that a disadvantaged student may face is a restricted language—he lacks a variety of ways of expressing the same thought. The student may have a set pattern of responding and simply transfer that response to a variety of situations, e.g., as "yeah man" or I bĕ cha."

A second language problem is that grammar and syntax change as the student forms a short-cut expression for a long sentence. The student may simply reduce a major thought into a simple declarative statement. A young first grader ran to his teacher and yelled, "'Me bus lefted." When calmed down, he was able to respond a little more coherently and related the fact that his bus had left him behind. Bereiter and Engelmann (1966) note a similar problem with a child who said "Da-re-truh" for "That is a red truck." Such a "giant word" is typical of the disadvantaged reader's language; he runs words together so that the sound unit "says" the complete thought. Often, the sound unit must be taken apart and restructured if one is to understand the intended message.

---

* J. A. Figurel, ed., *Reading Goals for the Disadvantaged*, Newark, Delaware: International Reading Association, 1970, p. 6.

A third language problem for the disadvantaged learner is his lack of an adequate stock of vocabulary words to express his day-to-day experiences. Usually, the people in these students' homes lack a variety of language experiences; thus, students are unable to gain confidence with new words. Often, they hear words and try to add them to their conversation at an inappropriate time or with an incorrect meaning. One little boy, for example, was throwing an educationally inappropriate word at a consultant. The word was inappropriate, considering the sex of the consultant, but the student had heard it in his world, and he liked the shock value for the middle-class teachers who were working with him. At first, the consultant was taken aback, but he finally realized that the student was anxious to use his new word, although he misunderstood its meaning. The boy was not concerned with the correct use of the word: he was simply enjoying a new word and the reactions he was getting.

Obviously, language difficulties are a real problem for many disadvantaged groups. The extent of these language deficits varies according to the student's environment. A student may just lack variety in his vocabulary, or he may have the full range of problems related to misunderstood vocabulary, syntax problems, and restricted language. Such a student may also have difficulty with a teacher who is unfamiliar with his speech patterns and does not understand what he is saying. This lack of communication could be crucial in the reading situation. Basically, when his language is inadequate for the learning task, the student may fail unless he is helped.

*Experience problems*

Experiences build from day to day and tend to be cumulative in their effect. Some educators question enrichment programs that are designed to compensate for all the missing experiences in a short time. It simply may not be possible to overcome experiential lags with enrichment activities that are concentrated within a short period. Obviously, when you approach any new material, you need some understanding of the context before you delve into the material. Before an inner-city child can read about a goat frolicking on a farm, he must first have some understanding of a farm and a goat. Simply reading the word aloud from a book will not indicate understanding or broaden the student's knowledge about the farm and the animals there. It is clear that certain levels of understanding must precede an attempt to break the reading code. Without this understanding, the disadvantaged child might have problems with the reading materials.

Crow, Murry, and Smythe (1966) support the need for experience:

> The child entering school brings learnings absorbed from his family, his peers, and other significant factors of influence, including motor and verbal skills, the cognitive process, and abilities and attitudes that hinder or facilitate successful school achievement.

> The qualities required to solve intellectual problems depend in a large measure on the nature of preschool experiences. Children are reared in homes where

industry and independence are not stressed,—where parents have not emphasized the need for school achievement, where parents themselves neither read nor see the value of their children's being able to read. Children from these home settings will enter school uninterested in the activities of the school, including that of reading.*

When you consider the experiences necessary for reading, you may tend to think of all the readiness activities that are incorporated into the initial steps of most reading programs. However, these are only a part of a child's experiential needs. Instead, think of the child as a member of the class, an individual learner, a sharer, a teacher, and a helper. Consider all of the experiences which enable him to share, lead, function independently, be supportive, and all the other necessary skills that contribute to learning. All of these aspects of experience are at least as much involved with success as is the ability to find the missing dog's ears or to tell the difference between the letters *r*, *h*, *n*, or *m*.

The disadvantaged learner has an experiential lag in the behaviors and knowledge necessary for success in school. Lack of experience, like language, is not an educational need you can fill in a few weeks by cramming experiences into a student. Rather, inexperience *is* a reality to be recognized, coped with, remedied, and, if possible, overcome. The experiential demands of any educational task should be considered in light of the disadvantaged learner's needs prior to instruction.

## Strengths

When considering disadvantaged students, there is a tendency to see only the things that need to be remedied before they can learn. We tend to forget that they have strengths upon which we can build. Let us now consider some strengths that can be developed to help such children learn.

### Concrete experiences

It should be clear that children who have weak conceptual systems and gaps in their knowledge need concrete experiences when they are learning. Concrete learning means being involved with realities rather than with just abstractions. When learning about farm animals, for example, the most concrete experience for a disadvantaged child would be to bring him into contact with such animals in their natural or nearly natural setting—a trip to a farm or to a zoo which has farm animals. Here, he would see different aspects of farm life and animal care, and he would be allowed to touch and investigate the animals and their surroundings. If such a trip were impossible, a motion picture would be a good alternative. Slides, pictures, television, tangible objects, and trips are also excellent ways to make learning more meaningful to those who learn best from concrete experiences.

Cheyney (1967) discusses "problem oriented" learning tasks that also stress concrete involvement. Through such an approach, the aims of instruction can be geared to specific needs, in contrast to the straight textbook approach found in many schools today. Cheyney suggests the use of projects, games, or mock situations in which physical involvement in learning is more likely to occur. Role-playing is an excellent concrete experience by which to draw children into the learning situation as either participants or active listeners. Role-playing gives each child a chance to involve his imagination, to use and enrich his language skills, and to understand relationships that are necessary for proper social functioning. Puppets are another alternative by which students can act out common social interactions. The student can let the puppet say what he, himself, finds hard to express. And he can learn from his own reactions and from others' reactions to him in this unique setting. Another good alternative form of concrete learning experience is to have students build objects to use in class or to take home for their own.

Many teachers use cooking as a learning tool, because while cooking, the child is:

1. motivated (he gets to eat the final outcome)

2. involved in the progress of the entire project

3. guided through a structured learning setting in which the outcome requires a certain amount of discipline

4. interested in the learning activities themselves.

The main purpose for concrete teaching is to give the student the actual experiences he needs for generalization and abstraction. In this way, the teacher helps the child build concepts, make specific generalizations, and build up to more complex ones. The teacher stresses the practical aspects of what is being learned and expands the student's vocabulary understandings throughout each new lesson. This concrete approach makes use of visual skills, tactile and kinesthetic reinforcement, and motoric involvement to complement the aural and oral method of teaching.

*Induction*

Cheyney (1967) notes that the

culturally disadvantaged are inductive rather than deductive in their approach to learning. More specifically, they reason from parts to wholes or particulars to generals. Their culture does not help them deduce, i.e., derive a conclusion by generalities or given premises. This is why many teachers find them doing well in computational mathematics, but poorly in thought problems.*

Children having limited experiences tend to see not universal principles, but rather the individual parts that make up a whole situation. Their paucity of experience, lack of vocabulary, and poor conceptual abilities may limit them as they attempt to perceive a whole relationship.

---

* A. B. Cheyney, *Teaching Culturally Disadvantaged in the Elementary School*, Columbus, Ohio: Charles E. Merrill, 1967, p. 47. Reprinted by permission.

In teaching, this limitation requires that a great deal of time be spent in developing small, meaningful parts of a whole in order to help the student generalize about a whole relationship. Concrete experiences are used to reinforce the concepts being learned. Initial attempts at teaching generalizations should be simple, using limited individual concepts to make up the whole. Examples of simplified whole relationships will help you avoid complex concepts that may be distracting or confusing to the learner. Many writers suggest using programmed instruction with disadvantaged readers because of their pronounced inductive abilities. Phonemic approaches that use word families are also suggested, because they are inductive in nature and tend to represent consistent sound patterns which aid in learning word attack. The language-experience approach is still another possibility. In this approach, the student develops his own reading materials which relate to the parts of a situation he understands.

*Physical involvement*

Learning is reinforced by body movements. Kephart (1971) notes:

> It is logical to assume that all behavior is basically motor, that the prerequisites of any kind of behavior are muscular or motor responses. Behavior develops out of muscular activity, and so-called higher forms of behavior are dependent upon lower forms of behavior, thus making even these higher activities dependent upon the basic structure of the muscular activity upon which they are built.*

Our society has placed emphasis on verbal abilities, but has neglected the rest of the body as an instrument of learning. In recent years, the concept of using the body to reinforce learning has been finding more acceptance in remedial and special learning settings. Tactile-kinesthetic approaches are being emphasized to help deviant learners. Such practices as writing letters in the air or on the board in large chalk letters are used to develop large muscle patterns which can aid and reinforce visual patterns. Rhythm and musical techniques are also used in teaching such things as multiplication. EMR (Educatable Mentally Retarded) children are receiving more emphasis on physical fitness as a factor supportive of learning. It appears that well-organized, healthy bodies and successful concrete experiences can positively reinforce learning in many students.

More than anything else, motoric skill programs achieve two positive results: (1) further sensory reinforcement to aid learning and, (2) success experiences in learning settings which build egos along with the desire to participate in further learning activities. Kephart (1971) suggests that motor learning and spatial knowledge reinforce each other. Through movement, the child gains knowledge of his surroundings and makes generalizations about his environment.

---

* N. C. Kephart, *The Slow Learner in the Classroom*, 2nd ed., Columbus, Ohio, Charles E. Merrill, 1971, p. 79. Reprinted by permission.

Programs of motor learning, as they are related to education, should start where the child is in the learning process and carry through to the development of the major generalizations. The importance of space relationships in relation to generalizations has been emphasized ... thus, in teaching motor responses, the spatial aspects of the activity must be stressed and a spatial component must be introduced into the program.*

### Visualization and spatial orientation

The disadvantaged student appears to be able to hold space relationships in his mind and to use visual skills to reinforce learning. Cheyney (1967) indicates that the ability to use spatial conceptualization is a type of thinking related to the problem-centered or concrete approach suggested for these students. Such approaches to learning tend to reinforce the ability of the eye and the hand to work together harmoniously.

The talent for visualizing and understanding spatial relationships can be used to advantage in teaching these students. Reinforcing instruction with visuals, designing pictures to explain concepts, using materials to construct the content of the lesson, and making use of other activities that involve the use of materials and hands to give any lesson a practical outlet—all are encouraged.

### Adjusting to the consequences of the handicaps and strengths

The practical ability of the teacher to adjust the curriculum to the special learning needs of disadvantaged students is vital to meeting their needs. It is necessary for the school to supply the following:

1. out-of-school experiences and personnel
2. field trips and excursions
3. adjusted curriculum and teaching materials
4. audio-visual materials and devices.

Such adjustments will also help open the learning setting, letting these students use the abilities they already possess to accommodate the school's learning requirements. The availability of adequate experiential teaching materials in a system's central library will also be important to meeting special needs. And audio-visual devices should be readily available within the school for use with disadvantaged learners.

The following suggestions should be considered when attempting to help these students learn new materials and concepts:

1. *Evaluate the readiness requirements of any lesson in terms of the disadvantaged student's particular needs.* Since experiences are essential to learning new content, the teacher cannot assume that these students already possess the concepts con-

---

\*    *Ibid.*, p. 103. Reprinted by permission.

tained in the new materials. Extended periods of readiness, involving concrete experiences, will be necessary to reinforce the new concepts. To some degree, mastery of certain factors should be considered a prerequisite to teaching particular new concepts. Such an approach will help insure the motivation for success such students need.

2. *Consider using a total language approach to develop and reinforce language skills.* Since reading is one of the language skills, developing all skills concurrently will help the students master language concepts and usage. The language-experience materials published by Encyclopedia Britannica are one approach that attempts to do this in a logical, set pattern. Throughout the set of guides, the child reads what he or his classmates write about. The content is life-related, and the child usually has adequate vocabulary to translate what he has dictated or recorded. Writing or typing the stories aid in learning the concept that words are units of meaning. The child learns that speaking and writing "make" the code, whereas listening and reading "break" the code.

3. *Include in the contents of early reading programs subjects directly related to the daily lives of the students so that they can identify with the material.* Too often, teachers present disadvantaged students with materials completely unrelated to their life styles or experiences. In their world, no Dick or Jane exists with an ultra clean euphoric environment and happy endings to all life's experiences. Newer materials are geared toward the multiethnic concept, but even these are not always suitable for some groups of disadvantaged students. When you encounter the latter situation, you will have to either keep looking for appropriate materials or make your own. A good teacher would, hopefully, work extensively with a disadvantaged student and discuss the contents of his reading materials to make sure his interest remained high.

4. *Gear instruction to specific needs as determined by diagnosis.* As do all children, disadvantaged students need a careful evaluation of their strengths and weaknesses to ensure a sound instructional program based on their needs. You may have to devise your own system of evaluation for a full understanding of these students, since most standardized tests are not geared for diagnosis of disadvantaged students' skills or special deficiencies. With disadvantaged children, the sensory channels should be screened to detect any acuity or more serious sensory problem which might hinder instruction. Methodology may depend on the type of sensory blocking; for example, a child with a high-frequency hearing loss or a serious speech problem might not respond well to a phonics approach.

5. *Select instructional materials that emphasize the students' strengths.* Since deprivation does mean that certain areas of weakness may predominate in a child's learning problem, it is wise to teach a child so that he will experience the most success to aid and encourage learning. These children do have strengths. It is wise to use techniques that take advantage of these strengths and help the students build positive attitudes toward themselves and their learning environment.

6. *Structure instruction to specific outcomes.* Students who have trouble learning or reading need structure to give them security and something to fall back on when faced with changes. Structure provides them with a chance to build successful experiences which will also fortify them for changes. Some educators believe that either the open classroom or language experience is an unstructured approach. This should not be the case. Actually, both approaches need a strong teacher to guide and control the learning situation. If either approach is not controlled, learning experiences become haphazard and don't offer students a positive goal or the proper direction for reaching their goal. When students and teacher are both working toward the same goal, the student feels more secure in his classroom. Most disadvantaged students do need practice and repetition in the initial stages of learning to help them overcome some of their inadequacies. Such approaches do offer the teacher a way to meet their needs for structure and security in the learning setting, while also helping them achieve mastery and success.

7. *The teacher's personality should be consistent with the needs of her disadvantaged pupils.* The teacher is the most important educational resource; therefore, it is very important for disadvantaged students to have a teacher who really wants to work with them to overcome their educational handicaps and all the related problems they bring to school. According to Cheyney (1967):

> If any one quality stands out as necessary it might be described as "respect for the pupil." Some authorities believe the old style, strict, highly structured teacher has the most to offer these children, whereas others look for reformers, teachers with patience, understanding, sensitivity, good judgment, and a sense of humor.*

Teachers need to feel a bit of missionary zeal toward their work. Certainly, they have to be willing to put the needs of their students first. This may require extra work, but watching these students grow is a very exciting and rewarding experience for the teacher. She must also possess a lot of understanding along with a sense of humor if she is going to cope with the ways that deprived students fight back at a world that causes them much frustration.

It is also important to find teachers who can appreciate the culture of the disadvantaged student, although this may be difficult because most teachers come from middle-class environments. Students quickly detect an attitude of disrespect from anyone who looks down on them. The teacher may have to adjust her own thinking and not react judgmentally to attitudes and values that are diametrically opposed to her own. In other words, she must be "unflappable" and keep her balance when her basic beliefs are being challenged.

The training of paraprofessionals from the immediate neighborhood of these children is a realistic avenue by which they can be reached. A sensitive paraprofessional, directed by a teacher, can break instructional materials down to the communication level of individual children and thus bridge the cultural gap.

---

\* A. B. Cheyney, *Teaching Culturally Disadvantaged in the Elementary School*, Columbus, Ohio: Charles E. Merrill, p. 38. Reprinted by permission.

9. *Involvement of the parents in classroom activities will reinforce the learning situation.* Since the student has to function in two environments—the school and his home—it is imperative that the people in both environments understand each other. By encouraging parents to participate in school activities and workshops, you help them to understand the goals of the school and identify with what is being done to instruct their children. Such activities help the parents build a positive attitude toward the classroom, an attitude quickly picked up by the child. Parents can also participate in trips to zoos, shopping centers, banks, parks, elevators and escalators, planes, trains, and numerous other important places. If parents learn to participate in such activities, they may begin to take a more active role in exposing their children to such vital experiences outside the school. Involving the parents in role-playing activities, puppet shows, story telling, and other language activities can teach parents the value of effective communication, and hopefully, they will carry this attitude into the homes. If parents are involved in physical activities such as art work, dancing, music, and other motoric events, they may also develop these activities in the home. This participation teaches the parents to be involved with the development of their children. It also builds empathy and understanding between the teacher and the parents and ultimately means that the students will learn more effectively.

## Slow Learners

Some of your students will have difficulty learning because of their limited verbal-intellectual abilities. These students can learn, but they will progress at a slower pace than your more typical students. These slower students are usually frustrated by their continual failure in meeting unreasonable educational demands. Their slowness in acquiring specific learning skills also frustrates their teachers.

You can expect about 15 percent of your students to fall within the *slow learner* category. Some of them may be placed in special classes for more individual help, but workers in the field of special education have recently indicated that most slow learners benefit more from classroom experiences with normal children. Now, therefore, emphasis is being placed on putting these students back into the mainstream of normal classroom activity. Concurrently, there is a demand for an adjusted curriculum so that each child, whether a slow or quick learner, is taught with materials that are meaningful to him.

Slow learners have been separated into two basic groups—*EMR* (Educable Mentally Retarded) and *dull normal*—according to their performance on an individual intelligence test. Scores from 60 to 75 are indicative of the EMR student, while scores from 75 to 90 classify the dull normal child who is capable of functioning in the normal classroom. IQ scores are really a poor indication of a student's ability to function from day to day, but they do measure the level of the student's verbal skills. The scores enable the teacher to anticipate the probable reactions that a student will have to various learning tasks.

*Nature*

Generally, the slow student's educational growth appears normal, but his pace of development is slower than that of the average child. This point seems to be forgotten in the regular classroom, and the child is often described as "lazy" or "dumb." The use of these terms is unfortunate, for the untruths they represent may be an easy out for a teacher who is not willing to understand these students. They can learn, but they learn at a slower pace and therefore require longer periods of readiness and instruction to accomplish what their peers may do more quickly.

Most often, neither neurological complications nor disruptive or traumatic experiences seem to cause or be part of the learning problem. Although they tend to have more minor physical problems than do other children, factors do not appear to be causative. They seem to have more trouble with sensory problems, but these are not necessarily contributors to their impaired learning rate. Since these slow learners come from a variety of home environments, deprivation of early stimulation does not appear necessarily to be involved, either. Their syndrome does not include the kinds of genetic defects that you find with the mongoloid child. Slow learners simply do not learn as rapidly or in the same style as do their more capable peers.

*Lowered intellectual abilities*

Slow learners can be identified by their scores on verbal intelligence tests. Most authorities agree that slow learners have IQs ranging from 75 to 90. Other tests developed to identify these students indicate weaknesses in some major types of language and learning avenues. One major intellectual deficiency may be an inability to generalize from experiences. Kephart (1971) says:

> It is in the development of generalization in which the slow learning child frequently has his greatest difficulty. He learns facts and acquires specific skills with relative ease. His problem comes in integrating and organizing these data. They remain isolated and largely independent. They are called up only when a particular stimulus occurs. When he needs quantities of data to solve a problem, he must inventory his knowledge item by item, selecting and rejecting each in turn.
>
> As a result, in any assigned task he is apt to overlook a fact or piece of information which he has been taught and knows well. He can read a word on a page at one moment and fail completely to recognize the same word at the next moment. His conversation is frequently a string of loosely related ideas which carries him further and further from the point. He puts together things which do not belong together, and composite wholes such as forms of words fall apart on him.*

---

* N. C. Kephart, *The Slow Learner in the Classroom*, 2d ed., Columbus, Ohio: Charles E. Merrill, 1971, p. 52. Reprinted by permission.

Such weaknesses in the thought processes negatively affect learning activities and reading requirements.

Although these children may be slow in their mental functioning, they may react quickly to failure. Their depressed scores may reflect the failure and frustration they experienced with verbal items in previous learning situations. These students do have strengths—which are not measured in our more commonly used intellectual measures—for which they need recognition in an overall evaluation. Usually, slow learners adjust to society and make their own way, thus indicating some form of practical intelligence not measured by tests available today.

## Ego Involvement

Slow learners usually experience failure and frustration when their needs or existence are not recognized in the classroom. Strang, McCullough, and Traxler (1967) described the slow child as a "burnt child—a child who has tried to learn to read and failed." The term "burnt" is indicative of what failure can do to a child. It can hurt the student to such a degree that all learning and school interaction are negatively affected. Zintz (1970) notes that "slow learners as a total group, may exhibit behavioral characteristics that have resulted from continual failure experiences in the classroom, poor motivation, dislike of school, compensations for academic failure, and dropping out of school" (p. 568).

Slow learners can react to continued failure just as strongly as normal students can. They suffer hurt and develop negative ego involvements just like any other child. They simply may not have enough successful experiences to fall back on to quickly rebuild their egos without help from understanding teachers.

## Educational career

The education of all deviant learners requires an adjustment in curriculum and attitudes; otherwise, the educational career of these students is in jeopardy. The slow student depends on the teacher and the school to adjust to his needs and strengths so that he can realize his potential without frustration and failure. With such adjustment, he may do well and progress slowly toward his goals. Indeed, Kirk (1940) has stressed the absolute necessity for these students to have an "adjusted curriculum." However, if he is unjustly compared to or expected to compete with normally paced learners, he may eventually fail. The slow learner desperately needs time and a recognition of his particular needs if he is to avoid becoming an early dropout.

The slow learner should not sit idly in class and wait for some vague point at which he is ready to learn. He should be taught many varied prerequisite types of behavior which reinforce learning and encourage its development. Dechant (1970) says that starting before the slow learner is ready

> is often a waste of time for both the teacher and the pupil and will result in pupil discouragement. The extended readiness program of the slow learner should emphasize social interaction, storytelling, arts and crafts, dramatizing,

> music, and recreational activities. Reading charts built from direct experiences of the children are especially useful. These charts will be read and reread with pride and satisfaction by pupils ... In the early stages of learning, listening will need to be stressed more than reading.*

These children need educational experiences built around their peculiar learning patterns, and they need successful experiences if they are to thrive in any educational setting.

## Special learning needs

Slow learners need *simplicity* in all their work. All lessons, tests, reading meterials, and instructional devices should strive to incorporate this principle into the teaching approches used with these children. Too often, they are overwhelmed by the complicated ways teachers present materials to be learned. Strang, McCullough, and Traxler (1967), for example, reported responses of some slow learners to the instruction they were receiving in the regular class setting. One child asked that the teachers explain more. "A little bit of work explained is better than a lot of work without any explanation." Simple but adequate directions are necessary for their success.

Slow learners also need *varied ways of attacking a problem* and *practice* built into instruction to help them internalize what they are learning. Practice means that you find many new ways to do the same skill. Kephart (1971) stressed the difference between redundancy and practice. Redundancy is doing a thing over and over in the same way until it is mastered. Practice, on the other hand, involves learning a skill with new materials or new ways until it is mastered.

Slow learners need *concrete experiences* to help them handle new learning requirements. Such experiences relate to the types of mental processes involved in learning. Since these students have trouble generalizing and transferring knowledge, it is best to reinforce learning with a number of techniques. Inductive teaching procedures in conjunction with both concrete and motoric types of reinforcement may be essential for developing concepts with slow learners.

The slower-learning pupil needs *shorter assignments and short-term goals* for all instructional procedures. He needs less work in an assignment and quicker feedback on his work. If the student is on a high-success schedule, the failure he experiences with new material in a lesson should be minimal. He should receive reinforcement through numerous successes as he works. Too much work, too quickly, might cause failure.

The slow learner needs the *comfort* and *assurance that routine creates*, and any changes in his routine must be handled gently and slowly. These students find security in what they do well. They resist anyone or anything that tries to "rock their boat." If you alter a routine or instructional technique, do so slowly, building readiness for new activities as you withdraw the old, familiar, and cherished ways. The old and familiar act as a "security blanket" for the slow learner. Just as a child

---

\*    E. V. Dechant, *Improving the Teaching of Reading*, Englewood Cliffs, N. J.: Prentice-Hall, 1970, p. 493. Reprinted by permission.

has difficulty giving up his blanket, the slow learner holds on to the familiar with which he is happy and secure.

The slow learner needs *a greater amount of oral reinforcement* early in his learning situation. Since the student often depends on listening as an avenue to learning, you can reinforce this strength in your teaching materials. Many teachers and specialists recommend that we use less oral reading with our normal learners. This is probably wise. With slower learners, however, oral work reinforces what they are learning. Dechant (1970) suggests you might even encourage lip movements, vocalizations, and pointing at words. Although such approaches might be unacceptable with other learners, they are necessary for the slower ones.

## Adjusting to the consequences of the handicap

The emphasis of your teaching with a slow learner must be on practicality and understanding. First, understand his nature and his needs. He *can* learn, although at a slower pace, and he needs an adjusted curriculum. The experiences you build for him—which must be real and practical—determine his success or failure. The following suggestions will help you adjust to the slower-learning student's needs within the classroom:

1. *The slow learner should feel that he is a contributing member of the classroom.* Since the slow student is likely to have experienced frequent frustration, it is wise to first build his self-image as a successful learner. Reinforce those things he does well, and underplay some of his weak areas. Too often, teachers reward only those academic achievements that contribute to the verbal learning of the brighter students. Teachers should also stress some of the practical things that underachievers do well. For a long time, society has looked down on those who earned a living by using their hands. Today, many of these people are in such demand that they can earn more than some teachers with a degree. So, within the value system of the classroom, slower learners should feel that practical contributions are as valuable as those of the quicker-learning students.

2. *Materials and approaches for instruction should be adjusted to the learning style and pace of the slowr-learning student.* In selecting any material, look for approaches that stress induction, simple directions, highly motivating contents on a practical level, and various ways to handle the same information for the student's practice. Finding material to fit these criteria may be difficult, and you may have to rely on your own creative ability to rewrite instructions and construct new activities and materials.

3. *A complete developmental program should be planned for the slow learner, with special attention being given to various practice methods and allowance for their slower rate of accomplishment.* It isn't necessary to plan different types of reading programs for the slower learners; however, the overall plan must incorporate more exercises in skill development and allow the slow learner to move at his own pace. In some instances the length and the directions that accompany the skill lessons might need adjustment to individual needs. It is probable that slow learners will be able to use

many of the same skill lessons as their more normally paced seers, but the level of expected responding will need to be adjusted within the range of the slower student's capabilities. Oral reinforcement through group work, as mentioned previously, is a strong learning tool. When independent lessons are not a part of the curriculum, it is wise to schedule plenty of interaction between teacher and groups to encourage involvement and feedback.

4. *Slower learners should be developing specific needs as determined by an adequate diagnosis.* These students need to work on specifics, just as other students do. For such students, teacher-made diagnostic devices may be more reliable than standardized tests to assess their skill needs. These students may react more positively to a short worksheet than to a long test. Since sensory involvements are a part of the slow-learning syndrome, all sensory avenues should be evaluated in light of instructional needs and materials.

5. *The classroom should offer security, continuity, and challenge for the slow learner.* Because of the emotional needs of these students, the classroom should satisfy their urgent need for security. Evaluate distractions and pressures and make adjustments to avoid troublesome situations for your special learners.

6. *A system of tangible rewards for achievement is usually productive with slower learners.* Behavior-modification techniques are very successful with slower learners when you offer such things as candy, objects, or money when they successfully complete an assignment. Motivation is the key. Often, slower learners lack sufficient motivation to handle difficult learning tasks; rewards create a desire to achieve. For a long time, educators frowned on the use of extrinsic rewards as a basis for intrinsic motivation. Today, however, the use of extrinsic rewards, e.g., candy and games, is regarded as acceptable for the motivation needed by the slower learner. Teachers are finding that these students respond positively to learning situations in which they have an opportunity to earn a reward that is particularly meaningful to them.

7. *An empathetic teacher can help the slow learner as he moves through the learning-reading process.* An understanding teacher who obviously values all her students regardless of their problems will help the slow learner. If the student feels that the teacher likes him and expects him to learn, he will try harder to meet her expectations. If the student perceives that he is thought of as stupid, he will play the role and not try to change his teacher's mind. The child's perception of how the teacher feels about him is critical. But remember: You can't fake real feelings!

8. *A classroom atmosphere of acceptance and support is vital if the slow learner is to thrive.* Many adjustments must be made in the educational demands placed on slower-learning pupils. In addition, the school atmosphere must be geared toward allowing the slower learner to function within his capabilities and without unreasonable demands being placed on him. What is needed is a variety of instructional materials that can be easily adjusted to meet individual needs.

## Special Instructional Approaches

As a sensitive, thoughtful teacher, you will recognize the need to adjust your instructional approach to cope with individual learning problems. Most *new* or *different* approaches incorporate sound teaching suggestions in their methodology. There is no substitute for good teaching aimed at a student's strengths and needs. Good teaching implies modifying your instructional approach until you find the best learning route for an individual child. For many children, no *special* approach is required, just adjusted instruction based on a pupil's specific needs and strengths.

Some students, in order to learn, may respond only to highly structured teaching methods. A number of these are available to you. Many times, however, these approaches and methods require your working on a one-to-one basis with the student. They may also require a special setting or equipment which may not be practical in your classroom. Therefore, when you consider any special method or approach, beware of the practical limits of your situation—teaching space, curriculum demands, and individual needs.

The following is not a *how to* section; rather, it is an overview of various approaches that can be adjusted for individualized instruction. The references listed will help if you want to study any of these approaches more thoroughly. Some of the approaches discussed are of questionable value. But you should know about them in order to have some alternatives available at certain times.

### Multisensory approaches

Most learning is accomplished through our visual (V) and auditory (A) senses. Some children, however, need reinforcement through other sensory avenues to help them effectively retain and retrieve information. Tactile (T) and kinesthetic (K) senses, used in some approaches, involve touch and movement in the learning process. Motor activities also enhance learning. The abbreviations VAK and VAKT represent the methods that involve tactile and/or kinesthetic senses in addition to the more familiar visual and auditory responses. You will find a discussion of these techniques in Johnson (1966).

#### *Fernald-Keller approach*

This is perhaps the most widely known and accepted multisensory approach to learning. Frierson and Barbe (1967) state that initially, the approach uses word-tracing, the "assimilation of simultaneous visual and kinesthetic stimuli as an aid to retrieval." As a student advances through various stages of this approach, extrasensory reinforcement is dropped, and visual and auditory avenues are stressed for all additional learning.

Some applications of the Fernald approach suggest the use of sand or salt boxes for the initial tracing period in order to promote learning through tactile reinforcement. Another modification is the use of manuscript instead of cursive letters during the tracing stage. Manuscript letters more closely duplicate symbols in books, and the student may learn more about word-form constancy through using such manuscript letters exclusively. Discussions of the Fernald approach are available in Bond and Tinker (1967), Otto, McMenemy, and Smith (1973), and Myers and Hammill (1961).

### Cruickshank approach

This approach (Cruickshank 1961) is directed to the student with neurological complications. In this approach: (1) visual and auditory stimuli are reduced, (2) the environmental setting offers reduced stimulation, (3) the instructional program is highly structured, (4) the instructional materials are highly motivating, and (5) success is emphasized.

The instructional program stresses color perception, perceptual skills, integrative skills, and visual motor skills. It incorporates blocks, stencils, pegboards, color clues, puzzles, and perceptual training devices to involve all of the student's sensory channels in learning. In reading, for example, sounding techniques and sandpaper letters are used to reinforce sound-symbol relationships. Jump ropes, balance beams, walking blocks, and many other devices are also used to involve motoric response in the learning setting.

### Lehtinen approach

This approach focuses on the student whose needs may have roots in a neurological problem. Because Lehtinen had worked with Strauss, she therefore aimed her remedial approach at the child with the Strauss Syndrome, i.e., the hyperactive child. Strauss and Lehtinen (1947) suggested that every hyperactive child can be helped in the regular classroom if the environment is adjusted.

Teaching aids based on the Lehtinen approach include motor activities, sorting, cutting, printing or writing, and manipulating objects and gadgets. Lehtinen makes a large distinction between methods and materials: the materials are only a vehicle to reinforce learning which takes place while using the method. In reading, for example, auditory discrimination, visual discrimination, and writing are integrated to reinforce one another, Color-coding of the letters and sounds is used to provide additional clues to learning. Words are initially stamped out letter by letter to spell words. The use of colored stamps can help the child to retain the structure of the word. Writing is then used to reinforce word forms and facilitate memory.

### Kephart approach

Another approach developed for deviant or slow learners is discussed by Kephart (1960, 1971). The purposes of the learning activities are to: (1) master basic motor skills, (2) build perceptual skills, (3) learn integrative and generalizing skills, (4) train visual and motor skills at the chalkboard, (5) develop directionality through special exercises, and (6) develop form perception. Kephart stresses the values of building successes for the student by beginning with simple tasks and moving toward more advanced tasks. While the approach emphasizes visual-motor abilities, reading is developed electrically. The materials selected should complement the overall activities and reinforce the skills under development.

## Delacato approach

This approach emphasizes the developmental stages of neurological makeup. Delacato believes that immature movement and posture indicate that the spinal cord, pons, midbrain, and cerebral cortex are positively involved in reading failure. He places importance on neurological maturity and hemisphere dominance as determining factors in reading ability.

Depending on the individual case, corrective measures may involve: creeping and crawling, sleeping in a given position, or suppressing an eye, arm, or foot that is involved in crossed dominance. Exercises to develop neurological organization and dominance suggested by Delacato (1966) can range from: flip-flops, cross-pattern crawl, cross-pattern creep, cross-pattern walk, trampoline exercises, sleeping positions, listening to stories, listening to folk songs and nursery rhymes, to eye-hand coordination exercises. This approach, however, has been discredited by many highly concerned and respected workers in the field.

## Phonic, phonemic, and spelling approaches

Some approaches to teaching reading are based on the sound-symbol association and regular patterns found in many American-English words. Controversy over the use of these methods continues. For some children, however, these approaches may have particular value.

### Gillingham approach

Gillingham's alphabetical system is based on the theories of Orton (Gillingham and Stillman, 1965). Phonics, spelling, writing, and dictation are used to reinforce reading behavior. Emphasis is placed on learning through visual and auditory avenues with some reinforcement of writing and small muscle movement. First, the sound-symbol relationships are introduced. Each phonogram is presented in a key word. When the student has mastered a certain number of letter-sounds, short, phonetically regular words are introduced. Word cards and spelling are then introduced to reinforce the words. Next, selected stories that contain the words within the spelling patterns of the mastered letters are presented. Finally, new letters are introduced, and the process is repeated and expanded. However, this approach is not complete and should be used only as in aid to developing phonic skills.

### McGinnis approach

Although this approach could be classified as multisensory, the reading instruction does rely heavily on sound-symbol relationships. McGinnis tackles the language problems faced by aphasia cases. Myers and Hammill (1969) call it the "Association Method" because it systematically develops and associates each of several reading and communication skills. They note five major principles in the method:

1. words are taught by a phonetic or elemental approach

2. each sound is learned through emphasis on precise articulation

3. the correct articulation of each sound is associated with the corresponding letter-symbol written in cursive script

4. expression is used as the foundation, or starting point, for building language skills

5. systematic sensorimotor associations are utilized.

McGinnis (1963) developed her method for the aphasic child who lacks adequate speech development. The initial part of the program concentrates on speech, then branches out to reading and other subjects.

### Let's Read

Bloomfield devised an approach to reading based on phonemically regular word patterns. This system is based on the following principles:

1. Language is basically an oral process.

2. Our language is based on an alphabetic code system that can be broken.

3. Consistent and systematic patterns recur in our language that can aid in the decoding process.

*Let's Read* presents the reading materials in an orderly sequence, starting with the alphabet and progressing through the most commonly used patterns—*an, at, ad,* and *ap*. The child slowly masters the phonemically regular units by building words through initial consonant substitution. Aukerman (1971) points out that the child goes through some 35 to 40 weeks of nothing but pronunciation of phonemically regular words and nonsense syllables. The material contains 245 lessions which introduce about 5000 words. There is a steady progression from small units to more difficult ones, and phonemic regularity is stressed. A few irregular sound-symbol relationships are developed. Emphasis is placed on sounding and spelling patterns to reinforce memory and mastery.

### Early-To-Read i.t.a. program

This is the American adaptation of the *initial teaching alphabet* used in England (Mazurkiewicz, 1964). Technically, i.t.a. is not a method; it is only an alphabet. Several additional symbols were added to the alphabet so that each of the most basic 44 sounds in our language has a symbol. The use of only lower-case letters also simplifies the system for young readers. An enlarged manuscript letter functions as a capital letter. In this way, the student has only 44 symbols to learn. The assumption is that once a child has learned the sound-symbol relationships that are regular, irregularities are a lot less confusing. The i.t.a. alphabet supposedly helps the student have an easy first reading experience, but it is not a replacement for our present alphabet. A transitional reader brings the student back to the regular alphabet (traditional orthography). The American approach to i.t.a. places heavy emphasis on sound skills, or phonics.

*Words in color*

This approach emphasizes sound-symbol relationship, but it also offers color clues as additional reinforcers. The student has to decode the symbols and translate them into speech sounds. The 21 charts of colored letters help teach the 47 sounds that Caleb Gattegno, the originator of the approach, believes are important to American English. There are also 47 shades of color to reinforce and teach the 47 sounds. In this way, Gattegno deals with the irregularities in the sound-symbol approach by using color to replace the basic irregularities in traditional orthography and spelling. You will find a discussion of this approach in Aukermann (1971) and Zintz (1970).

*Spalding approach*

This phonic and spelling approach, called the Unified Phonic Method, at first places emphasis on writing the sounds of spoken language. Then, spelling and writing are used to teach word patterns and to build motor patterns. Spalding feels that visual recall, along with kinesthetic and auditory recall, are vital to word retention. In the process of teaching, the student first learns to write the patterns he hears; then, he learns to spell the words. Only after these first two steps does the child use skills in reading. This is a highly structured approach suggested by Spalding (1957) for regular classroom use. However, it has become more of a remedial technique for students with special learning needs.

## Content approaches

Some approaches depend on specific contents and methods to develop reading behaviors. Some of these approaches you have just read about are like that; their contents are spelled out and should usually be followed as suggested. However, they are classified under the heading that pinpoints their strongest feature.

*Programed reading*

This is basically a phonemic approach with a set content. The contents are locked in by the method of presentation. The student learns letters, discrete words, sentences, and word attack. He uses a workbook with a plastic sheet to protect the printed copy. As he works, the student gets immediate feedback on the accuracy of his response. As in Bloomfield's *Let's Read* approach, phonemically regular words reinforce sound-symbol relationships. The high degree of consistency makes this approach an excellent device for some children (Aukerman 1971). There is also a tremendous amount of repetition to aid students who need a great deal of reinforcement.

*Language experiences in reading*

Allen (1966) has very carefully structured an approach using the language and thinking of each individual child as a basis for reading instruction. The whole philosophy of Allen's approach is built on the following four points:

1. What I think about, I can talk about;
2. What I say, I can write—or someone can write for me;
3. What I can write, I can read—or others can read, too;
4. I can read what I have written; and I can also read what others have written for me to read.*

The materials available build skill development through specific activities. Workbooks ensure common skill experiences. Aukerman (1970) says that the purpose of Language Experience in Reading (L.E.I.R) is to lead the student into reading through a variety of ways: listening to poems and stories; expressing himself in pictures, words, and sentences; perceiving the relationship of words to each other in our language; understanding the construction of words through spelling and writing; and hearing and reading a wide variety of stories and poems by different writers. The Allen approach uses the language of the student so that sentence structure and vocabulary are limited to individual patterns. Although syntax may be different from standard English, spelling remains standard.

In conclusion, you must always sift and sort the various methods and their materials in order to choose the best learning route for each student with special learning needs. In this way, reading instruction can be focused on the student and his particular needs or problems.

## References

Allen, R. V. and C. Allen. *Language Experiences in Reading*, Chicago: Encyclopedia Britannica Educational Corp., 1966.

Aukerman, R. C. *Approaches to Beginning Reading*, New York: Wiley, 1971.

Bereiter, C. and S. Engelmann. *Teaching Disadvantaged Children in The Preschool*, Englewood Cliffs, New Jersey: Prentice-Hall, 1966.

Bond, G. L. and M. A. Tinker. *Reading Difficulties: Their Diagnosis and Correction*, New York: Appleton-Century-Crofts, 1967.

Cheyney, A. B. *Teaching Culturally Disadvantaged in the Elementary School*, Columbus, Ohio: Charles E. Merrill, 1967.

Clements, S. D. "Minimal brain dysfunction in children," N.I.N.B.D. Monograph No. 3, U.S. Department of Health, Education and Welfare, 1966.

Coleman, J. D. *Abnormal Psychology and Modern Life*, Chicago: Scott, Foresman, 1964.

Crow, L. D., W. I. Murry, and H. H. Smythe. *Educating the Culturally Disadvantaged Child*, New York: David McKay, 1966.

---

*    R. V. Allen and C. Allen, *Language Experiences in Reading*, Chicago: Encyclopedia Britannica Press, 1966, p. 6. Reprinted by permission.

Cruickshank, W. A. *Teaching Reading for Brain-Injured and Hyperactive Children*, Syracuse, N.Y.: Syracuse University Press, 1961.

Dechant, E. V. *Improving the Teaching of Reading*, Englewood Cliffs, New Jersey: Prentice-Hall, 1970.

Delacato, C. H. *Neurological Organization and Reading*, Springfield, Illinois: Charles C. Thomam, 1966.

Figurel, J. A., ed. *Reading Goals for the Disadvantaged*. Newark, Delaware: International Reading Association, 1970, (pp. 1–10).

Frierson, E. C. and W. B. Barbe. *Educating Children with Learning Disabilities*, Columbus, Ohio: Charles E. Merrill, 1969.

Gillingham, A. and B Stillman. *Remedial Training for Children With Specific Disabilities in Reading, Spelling and Penmanship*, Cambridge, Massachusetts: Educators Publishing Company, 1965.

Harris, A. J. *How to Increase Reading Ability*, New York: David McKay, 1970.

Johnson, M. S. "Tracing and kinesthetic techniques," *The Disabled Reader: Education of the Dyslexic Child*, ed. J. Money. Baltimore: John Hopkins Press, 1966, pp. 147–160.

Kaluger, G. and C. J. Kolson. *Reading and Learning Disabilities*. Columbus, Ohio: Charles E. Merrill, 1969.

Kephart, N. C. *The Slow Learner in the Classroom*, 2nd ed., Columbus, Ohio: Charles E. Merrill, 1971.

Kirk, S. A. *Teaching Reading to Slow-Learning Children*, Cambridge, Massachusetts: Riverside Press, 1940.

Mazurkiewicz, A. J. and H. J. Tanyzer. *Early to Read i.t.a. Program*, New York: Initial Teaching Alphabet Publications, 1964.

McGinnis, M. A. *Aphasic Children*, Washington, D.C.: Volta Bureau, 1963.

Myers, P. I. and D. D. Hammill. *Methods for Learning Disorders*. New York: Wiley, 1969.

Otto, W., R. A. McMenemy, and R. J. Smith. *Corrective and Remedial Teaching*, 2d ed. Boston: Houghton Mifflin, 1973.

Spalding, R. B. and W. T. Spalding. *The Writing Road to Reading*, New York: Morrow, 1957.

Strang, R., C. M. McCullough, and A. E. Traxler. *The Improvement of Reading*, New York: McGraw-Hill, 1967.

Strauss, A. A. and L. E. Lehtinen. *Psychopathology and Education of the Brain-Injured Child*, New York: Grune and Stratton, 1947.

Zintz, M. W. *The Reading Process*, Dubuque, Iowa: Wm. C. Brown, 1970.

# 14 / Improvement of reading instruction

## Introduction

*Scene*:  a teachers' lounge in Early Seventies style. A hand-operated duplicator stands on the table.

*Garcin*:  (enters, accompanied by the reading teacher and glances around). "Hm! We've got to do something about reading."

*Reading Teacher*:  "Yes, Mr. Garcin."

*Garcin*:  "You know that some teachers think you have a soft snap—working with a few kids at a time—teaching only isolated skills."

*Reading Teacher*:  "That's not fair. I have the children that the teachers find difficult. It's not easy to diagnose each child's needs and to plan an appropriate individualized sequence for him. Besides————"

*Garcin*:  "Okay. Okay. But I'm getting some flack. They say a reading teacher ought to upgrade the entire program, not just work with a few kids—many who won't even stay in this school."

*Reading Teacher*:  "I have advised you about the materials we should have."

*Garcin*:  "But you should hear the superintendent's favorite speech. Since 80% of instructional cost is in teachers' salaries, our cost effectiveness must center on teachers. Either increase their productivity or think about cutting staff—look for other ways of doing the job."

*Reading Teacher*:  "Are you saying you want me to train teachers instead of teaching children?"

*Garcin*:    (on the point of answering "both," but then his eyes fall on Inez). "Let's talk about it."

*Reading Teacher*:    (turning to Inez). "To tell the truth, I'm not sure the teachers want help in reading. Mae thinks she knows more about teaching reading than anyone, and the new first-grade teacher doesn't want anyone watching her teaching. She says it makes her nervous."

*Inez*:    "If we're honest, all of us can use help. I remember what Miss Kresy did for me my first year. The point is, however, it must be seen as help and not as a threat. I don't want anyone coming in and criticizing the way I teach —either to my face or to others behind my back. I know that Mr. Garcin has to rate us, so I probably tend to show him my success, not to call him in to watch me teach something I'm not sure about."

*Garcin*:    "'Rating,' 'appraisal,' 'accountability'—teachers hate these words or the conjectures they elicit. You know I'm no torturer. I don't want to make anyone cry, but I don't want to be a copout either. Sure, I can make more points with teachers if I promised them only goodies—new materials, more free time, smaller classes. But look at it this way—if there is some-one on the staff who can't get kids to achieve in reading or do much for their incentive to learn, you'd want me to get help for that teacher, and shouldn't I let that teacher go if after a reasonable effort there is no differ-ence? Shouldn't I put the school and the kids first?"

Improvement in the teaching of reading occurs directly in two key ways. First, there is improvement when instructional intents become more defensible, that is, when the instructional outcomes—skills, attitudes, habits—sought by teachers are recognized as important to reading and appropriate for a given learner. For example, we believe that a teacher is improving when he/she forsakes trying to get children to walk a narrow plank (literally), believing that such a psychomotor performance falls under the rubric "reading," and instead seeks to equip learners with a skill for recognizing a letter-sound correspondence. Second, there is improve-ment when one's instruction is modified, e.g., changed methods, instructional sequence, materials, management practices, so that the intended results are achieved by more learners in less time (and with no undesirable side effects).

Improvement is often thought to occur indirectly as a consequence of adminis-trative actions such as an accountability plan, monitoring of reading scores, tutorial experiences, new courses for teachers, mandatory hours of reading instruction, and providing different facilities and staff assignments for teaching. These kinds of actions, however, do not constitute improvements unless they can be shown to be related to pupil growth in reading. They are not ends to be prized, but means to be appraised. Situations such as that depicted in the scene above spark issues and problems of what constitutes improvement in reading instruction and how this improvement can best occur. The purpose of this chapter is to provide a conceptual framework and description of newer ways by which clinical professors of reading, administrators, supervisors, and teachers can both constructively resolve many of the issues and fulfill roles that make a difference in what and how children learn from instruction in reading.

Beginning with the general problem area of making decisions about teachers of reading (this focus on teaching rather than on materials and organization rests on the assumption that teachers are presently the chief instruments of instruction), we will categorize their decisions, specify the information required for making the decisions, and describe the tools that are available for collecting the necessary information. We will then examine in some detail newer approaches which have been found useful in improvement programs.

## Making Decisions about Teachers of Reading

### Different purposes for evaluating teachers

Decisions involve evaluating courses of action and making a choice. Judgments about teachers are made by teacher educators, school personnel officers, supervisors, principals, and teachers themselves. To make sense of the diverse judgments, we must make distinctions in purpose. The administrator looks for information about how effective a teacher is so that he will be able to make better decisions about which of many teacher applicants to employ, what group of pupils should be assigned to which teacher, and who should and should not be recommended as a permanent teacher. The quality of these kinds of administrative decisions is believed to be related to improving reading in school at the classroom level. Supervisors, consultants, and teachers want to know the present pedagogical practices of the individual teacher and the consequences of these practices in order to determine which of that teacher's instructional procedures to reinforce, eliminate, or modify so that there is better pupil achievement.

Novices, in their initial courses and student teaching, usually judge themselves as inadequate in the teaching of reading (that's why they are in the program). Their purpose is to acquire knowledge about what should be taught and what practical procedures to use in teaching reading.

### Decisions have not been based on requisite information

The pursuit of one purpose may impede the pursuit of another. In order to improve in reading, one usually has to "take a risk," be willing to reveal a personal deficiency—a gap in one's behavior. It's difficult to get teachers (student teachers or experienced teachers) to expose their weaknesses when they believe that the information will be used not only for helping them improve, but also become the basis for a grade or judgment that will affect a decision about their employment or the esteem of their colleagues. Also, judgments made about a teacher are only as good as the information collected. Until recently, those making decisions about teachers of reading have not given much thought to what is required for making valid decisions about a teacher and accordingly, they have not arranged for the collection of critical data. Administrators, supervisors, and others have tended to rely on such instruments as classroom observations, checklists, paper-and-pencil tests, interviews, and the like. The use of newer tools, such as those associated with systematic observation and analysis, simulation, contract plans, and performance tests, creates an opportunity to correct this lack of information.

However, there is a special problem in collecting information that will not be resolved by the newer methodological aides. We refer to the fact that many decisions about a teacher of reading demand more information than merely facts relating to that teacher's ability to teach reading. There are variables that are probably irrelevant to teaching competence but are important in making the decision, say, to employ the teacher. Age, sex, years taught, degrees held, grades received, and ethnic background are cases in point. These factors may be important for political and other reasons, and their inclusion in making decisions may be warranted on other than instructional grounds. However, knowledge of such factors is not sufficient for making a decision about a teacher of reading. Every decision about a person as a teacher of reading should take into account evidence of competency to produce specified changes in the reading behavior of learners.

### Procedures for Collecting Information about Teacher Effectiveness

#### Self-assessment, including use of video taped lessons

Self-assessment is generally conducted as follows: First, a teacher responds to a checklist containing such factors as: Do I do too much talking? Am I relying on one or two articulate pupils for most of the responses? Do I provide a purpose for learning? Are my lessons characterized by originality and a variety of approaches? Most questions of this kind assume that the practice is inherently good or bad independently of children's learning. Second, a video tape (or simply an audio tape) is made as the teacher conducts a brief reading lesson with a few children. After the session, the teacher "evaluates" the lesson alone in private, with a peer, or with a supervisor. Theoretically, the video tape allows a teacher to pay attention not only to what he *intends or thinks he does*, but also to what *he can be seen doing*. The record itself, however, is only as good as the accompanying analysis. At times, the teacher may review the record to see if a "troublesome" habit, e.g., failure to provide feedback to learners, is being overcome. At other times, the record is used to identify previously unrecognized deficiencies. The teacher must not only be able to recognize both pupil and teacher behavior, e.g., use of *how* and *why* questions, use of pupil names, providing of both positive and negative examples of the concept being taught, but also have the imaginative power to infer how these acts relate to the learning of pupils.

Self-assessment is defended on the grounds that change in one's teaching behavior is a personal responsibility that cannot be imposed by others and that teachers are self-directing in their eagerness to improve. It's not that simple, however. In order for self-confrontation to be successful, discrepancies between actual and ideal performances must be made clear. Without specialized help, some teachers employ nonadaptive defenses—perceiving ideal performance states as unrealistic and perceiving information about their own performance as invalid. Those who possess self-confidence and set realistic goals for change sometimes change their classroom performances more effectively after self-assessment. However, the viewing of one's own behavior on tape, for example, is not by itself likely to result in improved instruction. Most teachers tend to criticize superficialities—personal mannerisms, appearance, voice, and use of materials.

A summary of results from studies of the effects of self-viewing—video tape or film—is reported in the work of Salomon and MacDonald (1970). The investigators found that when no model of good teaching was presented, satisfaction with one's own performance determined what was noticed on the screen, how it was evaluated, and the nature of any attitudinal change. Self-viewing will not produce any desirable changes unless it provides information about the amount of departure from a standard which has been accepted by the viewer. Also, there is a tendency for teachers to overrate themselves, and there are negligible relationships of self-assessment with other criteria such as pupil rating and pupil growth.

## Rating scales

The measurement of teaching effectiveness by using rating scales is suspect. It is not uncommon to find such vaguely worded items on these scales as "planning and organizing appropriately," "instructional skills," "classroom control," "awareness of individual needs," and "motivation." The compounding of instruction with political and other considerations is recognizable in those scales that call for evaluating the teacher on the basis of staff relations, ethics, professional attitudes, loyalty to the school, cooperation, initiative, and community activity. Halo, lack of operational definitions, failure to control for sampling of teacher behavior, and effect of observer on teacher performance are some of the limitations that make rating scales of doubtful worth in the hands of administrators, supervisors, and fellow teachers.

## Pupil reports

The many uses of student reports—instructional improvement, teacher assessment, description of teacher practices—make this measure a fruitful one. Data from pupils will have more positive effect on teachers than data received from any other source (Schmuck, 1969). When one desires day-to-day observation of the teacher's behavior without the presence of outside observers, the use of pupil accomplices is one answer. Reliability of pupil observations is increased when pupils focus on discrete observable behavior. Even five- and six-year-old children are reliable identifiers of instances of negative teacher differentiation among pupils, e.g., "Who doesn't get to read so often in your reading group?" If interested in overall assessment of the teacher, one might wonder if pupils wouldn't rate the same teacher differently depending on their sex, grade received, and progress made. Studies such as those by Davidoff (1970) suggest that these factors have little relation to the ratings given and that pupil opinion of teacher behavior is very stable over time.

The validity of student ratings is a problem, however. Considerable halo effect is found when pupils rate their teacher on several traits. As expressions of feeling, pupil ratings unquestionably have validity. They can be useful indicators that learners do or do not have favorable attitudes toward given activities in reading, particular skill lessons, and the teacher who taught them. Even such a simple reporting form as the one that follows provides information about affect and can be used by a teacher in deciding whether or not a reading task has been well received.

Circle the face that shows how you feel about the lesson:

A teacher's self-confrontation is likely to be internalized if he decides on what data to collect about his classroom performance and if these data are collected from his pupils. Usually, a teacher will get honest, unintimidated feedback from pupils about how they feel about a new practice. If one thinks that pupils might be reluctant to share true feelings, steps should be taken to assure pupils of the anonymity of their responses.

## Systematic observations

There is a plethora of instruments that purport to be useful in analyzing instructional acts. In their anthology, *Mirrors for Behavior*, Simon and Boyer (1970) describe 79 instruments for classifying the dynamics of instruction. Most of the instruments require the user to learn a complicated system for coding particular teaching behaviors or instances within a category. Therefore, we predict that these instruments will have chief value for researchers interested in describing teaching. Exceptions are the well-publicized *Interaction Analysis System* (Flanders, 1967) and systems that apply specifically to the teaching of reading, e.g., Davidson's system for studying the effect of teacher-pupil interaction on the development of critical reading skills (Davidson, 1968). Flanders' system allows one to analyze verbal communication between pupils and teacher and to judge the degree to which a teacher is exercising direct, as opposed to indirect, influence on pupils, e.g., soliciting opinions from pupils, praising, accepting feelings. There is much argument about whether or not a teacher who engages in indirect rather than direct influence is more effective (Rosenshine, 1970).

We would like to reiterate that there are many purposes for studying teacher behavior. A few will use systematic observation solely for nonjudgmental description—to describe what goes on; others will use these systems as aids for fixing attention on factors in the teaching act that would not otherwise be noted—factors that might be manipulated (tested, or tried out) in subsequent lessons to see if better effects can be achieved. And there are those, too, who won't make the effort to assess results as shown by pupil growth but settle for judging teachers by the processes of instruction they use. The latter practice is to be avoided, since it is unlikely that one particular teaching process will invariably produce pupil growth, considering the idiosyncratic backgrounds of teachers and pupils, the great range in objectives in reading, and the immense variation in environments where teaching occurs.

## Personal attributes and history

There is no end to the desirable qualities sought in a teacher of reading. As long as "good teacher" is associated with "good person," the problem of teacher improvement is unmanageable. The single most important deficiency in improvement programs is the failure to use pupil progress as a criterion and instead to rely on *a priori* measures of personal attributes such as personality, education, and background. We should not assume that teachers can achieve desired results with learners just because they have satisfactorily completed courses in psychology, linguistics, and teaching of reading. Neither is it sufficient that teachers cherish literature and that when they read stories, their voices sing—showing life as laughter, sadness, exhilaration, and despair.

Lack of success in predicting teacher effectiveness in the teaching of reading arises because decision makers have tried to predict an unstable criterion variable on the basis of an illogical predictor. We have already indicated some of the great range in outcomes that might follow from instruction in reading. Consider, too, Goethe's comment in his eightieth year, "The dear people do not know how long it takes to learn to read. I have been at it all my life and I cannot say I have reached the goal."

It is very unlikely that any personal or instructional variable will correlate highly with all the skills associated with "reading." Specific instructional objectives and criterion-referenced tests contribute to the stability of our criteria for reading, thereby increasing the chances of finding relations between selected qualities of the teacher and certain skills of reading. Nevertheless, the definitions of these qualities must also become more operational before reliable consequences can be sought. Such factors as grooming, emotional stability, health, use of English, and humor, for example, are unlikely to predict a teacher's success in teaching. The meanings of these terms are too imprecise and conflicting, e.g., tolerance for cultural diversity versus commitment to elevating reading tastes. Typically, when an administrator says that a teacher is original or thorough, he is stating his emotional feeling about the teacher. Since the quality is largely in the eye of the beholder, the best that can be said is that because the administrator sees such values in the teacher, this perception may predict teacher retention as contrasted with teaching effectiveness.

Those who certify teachers as competent to teach reading have tended to rely on proximate criteria indicating that the candidate has had experience in teaching and clinical situations and that he has completed courses in reading, psychology, diagnosis and correction of reading disabilities, test construction, and interpretation. There is no universally accepted specific competency to be acquired from courses. Written tests of competency vary considerably in what they measure. The candidate may have to answer factual questions and apply:

1. concepts drawn from disciplines (psychology, linguistics, sociology) which appear to relate to the teaching of reading. For example:

   Juan, a native speaker of Spanish, is presented with the sentence:
   "Put your feet on this mat and then move your left foot to the right."

   Based on linguistic contrastive analysis of Spanish and English, which one of the following is likely to seriously interfere with Juan's comprehension of the sentence?

   a) word order
   b) inflection (plurals)
   c) intonation

2. information common to the pedagogy of reading. For example:

   Provide three examples of how a lesson in phonics can be taught.
   Use the following approaches in making up your examples: (1) analytic, (2) synthetic, and (3) spelling pattern.

3. tools commonly found in classroom and clinical practice. For example:

   Describe how you would construct and interpret an informal reading inventory for use with pupils of your own choice.

4. content from humanistic studies. For example:

   List five books that you might read aloud to pupils in a fifth-grade class in order to illustrate symbolism in literature. Specify the symbolism to be found in each selection.

Recent court decisions have emphasized that examinations taken by teachers for employment purposes must measure the knowledge and skills essential to the position, not just content taught in professional courses. The ability to perform well on written tests such as those illustrated above is not a valid measure of ability to teach reading. This is not to say that such ability is not important to the teacher of reading. On the contrary, many "learnings" from course work and laboratory practice can be logically related to on-the-job decisions about what and how to teach. One should not, however, arbitrarily assume that presage criteria, teacher characteristics, and knowledge of subject matter either accurately reveal the teacher's actual classroom behavior or predict the growth in reading of pupils under that teacher's directions.

Durrell has called attention to the dilemma of identifying the particular components that should be included in programs for teacher preparation, indicating the great difference in components selected in various programs. He has also reported that there is only a low positive correlation between scores identifying teachers as highly achieving as shown by pupil growth and scores identifying teachers as highly rated as evidenced by observed practice, i.e., providing for individual differences, giving specific instructions suited to pupil subskill weaknesses, showing economy in the use of learning time, and displaying enrichment practices (Durrell, 1969).

## Performance tests

Successful completion of a performance test is evidence that a teacher can promote desirable learning among pupils. Typically, performance testing means giving a teacher one or more instructional tasks (objectives) and a sample of the measure to be administered to pupils after the teaching has occurred. The posttest itself is not given to the teacher, because assessment must be based on the teacher's ability to teach a generalizable reading skill, not merely respond to particular test items. The instructional tactics are left to the teacher. The teacher is allowed a specific period of time for planning the lesson(s) and for the teaching. Often, the tasks selected are those that can be taught by competent teachers in a short period of time, typically 15–20 minutes. Tasks that require several days or weeks of instruction are, of course, also possible. Prior to instruction, pupils are pretested to determine their level of attainment with respect to the objective and its prerequisites. Figure 14.1 is an example of an objective for a performance test that appears in a collection of performance tests issued by Instructional Appraisal Services (Learning Improvement Kits, Instructional Appraisal Service, 1972).

Performance tests can be used to answer administrative questions, e.g., is teacher X better than teacher Z? Which teachers are able to produce learning for a population of learners at a minimal acceptable level under controlled conditions?—performance tests can also be used to answer self-improvement questions, e.g., Among a number of teaching tasks in reading, which am I able to achieve? Can I get better results when I follow suggested procedures for teaching to a particular objective?

When it is necessary to differentiate among teachers, e.g., when a few new teachers are to be employed from many applicants, it is important to have data indicating relative teaching power. In the past, such data were hard to get, because the competing teachers did not have comparable groups of pupils and there was little control over time for preparation and conditions of presentation. In order to compare teachers, the challenges presented to them should be comparable. Provision for equalizing test difficulty among the teachers occurs when all teachers are given the same objective, when there is pretesting and random assignment of learners to teachers (groups of pupils can be rotated among teachers to learn different skills so that it can be clearly demonstrated that the exceptional effects are produced by

Mini-Lesson on SOUNDING THE LETTER C*

Your task is to teach the children a rule for determining whether the letter *c* in a word should be sounded like a *k* as in *"kite"* or like an *s* as in *"sun."* The words used in the children's test will follow this rule:

> The letter *c* is pronounced as an *s* when immediately followed by an *i, e,* or *y;* otherwise, it is pronounced as a *k.*

Your instructional objective is:

> Given a list of unfamiliar words containing the letter *c* and following the phonetic rule stated above, the children will be able to indicate whether the *c* takes the *k* or *s* sound by circling a picture of either a kite or a sun.

A sample of the kind of questions which will be used to determine if this objective has been met is given below.

*Directions* (to be read aloud by the test administrator):

> All the words on this page have a letter *c* in them. If the *c* makes a ____ (sound out a *k*) sound as in kite, circle the kite. If the *c* makes a ____ (sound out an *s*) sound as in sun, draw a circle around the sun.

* This lesson is designed for very young children who have NOT had instruction on the phonetic rule stated here.

*Sample items:*

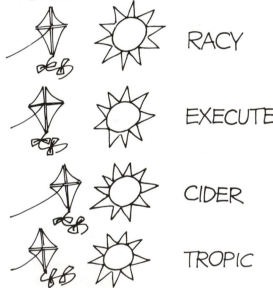

RACY

EXECUTE

CIDER

TROPIC

*Answers*: The kite should be circled before the words "execute" and "tropic"; the sun should be circled before the words "racy" and "cider."

In addition to this kind of question, the children will be asked to indicate the degree to which they found the lesson interesting.

*Fig. 14.1   Example of an objective for a performance test. (Reprinted by permission of Instructional Appraisal Service, Ithaca, N.Y.)*

the teacher and not by the inherent makeup of pupils), and when there is control for the time and setting in which the teaching occurs.

The mean posttest scores earned by groups of pupils become indicators of teacher's effectiveness. Reliability of performance tests is increased by permitting the teacher to teach a number of lessons which feature different kinds of objectives, e.g., comprehension as well as word-recognition skills. Teachers can then be ranked on their ability to reach particular instructional goals as well as their generalized teaching power.

On the other hand, the performance test can be used as a diagnostic measure. Rather than ranking teachers, the test results can be applied to provide teachers with information about which skills they cannot teach well. When coupled with analysis of the teaching lesson, the teaching process can be linked to information about how to get better results.

Thus far we have described performance tests as instruments that indicate ability to promote learner attainment of specific instructional objectives. The American Association of Colleges for Teacher Education Committee on Perform-ance-Based Teacher Education includes among its survey of performance tests those that only require the teacher to exhibit behaviors known to promote learning (AACTE, 1972). For instance, a teacher might be expected to teach a minilesson demonstrating both closed and open questioning techniques. (An example of a closed question is, "What letter do you see at the end of this word?"; an open question is, "What might cause someone to avoid his friends?") The difficulty with per-formance tests that measure a teaching skill independent of pupil gain is that there is little agreement about which teaching skills are valid. There are no scientific laws for teaching; there are only categories of instructional variables—movement, inflection of voice, use of pupil ideas, praise, structuring comments—which direct our attention to dimensions of teaching that would otherwise be overlooked. These variables suggest more possibilities to check out in instructing particular learners in specific tasks.

## Contract plans

A newer alternative for assessing teacher competency involves a teacher-adminis-trator agreement regarding pupil gain in reading. Although contract plans vary widely, most of them involve the teacher's agreement to be responsible for pupil attainment of selected instructional objectives. Prior to this agreement, an assess-ment is made of the status of a class with respect to these objectives. The agree-ment specifies what will constitute acceptable performance of the class on measures of objectives after instruction. Item sampling is considered an economical way to get sensitive pre- and post-instructional measures. Criterion-referenced tests for each of the objectives are distributed among the children in a class. Each child responds to only a few test items. For example, a teacher might have twenty objec-tives and three test items for each objective; in a classroom of thirty pupils, each child might be given only two items (different items for each child). The number of correct answers out of sixty would thus be the starting benchmark for the class. The same items can be randomly assigned at the end of the term; the resulting number correct would indicate the progress made by the class as a whole toward the stated objectives. The measures are much more likely to show change in pupil status than are pre- and post-test scores on standardized tests.

Obviously, item sampling is especially useful for collecting evidence about teacher effectiveness. On the other hand, the teacher whose purpose is to make instructional decisions on behalf of individual learners would not use this technique for the prerequisite individual diagnoses. In order to determine an individual's status, the learner must respond to many items, usually representing fewer, yet a comprehensive range of, objectives.

The contract plan allows teacher and administrator to agree that objectives selected for the class are indeed important and appropriate for the majority of children in a given classroom. In addition, the teacher may choose to have the contract credit the teacher with the progress of individuals or subgroups in mastering selected reading tasks. In any event, the teacher and administrator agree in advance on what they will accept as evidence that the teacher has been successful in developing student skills and attitudes in reading. The contract counters the prevailing practice of trying to make *ex post facto* judgments about both the desirability of skills taught during a term and the amount of progress that would warrant merit.

In saying that a contract plan allows the individual teacher to choose from among a number of approved objectives, we mean that the teacher need not choose those tasks which are either too advanced or have already been mastered by the students. Pupil characteristics and prior learning should be taken into account in setting expected growth rates. The contract may be revised subsequently to permit the substitution of objectives more appropriate for the particular learners. Such revision occurs when new information about the learner comes to light after instruction has commenced.

Although we recommend the use of criterion-referenced tests and some form of matrix sampling, i.e., item or pupil sampling, other techniques for measuring pupil progress can be employed. A standardized test might be given. However, such a test is less likely to show changes in pupil ability to perform and probably will not measure all the tasks taught during the term.

Other options in designing contract plans include teacher agreement that pupils will achieve scores that fall within the standard distribution of scores in like classrooms (comparison among teachers) or will make statistically greater gains during the current year than did similar classes the previous year (teacher serving as own control). Evidence that a teacher is able to improve the results from one year to the next implies that the teacher is capable of learning how to be a better teacher— a value to consider when making decisions about that teacher. The contract plan also permits the collecting of evidence for both planned and unplanned effects of instruction, and a teacher may be encouraged to pursue, without fear of penalty if unattained, high-risk objectives, i.e., goals known to be very difficult to reach, such as a learner's changed self-concept or attitude toward reading.

## A Model for Helping Teachers Become Better Teachers of Reading

A teacher becomes better when instructional intents (objectives) are more warranted and when instruction results in the attainment of these intents by more children without undesirable concomitants. How, then, can a teacher be helped to select better objectives and to modify teaching strategies so that greater achievement occurs?

One answer focuses on a framework termed the *improvement cycle*. Professor Robert Anderson and his associates at Harvard University have pioneered the development of a supervisory structure by which a teacher or group of teachers can examine teaching in a most productive fashion. During an improvement cycle, a teacher submits a lesson plan containing preassessment data and objectives to a team of fellow teachers. The team observes the lesson and then meets to study the lesson and to confer with the teacher. Although there are wide variations in the conduct of the cycle, it generally comprises certain phases.

### Preobservational phase

Prior to observing a teaching act, the observer team meets with the person who will be doing the teaching. This preobservational conference allows the teacher to clarify instructional intent for the particular lesson, e.g., what the objectives are, how they relate to longer-term goals. Often in these conferences, the teacher will recognize that an objective selected is not appropriate. Therefore, the conference is usually scheduled far enough in advance of the teaching act so that a more suitable objective can be formulated and so that the requisite planning can take place. A student teacher, for instance, entered a preobservational conference with the following objective for a 20-minute lesson with children beginning to learn how to read.

> Given a written paragraph which he has not seen before, the learner will be able to respond to questions that can be answered directly or inferred from the material.

> "When I'm home alone,
> I think about lots of things.
> I think about my pets.
> I have a fish, a pup, and a cat."
> What did she have a lot of?

Discussion of children's prior work revealed that children could not recognize such sight words as *about*; they had neither been taught the spelling patterns *at*, *up*, nor had they used the consonants *f* and *p*, even in substitution exercises. Use of the apostrophe (contraction), comma, and period were also unfamiliar to the pupils. Consequently, this student teacher decided to keep the objective as a long-range objective, but focus the forthcoming 20-minute lesson on a specific objective consistent with one or more of the revealed "needs" rather than to try to teach many prerequisite tasks within the single lesson.

Other preobservation conferences have led to changes in teacher objectives after the teacher has reflected on such factors as pupil interest, the fact that many pupils have already mastered the objective, or apparent triviality of the objective. The preobservational conference is also, of course, an opportunity for the "helping" teachers or supervisors to clarify what their roles will be during the succeeding phases of the conference and to respond to any special request from the teacher.

## Observation phase

During a lesson, observers attempt to record what the teacher and pupils say and do. Exact questions are posed and the answers given are written down. Words of praise, directions given, and comments are recorded as part of the record, as are nonverbal observations—movements and actions. The emphasis during the observation is on the collection of *data* (that which can be seen or heard and requires no inference); the observation phase is not the time for making inferences, generalizations, or judgments.

The list that follows gives some examples of what is and what is not recorded during an observation.

| *Record* (data) | *Not recorded* (inference) |
|---|---|
| The boy is tearing the worksheet into little pieces. | The boy does not like the lesson. |
| The girl turned to page 6, not 10. | The girl is confused by the explanation. |
| The boy said *cat* is *kitten*. | The boy is having trouble reading aloud. |
| The child did not volunteer to read. | The child is ashamed to read aloud. |
| The teacher said, "Jimmy, you are forgetting that words like *afterwards*, *before*, and *later* signal a change in time. | The teacher is scolding the child. |

Data are necessary for deriving valid inferences. Furthermore, it is helpful to present data to a teacher rather than to confront him with inferences alone. Without data, a teacher often feels unfairly judged (the teacher may be able to provide more valid inferences than the observer when given the data). Also, data indicate what specifically might be changed. A written record allows for careful subsequent analysis which gives rise to instructional patterns worth attention.

## Analysis and strategy

Before meeting with the teachers, the observer team studies the record in order to find what might be most useful to share with the teachers. The analysis is conducted in the light of the objectives stated in the preobservational conference, although teacher attainment of these results is not the important issue. The rationale for an improvement cycle is to help a teacher find new ways of teaching, not to make a big deal about whether or not the teacher got the expected results with learners. To what extent did the learners achieve the instructional objective(s)? If learners did not achieve as intended, what was seen that has heuristic values? In other words, suggest something that the teacher might try to get better results. Also, what was observed in the lesson that indicates a need for objectives not previously considered? Questions such as these show how an analysis session might proceed. The idea is to not only help a teacher achieve better results in teaching a particular task, but also share some ideas that might pay off in better results in a range of future lessons. Participants in the analysis session study the data and attempt to form generalizations from the data. To this end, a variety of constructs—criteria, instructional paradigms, categories for interaction instruments—can be used. The ten learning principles identified in Chapter 3 are of particular value in conducting an analysis of a teaching act.

Strange as it seems, teachers frequently do not give pupils an opportunity to practice the skill equivalent to that called for in the instructional objective. Instead, they encourage practice of a prerequisite task or perhaps practice of an analogous task, i.e., activities that may be necessary, but not sufficient. One of the simplest and most effective procedures for conducting analysis of lessons is to look at the data to see how many opportunities all pupils had to perform the task stated in the objective. Anyone can do this if he can differentiate analogous, equivalent, and prerequisite tasks. For example, stated below are objectives for three different lessons and a record of what the teacher did in teaching to the specified objective. See if you can identify the lessons in which there is equivalent practice.

| *Objective* | *Activity* |
|---|---|
| Given sets of sentences, each set consisting of one general statement and two supporting statements, the learner can select the general statement | Teacher presented sets of statements such as the following and asked pupils to select the general statement.<br><br>a) The Husky pulls the sled.<br><br>b) The St. Bernard brings food to the traveler.<br><br>c) Dogs work. |
| Given printed words that end with the *et* pattern, the learner can say another word that ends with the same pattern. | Teacher said: "*net, get, wet,*" and asked pupils to write another word that ends like *net, get, wet.* |
| Given common physical descriptions, e.g., big smile, clenched fist, shaking knees, learner can tell the probable emotional state that accompanies the description | Teacher asked pupils to tell about the times when they were most happy, frightened, and surprised. |

Objective 1 in this list is an instance of equivalent practice. A teacher who wants to get better results should be sure that learners have equivalent practice.

In addition to analyzing the lesson, those who help a teacher also plan strategy for presenting their analysis to the teacher. When eavesdropping on a strategy session, these questions are heard: How many suggestions do you think the teacher is likely to entertain now? Which of your suggestions might be too threatening? Which suggestions require more follow-up than can be given at this time? Is it better for the teacher to make his own analysis of the facts before we give ours? Who will take responsibility for showing the teacher evidence that suggests favoritism among pupils? Just exactly what would we like the teacher to do differently as a result of our meeting?

## Postobservation conference

A good postobservational conference should result in the teacher's walking away from the conference with both ideas that he is willing and able to try in subsequent lessons and new objectives for pupils. Typically, not only does the teacher benefit from the analysis and suggestions made, but the participants, too, find that the group activity helps them reflect more on their own teaching and prompts them to behave differently when teaching their own lessons.

Evidence that the model can articulate serious problems of instruction is found in the work of Goldhammer (1969). Also, extensive descriptions of supervisors operating within the model are available (McNeil, 1970 and Weller, 1971).

## Conclusion

Improvement in the teaching of reading calls for decisions by many different people. Much of the vital information—facts, data—needed for making defensible decisions about teachers of reading has been wanting. The casual collecting of information and indiscriminate use of instruments such as rating scales and self-assessment is not a sound basis for bringing about better instruction. Several newer tools and a framework for their application may yet transform the rigidity of yesterday's answers. Those using performance tests and contract plans promise to close the gap in providing data about the effect of a teacher as shown in pupils' progress; supervisors with systematic observation schedules are trying to illuminate powerful teaching patterns worthy of evaluation.

In the future we expect to see a closer match between: (1) particular decisions, (2) requisite information, and (3) use of the correct instrument for getting the information. For purposes of assignment, Principal X may want to know which of several teachers can best teach the children in the school to pronounce vowel sounds in unfamiliar words. He will therefore select a performance test that measures this skill—a test that differentiates among teachers, yet gives all teachers an equal chance. Supervisor Y wants to help a teacher who is not attaining the desired results. A systematic observation instrument used within the framework of the improvement cycle can lead to a fruitful record and analysis for the teacher.

The challenge remains, however, to organize an improvement program in which combinations of measures can be employed, each yielding a unique set of data. Unlike the state of affairs depicted in our opening scene, a school can be organized to meet both a variety of improvement needs and accountability demands.

Teacher and administrator can set end-of-term goals under a contract plan, thereby satisfying both the teacher's goal preferences and the administrator's preoccupation with protecting children. Parallel to the emphasis on achievement, there can be opportunities for teacher improvement. There should be improvement cycles and minilessons conducted either with peers or solo, in which the teacher is encouraged to take risks and to learn new teaching skills without fear that failure will be reported as data to be considered in rating the teacher. Inasmuch as there is now more pressure on teachers to get results, there must be an opportunity for teachers to identify teaching tasks on which they are not competent and to receive help in learning how to teach these tasks. Further, teachers must be encouraged to express, without penalty, fears about their instructional adequacy in order to receive technical and emotional support.

## References

American Association of Colleges for Teacher Education, Committee on Performance-Based Teacher Education. *A Resumé of Performance-based Teacher Education: What is the State of the Art?*, ed. Stanley Elam, Washington, D.C., March 1972.

Davidoff, S. H. *The Development of an Instrument Designed to Secure Student Assessment of Teaching Behaviors that Correlate with Objective Measures of Student Achievement*, Office of Research and Evaluation, The School District of Philadelphia, March 1970.

Davidson, R. L. "The effects of an interaction analysis system on the development of critical reading in elementary school children," *Classroom Interaction Newsletter* **12**, (May 1968): 12–13.

Durrell, D. D. "Government support of in-service programs in reading: pros and cons," in *Reading and Realism*, ed. J. Allen Figurel, Newark, Delaware: International Reading Association, 1969.

Flanders, N. A. "Teacher influence, pupil attitudes, and achievement." U.S. Office of Education Cooperative Research Monograph No. 12, OE-25040, Washington, D.C.: USOE, 1965, pp. 50–65.

Goldhammer, R. *Clinical Supervision*, New York: Holt, Rinehart and Winston, 1969.

McNeil, J. D. *Toward Accountable Teachers: Their Appraisal and Improvement*, New York: Holt, Rinehart and Winston, 1971.

Rosenshine, B. "Interaction analysis: a tardy comment," *Phi Delta Kappan* **51**, (April 1970): 445–446.

Salomon, G. and F. J. McDonald. "Pretest and posttest reactions to self-viewing one's teaching performance on video tape," *Journal of Educational Psychology* **61**, 4 (1970): 280–286.

Schmuck, R. A. "Self-confrontation of teachers," in *Conceptual Base of Program 1: Specialist in Continuing Education (SCE)*, Northfield, Illinois: Cooperative Educational Research Laboratory, Inc., HEW Contract OEC-3-3-061391-3061, July 1969, pp. 52–78.

Simon, A. and E. G. Boyer, eds. "Mirrors for behavior: an anthology of observation instruments," *Classroom Interaction Newsletter,* Special Edition, vols. A and B, Spring 1970.

Teaching Improvement Kits. Instructional Appraisal Service, 105 Christopher Place, Ithaca, New York, 14850.

Weller, R. H. *Verbal Communication in Instructional Supervision,* New York: Teachers College Press, Teachers College, Columbia University, 1971.

# Index